Operation Iraqi Freedom and the New Iraq

INSIGHTS AND FORECASTS

EDITED BY

Michael Knights

Published in 2004 in the United States of America by The Washington Institute for Near East Policy, 1828 L Street NW, Suite 1050, Washington, DC 20036.

Library of Congress Cataloging-in-Publication Data

Operation Iraqi Freedom and the new Iraq : insights and forecasts /
edited by Michael Knights.

p. cm.

Includes index.

ISBN 0-944029-93-0

1. Iraq War, 2003. 2. Iraq-Politics and government-20th century. 3. Iraq-Politics and government-2003- 4. United States-Foreign relations-Iraq. 5. Iraq-Foreign relations-United States. 6. United States-Foreign relations-2001- 7. United States-History, Military-21st century. I. Knights, Michael. II. Washington Institute for Near East Policy.

DS79.76.O635 2004

956.7044′3-dc22 2004017805

Cover photo ©AP Wide World Photos

Table of Contents

Contributors **1**

The Washington Institute Executive Committee, Advisors & Staff **2**

Maps **3**

INTRODUCTORY ESSAY *MICHAEL KNIGHTS* **7**

Part One: Historical Antecedents **11**

Introduction *Michael Eisenstadt* 13

1. U.S. Policy in Post-Saddam Iraq: Lessons from the British Experience *Michael Eisenstadt* 15

Part Two: Operation Iraqi Freedom **27**

Introduction *Michael Knights* 29

2. What Kind of Defense Might Iraq Mount? *Jeffrey White* 32
3. Infrastructure Targeting and Postwar Iraq *Michael Knights* 35
4. The Complexities of a Military Coup against Saddam *Jeffrey White* 38
5. The Long View of No-Fly and No-Augmentation Zones *Michael Knights* 41
6. Iraq Fights Its War 'Outside-In' *Jeffrey White* 44
7. Iraqi Strategy and the Battle for Baghdad *Michael Eisenstadt* 47
8. War in Iraq: A Preliminary Assessment *Jeffrey White* 50
9. Basing Restrictions Shape Concept and Conduct of War *Michael Knights* 53
10. Fighting the War to Win the Peace in a Post-Saddam Iraq *Michael Eisenstadt and Jeffrey White* 56
11. The End of Saddam's Regime *Jeffrey White* 59
12. Operation Iraqi Freedom: One Year On *Michael Knights* 62
13. Middle East Weapons Proliferation: Lessons from Iraq and Beyond *David Albright and Michael Eisenstadt* 65
14. Sitting on Bayonets: America's Postwar Challenges in Iraq *Michael Eisenstadt* 68

Part Three: The Sunni Resistance **75**

Introduction *Jeffrey White* 77

15. Ansar al-Islam: Iraq's al-Qaeda Connection *Jonathan Schanzer* 81
16. Foreign Irregulars in Iraq: The Next Jihad? *Jonathan Schanzer* 84

17. The Emergence of Resistance in Iraq *Jeffrey White* 87
18. Patterns of Sunni Resistance in Iraq *Jeffrey White and Michael Schmidmayr* 90
19. Resistance in Iraq *Jeffrey White and Michael Schmidmayr* 93
20. Resistance in Iraq: Emerging Capabilities and Threats *Jeffrey White* 114
21. Insurgency in Iraq: Implications and Challenges *Michael Eisenstadt, Jeffrey White, and Michael Knights* 117
22. The Implications of Saddam's Capture for the Resistance in Iraq *Jeffrey White* 121
23. Eyewitness Perspectives Assessing Progress in Iraq: Security and Extremism *Jeffrey White and Jonathan Schanzer* 124
24. Faces of Resistance *Jeffrey White* 128
25. Al-Qaeda's Deadly Gamble *Jonathan Schanzer* 131
26. The Battle for Fallujah and Sunni Resistance *Jeffrey White and Ryan Phillips* 133
27. Iraqi Violence: Shiite-Sunni Collision or Collusion? *Jonathan Schanzer and Ryan Phillips* 136
28. Crisis in Iraq: Assessments and Implications *Jeffrey White and Michael Knights* 139
29. Insurgent Operations against the Highways in Iraq *Jeffrey White and Ryan Phillips* 142
30. Ansar al-Islam: Back in Iraq *Jonathan Schanzer* 145

Part Four: The Shiite Opposition 157

Introduction *Jeffrey White* 159
31. Shiite Opposition in Iraq: An Emerging Challenge *Jeffrey White and Michael Schmidmayr* 162
32. To the Brink: Muqtada al-Sadr Challenges the United States *Jeffrey White* 165
33. Over the Brink in Iraq: Muqtada al-Sadr Confronts the Coalition *Jeffrey White* 168
34. United States Should Choose Time, Place to Confront Radical Cleric *Michael Knights* 172
35. The Revolt of Muqtada al-Sadr: Characteristics and Implications *Jeffrey White and Ryan Phillips* 174
36. Muqtada al-Sadr's Continuing Challenge to the Coalition (Part I): The U.S. Military Response *Jeffrey White and Ryan Phillips* 177
37. Muqtada al-Sadr's Continuing Challenge to the Coalition (Part II): An Adaptive Enemy *Jeffrey White and Ryan Phillips* 180
38. Security and Politics *Patrick Clawson* 184
39. Sadrist Revolt Provides Lessons for Counterinsurgency in Iraq *Jeffrey White and Ryan Phillips* 187

Part Five: Postwar Coalition Security Policy 199
Introduction *Michael Knights* 201
40. Envisioning a Post-Saddam Iraqi Military *Michael Eisenstadt and Kenneth Pollack* 205
41. The Future Shape of Military Operations in Support of Postwar Stabilization in Iraq *Michael Knights*..208
42. The New Iraqi Army: Problems and Prospects *Jeffrey White*.................................211
43. Economics of Iraqi Security: Assessing the Value of Security Spending *Michael Knights* 214
44. Militias and the Monopoly of Force in Transitional Iraq *Michael Knights*.............217
45. Setting Realistic Expectations for Iraq's Security Forces *Michael Knights*..............220
46. Lessons of the Iraq War and Its Aftermath *David Petraeus* 223
47. The Multinational Divisions in Iraq: Lessons Learned *Michael Knights*.................226
48. Crisis in Iraq: Military Lessons for the Coalition *Michael Eisenstadt*......................229
49. Short-term Stabilisation in Iraq Could Have Long-Term Costs *Michael Knights* 232
50. The Transfer of Sovereignty in Iraq: Prospects for a Security Agreement *Michael Eisenstadt and Michael Knights* 239

Part Six: Post-Saddam Economics and Politics 243
Introduction *Patrick Clawson* 245
51. What Next after Saddam? 247
52. Building a New Iraq 255
53. The Shiites and the Future of Iraq *Yitzhak Nakash*...259
54. Turkmens, the Soft Underbelly of the War in Northern Iraq *Soner Cagaptay* 262
55. Iraq's Ruptured Pipeline to Peace *Michael Knights*...265
56. Give the Sunnis a Break—and a Stake *Michael Eisenstadt*......................................267
57. How Iraqis View U.S. Role Is Key to Evaluating Progress in Iraq *Patrick Clawson* 269
58. Economics of Iraqi Security: Employment *Michael Knights*.................................272
59. Economics of Iraqi Security: Financing Reconstruction *Patrick Clawson* 275
60. Trying a Tyrant: Should the Iraqis Alone Sit in Judgment of Saddam? *Ruth Wedgwood and Neil Kritz*...279
61. Iraqi Kurdistan and the Transition, Post–Coalition Provisional Authority *Barham Salih*...282
62. Eyewitness Perspectives Assessing Progress in Iraq: Politics, Transition, and the Kurds *Patrick Clawson and Soner Cagaptay* 285
63. The Iraqi Bill of Rights in Regional Perspective *Patrick Clawson*...........................290
64. Kurds Aim to Secure Continued Regional Control *Michael Knights*......................293
65. Iraq for the Iraqis: How and When *Patrick Clawson*...299

66. Challenges in Iraq: Learning from Yemen? *Jonathan Schanzer* 305
67. Sovereignty Now *Dennis Ross* 308
68. Iraq Reconstruction *Jonathan Schanzer* 310

Part Seven: Regional Implications 321

Introduction *Patrick Clawson* 323
69. A Terrorist Front in Iraq? *Matthew Levitt, Roger Cressey, and Avi Jorisch* 325
70. Arabs View the War: Images, Attitudes, and Opinions *Hafez al-Mirazi, Mouafac Harb, and Jonathan Schanzer* 328
71. First Steps to Remake Iraq *Patrick Clawson* 331
72. Impact of Success in Iraq on Gulf States *Simon Henderson* 334
73. Iraq and Iran: Crosswinds? *A. William Samii and Nasser Hadian* 336
74. An Arab Liberal Looks at the Post-Saddam Middle East *Hazem Saghie* 339
75. Can Americans, Turks, and Kurds Get Along in Northern Iraq? A Vision *Soner Cagaptay* 342
76. Iran's Threat to Coalition Forces in Iraq *Raymond Tanter* 345
77. USA Ties Terrorist Attacks in Iraq to Extensive Zarqawi Network *Matthew Levitt* 348
78. Tehran's Hidden Hand: Iran's Mounting Threats in Iraq *Jonathan Schanzer* 353
79. Incident in the Shatt al-Arab Waterway: Iran's Border Sensitivities *Simon Henderson* 356
80. Allied Forces *Soner Cagaptay* 359

Chronology 363

Index 369

Contributors

Michael Knights is the Mendelow Defense Fellow at The Washington Institute, specializing in the military and security affairs of Iraq, Iran, and the Gulf Cooperation Council states. Working with the U.S. Department of Defense, Dr. Knights has undertaken extensive research on lessons learned from U.S. military operations in Iraq since 1990. He earned his doctorate at the Department of War Studies, King's College London, and has worked as a defense journalist for the *Gulf States Newsletter* and *Jane's Intelligence Review*.

Patrick Clawson is deputy director of The Washington Institute and senior editor of *Middle East Quarterly*. A frequent writer and commentator on U.S. Iraq policy, he served previously as a senior research professor at the National Defense University's Institute for National Strategic Studies and as a research economist at the International Monetary Fund and the World Bank. He is the editor, most recently, of *How to Build a New Iraq after Saddam* (The Washington Institute, 2002).

Michael Eisenstadt is a senior fellow at The Washington Institute. A reserve officer in the U.S. Army, he served on active duty in 2001-2002 at United States Central Command (USCENTCOM). He has published widely on Middle Eastern military and security issues, including *U.S. Policy in Post-Saddam Iraq: Lessons from the British Experience*, coedited with Eric Mathewson (The Washington Institute, 2003).

Jeffrey White is an associate of The Washington Institute specializing in the military and security affairs of Iraq and the Levant. Before joining the Institute, he completed a thirty-four-year career with the Defense Intelligence Agency, serving in a variety of senior analytical and leadership positions, writing extensively for senior defense officials including the secretary of defense and the chairman of the Joint Chiefs of Staff, and participating in operational and policy planning. He is the author of a forthcoming study on the Sunni-based resistance in Iraq.

Iraq: Provinces and Capitals
TURKEY
SYRIA
IRAN
SAUDI ARABIA
KUWAIT
Persian Gulf
DAHUK
Dahuk
IRBIL
Irbil
Mosul
MOSUL (NINAWA)
Kirkuk
KIRKUK (TAMIM)
SULAYMANIYA
Sulaymaniya
SALAHUDDIN
Samara
al-Qaim
DIYALA
Baquba
BAGHDAD
Baghdad
Ramadi
ANBAR
WASIT
Kut
Karbala
KARBALA
Hilla
BABIL
Diwaniya
QADISIYA
Najaf
NAJAF
Amara
MAYSAN
DHIQAR
Nasariya
Samawa
Basra
BASRA
MUTHANNA
N
0
200
miles

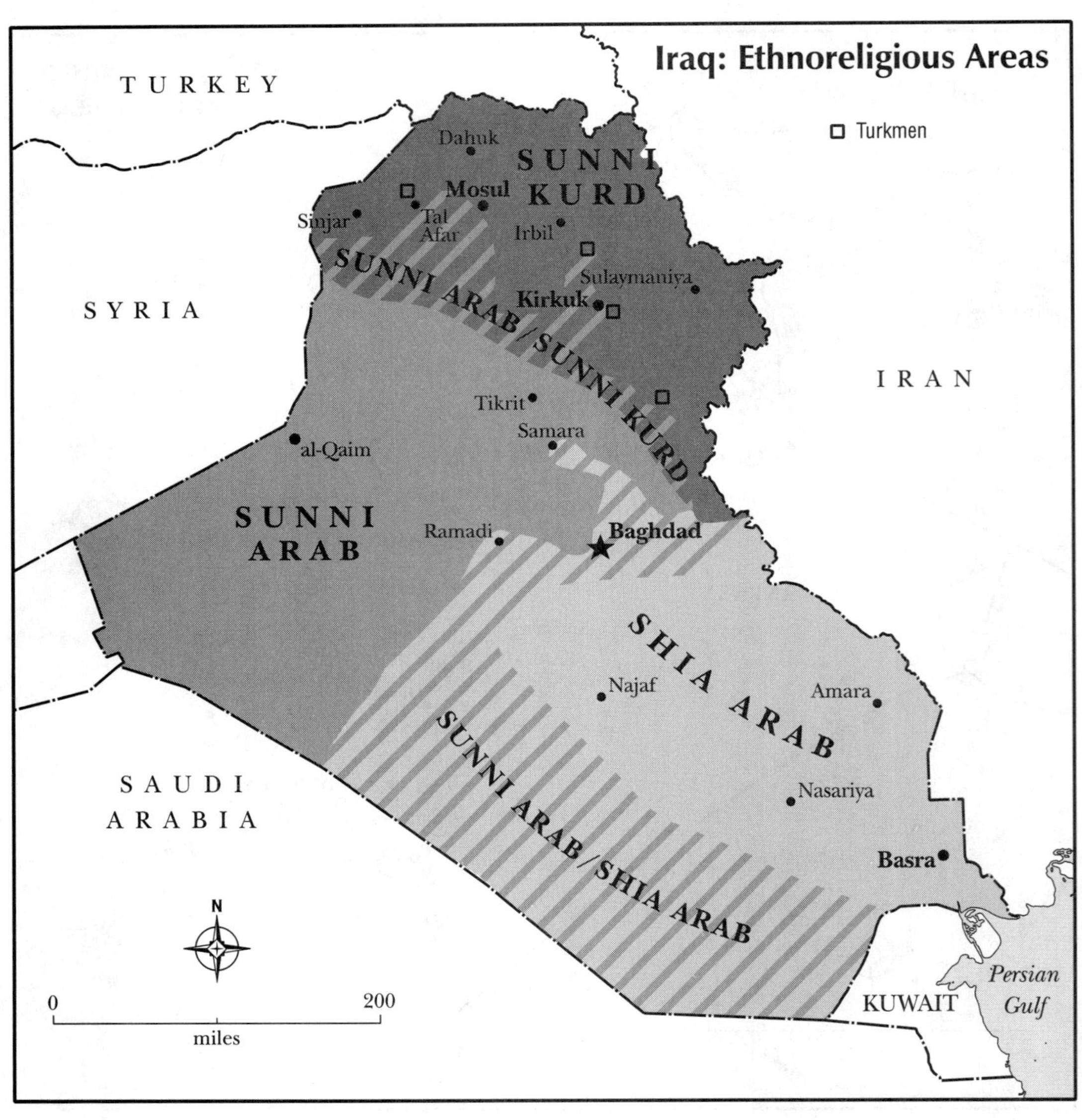

Iraq: Ethnoreligious Areas
Turkmen
TURKEY
SYRIA
IRAN
SAUDI ARABIA
KUWAIT
Persian Gulf
SUNNI KURD
SUNNI ARAB/SUNNI KURD
SUNNI ARAB
SHIA ARAB
SUNNI ARAB/SHIA ARAB
Dahuk
Mosul
Sinjar
Tal Afar
Irbil
Sulaymaniya
Kirkuk
Tikrit
Samara
al-Qaim
Ramadi
Baghdad
Najaf
Amara
Nasariya
Basra
N
0
200
miles

Iraq: Oil Infrastructure
Supergiant Oilfield (5 billion barrels in reserve)
Other Oilfield
Pipeline
Pump Station
Operational Refinery
Tanker Terminal
TURKEY
SYRIA
IRAN
IRAQ
SAUDI ARABIA
KUWAIT
Persian Gulf
Mosul
Kirkuk
Baghdad
Basra
Sufaya
Mushora
Ain Zalah
IT-2A
Butma
Gusair
Alan
Sasan
Ibrahim
Qallan
Adalya
IT-2
Jawan
Qasab
Najma
al-Qayara
Sadid
Demir Dagh
Taqtaq
Bay Hasan
Kirkuk
Chamchamal
Qara Chauq
Jambur
Kor Mor
IT-1A
Hamrin
Palkhana
Gilabat
K-2
Ajil
Qamarim
Chia Surkh
West Tikrit
Judaida
Nau Duman
Injana
Jaria Pika
T-1
K-3
Akkas
Iraq-Syria Pipeline
Kashim al-Ahmar
Mansuriya
Naft Khaneh
Balad
Falluja
East Baghdad
PS-4
Badra
Abu Ghurab
Dhafiriya
Buzurgan
Ahdab
Amara
Kumait
Jabal Fauqi
Marjan
al-Kifl
al-Dujayla
Huwaiza
PS-3
West Kifl
Rafidain
Halfaya
Noor
Iraq Strategic Pipeline
Gharraf
Rifae
Nasariya
Majnun
Samawa
PS-2
West Qurma
Nahi Umar
Subba
Rumayla North
Diwan
al-Ratawi
Siba
Salman
al-Luhays
Tuba
Khawr al-Amara (closed)
al-Raki
Safwan
Jerishan
Rumayla South
Mina al-Bakr
IPSA 2
Abu Khaima
N
0
200
miles

Iraq: No-fly Zones
No-fly Zones
TURKEY
IRAN
SYRIA
IRAQ
SAUDI ARABIA
KUWAIT
Persian Gulf
Zahko
Dahuk
Mosul
Irbil
36°
Sulaymaniya
Kirkuk
Halabja
Tigris R.
Euphrates R.
Tikrit
Samara
Baghdad
Ramadi
33°
Basra
N
0
200
miles

Michael Knights

Introductory Essay

When Operation Iraqi Freedom commenced on March 19, 2003, it was not the beginning of a conflict but the final act of one that had lasted almost thirteen years. Since Iraq's invasion of Kuwait on August 2, 1990, the military containment of Iraq had become a familiar and unwelcome feature of the post-Cold War era. The September 11 terrorist attacks on the United States had brought the Middle East to the center of U.S. national security strategy, and now the invasion of Iraq saw the United States and its coalition allies project major armed forces to the very heart of the Middle East. Although every leading media outlet and many instant experts focused their attention on Iraq, The Washington Institute found that there remained a strong demand for analysis by long-term regional specialists that could go beyond the headlines.

Beginning in March 2003, Institute coverage of Iraq concentrated on providing a realistic and balanced interpretation of the rapidly changing present and venturing an informed view of the future. We focused on the serious issues of prewar intelligence and prisoner abuse within the context of evolving U.S. policy in the Middle East. Throughout, our objective was (and remains) to provide useful policy analysis to U.S. decisionmakers. Thus, the Institute's coverage focused primarily on the political, military, and economic challenges that the coalition confronted on a daily basis.

This book is a companion to the Institute's 1991 *GulfWatch Anthology*, which compiled seventy-eight analyses written by Institute scholars during and immediately after the Gulf crisis of 1990-1991. The seventy-seven texts collected here represent a selection of the Institute's most significant written work on Iraq, produced, with few exceptions, between March 19, 2003, and June 28, 2004, the date of Iraq's formal transition to self-governance.[1]

This anthology serves two important purposes. First, for the reader's convenience, it draws together in one volume the Institute's prodigious work on Iraq from many sources, including The Washington Institute's flagship *PolicyWatch* series,[2] authoritative defense publications such as *Jane's Intelligence Review*, scholarly journals such as the *Middle East Quarterly*, and the opinion columns of major U.S. and European newspapers. Second, the anthology has added new value to the existing body of work through the introductory essays that begin each thematic part. These essays synthesize the key trends and developments evident in the political, military, and economic spheres. When gathered together and viewed as a continuous body of thought, the value of the products of the Institute's intensive coverage of Iraq is greatly increased.

For Institute scholars, the anthology offered an opportunity to step back from tracking new developments in Iraq and focus on the unanswered questions and unresolved issues of the invasion and occupation. Policy choices such as the contentious decision to disband the Iraqi military are placed in broader context. Expectations about the extent of Iraq's political transformation, the pace of security reform, and the country's ability to pay for its own economic reconstruction are critically assessed. Well-grounded judgments are rendered on issues of ongoing relevance, such as the significance of foreign fighters in the resistance and the roles played in Iraq by neighboring states such as Iran and Syria. Suspended in time, the Institute's analyses show which risks and challenges were known or foreseeable and which emerged without warning. This feature gives the anthology lasting value to those seeking to learn lessons from the intense and often bitter experiences of the invasion and its aftermath.

On March 1, 2003, The Washington Institute released *U.S. Policy in Post-Saddam Iraq: Lessons from the British Experience*, excerpts of which make up the first part of this anthology. That publication and other prewar analyses written by Institute scholars set the tone for the Institute's coverage of Iraq, making clear the potential pitfalls that faced an invading and occupying power.

In general, two apparently dichotomous impressions emerge from an analysis of the coalition experience in Iraq. On the one hand, U.S. and coalition military and civilian decisionmakers often knew only a fraction of what they needed to know about Iraq and Iraqis to make timely, high-quality decisions. On the other hand, with little attention paid to the lessons of the British experience or the contemporary history of Iraq's failed 1991 uprising, the West had forgotten much of what it had known and ignored much of what it could have learned about Iraq. Iraq's liberation and subsequent occupation (itself a dichotomy) was characterized by difficult choices between bad and worse alternatives. Every action or lack of action in Iraq had political costs as well as benefits, meaning that there was no ideal solution to most of the country's problems. Due partly to conditions outside its control and partly to policy choices, the coalition faced a far greater political, security, and economic vacuum in Iraq than it had anticipated, and early mistakes proved difficult to rectify. Indeed, the Iraq experience demonstrated that foreknowledge, detailed planning, and effective early adaptation of overarching plans are key prerequisites for future nation-building projects.

The Institute's coverage of Iraq documents the learning curve traced by the coalition, a painful process that eventually established a firm foundation for the new Iraqi Interim Government, the U.S. embassy, and the multinational forces. Much good and unheralded work was done by coalition military and civilian personnel throughout the occupation of Iraq, but it was not until the last few months—in some cases weeks—of coalition control that lasting and effective formulas for cooperation were developed in the areas of integrated security-forces training, streamlined disbursement of military aid, security coordination, and political partnership with legitimate Iraqi leaders. The future looks brighter: That is what visiting coalition military and political speakers have consistently told Institute audiences, and that is what the early performance of the new interim government suggests. It is striking that those who are in Iraq, those who are most familiar with the capabilities of Iraqis, are the most optimistic about the country's future.

No one doubts that the future will hold many challenges. Ensuring safe, fair, and free elections in winter 2004-2005 will provide the first major test for the new Iraq. Assuming the country can overcome this hurdle, 2005 will be a trying and decisive year, when many deferred issues concerning the fundamentals of the Iraqi state—in particular, the roles of religion and federalism—will resurface during the national debate over the formation of a new constitution. Violence will almost certainly be a feature of this debate, but to what extent is unclear and highly dependent on the outcome of the preceding elections. U.S. returnees from Iraq voice quiet confidence that free and fair voting held against a backdrop of an inclusive political campaign will result in the election of a surprising number of moderate, secular representatives. One of the primary lessons of the past year and a half is that the United States and its allies need to enable this silent majority of Iraqis to find their voice. Moreover, the past thirteen years have shown that the job of fostering security and freedom in Iraq does not and should not end. Accordingly, The Washington Institute will continue to focus on this important, vibrant, and now free country.

Michael Knights
Mendelow Defense Fellow
The Washington Institute

Notes

1. A comprehensive listing of The Washington Institute's written work on Iraq can be accessed at www.washingtoninstitute.org

2. *PolicyWatch* is a series of brief analytical essays on breaking events in the Middle East written by Washington Institute scholars and associates. These analyses are regularly published on the Institute's website at www.washingtoninstitute.org/watch/Policywatch/index.htm

Part One

Historical Antecedents

Michael Eisenstadt

Introduction

The U.S. invasion and occupation of Iraq, and the challenges that American policymakers confronted in their wake, were prefigured nearly a century before by the British invasion and occupation of the Ottoman provinces of Mesopotamia during World War I, followed by more than a decade of British rule (direct and then indirect), and finally by the granting of Iraq's independence in 1932.

The British experience holds contemporary relevance due to its enduring impact on Iraqi society and politics. The history of this period provides valuable insights into Iraqi political culture, the logic of foreign intervention, and the links between regional and domestic politics in the Middle East. Iraqis often perceive echoes of the past in contemporary developments, and there are a number of intriguing parallels between the British and American experiences in Iraq:

- The British promised the Arabs independence in return for their help in defeating the Ottoman Empire during World War I. These promises were, by and large, not kept, leading to a bloody revolt against British rule in Iraq in 1920. The U.S. invasion of Iraq was likewise accompanied by the promise of liberation and prosperity. The joy of liberation felt by many was, however, tempered by the subsequent chaos, looting, economic hardship, insecurity, and often humiliating occupation, which produced a nationalist and Islamic backlash that has fueled anti-American violence.
- One of the first challenges the British faced was finding a leader acceptable to broad segments of the population of the new Iraqi state. Lacking local candidates with wide popular appeal, Britain eventually installed a foreigner, Faysal bin Hussein (son of the Sharif of Mecca), on the throne of Iraq. The United States likewise faced a leadership vacuum in post-Saddam Iraq. As a result, the new Iraqi institutions of governance have drawn heavily on political exiles who returned to the country after the fall of Saddam Hussein.
- After World War I, political and financial constraints forced Britain to keep its military presence in Iraq to a minimum, and it was compelled to police the country "on the cheap," relying mainly on air power (in accordance with the British doctrine of "air control") and local Iraqi forces—the Iraq Levies—who came to be reviled for their ties to the British authorities. The United States has similarly tried to police Iraq with a force widely perceived as too small to keep the peace and secure the country's borders against terrorists, while the Iraqi security forces it created have been the target of Iraqi insurgents, who see them as a tool of the occupation.

Despite the passage of more than a year since the start of the U.S. occupation and the recent transfer of sovereignty to the Iraqi Interim Government, the legacy of the formative period of modern Iraqi history continues to influence how many Iraqis perceive the U.S. presence in Iraq. As a result, there is still much that U.S. policymakers could learn from the British experience.[1] Indeed, the burdens of the past will continue to weigh on the present, even as the United States and Britain work together to create a new Iraq.

Notes

1. For example, a discussion of how the past may affect future efforts to conclude a security agreement with Iraq can be found in chapter 50, "The Transfer of Sovereignty in Iraq: Prospects for a Security Agreement."

Michael Eisenstadt

1
U.S. Policy in Post-Saddam Iraq: Lessons from the British Experience

In the planning stages of the U.S-led war against Saddam Hussein's regime, policymakers and military planners studied the post-World War II occupation of Germany and Japan for lessons relevant to the reconstruction and transformation of Iraq. Although it is natural for Americans to draw on their own national experience for guidance and inspiration, there is merit in studying the British experience in Iraq as well. In addition to the numerous intriguing parallels between the British and American cases, the Iraqis are likely to view U.S. actions through the lens of their country's experience during the British era. Hence, it is vital that U.S. policymakers and military planners develop some sense of the history that preceded the current U.S. involvement in Iraq and that could shape its outcome.

British Goals and Achievements

The British era in Iraq lasted more than four decades, from 1914 to 1958. Britain's involvement in the country's affairs was most intense during World War I and the subsequent League of Nations mandate period, though its influence endured even after Iraq achieved independence in 1932. The British era ended with the 1958 coup that toppled the monarchy and forced the final departure of British advisors.

Britain's primary goal in Iraq was stability, which was necessary in order to secure British lines of communication with India; protect British interests in the potentially lucrative oil fields of Iran and Iraq; and preserve the political structures that underpinned the Iraqi monarchy, the main conduit of British influence. Yet, stability often proved elusive. Iraq experienced a major anti-British revolt in 1920; tribal and nationalist uprisings in Kurdistan in 1919-1920, 1923-1924, 1931-1932, and 1935-1936; and Shiite tribal rebellions in 1935-36. Moreover, several coups followed independence, including a 1941 takeover by pro-Nazi elements that resulted in reoccupation by British forces. Nevertheless, Britain managed to secure its interests in Iraq for nearly half a century, though ultimately at great cost to its long-term position there.

British influence in Iraq never extended far beyond a small circle that included the king, various tribal leaders, and a number of pro-British politicians and military officers. Yet,

Originally published as "Conclusion: Lessons for U.S. Policymakers," in Michael Eisenstadt and Eric Mathewson (eds.), *U.S. Policy in Post-Saddam Iraq: Lessons from the British Experience* (Washington, D.C. Washington Institute for Near East Policy, 2003).

Britain's impact on Iraq can still be felt today. On one hand, the British introduced constitutional government and established the rudiments of a modern administration, economy, and infrastructure. Moreover, during the 1920s, the British military—particularly the Royal Air Force—may have played a key role in holding Iraq together until it achieved independence.[1]

On the other hand, British policies and actions contributed to some of the more problematic features of Iraqi politics, including the consolidation of minority (Sunni Arab) rule; the establishment of a strong central government that stifled Kurdish and Shiite aspirations; and the involvement of the military in repression and domestic politics. These outcomes can be attributed in part to Britain's creation of a system of control rather than of governance—a system in which maintaining stability was more important than promoting democracy.

U.S. Objectives

The United States has adopted a far more ambitious agenda than that pursued by the British nearly a century ago. The political transformation of Iraq and the region lie at the heart of the Bush administration's approach. After ridding the country of Saddam's regime, U.S. officials have pledged to seek a stable, unified Iraq that is at peace with its neighbors; free of weapons of mass destruction and ties to terrorism; and led by a broad-based, representative government that is on the path to democracy.[2] The U.S. agenda also includes leveraging regime change in Iraq to pressure and deter Iran and Syria; to serve as a hedge against instability in Saudi Arabia; to establish conditions conducive to the resolution of the Arab-Israeli conflict; and to encourage political reform throughout a region much in need of change.

In undertaking this mission, the United States would do well to study the British experience. The British agenda was relatively modest, and major changes have occurred in Iraq, the region, and the world since then. Nevertheless, the British era offers relevant insights into the dynamics of Iraqi politics, the logic of foreign intervention, and the links between regional and domestic politics in the Middle East.

Iraqi Nationalism

Historical Background. Initially, British forces invading Mesopotamia during World War I were greeted with indifference by much of the Iraqi populace. Arab nationalism had not yet taken root in the Ottoman provinces of Basra, Baghdad, and Mosul; and the British pacified the population by improving economic conditions, paying off influential urban notables and tribal sheikhs, and governing with greater integrity and efficiency than had the Turks.[3]

Iraqi attitudes changed dramatically after the war, however. British policies alienated many tribesmen and less prominent sheikhs and threatened the socioeconomic status of the Shiite clerics of Najaf and Karbala.[4] Moreover, Britain showed no sign of leaving; in April 1920, it was assigned a League of Nations mandate over Iraq. Many Iraqis saw this extension of British rule as a betrayal of wartime promises of independence.

The consequent suspicion and hostility reached a peak in June 1920, when demonstrations were held in Baghdad and anti-British violence erupted in Shiite tribal areas of the middle and lower Euphrates regions. Britain did not completely quell the uprising until four months later, at the cost of 450 British killed and 1,250 wounded; Iraqi losses numbered some 8,450 killed or wounded.[5]

The 1920 revolt marked a turning point in British policy toward Iraq. A manifestation of both religious and incipient nationalist feeling against the British presence, the uprising demonstrated that direct rule was economically and politically unsustainable, and that an indigenous administration was needed to prepare the country for independence. The heavy costs of the revolt also influenced the ongoing debate in Britain regarding the empire's overseas commitments. The result was a dramatic reduction in the British military presence in Iraq.

Lessons Learned. Most Iraqis would welcome regime change, but few would take kindly to a large, open-ended U.S. presence. Iraqi nationalism remains a potent force, and the United States must be prepared for a wary, if not hostile, reception from the many Iraqis who are bitter about past U.S. "betrayals" (most notably, Washington's failure to support the post-Gulf War uprising in 1991), about the impact of sanctions on their country, and about U.S. policy toward Israel and the Palestinians. Iraqis may also harbor fears about U.S. intentions, with some believing that Washington aims to control Iraq's oil and others (particularly Sunni Arabs) concerned about U.S. plans to bring democracy to the country.

To demonstrate goodwill and mitigate Iraqi mistrust, the United States should pursue the following objectives as soon as is feasible:

- initiate humanitarian assistance and reconstruction;
- minimize the U.S. military footprint;
- involve Iraqis in governance;
- show that Iraq's oil is being used to benefit Iraqis; and
- leave Iraq once U.S. goals are met.

The main challenge for the United States will be remaining in Iraq long enough to achieve significant and lasting benefits without overstaying its welcome—thereby stoking anti-American sentiment. In practical terms, this means that U.S. objectives should be realistic and attainable within a relatively short timeframe—perhaps twelve to eighteen months, though preparations should be made to stay longer if conditions permit.

Loosening the Grip of the Iraqi State

Historical Background. During World War I, Britain made Baghdad the seat of its civil administration in Iraq, unifying three former Ottoman provinces that had not previously formed a coherent political or socioeconomic unit. The monarchy reinforced this tendency toward centralization, believing that only a strong government and a powerful military could hold the country's diverse population together.

The largely Sunni Arab ruling elite also looked to Arab nationalism as a means of unifying Iraqis under a single ideology and forging a new national identity. The Kurds and Shiites, however, saw these efforts as the elite's attempt to impose its hegemony, resulting in frequent bouts of unrest in the largely Kurdish north and Shiite south. Indeed, these centralizing policies paved the way for the authoritarian military regimes that controlled Iraq after 1958 and for the totalitarian rule of the civilian Ba'ath after 1968.

Lessons Learned. The United States will need to encourage the decentralization of political power in post-Saddam Iraq in order to prevent a return to authoritarian rule. From the outset, U.S. military and civil officials should bolster the surviving administrative machinery in the various provinces of Iraq (after purging them of regime loyalists) in order to reduce the influence of Baghdad; create the political space necessary for the emergence of local participatory government; and, perhaps, lay the groundwork for a federal political structure in a new Iraq.

From Minority Rule to Power Sharing

Historical Background. When the British set out to create an indigenous government in Iraq following the 1920 revolt, they leaned heavily on the largely Sunni Arab elite that had administered the country under Ottoman rule. The British believed that only this group had the necessary skills and experience to run the country.[6] They also believed that tribal Kurds and Shiites would resist the creation of a strong central government, given the Kurdish rebellion of 1919 and the major role that Shiite clerics and tribes had played in the 1920 revolt.

Although Britain's interests may have been well served by a minority-led government dependent on British support for its survival, minority rule turned out to be a recipe for instability and conflict between the central government and the Kurds and Shiites.

Under the monarchy, the government functioned as a "close oligarchy" of 200-300 individuals, mainly urban notables, military officers, and tribal sheikhs. Most were urban Sunni Arabs, with a few Kurds, Shiites, Christians, and Jews playing bit parts (although Shiites and Jews played dominant roles in certain sectors of the economy). The overwhelming majority of Iraqis were thus effectively shut out of politics, establishing a pattern of exclusion that survives to this day.

Lessons Learned. To break the nexus between minority rule on the one hand and instability and repression on the other, the United States should help Iraqis create a broad-based post-Saddam government that incorporates representatives of all major ethnic and religious groups, upholds the principles of participation and power sharing, and safeguards minority rights. Although such a reconfiguration in the balance of power would solve some of Iraq's problems, it would also create new challenges for the United States.

For instance, Washington will need to reassure Sunni Arabs that the removal of Tikritis (i.e., individuals from Saddam Hussein's hometown) and their allies from the government and military will not presage the disenfranchisement of the entire Sunni community. Even as the United States purges regime loyalists from the post-Saddam administration, it should cultivate and support those Sunnis who do not have strong ties to the old regime.

At the same time, Washington must help the Shiites make tangible progress toward achieving political influence commensurate with their demographic weight, lest they become alienated from the post-Saddam government and receptive to the entreaties of extremist groups or Tehran. Similarly, the Kurds must be persuaded to participate in the new central government in order to bolster the regime's legitimacy and avoid creating the impression that Kurdish autonomy within Iraq will be a stepping stone to a separate Kurdish state. Finally, the United States must identify and cultivate a new generation of moderate leaders (both secular and religious) who are willing to play by democratic rules.

'Outsiders,' 'Insiders,' and the Challenge of New Leadership

Historical Background. One of Britain's main challenges was finding an individual of sufficient stature and widespread appeal to serve as head of the new Iraqi state. At the Cairo Conference in March 1921, the British opted to install a foreigner—Faysal bin Hussein, son of the Sharif of Mecca—on the throne of Iraq. Faysal's emergence as the candidate of choice was due to several factors:

- Britain's desire to repay his family's wartime service and compensate him for the loss of his Arab Kingdom of Syria at the hands of the French in July 1920;
- his reputation as a genuine Arab war hero;
- his status as an "outsider" who was not associated with any Iraqi faction or region;
- his standing among the former Ottoman military officers and officials who had served with him in Damascus and who would soon form the backbone of the new administration in Iraq; and
- his status as a sayyed (descendant of the Prophet Muhammad), which made him acceptable to some Shiites.[7]

Although dependent on the British for survival, King Faysal I challenged them on key issues (e.g., by pushing for Iraqi independence and military conscription) out of personal conviction as well as political expediency. His less adroit successors made similar efforts to distance themselves from their foreign patrons. Nevertheless, the royal family's British connection earned them the enmity of many Iraqis and ultimately sealed their fate.

Lessons Learned. The United States should let the Iraqi people choose their own leaders, avoiding the perception that it is imposing its preferred candidates. At the same time, it should not hesitate to help Iraqis form a transitional government or establish new civil society institutions and structures; in fact, U.S. advice on such matters may prove critical. Moreover, "outsider" status should not be an obstacle to high office in a post-Saddam Iraq if the individual in question has ample qualifications, can forge strong ties with well-positioned "insiders," and can work with Washington without becoming too closely identified with U.S. positions or policies.

The Tribal Temptation

Historical Background. During the period of direct rule, the British sought security and stability in the countryside through alliances with tribal sheikhs. At the time, the tribes were heavily armed and numerous (some three-quarters of the population lived in tribal areas), constituting the most powerful element in Iraqi society. Yet, government-supported sheikhs often abused their newfound authority (e.g., by imposing burdensome taxes on their tribesmen). Hence, although this policy may have ensured short-term stability, it earned the British the enduring hostility of the tribesmen and contributed to the 1920 revolt and subsequent uprisings.

Lessons Learned. The United States might be tempted to strike alliances with congenial tribal sheikhs in order to stabilize the postwar countryside (though it is unclear how much real authority these sheikhs possess). Such alliances may help accomplish short-term security objectives, but they could also jeopardize long-term U.S. goals by undermining the authority of the post-Saddam government and reinforcing values and forms of social organization that are inimical to the emergence of pluralistic, representative government.[8]

In any event, if the United States seeks alliances with sheikhs, it should impose curbs on their arbitrary exercise of authority and facilitate the formation of institutions whose membership cuts across tribal boundaries. Such measures may help prevent the retribalization of Iraqi society, a trend that has been encouraged by Saddam Hussein.

Building Democracy

Historical Background. During the mandate period, Britain created the trappings of democratic government in Iraq, with a king, a council of ministers, and a parliament whose roles were defined by a constitution. In practice, however, this system primarily served the narrow interests of the British, the king, and the small circle of men who dominated Iraqi politics prior to and after independence.

Due to the absence of strong governmental institutions, politics during the monarchy were highly personalized. King Faysal I often played a role in the formation and dissolution of governments, impinging on the prerogatives of parliament and exceeding the broad powers granted to him by the constitution. Both the crown and the British sought to influence the outcome of parliamentary elections in order to secure positions for their preferred candidates. Moreover, many of those who served in parliament did so out of a desire for personal gain, not out of a commitment to public service.

Eventually, democracy came to be discredited in the eyes of many Iraqis because of political corruption, British meddling, and the government's failure to respond to their needs. During the reign of Faysal's son and immediate successor, King Ghazi, military coups became the primary means by which governments were changed, setting the stage for the eventual overthrow of the monarchy in 1958.

Lessons Learned. After three decades of totalitarian Baath rule, the Iraqi people may be ready to take the first steps toward establishing a functioning democracy. The British experience offers a number of relevant lessons:

- Although the United States can help Iraqis create a transitional administration and establish democratic structures and institutions, it must avoid the appearance of meddling in Iraqi politics. If democracy is to take root, it must be built primarily by Iraqis, in response to specific Iraqi conditions and needs.
- The establishment of democratic structures alone is insufficient to produce democratic processes or outcomes. The Iraqis must also create civil society institutions and strengthen basic freedoms, which are essential preconditions for building democracy. In addition, they must devote significant effort toward preventing corruption by fostering transparency, accountability, and the rule of law.
- The military could pose the greatest long-term threat to democracy in Iraq. In this context, the depoliticization of the officer corps may be Saddam's sole positive legacy; failure to preserve this accomplishment or obtain the military's commitment to uphold and defend a new Iraqi constitution could doom attempts to build a functioning democracy in Iraq.

Getting the Military Out of Internal Security . . . and Keeping It Out of Politics

Historical Background. Following the 1920 revolt, Britain dramatically curtailed its military presence in Iraq as part of a larger effort to cut expenses and scale down its overseas commitments. Responsibility for internal security was handed to the Royal Air Force and the Iraq Levies (a British-led force of approximately 4,000 soldiers, most of whom were Assyrian).[9]

The British insisted that the Iraqi army be kept small so that it would not threaten their position in Iraq. For its part, the Iraqi government wanted a strong army with which to impose its will on recalcitrant Kurds and Shiites, strengthen its hand vis-à-vis Britain, and bolster the process of nation building. This issue was a major point of contention for Britain and Iraq throughout the mandate period. Between 1921 and 1932, the army grew from 3,500 to 11,500 troops, but it was still smaller than many Iraqi officers and politicians would have liked.[10] Following independence, the army nearly quadrupled in size, expanding to 43,000 troops by 1941.[11] This growth occurred at a time when Britain's ability (and, perhaps, its inclination) to influence the selection and training of new Iraqi officers was greatly diminished.[12]

The premature death of King Faysal I in 1933 and the ascension of his inexperienced and politically inept son opened the field to civilian politicians who sought to turn the armed forces into an instrument of control and a weapon against political rivals. The military soon became engaged in repressing minorities and the regime's tribal opponents, beginning with the massacre of Assyrians in 1933 and the quashing of Kurdish and Shiite tribal uprisings in 1935-1936.

Such measures exacerbated tensions in Iraqi society and confirmed the perception shared by many Kurds and Shiites that the military was an instrument of Sunni Arab domination. At the same time, the officers who led these military actions became heroes in the eyes of certain Iraqis. With the added encouragement of civilian politicians, the officer corps came to view itself as a legitimate political actor. This set the stage for the series of coups that plagued Iraq between 1936 and 1941.

Lessons Learned. In order to ensure a stable, peaceful post-Saddam Iraq, several constraints will need to be placed on the Iraqi military. These include:

- barring the military from all internal security responsibilities;
- creating an apolitical, professional officer corps;
- placing legal curbs on political recruitment and ideological indoctrination within the military; and
- erecting normative and constitutional barriers to military intervention in politics.

Moreover, the United States must avoid using Iraqi military units that defect or surrender as a stabilization force in the aftermath of regime change. Such a step could alienate the Iraqi people, who might see it as presaging a return to authoritarian rule and a betrayal of U.S. promises of democracy. It could also create the impression that internal security is an appropriate mission for the Iraqi military. Therefore, coalition or other international forces should be used to ensure both internal and external security until a reformed Iraqi police force and a reconstituted military can assume their respective missions.

The United States must also confront the challenge of reeducating Iraq's officer corps and reorganizing the military. Because such measures are crucial to the stability and survival of a post-Saddam government, they should be undertaken sooner rather than later, while the United States has maximum leverage, even if they create resentment among some Iraqis.

The Impact of Regional and International Developments

Historical Background. Even in the 1920s and 1930s—long before the advent of satellite television and the internet—regional and international developments had a significant impact on Iraqi attitudes toward British policy. Britain's wartime promises to the Arabs, President Woodrow Wilson's Fourteen Points, and the formation of the League of Nations all raised Iraqi expectations of independence, making direct British rule over Iraq unsustainable. Moreover, Britain's support for a Jewish national home in Palestine, its unsuccessful attempts to manage the conflict between Arabs and Zionists, and—in particular—the outbreak of the 1936-1939 Arab revolt in Palestine stoked anti-British sentiment in Iraq and complicated Anglo-Iraqi relations.

Lessons Learned. Postwar Iraqi attitudes toward the United States will be affected by developments elsewhere in the region. Growing anti-Americanism, U.S. policy toward the Israeli-Palestinian conflict, and the U.S.-led war on terrorism may be particularly influential. For example, continuing Israeli-Palestinian violence could offset any goodwill generated by U.S. humanitarian assistance and reconstruction in Iraq. Hence, Washington must show those in the region that it is making an effort to address and resolve the conflict. Moreover, al-Qaeda terrorist attacks against U.S. interests elsewhere could embolden Iraqis who oppose the U.S. presence in their country. And should the United States target Hizballah in a future phase of the war on terror, factions of the Iraqi Shiite Islamic Dawa Party with longstanding ties to the Lebanon-based organization might respond by targeting U.S. personnel or interests in Iraq.

The Limits of Power and the Dangers of Overreach

The British experience in Iraq serves as a cautionary tale for U.S. policymakers. World War I left the British public weary, government coffers drained, and faith in Britain's imperial mission undermined. Although the public was in no mood for costly new commitments in the Middle East, many British officials nevertheless believed that they would be able to

> *re-shape the region in line with European political interests, ideas, and ideals. . . . [T]he British government had arrived at a compromise with British society, by the terms of which Britain could assert her mastery in the Middle East so long as she could do so at little cost. To British officials who underestimated the difficulties Britain would encounter in governing the region—who, indeed, had no conception of the magnitude of what they had undertaken—that meant Britain was in the Middle East to stay. In retrospect, however, it was an early indication that Britain was likely to leave.*[13]

The United States might encounter similar problems translating vision into reality in the Middle East. Already, ill portents abound regarding the prospects for the Bush administration's agenda in Iraq. The U.S. economy is faltering, the depth of domestic support for intervention is uncertain, and international opposition is strong. New phases in the war on terror and renewed proliferation concerns in Iran and North Korea loom on the horizon, while a lack of bipartisan support raises questions about the sustainability of the administration's plans in Iraq should the intervention bog down or the next election change the occupant of the White House. Such problems could make it difficult to maintain the focus required to sustain a major, long-term commitment to the reconstruction and transformation of Iraq.

Iraqis and other Middle Easterners continue to live with the legacy of decisions made by Britain eighty years ago. Similarly, decisions currently being made in Washington could affect the peoples of the region for decades to come. The stakes are high, the challenges in Iraq are formidable, and the domestic, regional, and international environment is inhospitable. As U.S. policymakers navigate the challenges ahead, one can only hope that they will be guided by wisdom, insight—and a solid grasp of history.

Notes

1. Hanna Batatu, *The Old Social Classes and the Revolutionary Movements of Iraq* (Princeton, N.J.: Princeton University Press, 1978), pp. 24-25.

2. President George W. Bush, speech before the American Enterprise Institute, Washington, D.C., February 26, 2003 (transcript available online at www.whitehouse.gov/news/releases/2003/02/20030226-11.html); Undersecretary of Defense for Policy Douglas J. Feith, testimony given during *The Future of Iraq:*

Hearing before the Senate Foreign Relations Committee, 108th Cong., 1st sess., February 11, 2003 (transcript available online at www.defenselink.mil/policy/speech/feb_11_03.html); Undersecretary of State for Political Affairs Mark Grossman, testimony given during *The Future of Iraq: Hearing before the Senate Foreign Relations Committee*, 108th Cong., 1st sess., February 11, 2003; National Security Advisor Condoleezza Rice, interview, Face the Nation, Columbia Broadcasting System, February 9, 2002.

3. Philip Willard Ireland, *Iraq: A Study in Political Development* (London: Jonathan Cape, 1937), pp. 75-77.

4. Yitzhak Nakash, *The Shi'is of Iraq* (Princeton, N.J.: Princeton University Press, 1994), pp. 66-72.

5. Ireland, *Iraq*, p. 273.

6. Charles Tripp, "Iraq: The Imperial Precedent," *Le Monde Diplomatique* (Paris), January 2003.

7. Charles Tripp, *A History of Iraq* (Cambridge: Cambridge University Press, 2000), pp. 48-49.

8. In Afghanistan, the United States has continued to work closely with warlords accused of past (and ongoing) human rights abuses and wartime excesses. In the words of Lt. Gen. Dan McNeill, the senior U.S. officer in country, such cooperation is justified because "they are providing a degree of security and stability out and away from Kabul." David Zucchino, "General Values Alliance with Afghan Warlords," *Los Angeles Times*, November 4, 2002. This approach holds obvious appeal for military officers who, when confronted with the bewildering complexities of an alien society's politics, prefer the apparent simplicity of dealing with a single individual standing atop a hierarchical organization that seems much like their own. (This analogy fails to capture the complexities and nonhierarchical nature of Arab tribal politics, though.) On the tension between tribalism and democracy in contemporary Afghanistan, see Abbas Jalbani, "A Return to Tribalism?" *Dawn*, September 12, 2002.

9. *Iraq and the Persian Gulf* (London: Naval Intelligence Division, the Admiralty, 1944), p. 295; Mohammad A. Tarbush, *The Role of the Military in Politics: A Case Study of Iraq to 1941* (London: Kegan Paul International, 1982), p. 76.

10. Peter Sluglett, *Britain in Iraq: 1914-1932* (London: Ithaca Press, 1976), p. 260.

11. Tripp, *A History of Iraq*, p. 78.

12. As a result of this rapid expansion, large numbers of lower-middle-class Iraqis became officers, among them the men who would overthrow the monarchy in 1958 and transform Iraqi politics over the subsequent decade. Hence, the military expansion that had been intended to strengthen the monarchy ultimately led to its

undoing. Mark Heller, “Politics and the Military in Iraq and Jordan, 1920-1958,” *Armed Forces and Society* 4, no. 1 (November 1977), pp. 83-85; Marion Farouk-Sluglett and Peter Sluglett, *Iraq since 1958: From Revolution to Dictatorship* (New York: I. B. Taurus, 1987), pp. 36-37.

13. David Fromkin, *A Peace to End All Peace: The Fall of the Ottoman Empire and the Creation of the Modern Middle East* (New York: Avon Books, 1989), pp. 561-562.

Part Two

Operation Iraqi Freedom

Michael Knights

Introduction

When Operation Iraqi Freedom (OIF) began on March 19, 2003, the broad outlines of coalition military strategy were well known. Thanks to years of no-fly-zone operations, which had been ramped up to new levels of intensity in June 2002, the coalition had air superiority even before the war began, allowing the near simultaneous commencement of land and air operations. Following the Turkish parliament's decision to refuse access to one U.S. division through northern Iraq, a lean four-division coalition ground force launched from Kuwait, seeking to close on Baghdad as rapidly as possible, bypassing other major cities. Coalition airstrikes on Iraqi government and civilian infrastructure were strictly limited. The war plan envisaged a primarily "inside-out" approach, identifying Baghdad as the Baath center of gravity and emphasizing the selective engagement of only those regime elements that were determined to resist the coalition. But, to quote Helmuth von Moltke, "No plan survives contact with the enemy," and Operation Iraqi Freedom was to be no exception. In fact, even as the war progressed it became apparent that major combat operations would be only the opening shot of a longer struggle to remove the threat posed by members and associates of the Baath regime.

The broad lines of Iraq's "counterstrategy" became evident in the first four days of the war. As Jeffrey White anticipated in his prewar analysis, Iraqi defensive strategy involved "fighting in as many places as possible, employing all armed elements that are willing and able to battle coalition ground forces." Iraq employed regime loyalists—the Fedayeen Saddam—to aggressively harass coalition lines of communication. White noted on March 25, 2003, that Iraq preferred to fight the war "outside-in," fighting coalition forces at multiple points simultaneously, from the country's borders to Baghdad. Thousands of weapons caches and ammunition storage points had been established all over the country in anticipation of a dispersed and protracted resistance effort. Baath loyalists displayed determination in pressing their attacks on coalition forces, even sallying forth from bypassed cities to attack coalition convoys. As White commented before and during the war, the potential existed for prolonged resistance to coalition operations.

Similarly, the Baath regime showed itself to be more resilient than anticipated, maintaining what White termed the "theater of government" and the apparent continuity of government functions. The regime did not collapse as soon as the war began, nor did it carry out widespread demolition of critical infrastructure or flood large areas. As Michael Eisenstadt noted one week into the war, regime actions suggested that Saddam Hussein and the Iraqi leadership saw the war as survivable, even winnable. The regime did not take the "Samson option"—that is, initiating spiteful acts of sabotage that would have invoked international censure and highlighted the difference between Iraqi national interests and those of the regime—but instead sought to maintain the visage of a legitimate government. A week before the battle of Baghdad, Eisenstadt suggested that the capture of the Iraqi capital would mean "the fall of the regime" but not necessarily "an end to resistance." Envisioning a "new phase" of the war to follow, Eisenstadt asked: "Will the regime collapse . . . or fade away to fight another day?" When Baghdad fell nine days later, there was no final stand, no Samson option, and the regime did indeed melt away.

The speed of the coalition advance and the selectiveness of its targeting of Iraqi forces enabled the rapid success of major combat operations during the war. A mere twenty-one days elapsed between the first coalition airstrikes and the destruction of Saddam's statue in al-Fardus Square on April 9. The four-division force had proven sufficient for the removal of the regime, but key questions regarding the decisiveness of combat operations were already emerging before the war had even ended. As Eisenstadt and White noted on April 2, a quick war threatened to yield "an unstable peace." On the one hand, speed and humaneness reduced coalition and Iraqi casualties; on the other hand, the campaign did not leave the regime undeniably "bowed, broken, and incapable of resuming operations against coalition forces or subverting a new Iraqi government." Due to the speed of the operation, the selective engagement of the enemy, and the lean forces that were deployed, fewer than 12,000 prisoners of war were captured. The majority of Iraqi leaders and combatants simply melted into the civilian community, prompting the Institute to note on April 11, "If the coalition has to root such figures out of small villages, tensions will undoubtedly increase between [coalition] forces and tribal elements." Although the end of major combat operations was announced on May 1, the larger mission of setting the conditions for the emergence of a broad-based post-Saddam government was far from complete.

Even before the final collapse of the Baath regime in early April, the coalition had begun a transition from war fighting to stabilization and support operations. In addition to providing humanitarian and reconstruction assistance, the coalition was expected to secure key infrastructure against endemic looting, to search for leadership figures and weapons of mass destruction (WMD), and to engage in force protection as a pattern of resistance attacks began to emerge. As would be the case with so many features of the campaign in Iraq, many contradictory requirements left the coalition with no easy choices. Force protection and other missions (e.g., humanitarian aid, reconstruction) were intimately connected yet sometimes appeared mutually exclusive. Balancing displays of authority and friendliness proved challenging in the dangerous and lawless postwar environment. The line between liberator and occupier was a fine one, and coalition forces were required to straddle it wherever they operated in Iraq. Institute analyses from the late-war period reflect the deep uncertainty felt at the time over how the Iraqi people would respond to the coalition presence.

Operation Iraqi Freedom was rich in operational lessons concerning the ability of coalition forces to maneuver quickly and to project firepower regardless of terrain or weather conditions. At the same time, it was also clear that coalition operational capabilities outstripped the ability of the U.S. and allied intelligence and planning communities to prepare strategic and operational decisionmakers for the war. Questions over the assessment of Iraq's WMD capabilities grew with time. The resilience of the regime was not anticipated, nor did coalition decisionmakers have any reliable way of gauging Iraqi popular opinion toward either the regime or the coalition. Perhaps most important, it was clear that no matter how operationally and tactically effective coalition forces were, military power alone was not sufficient to achieve Operation Iraqi Freedom's strategic objectives. In the immediate postwar period, it became clear that the occupation of Iraq represented a task even more challenging than the defeat of the Baath military. Stabilizing the country would require faster and more regular adaptation, larger forces, and, ultimately, greater sacrifice in terms of coalition casualties. It would require, as the Institute noted, "the same blend of forethought, calculated risk, and determined execution" as the war-fighting phase.

Jeffrey White

2
What Kind of Defense Might Iraq Mount?

If the United States and the "coalition of the willing" go to war, the result will be a comprehensive defeat of the Iraqi regime and its military and security forces. What is not so clear is how smoothly the military campaign will proceed. Many commentators seem to assume that any serious problems would emerge only after the war was over. Yet, could the Iraqis mount enough defense to cause problems during the war itself? How might they defend themselves, and why might they have some success?

Countering the Coalition's Strategy

Based on available information about U.S. war planning, coalition operations in Iraq would consist of several elements: speed; precision strikes; overwhelming force; operations on multiple fronts; special forces activities; psychological warfare; bypassing nonthreatening Iraqi units; minimizing civilian casualties and damage to economic infrastructure; and capturing the regime's leadership and any facilities or individuals associated with weapons of mass destruction. The coalition's intention would be to rapidly collapse the pillars of the regime while inflicting minimal damage on the economy and society.

The internal requirements of this strategy give the Iraqis some possibilities for resistance. The Iraqi "counterstrategy" outlined below, some elements of which are already being implemented, does not require Baghdad to initiate any highly provocative actions such as chemical attacks on coalition forces in Kuwait or missile strikes on Israel. Yet, to the extent that the Iraqis can carry out some of these countermeasures, the coalition's success will likely come more slowly and at a higher cost.

Potential Iraqi Defensive Strategy

Recognizing that they will not be able to move their forces strategically or even operationally once the war has begun, the Iraqis may limit themselves to fighting locally. Based on the 1999 NATO military operations in Kosovo and on their own experiences during the 1991 Gulf War, they doubtlessly understand that moving units would be detected quickly and destroyed. By placing combat units along key lines of communication (LOCs) and in strategically important areas before hostilities begin, the Iraqis can increase their chances of engaging coalition forces under the best circumstances: terrain of their choosing, with minimum exposure and advance preparation. In fact, several key Iraqi units are already deployed more or less in this manner. Such a tactic could

Originally published as *PolicyWatch* no. 720, March 5, 2003.

also provide them with perhaps the best opportunities to use chemical weapons. The Iraqis are not going to win any major battles simply by fighting locally, but they could increase the coalition's losses in terms of casualties and time.

Iraqi defensive strategy may also involve fighting in as many places as possible, employing all armed elements that are willing and able to battle coalition ground forces. These elements could include the Special Republican Guard in Baghdad; Republican Guard divisions in key cities and along key LOCs; several of the regular army's heavy divisions (e.g., those at Amara and Samawa); and various "popular" forces (e.g., Baath Party and tribal elements). Although these forces would vary widely in capabilities and cohesiveness, they present the possibility of varying degrees of resistance at multiple points, which could slow the coalition's operations and take some toll on its forces.

The Iraqis will also expect intensified coalition operations against the regime's ability to direct its forces and keep them loyal. They have considerable experience with attacks on their command system and could take several measures to mitigate the effects. Contingency plans could be established in the event that communication links with Baghdad are severed, including the devolution of some authority to lower levels of the military and civilian bureaucracies, along with the use of couriers to carry orders and reports. In order to offset the coalition's psychological warfare campaign, the Iraqis could stress national resistance and perhaps loyalty to Saddam Hussein rather than to the regime. If unit loyalty is questionable, commanders could be replaced or rotated, and units could be redeployed.

The Iraqis will also be looking to achieve some victories, even small ones, and the coalition's special operations may give them a chance to do so. Based on their own experience in 1991, on recent special operations in Afghanistan, and on media analysis of coalition plans and capabilities, the Iraqis probably have a good idea of what to expect from the coalition's special forces. Elements of the Republican Guard and regular army, as well as tribal and militia forces, would all pose threats to special operations, which, as was seen in Afghanistan, are inherently risky. Even the potential destruction or capture of a few special forces units would complicate coalition operations.

Iraqi forces are also likely to use both the terrain and the population for cover. Much has been made of urban environments posing a potential problem for the coalition, but other physical and cultural elements could prove important as well. For example, Iraq is dotted with hundreds of villages, all of which are possible points of resistance, with both physical structures and civilians to hide behind. Although many of these villages could be bypassed, coalition forces may have to fight for some of them. Iraqi authorities are already issuing orders to keep the population in place, and to the extent that they are successful in these efforts, they will present the coalition with some difficult military and political choices.

Baghdad could also encourage genuine popular resistance. Various commentators assume that Saddam is so widely, albeit secretly, opposed that the population will generally not resist the coalition. What if this assumption is wrong, though, even if only in a few areas? Some Iraqis are likely to see coalition operations as an invasion of Iraq, not just an attack on Saddam's regime, and they may react accordingly by actively resisting. Popular resistance could be particular troublesome for coalition logistics units, which will be operating over hundreds of miles and which are more vulnerable than combat units to attack by irregulars.

In addition, the Iraqis can be expected to do everything they can to impede the movements of coalition forces. They could employ several such measures just before and during the early stages of a war, including flooding, airfield denial, destruction of bridges, and use of persistent chemical agents to deny assembly and approach areas. Although the coalition has tremendous mobility in the form of air transport, its heavy forces (along with logistical support elements) will be moving on the ground, often over Iraqi roads and bridges. Even partial denials of such infrastructure would likely complicate coalition operations.

Finally, the Iraqis can trade space, not necessarily for time, but for dissipation of the coalition's efforts. Although the coalition may have as many as fourteen divisions to both crush Iraqi military resistance and secure large areas, its forces will also have to watch bypassed Iraqi units (even those sitting in garrisons), protect LOCs and rear echelon units, control urban areas, and prevent potential Kurdish and Shiite opportunism.

Conclusion

Perhaps the Iraqis will be unable to carry out any of the above tactics, and coalition operations will unfold as planned. Yet, an old truism says that no plan survives the test of battle, and the hoary concept of "friction"—the cumulative effects of small problems in military operations—may yet rear its head in twenty-first century warfare. Saddam and his regime will be defeated, but the military campaign could be slower and more painful than some anticipate. A rather different question remains, though: what would be Iraq's strategic objective in mounting such a defense, beyond delaying the inevitable? This will be the subject of a forthcoming *PolicyWatch.*

Michael Knights

3
Infrastructure Targeting and Postwar Iraq

Using new operational concepts in concert with rapidly maturing strike technologies, the U.S. military will attempt to seamlessly dovetail the destructive process of warfare with the reconstructive effort of nation building in any future air operations against Iraq. Lessons learned from air campaigns conducted in Iraq during the 1990s have laid the foundation for a more finessed approach to infrastructure targeting.

Changes in Targeting from Desert Storm to Desert Fox

In Operation Desert Storm, a ground offensive was supported with extensive airstrikes on every significant element of Iraq's dual-use power, communications, transportation, and industrial sectors. In a war that had the potential to become protracted, it made sense to destroy Iraq's ability to refine oil and produce ammunition, as well as its stockpiled reserves. At the same time, U.S. Air Force planners sought to cause only temporary damage to Iraq's economic infrastructure by precisely targeting easy-to-replace elements of key facilities rather than destroying such facilities outright.

Yet, these plans were thwarted by standard operating procedures that were deeply ingrained in the military community. Wary of underestimating Iraq, Desert Storm planners inflicted massive damage on the country's economic infrastructure. For example, instead of targeting rapidly replaceable electricity transformer yards and refined oil storage sites, U.S. forces destroyed hard-to-replace generator halls and cracking (distillation) towers. Initially, Tomahawk cruise missiles were used to dispense carbon graphite filaments over power stations, minimizing permanent damage while still causing blackouts. Yet, these sites were later used as bomb dumps for carrier-based aircraft returning to ship, rendering the less-destructive effects of the cruise missile strikes meaningless. Desert Storm also highlighted the unforeseen consequences of disrupting the highly interconnected critical infrastructure of a modern industrialized country, as attacks on dual-use power facilities caused cascading damage throughout the water purification and sanitation systems, exacerbating a public health crisis.

In the years following Desert Storm, these lessons were rapidly incorporated into targeting policy. During the four-day Operation Desert Fox in December 1998, the military took great pains to focus its strikes on Saddam Hussein's regime rather than on

Originally published as *PolicyWatch* no. 725, March 14, 2003.

dual-use infrastructure. While numerous Baath security, intelligence, and military targets were destroyed, power and telephone systems were spared. The sole economic target, authorized after hard bargaining by Desert Fox planners, was an oil refinery linked to smuggling. This target was temporarily crippled in a strike designed by the Joint Warfare Analysis Center, which engineered a targeting solution that disabled the site for six months while minimizing pollution. Five months after Desert Fox, new types of carbon graphite munitions were used to disable Serbian electrical networks during Operation Allied Force, greatly reducing permanent damage. Moreover, current reports indicate that radio frequency (RF) devices that use electromagnetic pulse effects to disrupt advanced electronics are being weaponized for deployment in cruise missiles and guided bombs in the event of a new war in Iraq.

Targeting Iraq in 2003

Given the fact that the Iraqi military has been greatly reduced, U.S. Air Force planners recognize that the current operational problem is how to quickly overcome a static Iraqi defense in support of a high-intensity ground war that would likely begin nearly simultaneously with an air campaign. In such a situation, slowly maturing attacks on Iraqi dual-use industrial infrastructure would not be particularly useful from a military point of view. Military planners now recognize that targeting certain forms of infrastructure (e.g., the national electrical grid or public telecommunications) causes more disruption to civilians than to the enemy military and hence may not meaningfully reduce the risk to allied forces. Moreover, such attacks may cause collateral damage—a particularly sensitive issue given Washington's uncertain mandate for war. According to a February 5, 2003, Pentagon briefing, strikes against dual-use facilities are now automatically considered to cause collateral damage, and thus require special authorization.

Moreover, according to the U.S. Agency for International Development's (USAID) "Vision for Post-Conflict Iraq," the United States will strive to ensure that critical infrastructure remains operational following a war, with most transport links and water, sanitation, and electrical services functioning, especially in urban areas. Within eighteen months after a war, USAID plans to rebuild Iraqi infrastructure completely, even improving on prewar conditions. This will require limited infrastructure targeting in each sector:

Power. Strikes against Iraq's electricity grid will probably be limited, focusing on power transmission to specific government and military facilities. RF and other nonkinetic weapons are likely to be used to minimize permanent damage.

Water/Sanitation. USAID is preparing to deploy generators to key water and sanitation facilities in case of disruption, while personnel from the U.S. Army Corps of Engineers and firms such as Contrack and Morganti will be on hand within sixty days of war's end to operate Iraq's ten major facilities.

Transportation. Iraq's transportation network is unlikely to be dismembered as it was in 1991, when over forty road and rail bridges and all major airports were destroyed. For one thing, transport nodes are necessary for allied offensive and logistical operations. In addition, more precise twenty-four-hour, all-weather intelligence, surveillance, reconnaissance, and strike technologies will allow on-call air forces to interdict Iraqi movement without destroying basic infrastructure such as bridges. Moreover, an intact transportation network will be required immediately after a war, as USAID aims to restore humanitarian access to major seaports (e.g., Umm Qasr), airports (e.g., Basra), and the rail network in order to ensure rapid resumption of UN oil-for-food deliveries and domestic fuel distribution.

Petrol, Oil, and Lubricants. The need for a functioning transportation system and an expedient return of Iraqi oil to market following a war make it unlikely that facilities such as oil refineries will be extensively targeted. Initially, damage to downstream oil industry infrastructure will likely be tended to by the U.S. Army Corps of Engineers and civilian contractors Kellogg, Brown, and Root, Inc.

Communications. Certain types of telecommunications facilities have already been extensively targeted (e.g., microwave relay, tropospheric scatter, fiber-optic). The public telephone network has been spared in all airstrikes since 1991 and is unlikely to be comprehensively targeted in the future. Yet, Iraq's radio and television jamming and transmission facilities will likely be destroyed in order to open the airwaves for extensive U.S. psychological operations. RF weapons may be used in attacks on government communications infrastructure, leaving large (yet isolated) segments of the system undamaged but functionally dead.

Implications

U.S. forces will face many wild cards. For example, Iraqi sabotage of oil infrastructure and bridges could reverse the effectiveness of finessed U.S. targeting policies, while a prolonged conflict could necessitate wider strikes on industrial facilities or infrastructure defended by the regime. Nevertheless, current U.S. targeting plans represent an unprecedented attempt to move seamlessly from war to reconstruction. In fact, psychological operations may be the only U.S. military measures that directly target the Iraqi public and key constituencies in the Iraqi regular military and militia (as distinct from the Republican Guard). As in the Desert Fox strikes, the regime's leadership, security forces, and weapons-of-mass-destruction materiel will constitute a large share of the preplanned targets. Such a strategy will help spare infrastructure and avoid the overkill wrought by Desert Storm.

Jeffrey White

4 The Complexities of a Military Coup against Saddam

There has been much speculation that under certain circumstances—either just before a war or in the early stages of a coalition operation—some elements of the Iraqi military would move against Saddam Hussein and his regime. A coup against Saddam would in fact be a highly complex event with uncertain benefits for the coalition. Whether or not such an action were to begin before or after the onset of war, specific requirements would have to be met and serious obstacles overcome in order to achieve a successful end result. The history of failed coups against Saddam suggests just how uncertain the prospects would be for such a result.

Requirements

- There must be some motivation for taking the enormous risks inherent in a coup. Self-interest or group interest, revenge, nationalism, honor, or morality are all reasons Iraqi commanders might decide to move against Saddam's regime. Most likely, commanders would be motivated by a mixture of these elements, for example, the hope of improving their own survival prospects in a post-Saddam scenario, combined with deep feelings of moral opposition to the regime.
- The conspirators must have some measure of agreement on an objective: to replace Saddam and his inner circle, to sweep the entire regime away, or to simply ward off defeat and occupation.
- Secrecy must be maintained. In plotting against such a formidable system, there is an inherent tension between the number of complicit plotters and the security of the plot itself; having too few in the loop risks ineffective coordination and execution, while having too many risks discovery. Tension also exists between the time needed to plan and prepare a coup, and the opportunity for detection. Coup plans long in the making are more likely to be either betrayed or discovered.
- Coup forces must have adequate combat power to engage whatever military and security elements remain loyal to the regime and to secure the apparatus of state control. In the Iraqi context, this is a particularly steep requirement because of the extensive set of military, paramilitary, and security forces that Saddam could activate to

Originally published as *PolicyWatch* no. 727, March 17, 2003.

counter a coup, as well as the large and overlapping organizations of the state that would have to be brought under control.

- There must be an opportunity to act. Some contexts are better than others for a coup, and—if Iraqi history is any guide—minimal prospects will present themselves unless the regime is shaken, as it was in 1998 during Operation Desert Fox. On the other hand, once the regime is under attack implementing any plan may prove more difficult. For example, "shock and awe" may affect those intending to move against the regime under the cover of coalition operations. In this context, the location of leaders—the principal targets in any coup—may also become more uncertain, military movement and communication more difficult, and regime authority less centralized, all making it more difficult for a coup to proceed smoothly and rapidly.
- Key players—individuals or units—in the coup must be close enough to the centers of power to act rapidly. Minimizing the warning and reaction time of the regime and, if coalition operations are underway, minimizing exposure to attack, will be important. There could actually be a "race" between coup forces and coalition forces advancing on Baghdad.
- Related to proximity is the requirement for mobility. Coup leaders and forces must be able to move quickly and coherently toward important targets. They must have tactical mobility and be able to move under fire, implying that armored or mechanized force will be needed. Of course, the movement of such units will also draw the most interest from, and potential attacks by, the coalition.
- Coup plotters face formidable knowledge requirements. They must know who and what to secure and where the key leadership targets will be at the time of the plot's execution. They must know where key personalities and organizations stand relative to the regime, as well as what these elements are likely to do during the coup: join, wait, or fight on the side of the regime.
- Coup forces must be organized for the mission, have a coherent plan for the operation, and achieve coordination with appropriate military, political, and possibly external elements.
- The conspirators must be both decisive and cold-blooded. They must act at the precise time with the necessary initiative, carrying out the likely requirement—killing—in order to accomplish the mission. Unless coup participants can match the determination and ruthlessness of the regime they will probably fail. Ruthlessness is not lacking among Iraqi military commanders, but decisiveness and initiative are rarer qualities.

Obstacles

A coup that meets the above requirements for success will still face formidable obstacles, some obvious and others more subtle.

- Security forces loyal to Saddam must be neutralized. But the existence of large and overlapping security, military, and paramilitary organizations close to the regime makes it likely that at least some of these forces would resist. This could mean serious fighting with an uncertain outcome. The security services themselves represent a special problem in the current context, in that they have been alerted to the danger of a coup and are doubtlessly meticulous in their search for conspiracies.

- The personal security measures for Saddam and other senior leaders—multifaceted and sophisticated even under normal circumstances—will likely be enhanced in a war context, making it even more difficult to fix leadership locations and anticipate movements. Failure to rapidly secure the top leadership will doom the coup.
- A coup will have its own psychological environment in which issues of loyalty, fear, honor, and Saddam's personal psychological dominance will play out. Even at the last minute, circumstances can change and plotters can alter their commitments, depending upon individual risk-taking preferences. How individuals react at the decisive moment will be unpredictable.

Implications

The complexity of conducting a serious military stroke against Saddam Hussein's regime suggests certain implications. First a "staff coup," or a move by headquarters personnel or elements, is unlikely to be successful. Staff officers can plan, organize, and even launch a coup, but they cannot sustain it against organized and disciplined regime forces. Combat power is needed, which must come from units close to Baghdad. This suggests that only Republican Guard elements can realistically serve as the basis for a robust coup. Some combination of staff—possibly from Republican Guard corps headquarters located north and south of Baghdad and from one or more of the Guard divisions in central Iraq—would have the best chance. Combat forces below the division level would likely be too small, and regular Iraqi armed forces are too far away.

For the coalition, a coup attempt—whether before or during an operation—could prove embarrassing. With a coup underway, the coalition would be challenged to determine exactly what was going on, who was involved, what chances there were for success, and what to do about it. All of these determinations would have to be made in a compressed time frame—such as the July 1944 failed coup attempt against the Nazi regime in Berlin, which lasted only about twelve hours—without much time for intelligence collection, decisionmaking, or implementation.

Finally, at the end of the day, someone unattractive could emerge as the winner. In this scenario, the coalition might face a successor loudly proclaiming the end of Saddam but still highly complicit in the crimes of the regime. Who that someone might be and what might happen as the coup progresses is a subject for follow-on analysis.

Michael Knights

5
The Long View of No-Fly and No-Augmentation Zones

Coalition ground forces entered Iraq on the first day of Operation Iraqi Freedom, in contrast to Operation Desert Storm in 1991, when the ground assault followed forty-three days of airstrikes involving an average of 2,500 sorties per day. This difference was due in large part to the fact that much of the work of preparing the battlefield had been completed well before the current operation began. Specifically, coalition air forces have long engaged in large-scale activities in Iraq's no-fly and no-augmentation zones, flying as many as 1,000 sorties per day—substantially more than the 700 sorties flown during the first day of Operation Iraqi Freedom.

Background

Although the northern and southern no-fly zones are linked to UN Security Council Resolutions 688 (April 1991) and 949 (October 1994), the legality of enforcement operations was regularly challenged because the resolutions do not explicitly mention such zones. Yet, Resolution 949 does explicitly authorize what is often referred to as a "no-drive zone" (or what might better be termed a "no-augmentation zone") in southern Iraq. When it was issued in 1994, the resolution demanded "that Iraq immediately complete the withdrawal of all military units recently deployed to southern Iraq to their original positions and that Iraq not again utilize its military or any other forces in a hostile or provocative manner to threaten its neighbors." Hence, the southern no-fly zone is also a no-augmentation zone, meaning that U.S. forces are authorized to counter both air- and ground-based threats there.

Over the past eleven years, violations in these zones have resulted in an average of 34,000 sorties per year over Iraq—the equivalent of fighting Desert Storm every three years. Iraqi resistance and U.S.-British responses in the no-fly zones steeply escalated following Operation Desert Fox in December 1998. The no-augmentation zone has been enforced less often, though attacks were launched against Iraqi anti-shipping missile (AShM) capabilities there in 1993 and 1998. Operations in the zones conditioned the international community to accept the routine use of force in peacetime. This

Originally published as *PolicyWatch* no. 730, March 24, 2003.

conditioning blurred the line between war and peace, particularly with regard to the still-evolving science of precision airstrikes, where the devil is in the details.

Preparing the Battlefield

Aerial policing in the Iraqi northern no-fly zone and southern no-fly and no-augmentation zones helped prepare the current battlefield in several ways:

- Air superiority was secured across most of the country (excluding Baghdad) before the war through the gradual degradation of the Iraqi air force and constant strikes against the static and mobile ground-based elements of Iraq's air defense systems.
- Information superiority was maintained through the reduction of Iraqi aerial reconnaissance capabilities; attacks on Iraq's general command, control, and communications systems; and, most recently, attacks on mobile radar units at the Iraqi border, which facilitated tactical surprise by reducing Iraq's early warning capabilities.
- Psychological operations have greatly benefited from leaflet drops, as well as from the elimination of Iraq's air defenses, which has allowed U.S. EC-130E Commando Solo aircraft to broadcast information to Iraqis without interference.
- U.S. force protection capabilities were enhanced by recent attacks on Iraqi AshMs and surface-to-surface missiles (SSMs). For example, the January 13, 2003, destruction of AShM batteries in southern Iraq has allowed U.S. aircraft carriers to operate far closer to Iraq. In February, U.S. forces also began striking Iraqi Abadil and Astros SSM and artillery positions in the south and Frog-7 SSM batteries in the north. Resolution 949 was used to justify the attacks in the south, while in the north—which lacks a no-augmentation zone—the SSMs were deemed to pose an "airborne" threat to the Kurdish minorities and were attacked under the terms of the no-fly zone.

Refuting Criticism of the Zones

Open-ended aerial policing has major effects on readiness and retention that are not yet fully understood. It also carries operational risks to both friendly forces and noncombatants. The risk to friendly forces has been considerably reduced in the no-fly zones, as suggested by Iraq's inability to down a single manned aircraft in over a decade of aerial policing. One initial force protection measure was to limit the size of the no-fly zones in order to ensure that patrols retained adequate fuel supplies, remained within easy reach of search-and-rescue forces, and avoided the dense radar, missile, and artillery belts over central Iraq. Even these precautions left U.S. forces at a disadvantage; although enforcement of the no-fly zones ceased at certain latitudes, Iraqi threat rings did not. Consequently, Iraq often fired missiles and artillery into the no-fly zones and even into Kuwait. U.S. forces increasingly responded in kind, using a broadening range of air-launched stand-off weapons and unmanned aerial vehicles to diminish the sanctuary at the edges of the policing zones and reduce risks to friendly forces.

Moreover, precision-guided weapons and improved intelligence support have reduced the risk of harming noncombatants, while improved strike and collateral damage estimation technologies have allowed U.S. forces to operate under somewhat less stringent rules of engagement. The United States has also learned how to debunk false claims of collateral damage and civilian deaths, using tethered satellite imagery to record weapon impacts (for bomb damage assessment purposes) and releasing the footage to disprove Iraqi claims.

Aerial policing is often presented as a choice of gradualism over "shock and awe," yet the two strategies work well in synergy. Establishing air supremacy and suppressing enemy air defenses have historically been the slowest portions of air campaigns and a major impediment to both "shock and awe" and simultaneous air and ground operations. The no-fly and no-augmentation zones allowed the United States to undertake many of the most time-consuming processes of battlefield preparation before Operation Iraqi Freedom began, facilitating near-simultaneous air and ground operations and, if U.S. forces are fully unleashed, even greater parallel strikes against high-value target sets as a means of creating "shock and awe." Overall, the outcome of establishing no-fly and no-augmentation zones in Iraq suggests the utility of aerial policing in the gray zone between war and peace.

Jeffrey White

6
Iraq Fights Its War 'Outside-In'

Iraqi forces have been countering the U.S.-led Operation Iraqi Freedom with a form of "outside-in" strategy, defending their country from the periphery to the center. Although the coalition is winning every significant engagement and has penetrated to the heart of the country, Saddam Hussein's regime is not giving ground easily, and the costs of bringing it down will rise. The regime is demonstrating once again that it is a dynamic opponent, capable of understanding what it faces and coming up with surprises.

Iraqi Strategy

Iraq's war strategy appears to consist of several preplanned elements. The first of these is to stay in the fight as long as possible. This approach has entailed avoiding actions that would be tantamount to suicide (e.g., use of weapons of mass destruction against Israel or Kuwait, which was expected by many in the West) and preserving combat units by avoiding any large-scale strategic movement (e.g., from northern to southern Iraq) or operational maneuvers. In fact, the largest attempted maneuver to date was at the battalion level, showing that the Iraqis have learned valuable lessons from the 1991 Gulf War and subsequent crises.

The second major element of Iraqi strategy has been to trade space for both time and dissipation of the coalition's ground forces. The Iraqis are using the long distances from the border to Baghdad and the large volume of the country as a whole (the size of California) to absorb coalition effort. Coalition forces are committed in western, southern, and northern Iraq and have not completely secured the areas that they have passed through. This is evident from the repeated outbreak of fighting in southern Iraq and from reports that elements of the 101st Airborne Division have been assigned to convoy protection. These problems are exacerbated by the difficulty of reducing resistance in built-up areas such as Basra and Nasariya without risking significant coalition and civilian casualties.

Before the war, many military analysts emphasized the potential for a difficult fight in the urban terrain of Baghdad. Yet, the challenge of fighting in complex terrain is in fact much broader. For example, small cities, towns, and agricultural areas are presenting problems. In such areas, coalition forces must sort out the civilians from the combatants, even though many of the latter are in civilian dress. The regime has clearly decided to fight from within the country's own population, and this tactic will inevitably slow coalition ground operations. So far, the coalition has been unwilling to take the humanitarian and

Originally published as *PolicyWatch* no. 731, March 25, 2003.

political risks of fighting through the civilian population in order to get at Iraqi combatants. The Iraqis will exploit this restraint to the hilt. The coalition's precision attacks on a limited set of regime-associated targets in Baghdad have allowed the regime to portray a resilient population standing behind its government without having the morale of that population suffer from attacks on power, transportation, and other services vital to everyday life. Although there are good reasons for such restraint, the coalition's strategy in Baghdad is to the regime's advantage in the short run.

The regime has also conceded the air war to the coalition. Aside from mostly ineffective antiaircraft fire, nothing has been done to defend Iraqi airspace. In fact, Iraqi antiaircraft batteries have had their greatest effect in a counterhelicopter role and as direct-fire weapons in ground fighting, where they have the potential to pose a significant hazard to troops in lightly armored or "soft" vehicles. The Iraqis have also demonstrated skill in mobile missile and rocket operations. Although their occasional missile and rocket launches into Kuwait have had no direct military effect, such attacks divert coalition assets, keep Iraqis in the fight in a highly visible way, and might eventually strike a valuable target.

Finally, the Iraqis are showing that they can both achieve and exploit small victories. The drawing out of fighting at Umm Qasr, Basra, and Nasariya has allowed the regime to cite these cities as examples of heroic national resistance. Moreover, the U.S. combat losses at Nasariya have been broadcast widely as examples of Iraq's ability to inflict damage on the coalition. The losses themselves are small, but the images are large, and they are playing well on the Arab street.

Iraqi Military Operations

Broadly speaking, the Iraqi regime has implemented its strategy in the form of two major operations since the beginning of the war. In the south, it has conducted a delaying and dissipating action centered on the towns and cities and featuring local battles with only limited maneuvers. Moreover, Iraqi forces have not completely unraveled at their first encounters with the coalition. Even some regular army units (e.g., the 11th Infantry Division at Nasariya and the 51st Mechanized Division in Basra), or pieces of them, have resisted, while forces such as the Baath Party militia and the Fedayeen Saddam (neither of which has ever been given much credit for combat effectiveness) have apparently fought hard in some areas. At least one Baath militia commander has been killed during the fighting, and coalition reports have indicated that Fedayeen Saddam elements were involved in several engagements.

The second major operation has been the "battle for Baghdad." For the most part, this has been an air operation; the major fighting has yet to begin, and the Iraqis have thus far weathered some of the effects of "shock and awe." At least outwardly, the central government appears to be operating, whether or not Saddam is dead, wounded, or in hiding. There have been no significant breakdowns of civil order or uprisings by the population. Press conferences and briefings are being held, the government's handling of the first U.S. prisoners of war was rapid and coordinated, and the ability of the Baghdad security services to operate effectively was displayed in the recent hunt for reportedly downed coalition aviators. The regime was also able to send its foreign minister to the Arab summit in Cairo.

The Political Dimension

Iraqi nationalism has been a strong theme in the regime's wartime pronouncements, with the leadership appealing to images of heroic Iraqis fighting invaders. Such rhetoric seems to have had some effect, with certain Iraqi elements demonstrating a willingness to stand up to the coalition's overwhelming firepower. The regime has also been able to give at least the appearance of remaining in control, as indicated above. Its success in maintaining its diplomatic posts has contributed to this perception. Moreover, the regime has been able to get its story out to the Arab world and the West, its two most important audiences. Hence, Iraq is still holding ground in the information and image war; the regime was no doubt heartened to some degree by the response in the Arab street and by the international calls to end the war. Perhaps most important, Iraqi command and control, although degraded, is still working.

Implications

Precisely how long the Iraqis can sustain a coherent defense is uncertain, but it cannot be for very long. The absence of a northern front has made their task easier, but this advantage will soon come to an end. Whenever the coalition can find and fix Iraqi forces, and whenever these forces try to maneuver, they are either defeated by superior firepower or bypassed. As coalition forces close on Baghdad, the Iraqi defense is likely to become denser, presenting problems and opportunities for both sides. Although the regime will have no more space to trade, it will still be able to fight from behind the urban terrain and the Iraqi people.

Michael Eisenstadt

7
Iraqi Strategy and the Battle for Baghdad

Over the past two days, U.S. forces have battled elements of the four Republican Guard (RG) divisions that form the outer ring of Baghdad's defenses, initiating what may be the decisive phase of the coalition's invasion of Iraq. The possibility of urban combat in Baghdad is a daunting one, entailing risks not only for coalition forces, but for the Iraqi regime as well. Although the battle for Baghdad is likely to be the decisive phase of the current campaign, it is unlikely to be the final stage of this conflict. Rather, it will mark the transition to a new phase of what is likely to become a protracted struggle, one that could last as long as U.S. troops remain in Iraq.

Traveling in the Fast Lane

U.S. forces heading to Baghdad have made remarkable progress, in one of the most rapid sustained armored advances in the history of warfare (averaging about seventy-five miles per day for the first four days). By avoiding major Iraqi military formations and skirting major population centers, U.S. forces racing to Baghdad have surpassed the achievements of the Germans in Russia (1941) and North Africa (1942), the Soviets in the Ukraine (1944) and Manchuria (1945), Israel in the Sinai (1967), and the United States in Iraq during Operation Desert Storm (1991). They have met with unexpectedly stiff and persistent resistance in a number of areas, but losses remain relatively light. A review of personnel attrition rates indicates that, after six days of battle, approximately 20 coalition soldiers have been confirmed killed in action (an average of about 3 per day), whereas more than 150 coalition soldiers were killed during the four-day air-land campaign at the end of Operation Desert Storm (for an average of nearly 40 per day). These numbers provide some context for assessing the pace and intensity of Operation Iraqi Freedom, though, at the end of the day, what really matters is whether the United States has met its objectives of disarming Iraq, achieving regime change, and setting the conditions for the emergence of a stable, broad-based post-Saddam government. For this, impending operations in Baghdad could be of critical importance, though it is unclear whether they will facilitate a decisive outcome to the war.

Baghdad: End Point or Way Point?

The coming battle for Baghdad is often characterized in the United States as Saddam Hussein's last stand. In contrast, the Iraqi regime seems to see the looming battle as a

Originally published as *PolicyWatch* no. 733, March 26, 2003.

decisive, but by no means conclusive chapter in the current struggle. Defeat in Baghdad will mean the fall of the regime, but it will not necessarily mark an end to resistance. Instead, it will signal a new phase in the struggle against the United States.

Saddam has survived numerous close calls and crises (including the most recent known attempt to kill him at the outset of the current invasion), and he seems optimistic that this war is not only survivable, but winnable. This may explain the regime's apparent decision to avoid torching Iraq's oil fields, destroying its infrastructure, gassing civilians, producing massive refugee flows, or launching Scud missiles against Israel. The regime intends to remain in power, and it is therefore unwilling to destroy the country—at least for now. Moreover, it may believe that such actions would dramatically weaken its relatively favorable international position, which will be a vital asset in the coming phase of the war. And if Iraq's leaders are removed from power, the prospects for a comeback would be significantly harmed if they were to raze the country in the process.

Iraq's Strategy

Iraq's objectives in the coming battle for Baghdad will be to maximize coalition and Iraqi civilian casualties; fight the coalition to a military standoff; and prompt international diplomatic intervention to negotiate a ceasefire in order to end the carnage, thereby securing the regime's survival. International opinion and the regime's diplomatic skills will be crucial to the success of this strategy.

Iraq faces significant obstacles to prosecuting an effective urban warfare strategy. The four RG divisions around the capital have been deployed to slow and wear down U.S. forces, and the regime will probably avoid bringing them into Baghdad (at least while they remain more or less intact) for fear that they might undertake a coup. Should they attempt to fall back to the outskirts of Baghdad, they could suffer heavy losses en route as a result of coalition airstrikes (though the current sandstorm might provide concealment for some movements). Those units that make it back to Baghdad will probably lack sufficient numbers or time to establish effective defenses. This job will be left mainly to units of the lightly armed Special Republican Guard (SRG) (with 15,000-25,000 men and some 100 tanks), Special Security Organization (SSO) (with 5,000 men), and Fedayeen Saddam (with 20,000-40,000 men). These organizations have a major presence in Baghdad, know the city well, and could wage a protracted urban guerrilla war against coalition forces while senior members of the regime escape into the hinterlands.

Baghdad has a Shiite majority (concentrated mainly in the Saddam City and Kadhimiya districts) that is by and large hostile to the regime, and which might become actively involved in antiregime activities once coalition forces enter Baghdad. Organized proregime forces will have to watch both their front and rear, and they may find it difficult and dangerous to operate in certain parts of the city. This danger would be somewhat diminished if they were to eschew fixed defensive positions and operate as guerrillas in civilian clothes.

Baghdad poses formidable challenges for the United States as well. Many of the U.S. military's technological advantages would be neutralized in an urban environment. Moreover, even limited fighting in Baghdad could produce significant coalition and civilian casualties, while combat in a historic Arab capital would produce dramatic and jarring images that would further harm America's standing in the Arab world. U.S. forces will likely be met by snipers and bands of fighters in civilian clothes (consisting of a combination of RG, SRG, SSO, and Fedayeen Saddam personnel). Deputy Prime Minister Tariq Aziz has described Iraqi's concept of urban guerrilla warfare as follows: "[O]ur cities [will] be our swamps, and our buildings our jungles." Although the United States will almost certainly succeed in taking the capital, the question is, at what price?

Will the Regime Collapse . . . or Fade Away to Fight Another Day?

Although the regime may end in a rapid collapse, it is at least as likely that Iraqi leaders will simply go to ground and fade away. In either case, there is a good chance that some members of the current regime-most likely individuals affiliated with its security apparatus-will manage to slip out of Baghdad and return to their home regions (for most, this means the Sunni Triangle region north and northwest of Baghdad). Believing that they have not really been defeated-as many are likely to survive the war-they may try to organize a protracted, low-intensity insurgency against the U.S. presence, drawing support from the Sunni Arab community and Shiite tribes that have supported the regime in the past. Their goal would be to obstruct U.S. efforts to set up a transitional administration and thereby prevent the United States from "winning the peace" and implementing its exit strategy. Their tactics would likely include stoking anti-American sentiment, intimidating or assassinating Iraqis who deal with the United States, and discouraging potential members of a "coalition of the willing" whom Washington might try to enlist in efforts to create a stability force or a transitional administration.

The bottom line is that a definitive end to the current conflict is unlikely. Some kind of low-intensity struggle will probably continue for an indeterminate period—perhaps as long as U.S. forces remain in Iraq. Although the United States may succeed in dismantling the political and security structures of the current regime and de-Baathifying the government, it may have more difficulty expunging an insurgency that, like the government it evolved from, appeals to a powerful sense of Iraqi nationalism, draws strength from the U.S. presence, and derives its resiliency from tribal ties that are rooted in the very fabric of Iraqi society. For these reasons, the battle for Baghdad may mark only the beginning of the end of Saddam Hussein's regime.

Jeffrey White

8
War in Iraq: A Preliminary Assessment

Saddam Hussein's regime is under relentless attack, and its days are numbered. Exactly when or how the end will come is unclear but not in doubt. After a week of major combat, it is reasonable to assess the progress of this war: accomplishments by both sides, surprising—and not so surprising—elements, emerging patterns or trends, and battlefield implications.

Coalition Achievements

The coalition has accomplished much in a short time. In the mass of detailed reporting and compelling "real-time" television images, it is easy to lose track of the scope of the enterprise. For the first time since World War II, the United States and its allies have invaded a large and well-armed country with the express intention of toppling its government, disarming it, and reconstructing it. Coalition accomplishments include both military and political gains. Militarily, the Iraqi air defense system has been suppressed to the point that it can offer only token resistance, a necessary measure to allow freedom of action over Iraq. Coalition ground forces penetrated rapidly to the heart of the regime, and within four days were developing a direct threat to the enemy's capital. Iraqi command and control was significantly degraded, though not eliminated. No Scud missiles have been fired from western Iraq, and missiles fired at Kuwait have been intercepted and destroyed without damage to coalition targets. Most importantly, U.S. and British forces have won all battles and engagements with the exception of the ambush at Nasariya, and possibly the Apache helicopter operation against the Medina division. The combination of tactical skill, lethal weapons, and air superiority has precluded all attempts by the Iraqis to inflict any serious damage on the allies. Politically, the coalition has managed a complicated and potentially dangerous situation in the north, preventing Turkish-Kurdish tensions from erupting, acquiring an overflight agreement with Turkey, and laying the groundwork for opening a northern front.

Iraqi Achievements

Saddam's regime has not proven as brittle as many originally believed; when the coalition kicked in the front door the rotten edifice did not collapse. The Iraqis are still in the fight, which may be their greatest accomplishment to date. They have withstood a decapitation

Originally published as *PolicyWatch* no. 736, March 28, 2003.

strike and recovered from the effects of "shock and awe." They are not doing badly in the media war; some would say they are winning on that front. Spectacular broadcast images of a seemingly defenseless Baghdad under violent air attack are not received well in the Arab world or in those parts of the West in which antiwar sentiment is strong. Militarily, the Iraqis can claim a few small victories. The ambush of the logistics unit at Nasariya—resulting in both dead Americans and prisoners of war—and the capture of the Apache helicopter crew have been exploited for maximum advantage. The Iraqis have also taken advantage of the coalition's remarkable restraint in order to delay operations and continue resistance in areas that primary combat units have passed through. The regime has been able to retain the loyalty of most of its armed forces and much of the population. There has been no revolt against the regime from within and no uprisings of any consequence thus far; some Iraqis appear to be fighting for Iraq, if not the regime. Even some regular army units, which were not assessed as being particularly dedicated to the regime, have fought. Finally, the Iraqis retained for some time the ability to fire missiles and rockets at Kuwait, providing further, highly visible evidence that they are still in the fight.

Surprises

The first surprise of this war is the resiliency of the regime. Saddam and the Baath Party are facing their most comprehensive crisis, but they have not collapsed and are resisting in creative ways. Their military strategy has succeeded in complicating coalition operations, demonstrating that an evil regime can still be capable and effective. A second surprise has been the tenacity of local resistance. Most analysts believed that the only serious fighting would come from the Republican and Special Republican Guards. In fact, regular army units have fought at Nasariya and around Basra. Even more surprising has been the resistance mounted by paramilitary forces—the Fedayeen Saddam and Baath Party militia. These organizations were considered to be the regime "brown shirts," bullies capable of terrorizing the citizenry. But they have fought, and not just by firing a few shots at coalition rear-echelon elements. Armed primarily with assault rifles and rocket-propelled grenades, they have attacked and been killed in some numbers by major combat elements of U.S. and British ground forces.

Also surprising, at least to some analysts, has been the absence of predicted catastrophic actions. Saddam has not attacked Israel; there has been no use of chemical or biological weapons, no flooding, and no massive destruction of civil or economic infrastructure. In part, this may be due to the military and psychological operations of the coalition, and Saddam still has the potential to take some of these actions as he becomes desperate.

Nonsurprises

Many aspects of the conflict have gone as expected. The overwhelming flexibility, maneuverability, precision, and firepower of coalition forces have allowed them to range widely over Iraq, penetrate to the center of the country, and destroy Iraqi forces as they are encountered. Nonetheless, the resistance of some paramilitary elements and Iraq's decision to fight from within its own population have made operations more difficult. The coalition has almost completely contained the maneuverability of Iraqi forces. Most Iraqi operations have taken place at the tactical level—brigade or lower—without attempts at either operational maneuver or strategic movement. In short, the Iraqis have waited for the coalition to come to them.

Emergence

The Iraqis seem to be learning how to fight, where to fight, and whom to use in the fighting. They have learned to "hug" their civilians, forcing coalition troops to either take increased tactical risks or risk inflicting civilian casualties. Iraqis are also utilizing paramilitary forces—many in civilian dress—to do much of the fighting. Tactically, Iraq is using infantry with light antitank weapons to engage coalition forces from cover at night, under favorable weather conditions, and when the tactical situation is advantageous. In at least one case, at Najaf, wire-guided antitank missiles were used, possibly the very modern and effective Russian-made KORONET. Iraqi troops are also employing light, automatic antiaircraft weapons in both a counterhelicopter role and against ground elements, capacities in which they have been effective in past wars. A large action by Apache helicopters of the 11th Aviation Regiment was met by a "storm of steel" from Iraqi antiaircraft artillery and small arms, with one helicopter lost and a number damaged, reportedly causing a U.S. tactical reassessment.

Conclusions

Drawing major conclusions from an unfinished war is hazardous, but a few elements are worth considering even at the early stages of this conflict. The end is not in doubt: a criminal and evil regime will be comprehensively defeated and dismantled. Estimating exactly when that end will come is more difficult. The fall of Baghdad will be decisive for the regime, but will not necessarily signal the end of all resistance by regime-associated elements. The final costs, especially in casualties, are also difficult to forecast. If casualties are the "currency of battle," the major battles of this war—against the Republican Guard and for Baghdad—have yet to be fought.

Michael Knights

9
Basing Restrictions Shape Concept and Conduct of War

With Saudi Arabian, Turkish, and Jordanian host-nation restrictions limiting coalition ground and air operations, the United States has begun to develop a range of Iraqi airfields as forward operating bases for combat aircraft. This is ironic considering that successive U.S. governments spent billions of dollars to develop an unparalleled basing environment to support U.S. power projection in the Gulf. Recent decisions by Saudi Arabia and Turkey—key U.S. allies—have arguably prevented Washington from waging a shorter and less costly war in terms of both blood and treasure. Yet, the United States has benefited greatly from its policy of diversifying basing assets in the smaller Gulf Cooperation Council (GCC) states, recognizing that Kuwait, Qatar, and Oman are dependable allies and that Iraq may one day replace Saudi Arabia as a key air base provider.

Background

As the German government has been keen to point out, and as GCC states are keen to obfuscate, some of the most significant military contributions to Operation Iraqi Freedom have come from states outside the "coalition of the willing," with Kuwait the only Arab state willing to be listed as one of the forty-four members of this nebulous grouping. Having long served as Iraq's small coastal opening into the Gulf, Kuwait is now providing the aperture through which the United States and Britain have had to move their major land forces—a far cry from the 1991 Gulf War, when the full breadth of Iraq's 488-kilometer Saudi border was available for land operations.

Ground Forces

Although Baghdad and Basra would have been major objectives in any war strategy, the coalition's inability to insert major ground forces through Saudi Arabia, Turkey, or Jordan has significantly reduced its choices concerning its axis of advance. One often-overlooked consequence of this restriction has been the loss of military access to crucial Saudi ports. While Kuwait's container terminal at Shuwaikh has twenty-one deepwater berths, Saudi Arabia's port complex at Dammam boasts thirty-nine, including six specifically designed to accommodate the roll-on, roll-off ferries being used to transport the Kuwait-bound armored vehicles of the 4th U.S. Infantry Division and other units.

Originally published as *PolicyWatch* no. 737, March 31, 2003.

Planners were also denied the opportunity to develop an alternative axis of approach (out of Saudi Arabia) avoiding the cities along the Euphrates river valley, which are now centers of high- and low-intensity Iraqi resistance. The possibility of developing a wide flanking threat using the 101st Air Assault Division from either Saudi Arabia or Jordan was forestalled early on, while the powerful 4th U.S. Infantry Division—arguably the most modern U.S. military unit—was effectively taken out of the war until mid-April due to the failure to secure Turkish basing rights, which denied Washington a powerful northern thrust and the ability to insert troops directly into the Baath heartland.

In other ways, however, the concentration of coalition ground forces in Kuwait has proven to be a blessing. Kuwait was perhaps the only Arab country that could rhetorically justify allowing such access to U.S. forces, given the Iraqi invasion and annexation in 1990. Moreover, strong Kuwaiti government force-protection measures have reduced the potential for attacks on deployed coalition personnel. A significant portion of the country has been turned into a militarized zone. Kuwaiti checkpoints dot key highways; the Kuwaiti Security Services and police forces launch preventative actions to preempt terrorist attacks; and Kuwaiti naval forces patrol the entrance to the Shatt al-Arab waterway, in one case protecting U.S. forces by destroying an Iraqi dhow believed to carry saboteurs. Although such measures have caused considerable damage to agricultural land and road infrastructure, Kuwait's citizens can harbor no illusions about their national stance—Kuwait made the war possible and has supported it ungrudgingly.

Air and Missile Forces

Basing restrictions have also complicated the task of providing the high sortie rates required during the unfolding assault on Republican Guard divisions near Baghdad, with the smaller GCC states, aircraft carriers, and forward bases in Iraq taking up the shortfall caused by Saudi restrictions. Kuwait and Oman have allowed unrestricted overflight and basing of combat aircraft, while Qatar has provided full basing rights at the al-Udeid Air Base. In contrast, the United Arab Emirates has permitted only reconnaissance assets to operate out of its territory. Although Saudi Arabia has provided command and control facilities from Prince Sultan Air Base and allowed all-important tanker, surveillance, combat search-and-rescue, and Suppression of Enemy Air Defenses (SEAD) aircraft to operate from its territory, it has closed its bases and airspace to strike aircraft. Moreover, both Saudi Arabia and Turkey have closed Tomahawk cruise missile launch baskets in the Red and Mediterranean Seas, respectively (although Riyadh has agreed to missile-overflight rights along specified routes). Turkey has also tightly limited any use of Incirlik Air Base for strikes in Iraq, even restricting overflight rights by placing limits on tanker sorties.

The key limitation for land-based air forces has been the shortage of bases near the Iraqi border that can be used for bombing missions. Kuwait has absorbed as many combat aircraft as possible, but this solution has resulted in serious overcrowding of the airspace. Both airfield security and flight safety are at risk under such conditions, particularly given the fact that Iraqi and U.S. missiles fly through the same airspace. The danger of this situation was highlighted by the recent downing of a returning British Tornado GR4 by a U.S. Patriot missile.

With the majority of strike assets forced to operate from U.S. aircraft carriers, Diego Garcia, Britain, Oman, and Qatar, the key effects of Saudi Arabia's unwillingness to base additional forces have been to reduce the sortie rate, decrease the availability of on-call close air support, and increase support requirements (e.g., tankers). To solve this problem, the United States has developed numerous captured Iraqi airfields as forward air bases that can generate higher sortie rates and provide sufficient close air support as forces engage in large clashes near Baghdad. Although this strategy entails a higher risk of air base attacks and imposes a considerable support burden, it provides the requisite proximity.

Regional States Shape the U.S. Plan

As expected, the war has shed interesting light on the limitations of both U.S. unilateralism and host-nation leverage. Without Kuwait, Operation Iraqi Freedom clearly could not have involved a credible ground element. Saudi Arabia and Turkey defined the axis of advance and caused unexpected levels of logistical bottlenecking by denying access to their ports. Nevertheless, barring Kuwait's crucial role, regional states have learned that they cannot stop U.S. military operations by restricting basing rights—they can only make them longer, more difficult, and more costly to the United States in terms of blood and treasure.

Michael Eisenstadt and Jeffrey White

10
Fighting the War to Win the Peace in a Post-Saddam Iraq

As the coalition prepares for the decisive phase of the war against Saddam Hussein's regime, it is crucial that combat operations set the conditions for achieving U.S. war aims and—just as important—winning the peace afterward. The principal war aims are: 1) eliminating Iraq's weapons of mass destruction (WMD); 2) achieving regime change; and 3) setting the conditions for the emergence of a stable, broad-based post-Saddam government. Moreover, prospects for winning the peace will be greatly enhanced if the coalition moves quickly to improve postwar living conditions for the largest possible number of Iraqis; to establish a modicum of stability in the country; and to create conditions wherein coalition forces are viewed not as occupiers, but as partners for building a new Iraq. How should the coalition fight the war in order to achieve these objectives?

Achieve Decisive Victory

The coalition must decisively defeat the regime and its forces, leaving them bowed, broken, and incapable of resuming operations against coalition forces or subverting a new Iraqi government. Paradoxically, a difficult war could improve prospects for an easy peace. A rapid collapse of the regime during the first days of the war could have prevented the coalition from achieving such a decisive victory and created problems down the road. The progress of the war to date, whether slower than expected or "on plan," is allowing the coalition to defeat the regime comprehensively and inflict heavy losses on its most hardcore elements. If coalition forces can finish the campaign without large numbers of civilian casualties, they will create more favorable conditions for postwar policy successes.

Keep the War Short

The longer the war lasts, the more likely it is that coalition forces will make missteps that generate antipathy among the Iraqi people. Paradoxically, while time is an ally in efforts to decisively defeat the regime, it is an enemy in efforts to minimize harm to civilians, win Iraqi "hearts and minds," and limit the impact of the regime's efforts to stir up passions in the Arab world against the coalition and the established regional political order.

Originally published as *PolicyWatch* no. 739, April 2, 2003.

Eliminate Key Members of the Regime

The coalition must do everything possible to kill or apprehend senior members of the regime. Nothing will more quickly establish U.S. credibility and break the barrier of fear that holds the Iraqi people in thrall than the demonstrable demise of Saddam Hussein and his chief lieutenants. In addition, the coalition must pursue key members of the Iraqi security services; due to their temperament and training, such individuals could lead a postwar resistance against coalition forces and subvert a post-Saddam government.

Seize and Secure WMD

The coalition must, to the greatest extent possible, prevent the diversion of Iraqi WMD to elements of the regime that may be planning an insurgency against coalition forces or a comeback after the regime has been toppled. It must also prevent the leakage of WMD or personnel with knowledge of how to produce or weaponize related materiel to neighboring states or terrorist groups. Toward this end, coalition forces must apprehend officials, scientists, and industrialists involved in Iraq's WMD programs in order to break up the intellectual basis for such programs and prevent these individuals from seeking similar reemployment elsewhere.

Gain the Confidence of the Iraqi People

Gaining and keeping the confidence of the Iraqi public will be necessary if the coalition is to succeed in the reconstruction and political transformation of Iraq. Many Iraqis are wary, if not outwardly hostile, toward the coalition, partly out of fear of Saddam's regime, but mostly due to bitterness over their perceived abandonment by the United States in 1991, the impact of sanctions, and suspicions regarding U.S. motivations (i.e., fears that Washington covets Iraq's oil). The coalition will have to overcome this legacy of mistrust. Coalition forces must avoid heavy-handed behavior toward Iraqi civilians, even though Iraqi tactics (e.g., use of soldiers in civilian clothes and suicide bombers) will make this difficult and coalition security measures will likely be perceived as onerous and objectionable. Coalition forces must also continue to adhere to significant restrictions on targeting in order to minimize collateral damage. Moreover, the coalition must commence large-scale humanitarian assistance operations as soon as is feasible, in as many areas as possible, in order to begin changing Iraqi attitudes. Although it may not be possible to win the hearts and minds of many Iraqis, it may be possible to establish a productive partnership founded on shared interests in Iraq's reconstruction and transformation.

Prevent Retribution and Score Settling

One of the legacies of Saddam's rule is deep enmity across virtually all elements of Iraqi society. Tribal, sectarian, and ethnic antagonism and suspicion have been fostered by regime policies and have left a web of old scores to be settled and outrages to be avenged, on both the individual and group levels. Preventing violence will be critical to achieving stability in Iraq; preserving the country's civilian infrastructure; preventing the reopening of old wounds and the creation of new ones; and facilitating a transition to effective local rule. This requirement will place severe demands on coalition administrators to identify, head off, settle, or suppress communal violence while adroitly avoiding the appearance of favoritism toward any particular group.

Deter Intervention by Meddling Neighbors

Iraq's neighbors have a significant stake in the outcome of the war, and some may be tempted to influence its course or aftermath. Washington has publicly warned Syria and Iran against troublemaking. Syria has reportedly provided military equipment to Iraq, allowed Arab war volunteers to transit its territory, provided refuge to the families of senior Iraqi officials, and accepted Iraqi WMD-related materials for safekeeping. Doubtlessly, Iran is employing intelligence and special forces personnel along its border and inside Iraq to obtain information and influence events in Iraq. The injection of Iranian-backed Shiite forces—the Badr Brigades—into what promises to be a fragile and volatile postwar situation in southern Iraq could be a major challenge for the coalition. In the north, Turkish intentions remain unclear. Beyond its decision to deny access to coalition ground forces, Turkey has avoided actions that would further complicate coalition operations. The Turks are most concerned that a war could result in autonomy or independence for Iraq's Kurds. An expanding coalition presence in northern Iraq could make it more difficult and expensive for Turkey to intervene, but might not suffice to deter such an eventuality.

Conclusion

The coalition faces difficult challenges as it tries to fight the war in a way that enables it to win the peace. A quick defeat of the regime could lead to an unstable peace. Conversely, a comprehensive victory could establish the preconditions for a more stable peace, but getting there would take time and would likely exact a higher toll on the Iraqi people, possibly engendering resentment against the coalition. It could also provide the regime's propaganda machine with additional opportunities to incite the Arab street, with unforeseeable long-term consequences for the stability of friendly regimes in the region. How the United States fights the remainder of the war will determine how these contradictions are resolved, and will have profound implications for the outcome of the war and the nature of the peace that will follow.

Jeffrey White

11
The End of Saddam's Regime

"Bloody thou art, bloody will be thy end"—like Shakespeare's quintessential villain Richard III, Saddam Hussein is being toppled by a combination of forces he called into existence through his own evil actions. Unlike Richard, Saddam's final act will lack heroic qualities. Clearly, the regime's disintegration is accelerating; all that is left is for the final act to be played out.

The Regime's Downward Rush

The freedom of action enjoyed by coalition ground forces is now approaching that of its air forces. Iraq's cities and countryside are open to pretty much any operation the coalition desires, with the primary limitation being the number of troops available. This limitation will be largely erased with the deployment of combat elements of the 4th Infantry Division. Although local resistance and some attrition can still be expected, coalition combat forces can go where they want to go and do what they want to do. The highly disproportionate casualties inflicted on Iraqi forces during operations in Basra and Baghdad over the weekend are evidence of this fact. Basra has basically fallen and Baghdad seems not far behind.

The pillars of the regime—the Republican Guard, Special Republican Guard, Fedayeen Saddam, and Baath Party—are experiencing an accelerating collapse as well. All of these organizations have been specially targeted and heavily damaged by coalition operations. Much of this has been done through the precise application of air power, but ground forces are increasingly adding their weight. The heavy casualties inflicted by elements of the 3rd Infantry Division on its first excursion into Baghdad proper, along with the highly successful British operations in Basra, are both indicative of the unmatchable firepower and skill that the Iraqis face. Since the beginning of the campaign for Baghdad, the Iraqi defenses have gone from brittle to shattered. Surrenders are increasing, and regime elements now control only the ground they stand on. Increasingly, they are taking cover in shrines, hospitals, and schools—"no-strike" areas for the coalition—but this hardly represents the basis for a coherent defense.

Indeed, Iraqi tactics have proven increasingly futile. Piecemeal counterattacks, static defense, kamikaze trucks, and suicide bombers have all failed to alter the grim tactical and operational realities for the Iraqis. On the contrary, these tactics are serving to kill regime diehards in some numbers, a potentially important element for postwar stability.

Originally published as *PolicyWatch* no. 744, April 7, 2003.

In a very positive sign, Iraqi civilians are helping the coalition uncover both evidence of the regime's crimes and those responsible for them. For example, elements of the regime have systematically used schools and hospitals for military purposes, including in all likelihood the interrogation and torture of prisoners.

Members of the regime also appear to be seeking avenues of escape. Civilian and military officials have reportedly been fleeing toward Syria with money and valuables. Ordinary citizens are fleeing Baghdad and Basra as well, indicating how the general public may perceive the situation. Similarly, the departure of the Russian ambassador and his staff attests to their assessment of the regime's ability to defend itself. These actions suggest that the regime could collapse at any time due to the effects of several factors: the mounting toll of military operations; an uprising in the Shiite areas of Baghdad; a military coup; or leadership casualties and flight. Some of these mechanisms appear to have been at work in Basra as well.

Attrition of regime leaders seems to be on the rise and approaching important levels. Ali Hasan al-Majid, known as "Chemical Ali," is apparently dead. A senior Republican Guard commander has been killed, and many other leaders in the regime's key forces have likely been killed in the towns and cities where resistance has been strongest. Several such figures have been captured. Moreover, coalition special forces are reportedly hunting key regime figures, and as defenses in Baghdad become more disorganized, their chances for success increase. Even without the capture or killing of the most senior leadership, losses among the lower cadres weaken both the regime's ability to resist and its hold on the Iraqi people.

Underlying all of these aspects is the fundamental failure of Saddam's strategy. The international community, including the UN, did not prevent the "coalition of the willing" from going to war to change the regime. Low casualties among both coalition forces and the Iraqi civilian population have prevented issues of attrition, morale, and public opinion from becoming a real factor in limiting coalition operations. The speed of coalition operations has not allowed time for external forces—the Arab street, European opinion, and diplomatic intervention—to take effect. Such precision execution has also kept the image of the war largely, although not completely, under control.

So what is left for Saddam and his henchmen? The regime still exercises some hold over its forces and the people. Despite the terrific pounding it has taken, the regime carries on in some important ways. It still has a presence in the media. There is still the possibility of serious city fighting in Baghdad; the result of that fighting is not in doubt, only the costs. The United States has ruled out anything but unconditional surrender, and neither France, Russia, nor the UN are likely to change that stance.

The End Game

Saddam has avoided actions that would be tantamount to regime suicide, leaving much infrastructure in place, refraining from causing ecological disasters, and avoiding massive retaliation by the coalition or others for the use of weapons of mass destruction. These "nonactions" suggest that he planned to be around after the war. But what role is he playing now? Publicly the regime has mounted a "theater of leadership," presenting Saddam in videotaped meetings and addresses, messages read by regime officials exhorting the people to fight, and staged public appearances. All of these measures have had an aura of unreality about them. Assuming he is still alive, Saddam's role is in reality a "false-heroic" one. Despite his titles and military imagery, he will not die leading the defense of Iraq, Baghdad, or anything else. Because he is a survivor above all else, attempted flight or, in extremis, surrender, seem more likely. The regime is manipulating loyalty and fear to keep its supporters fighting, allowing Iraqis to die in some numbers so that the leadership will be able to choose one of these options. Saddam and others may already have positioned themselves for a getaway, with Syria being the most likely exit route.

Saddam's escape, perhaps even his capture, would not be healthy for the postwar situation. His end must be conclusive and public. The same applies to other key regime figures. The coalition must demonstrate to all the participants in, and audiences of, this war that the regime and its principal figures are gone, for good. There should be no remaining figures to serve as rallying points for postwar opposition and resistance. Similarly, if there is no clear-cut end, no "surrender," restoring order in Iraqi society could prove difficult, even if the coalition is able to end organized resistance; this possibility makes the creation of a credible regime in situ an important step. Moreover, even if the regime ceases to exist, a substructure of its cadres could live on in post-Saddam Iraq. Hence, people and organizations associated with the regime must be thoroughly purged after the war.

Michael Knights

12
Operation Iraqi Freedom: One Year On

Operation Iraqi Freedom and the months of military activity that followed it constitute a particularly rich case study from which to draw lessons pertinent to the ongoing debate about the transformation of the U.S. military. Encompassing the full range of modern military missions, the Iraq campaign was exceptional in the sense that some parts of the battlefield had already transitioned into security and stabilization operations even while high-intensity fighting raged on in other sectors. In fact, the war and its aftermath were punctuated by a series of dramatic transitions: from the "not peace, not war" period of no-fly-zone enforcement, to intense warfare, to security and stabilization operations, to counterinsurgency operations.

Decisive Military Effects?

Operation Iraqi Freedom highlighted both the strengths and limitations of military force as a tool of foreign policy. The war demonstrated that U.S.-led coalition forces can maneuver through any type of terrain or weather. In Baghdad and other cities, coalition armored forces effectively breached urban areas that had previously been regarded as impenetrable, while "joint fires"—that is, the synergistic use of airstrikes, artillery fire, attack helicopters, and other forms of firepower-prevented enemy forces from maneuvering or mounting a cohesive defense.

Yet, the subsequent occupation phase has underlined the limitations of military force. Throughout the 1990s, military analysts often noted that air power alone could not be decisive. One overarching lesson of the period following Operation Iraqi Freedom is that a ground campaign is not necessarily decisive either. In other words, military force is a necessary, but not sufficient, tool of foreign policy.

Knowing the Enemy

Prior to Operation Iraqi Freedom, the U.S. military had essentially conducted thirteen years of intensive surveillance in Iraq. This scrutiny helped the United States acquire an encyclopedic knowledge of Iraq's infrastructure and some elements of its operational capabilities and habits (particularly with regard to air defense). Beginning in the mid-1990s, this knowledge expanded to an improved understanding of the nature and structure of the regime and its elite constituents.

On March 15, 2004, Michael Knights addressed The Washington Institute's Special Policy Forum. This rapporteur's summary (originally published as *PolicyWatch* no. 843, March 17, 2004) was prepared by Bjorn Delaney.

Nevertheless, there was still much that the coalition did not know as Operation Iraqi Freedom began. Despite the fact that Iraq had been placed under closer and more persistent observation than almost any nation in the history of armed conflict, uncertainty remained over some of the regime's capabilities and plans, including those related to weapons of mass destruction. The extent of Iraq's use of asymmetrical guerrilla attacks was unexpected, as was its highly effective but relatively low-tech observer network (which contributed to the only major Iraqi military victory of the war, the repulse of U.S. attack helicopters on March 23). Although the U.S. military quickly adapted to these threats, the ability of such a closely watched opponent to adopt a new approach and achieve tactical surprise is instructive.

In fact, the U.S. military faced a sharp learning curve from the moment it entered Iraq. The country's terrain—which had been viewed from a distance and from above for many years—required extensive reinterpretation at ground level. As mentioned previously, urban areas that had long been regarded as the enemy's sanctuary from armored forces proved to be relatively hospitable environments for U.S. operations. At the same time, however, areas that appeared to be clear on maps turned out to be dangerous semiurban sprawl that concealed dense enemy defensive positions. Moreover, many heavy weapons, ground vehicles, and aircraft were not found until after the war, highlighting the fact that even weak militaries can be quite capable at concealment and deception. In this context, the maneuverability of coalition forces proved highly effective at forcing concealed Iraqi units from cover and exposing them to heavy firepower.

Before, during, and in the wake of Operation Iraqi Freedom, the coalition struggled to accurately gauge the fluid emotions of the Iraqi people, which were influenced by contending attitudes toward liberation and foreign occupation. Prewar assessments of the fragility of the Baath regime may have underestimated that regime's ability to maintain local control and manage the perceptions of Iraqis. Indeed, one key lesson for future conflicts is that authoritarian regimes may be far more robust than they seem. The links forged between dictatorships and their subjects over decades of rule are unlikely to be quickly or cleanly brushed aside by any military effort to topple the regimes in question.

Integrating the Lessons

The knowledge of enemy intentions and capabilities that the U.S. military had painstakingly constructed during thirteen years of containment had to be reconstructed rapidly during the postwar period, as insurgent groups constituted a vastly more complex and adaptive enemy than the Baath regime ever had. Indeed, coalition and insurgent coevolution has been the overriding trend in postwar operations. The coalition must therefore systematically process and preserve the knowledge gained (at great expense) by its troops over the past year, particularly as new forces are rotated into Iraq. The war and its aftermath have highlighted the extremely valuable, if dangerous, role that ground forces play in increasing the number of "sensors" available to the military intelligence system. As many official "Military Lessons Learned" reports have noted, however, the value of individual soldiers as sensors is closely tied to the quality of their communications equipment as well as their ability to communicate in native languages, cultivate human intelligence, and understand local politics. If these and other recently learned lessons can be integrated into forthcoming training and procurement decisions, Operation Iraqi Freedom and the postwar period could prove to be a truly transformative experience for the U.S. military.

David Albright and Michael Eisenstadt

13
Middle East Weapons Proliferation: Lessons from Iraq and Beyond

The culmination of Operation Iraqi Freedom has given rise to much debate concerning the exact nature of Iraq's weapons-of-mass-destruction (WMD) programs. Similarly, ongoing negotiations with Iran regarding its nuclear activities have also been dogged by imprecise intelligence and unclear strategies. Both of these cases have led many to realize that noncompliance with weapons inspections does not automatically indicate the existence of hidden weapons programs. Although the Senate Intelligence Committee has yet to issue its report on Iraqi WMD, one could reasonably argue that the situation in Iraq during the 1990s served as an example of how inspections can provide a powerful deterrent against covert WMD activity. At present, it is too early to establish with any certainty the exact nature of Iraqi WMD prior to the invasion. Just as some prewar analyses were mistaken when they claimed to know precisely where Iraq's weapons stockpiles were, it would now be erroneous to declare that the country possessed no WMD before the war or that such weapons are not present there today. One must remain open to various possibilities until history comes down conclusively on either side.

Iraqi WMD Before and During the War

Recent analysis of why Iraq did not use WMD during the war has raised several different theories as to the state of the country's WMD programs and Saddam Hussein's strategy regarding such weapons. Beginning in 1991, major portions of Iraq's relatively large stockpile of chemical and biological weapons were slowly uncovered and destroyed, due to both UN inspections and internal Iraqi calculations. By 1995-1996, Baghdad decided that it made little sense to maintain large WMD stockpiles, which were far too easy for inspectors to find and destroy. Hence, one could reasonably conclude that Iraq might have retained a small strategic reserve or breakout capability in its biological and, perhaps, chemical weapons programs. Under such a strategy, the former regime could have retained its nonconventional capabilities while still feigning full cooperation with the UN by permitting credible inspections. Such capabilities—and the specter of their potential

On June 24, 2004, David Albright and Michael Eisenstadt addressed The Washington Institute's Special Policy Forum. Mr. Albright, president of the Institute for Science and International Security, has served as an International Atomic Energy Agency weapons inspector in Iraq. This rapporteur's summary (originally published as *PolicyWatch* no. 880, June 30, 2004) was prepared by Neri Zilber.

use—could have helped Saddam save face regionally while simultaneously keeping his internal and external enemies at bay.

These possibilities lead to an obvious question: if the former regime possessed WMD prior to the invasion, why did it refrain from using them against coalition forces during the war, as was anticipated by many? Several different answers are plausible:

- The prewar prediction that the regime would deploy WMD may have been incorrect; i.e., Iraq either did not have such capabilities or was unable to use them due to technical or time constraints.
- The country's WMD programs may have been in disarray due to corruption and the social effects that international sanctions had on Iraqi scientists. In addition, one should not underestimate the effect that Hussein Kamel's defection and death in 1995 had on those programs, as he was an effective manager who had accounted for much of the initiative behind the project. Finally, Saddam's psychological state, especially rumors of his withdrawn nature in the run-up to the war, might have played a factor in the program's lack of initiative or corruption.
- The Iraqi political hierarchy might have decided that chemical or biological weapons would simply not be effective against the U.S. military, which was equipped to weather such attacks.
- The use of biological or chemical weapons did not fit with Saddam's political strategy for surviving the war. According to this strategy, if Iraqi conventional forces could have held off U.S. forces, especially outside of Baghdad, then Russia or France might have intervened on Iraq's behalf. Such a strategy would not have been politically feasible if Iraq resorted to WMD.
- Saddam might have been optimistic about the abilities of his conventional military forces and fully expected them to win the war. Under such a scenario, Iraq might have sent its WMD to Syria before the war with the intention of retrieving them after the invasion was successfully thwarted.

Iranian Intransigence and the Role of Inspections

Recent events in Iran and the nascent status of the country's nuclear weapons program have emphasized the need for a coherent U.S. policy regarding WMD proliferation in the Middle East. The Bush administration's current stance—that Iran has a secret nuclear weapons program that cannot be proven but must be destroyed—does not provide many concrete policy options for moving forward. Much of the purported intelligence regarding Iran's nuclear weapons program is distorted and inconclusive, and additional International Atomic Energy Agency (IAEA) inspections are needed. Moreover, the United States and European Union (EU) must collaborate on formulating a definitive timeline for Iranian cooperation and action, as well as serious punitive measures if Tehran fails to meet the terms of the agreement.

Inconclusive intelligence aside, one cannot discount Iran's apparent intransigence in October 2003 regarding its nuclear proliferation agreement with the EU. Although Tehran divulged some information about its nuclear activities, it may also have gained the diplomatic and political cover needed to hide more serious developments. Reported inconsistencies in Iran's initial disclosures included not revealing its activities related to the German-made P2 centrifuge, which is more effective at extracting enriched uranium than Iran's declared P1 centrifuge. Subsequently, Tehran admitted to conducting a small research program into the capabilities of the P2. Soon thereafter, however, evidence was uncovered indicating that the country had attempted to import large quantities of components for a working P2 machine. In addition, Tehran is not honoring its most recent commitments to the EU, which included refraining from further uranium enrichment, halting any efforts to build heavy-water reactors, and removing spent fuel rods from Iran. The Iranian nuclear program remains poised to resume centrifuge production for enrichment purposes, and evidence of uranium hexafluoride (used only in heavy-water reactors) has been found. Tensions are high, and the risk of confrontation is very real. Satellite photos of the Natanz nuclear site have shown a substantial hardening against land and air attacks, demonstrating that Iran is indeed worried about a preemptive strike on its WMD capabilities. At the same time, U.S. intelligence has assessed that it would take the Iranians until at least the end of this decade to assemble a working nuclear bomb.

The Worldwide Proliferation Threat

The IAEA has begun to grasp the global nature of WMD proliferation and the need for new measures in addition to inspections. As in the past, foreign aid and technical assistance will play an increasingly integral role in the buildup of viable WMD programs worldwide. The nuclear black market network run by former Pakistani nuclear chief Abdul Qadir Khan is but the most glaring example of individual entrepreneurship in the global WMD trade. To counteract this growing threat, the IAEA has begun to crack down on dual-use exports to certain countries by promoting a treaty-based export control system. Despite the weak regulations in place in many countries, the agency has had success with tightening controls in certain key nations. Yet, problems remain in other countries that have particularly weak domestic regulations and are new to the proliferation market. Pakistan is a clear example of this problem. The IAEA has taken steps to investigate the Khan network in the context of Iran. Yet, focusing similar attention on Iran's external sources of WMD equipment and expertise would give inspectors a better understanding of the Iranian nuclear program and its attempts at weaponization. One should not underestimate the effects of U.S. and international efforts to curb WMD proliferation. Nevertheless, a clearer understanding of the lessons from Iraq and Iran is imperative if these efforts are to succeed in the Middle East and beyond.

Michael Eisenstadt

14
Sitting on Bayonets: America's Postwar Challenges in Iraq

Wars are ill-judged by their military outcomes or by the political repercussions that may follow in their wake. They often unleash social and political forces the ultimate impact of which can only be discerned years on. And they frequently produce unintended consequences that can pose complex and vexing challenges of their own that may contain within them the seeds of future conflicts. Those pondering the implications of Operation Iraqi Freedom (OIF) one year on would do well to keep that in mind.

To a great extent, OIF was supposed to take care of the unfinished business of the Gulf War. It was intended to eliminate, once and for all, the regime of Saddam Hussein and the threat it posed to regional stability, and to set the stage for the emergence of a stable, peaceful Iraq, free of weapons of mass destruction, with a legitimate, representative government on the path to democracy.

The Iraq War had several additional objectives: leveraging regime change in Iraq to deter Iranian and Syrian support for terror; enabling the withdrawal of U.S. troops from Saudi Arabia, thereby eliminating a source of friction with the kingdom and a pretext for the jihadist's war on America; establishing conditions conducive to the resolution of the Arab-Israeli conflict; and clearing the way for political reform and democratization in the region-the putative cure for the dysfunctional Arab politics that led to 9/11.

The initial phase of OIF was an outstanding success. Coalition forces took Baghdad and toppled the regime of Saddam Hussein in three weeks, immediately yielding substantial benefits: the Iraqi people were liberated from a tyrant, the Middle East was freed from the threat posed by an aggressive regime and the United States was able to pull its troops out of Saudi Arabia. But the occupation of Iraq has been beset by troubles. Efforts to restore basic services, quash violent insurgencies in Sunni and Shi'i regions, and establish a legitimate Iraqi government, have encountered numerous difficulties. Instability and violence in Iraq will pose a new set of challenges for the people of that country, for the Middle East and for the United States. Meanwhile, efforts to revive Israeli-Palestinian negotiations have foundered.

Originally published in the *National Interest* no. 76 (Summer 2004). Reprinted with permission. The author would like to thank Jeff Cary, Ryan Phillips, and Bjorn Delaney for their research assistance in preparing this article.

While it is still too soon to judge how all this will end, or to assess the historical significance of this war, it is possible to discern some of its near-term consequences, and to speculate about their long-term impact on the United States, Iraq and the region.

Imperiled Transition

The nature of the war and the way in which it was fought had a direct impact on the character of its aftermath—particularly the emergence of the insurgency centered in the so-called "Sunni triangle", and the transformation of Iraq into a major battleground in the jihadists' war on the West.

Although the coalition quickly took Baghdad and rapidly occupied the rest of the country, it failed to achieve a key precondition for postwar stability: ensuring that Saddam's hardcore supporters were either killed or captured and that those who survived the war emerged from it broken and defeated. This was in part a function of the decision by U.S. commanders and policymakers to favor a small force employing speed and overwhelming precision fire to bring about the rapid collapse of the regime in place of a larger, slower force designed to defeat the enemy methodically. The military planners made the right decision. The latter option would have produced higher casualties, provided opponents of the war with more time to press for a halt to the fighting before America's war aims were met, and given Baghdad time to wage a "scorched earth" campaign. This outcome was also a function of Baghdad's reliance on Saddam's Fedayeen and Quds Army thugs as cannon fodder, enabling large numbers of hardcore members of the security services, the Special Republican Guard and the Ba'ath Party to survive the war unscathed.[1]

The United States, moreover, did not prepare adequately for "the war after the war." Insufficient effort and resources were devoted, at least initially, to the pursuit of many of the second- and third-tier regime personalities who went on to play key roles in the postwar insurgency. Likewise, because the coalition went in "light" in order to ensure surprise, it lacked (and still does) the numbers needed to secure large expanses of Iraq's borders against foreign jihadists entering the country from abroad, or to ensure security, law and order in the so-called "Sunni triangle" and elsewhere. As a result, local, tribal and party militias have proliferated to fill the security void.

The coalition now faces terrorist challenges from foreign and homegrown jihadists, and threats to stability from the militias. While the number of foreign jihadists may not be great, they often bring to bear expertise, experience, a perceptive grasp of how to cause mayhem and a commitment to die a martyr's death, all of which enable them to have an impact out of all proportion to their numbers. To their ranks should be added thousands of Iraqi salafists from the villages and towns of the "Sunni triangle", whose numbers swelled in the past decade as a result of official encouragement of religion (Saddam Hussein's so-called "faith campaign") and infusions of money and religious propaganda from Saudi Arabia and elsewhere. The existence of the militias will likewise create a heightened potential for violence as Iraqis jostle for political advantage as the transfer of sovereignty and elections draw near.

The attitude of many Iraqis toward the coalition has been a major complicating factor. While some Iraqis are indeed staunchly pro-American (especially the Kurds), the attitudes of most range from ambivalence to open hostility, due to past betrayals, recent and ongoing humiliations and U.S. support for Israel.

Shi'a in particular remember the failure of the United States to come to their rescue after encouraging them to revolt in 1991, while many Iraqis, particularly Sunnis, were humiliated by the defeat and dissolution of the Iraqi army and the heavy-handed tactics sometimes used by American occupation forces. Many Iraqis are apprehensive about U.S. plans for democracy; some Shi'a believe that the United States might eventually install a new Sunni strongman to ensure stability (the recent rehabilitation of former Ba'ath Party members have fed these fears), while many Sunnis believe that democracy will lead to their marginalization. These suspicions have been compounded by the perception that the failure to halt looting after the fall of the old regime and delays in restoring basic services are an American tactic to keep Iraqis down while it exploits Iraq's oil wealth. Recent revelations concerning abuse and torture of Iraqi detainees by American personnel deepened the hatred some Iraqis feel for the United States. Such resentments and the fear of retribution by former regime elements have almost certainly deterred many Iraqis from assisting the coalition.

The new Iraqi interim government will inherit the insurgency, the foreign terrorist threat and, most likely, the challenge of dealing with the militias, but will lack the means to deal with these problems on its own. For this reason, Coalition forces will almost certainly remain in Iraq for the foreseeable future, though this will likely be a source of friction between the Coalition and the Iraqi interim government, which will probably seek to limit the Coalition military's freedom of action. Populist politicians and extremists will likely use the issue to discredit political rivals, and the longer Coalition forces stay, the more the resentment against them is likely to grow.

Ties between Washington and Baghdad will likely be tense and difficult. A pro-American Iraq is not in the cards; the best that can be hoped for now is an uneasy partnership based on an unsentimental assessment of shared interests. Moreover, it is not impossible that an elected Iraqi government will seek the early departure of coalition forces-through peaceful or violent means. Indeed, there can be little doubt that the country's security problems will stress its fragile new institutions of governance and greatly complicate the transition from dictatorship to democracy in a country that faces numerous other problems.

American Credibility in the Aftermath

The image of American power and competence evinced by the rapid coalition military victory has been badly tarnished by the failure of the coalition rapidly to halt postwar looting, restore order, repair the country's crumbling infrastructure, face down anti-coalition insurgents and halt terror attacks. This might affect the credibility of future

American deterrent and coercive threats. Likewise, flawed pre-war claims regarding Iraq's WMD have raised questions about the credibility of American intelligence.

Ironically, while the coalition has not yet found WMD in Iraq, the war may have implications for proliferation elsewhere. There are persistent reports that Iraq transferred WMD or related equipment to Syria prior to the war and that some Iraqi weapons scientists may have left the country, finding refuge and, in some cases employment, in other states of former or current proliferation concern, like Libya, Syria and Iran. For now, it remains unclear whether the WMD programs of neighboring states benefited from regime change in Baghdad, although for Iran and North Korea, the war probably confirmed the importance of a nuclear deterrent when dealing with the United States. North Korea's apparent decision to expand its nuclear arsenal in the aftermath of OIF probably reflects this concern.

Conversely, by inducing Libya to dismantle its WMD programs and Iran to reveal nuclear procurement data in order to avert international pressure or U.S. military action, the war may have helped U.S. intelligence to grasp better the scope of the international supplier network run by Pakistani nuclear scientist Abdul Qadeer Khan.

Finally, the invasion of Iraq has undoubtedly complicated the War on Terror. The invasion and events connected with it (such as the abuse of Iraqi prisoners by U.S. personnel) deeply humiliated many Iraqis and Arabs, and for many, confirmed Osama bin Laden's image of the West. The Iraq War will likely provide a new crop of recruits for jihadist groups in the Middle East, Europe and Asia.

Due to a lack of border controls and a functioning central government, Iraq has emerged as a principle arena of operations for jihadist groups committed to the fight against the United States and the establishment of democracy in Iraq, and a staging ground for attacks against neighboring states such as Turkey and Jordan. Reestablishing control over Iraq's borders and halting the activities of such groups will pose major challenges to a new Iraqi government.

Reshaping the Middle East

The United States went into Iraq with the declared intention of transforming it into a democracy that could serve as a model for the region. However, developments in Iraq since the war have served to underscore the formidable obstacles facing such an undertaking in a deeply divided society that continues to be wracked by communal tensions and political violence.

The influential role played by Shi'i and Sunni clerics in post-Saddam Iraq has raised concerns that Iraq may be on the way to becoming an Islamic republic. Because Saddam Hussein tolerated-and after the Gulf War encouraged-religious observance, while ruthlessly suppressing secular parties other than the ruling Ba'ath, the mosque networks and the Islamists were the best-organized entities in Iraq after his fall. These groups and their associated militias moved quickly to fill the void of authority in Iraq that followed the demise of the Ba'ath regime. The coalition's willingness to treat clerics as authority figures has likewise reinforced the role of religion and the clergy in post-Saddam Iraq

(although the Islamists among them remain wary of the coalition's perceived commitment to secular democracy.)

For now, however, an "Islamic Republic" of Iraq seems an unlikely outcome. What is more certain is that Islam and Islamists are likely to play a greater role in public life in post-Saddam Iraq than at any other time in the modern history of the country, adding another layer of complexity to efforts to build a stable democracy based on cooperation and compromise among Iraqi's disparate sects and ethnic groups.

Furthermore, the unprecedented participation of Kurdish and Shi'a personalities and political parties in Iraq's cultural and political life is generating pressures for political change in neighboring states. This is likely to have dramatic implications for Iraq and the region. The enfranchisement of Iraq's Kurds has engendered concern by other Iraqis (particularly Turkomen and Shi'a) who fear that Kurdish gains will come at their expense, and may embolden Kurds in Syria, Turkey and Iran to demand greater political freedoms. The Shi'a revival has likewise alarmed many Iraqi Sunnis who fear marginalization and a loss of privilege and has apparently prompted foreign jihadists in Iraq to attack Shi'a worshippers and religious shrines in an effort to foment civil war. The rise of the Shi'a as a political force has also produced tensions with the Kurds concerning the role of religion in public life and the issue of federalism.

At the same time, there have been countervailing tendencies. In April 2004, Sunni and Shi'a insurgents fighting coalition forces made common cause, at least on a rhetorical and symbolic level. It remains to be seen whether a shared interest in fighting and expelling coalition forces can provide the basis for a military alliance.

The ascendancy of the Shi'a in Iraq has major implications for Iran. The reemergence of Najaf and Karbala as centers of Shi'i religious learning and bastions of the dominant quietistic tradition within Shi'i Islam could undermine the pre-eminent status that Qom (in Iran) has enjoyed in the Shi'i world since the 1920s, further delegitimizing Iran's doctrine of clerical rule.

On the other hand, the rise of the Shi'a could lay the groundwork for the expansion of Iranian influence in Iraq. During the war and after, operatives of Lebanese Hizballah were reportedly sent to southern Iraq to gather intelligence concerning coalition forces-likely at the behest of Tehran. Likewise, the Badr Organization (formerly the Badr Corps militia) of the Supreme Council for the Islamic Revolution in Iraq, which enjoys strong ties to Iran's Islamic Revolutionary Guard Corps, has established a significant presence in southern Iraq and Baghdad, potentially giving Tehran a degree of leverage over developments in Iraq. As a result, the Islamic Republic could, through its agents and allies, do great harm to coalition forces in Iraq, should it desire to do so. The ironic result is that the coalition military presence in Iraq limits rather than enhances, Washington's ability to pressure Tehran regarding support for terror and its nuclear program.

As to the future, an Iraq in which Kurds and Shi'a hold senior government positions is unlikely to consider Iran a significant threat and is apt to have normal, if not cordial, relations with Tehran—an outcome that might not be completely to Washington's liking.

Finally, the rise of Iraq's Shi'a could embolden Shi'a communities in the Gulf to press for greater political rights. While in some places this might generate momentum for change, in others it might engender a backlash by Sunnis who view Shi'a political aspirations with trepidation. The United States may well be blamed by both friends and enemies in the Arab-Islamic world for any social and political tensions generated by such demands, just as it has been accused of conspiring with the Shi'a to corrupt and undermine orthodox (Sunni) Islam by some Al-Qaeda types. In this way, U.S. policy in Iraq could affect relations with allies in the Middle East and efforts to encourage political reform throughout the region.

In response to U.S. efforts to democratize Iraq, several Arab regimes have announced their intention to pursue reforms or have introduced what are in many cases token measures calculated to accommodate popular demands for change and deflect American pressure for reform (though some of these steps had long been contemplated).

American calls for democracy have, however, been greeted with skepticism by some Iraqis, and by the numerous critics of U.S. policy in the Arab world. These critics suspect U.S. motives, reject the neo-imperial aspects of the "imposition" of democracy from without, and fear that political reform will empower Islamists. Despite these qualms, 9/11 and OIF have placed the issue of political reform and democratization front and center on the Arab political agenda, fueling demands for reform and change.

The opposition of autocratic elites to this new strand in American Middle East policy is not surprising. They have much to lose should democracy take root. The United States, however, has to find ways to continue to work with its autocratic allies in Egypt, Saudi Arabia and the Gulf—while prodding and pressing them to engage gradually in real reform and to open up their political systems without fomenting instability. Failure to do so will only ensure the perpetuation of a status quo that does not serve the long-term interests of the United States, its allies or the peoples of the region, deepening cynicism toward the United States. Having come this far, Washington cannot back off without doing additional harm to its interests in the Middle East, though recent revelations concerning the abuse of Iraqi prisoners by U.S. military personnel will further complicate these efforts.

The Way Ahead

The epochal events of the past year have already had a profound effect on the Arab-Islamic world. The long-term impact of these events, however, will be influenced, more than anything else, by whether the Coalition and the UN succeed in overseeing the formation of a legitimate (that is, elected) Iraqi government in the coming months.

The prospects for such an outcome are at best uncertain, and it seems likely that for the foreseeable future, Iraq will have a weak and divided central government. The demise of strong central government, in conjunction with the rise of local politics, may in fact prove to be Iraq's political salvation by providing a more healthy basis on which to build a viable, humane polity—if Iraq can avoid a descent into rampant political violence or civil war in the meantime.

Such an outcome will not, however, happen on its own. Coalition forces will continue to play a key role in preventing the political transition from being derailed by violence or hijacked by extremists. For this reason, they should stay in Iraq as long as they are needed and welcome. Growing impatience with the coalition presence, however, has already begun to limit its political and military influence (which was never as great as coalition officials liked to think.) Iraqis should be encouraged, when feasible, to find Iraqi solutions to their problems, and when coalition forces are needed, they should be used only after consulting with local and national Iraqi leaders. Care should be taken to avoid political collateral damage that could undermine the ability of the coalition to continue to play a critical role in shepherding the transition. Failure to do so could render the coalition presence untenable before the necessary Iraqi political and security structures have been put in place.

The Bush Administration must reconcile itself to its diminishing influence in Iraq and its inability to control or master the forces unleashed by its war there. But if the Administration acts with a realistic grasp of what is possible and intervenes only when and where essential, it may yet succeed in helping to create a new Iraq that may be far from a model democracy but still worthy of America's support.

Notes

1. A supporting attack from Turkey (as had been planned) would probably have not made a difference in this outcome. Although more Fedayeen and Ba'athi militiamen would almost certainly have been killed, the regime's loyalists in the north would have gone under ground, just as hardcore members in the south did when overrun.

Part Three

The Sunni Resistance

Jeffrey White

Introduction

Whatever notions the U.S. government and its coalition partners had that the liberation and reconstruction of Iraq would be relatively benign were shattered by the rapid onset of a dangerous Sunni-based resistance movement. Arguably, coalition authorities and the Iraqis cooperating with them never "caught up" with the resistance as a response to the occupation. Coalition officials publicly debated what they were facing, applied simplistic labels to what was, from the beginning, a complex phenomenon, and took actions that contributed to the growth and hardening of armed opposition rather than suppressing it. The coalition failed to fully understand the phenomenon, creating opportunities for resistance successes and coalition missteps. Some of these were to have profound consequences for the occupation and Iraq.

Although many important social, economic, and political elements have shaped the postwar environment in Iraq, the instability created by armed and violent elements was the principal driver. Resistance came to affect virtually every facet of Iraqi life, and security came to be the most important issue for Iraqis. Resistance actions quickly demonstrated the necessity for a large coalition troop presence, undermined an ambitious reconstruction timetable, hazardously accelerated the political transition process, engendered the rushed (and flawed) creation and deployment of the new Iraqi security forces, and wreaked mayhem and destruction on individuals and organizations working to rebuild the country.

The Sunni-based resistance in Iraq did not emerge fully formed. It has evolved over time in response to its own internal dynamics, coalition actions, and developing Iraqi institutions, all within a shattered Iraqi society. Except for a relatively small number of foreign fighters and terrorists (who probably constituted less than 5 percent of the total), resistance elements sprang from the Iraqi population, especially among those who had been attached in one way or another to the old regime but who were also adherents of widespread affinities and cohort groups. This factor allowed for the ready propagation of resistance ideas, tools, and methods. Resistance operatives included Baathists, foreign fighters, jihadists, criminals, mercenaries, and aggrieved Iraqis. This mixture was recognizable by summer 2003. At no time during this period did foreigners appear to have constituted a significant proportion of active resisters. Moreover, beyond the active resisters was a wider circle of active and passive supporters—people and groups that would provide logistical support and information in addition to serving as a base for recruiting.

This strategy of "fighting from within the population" had complex results. It imposed severe limitations on coalition intelligence gathering and combat operations. It also ensured that when coalition forces did strike at resistance elements the costs would be borne by many people, not just those directly involved in armed opposition. Naturally, this created animosity toward coalition forces and sympathy for the resistance.

Against the resistance were arrayed the forces of the coalition: the military, the Coalition Provisional Authority, and the Iraqis cooperating with them. As the occupation wore on, the Iraqi component of these forces increasingly became a major target of resistance operations, reflecting efforts by the resistance to adapt to the changing political and security environment.

There were also Iraqis who simply were not involved, or at least not involved very much, in the struggle. These individuals, perhaps the largest in terms of numbers, represented an area of competition between the resistance and the occupation. If there were "hearts and minds" to be won, it was here.

The agents of the resistance landscape were linked by a dense web of connections, and their actions were propelled by military, political, social, and economic processes. Resistance spread through traditional social networks, including family and tribal connections, which proved difficult for coalition forces to penetrate and dismantle. While the coalition worked to obtain intelligence on the resistance, the resistance infiltrated the newly created Iraqi security services. Resistance, coalition, and Iraqi actions reverberated throughout Iraqi society, with both intended and unintended consequences. Coalition military operations aimed at reducing resistance instead generated greater sympathy for it in heavily affected Sunni cities and towns, while de-Baathification efforts served to convert members of the Baath Party into resistance supporters. At the same time, terrorist suicide bombings antagonized Iraqis and turned many against the resistance. Religious fervor in the form of radical Islamic fundamentalism emerged quickly in conservative Sunni areas and became an important driver of local resistance activity, as seen in Falluja.

In the forge of occupation the resistance did not remain unchanged. It adapted rapidly to the shifting environment—faster than either the coalition or Iraq's new political and military institutions. Aggressive intelligence-based coalition military operations imposed a kind of Darwinian process on the resistance. The killing of resistance fighters and elimination of resistance leadership by death or capture forced resistance elements to burrow deeper, recruit new fighters, and replace lost leaders while still remaining operationally effective. Despite all efforts to contain and suppress it, the resistance remained active throughout the Sunni areas.

Structurally, the resistance appears to have begun as a loosely connected group of local cells, led principally by members of the old regime and those associated with them. Over time this loose network has apparently become tighter, although still not centrally directed. Operationally, the resistance broadened the scope of its actions until, by the end of June 2004, it came to pose a comprehensive threat. Resistance elements routinely attacked coalition forces; Iraqi government personnel, organizations, and facilities; external organizations seeking to stabilize Iraq or contribute to its reconstruction; and a broad range of foreigners working in the country. The resistance also showed greater tactical proficiency beginning in fall 2003, engaging in activities that involved larger numbers of personnel, enhanced weapons skills, and increased organizational and operational complexity. The growth of resistance capabilities was fully realized in the April 2004 fighting in Falluja and elsewhere in the Sunni Triangle.

Falluja represents a microcosm of the resistance as it has developed to date. Disparate armed elements, apparently under the loose leadership of local religious and tribal figures and with the support of at least some of the population, fought hard enough to delay coalition military successes. This provided enough time to transform the situation from a coalition initiative to crush opposition centered in Falluja to a public siege and battle of political attrition that did not favor the coalition. Falluja has slipped outside of coalition and Iraqi government control at least for the near term, and shows every sign of being a haven for forces opposed to U.S. objectives in Iraq and the Middle East.

The resistance has not been completely alone in its fight against the occupation. In particular, support from across the Syrian border seems to have played a role. Syria looks in some measure like a secure base for the resistance. Money, people, arms, and other assistance appear to be moving across the border, and there is suspicion that a number of senior leadership figures of the resistance now reside in Syria. Moral and financial support are also reportedly being transferred from fundamentalists in Saudi Arabia to so-called Islamic radicals in Iraq.

The resistance is much more complex than any simple sound-bite description such as "regime dead-enders," "terrorists," or "Islamic fundamentalists" conveys. The resistance now has a well-articulated structure, sustainable leadership, diverse membership, and assets in the form of arms and money. It has adequate logistical support to generate significant numbers of fighters when required and to maintain them for longer periods of time. It has relatively secure means to communicate across the Sunni Triangle to the population it wishes to influence and to external supporters.

What does the course of the struggle up to the coalition's June 28, 2004, transfer of authority say about the future of Iraq? While there is a wide range of paths that the resistance could follow, it seems probable that it will evolve into an armed and violent political faction within the new Iraq—a faction that represents at least a portion of the Sunni population and that is heavily influenced by members and associates of the former regime and by radical Islamic elements. The public face of this faction will likely emerge in the form of individual leaders or parties associated with the struggle against the occupation and the new Iraqi government. Any such marriage of armed resistance and politically active Sunnis could become a persistent threat to political stability in Iraq.

The emergence of the resistance and the associated phenomenon of terrorism against the coalition and Iraqis were the subjects of extensive and, in retrospect, accurate assessment by Washington Institute scholars. Their frequent analyses identified the potential for resistance, signaled its onset, examined its components, projected its course, and assessed its implications for Iraq and for U.S. objectives there. Extensive coverage was also devoted to the terrorism-related aspects of the resistance and their links to broader terrorism issues. This body of analysis continues to grow, representing a living history of a critical stage in Iraqi and Middle Eastern history.

Jonathan Schanzer

15
Ansar al-Islam: Iraq's Al-Qaeda Connection

Ansar al-Islam, an al-Qaeda affiliate active in Iraqi Kurdistan since September 2001, is a prototype of America's enemies in the "war on terror." The group serves as a testament to the global spread of al-Qaeda affiliates, achieved through exploitation of weak central authorities and a utilitarian willingness to work with seemingly differing ideologies for a common cause. Lengthy reports on Ansar have appeared in the *New York Times, Washington Post,* and *Los Angeles Times,* and Kurdish leaders have given Washington a plethora of intelligence on the group. Nevertheless, Ansar has yet to appear on official U.S. terrorism lists. Meanwhile, political complexities would make military action against the group difficult, at best. Hence, this small force of 650 fighters is a textbook example of the ongoing challenges posed by the war on terror.

Northern Iraq's al-Qaeda

In August 2001, leaders of several Kurdish Islamist factions reportedly visited the al-Qaeda leadership in Afghanistan with the goal of creating an alternate base for the organization in northern Iraq. Their intentions were echoed in a document found in an al-Qaeda guest house in Afghanistan vowing to "expel those Jews and Christians from Kurdistan and join the way of Jihad, [and] rule every piece of land . . . with the Islamic Shari'a rule." Soon thereafter, Ansar al-Islam was created using $300,000 to $600,000 in al-Qaeda seed money, in addition to funds from Saudi Arabia.

Today, Ansar operates in fortified mountain positions along the Iran-Iraq border known as "Little Tora Bora" (after the Taliban stronghold in Afghanistan). There, the group's Kurdish, Iraqi, Lebanese, Jordanian, Moroccan, Syrian, Palestinian, and Afghan members train in a wide array of guerrilla tactics. Approximately thirty al-Qaeda members reportedly joined Ansar upon the group's inception in 2001; that number is now as high as 120. Armed with heavy machine guns, mortars, and antiaircraft weaponry, the group fulfills al-Qaeda lieutenant Ayman al-Zawahiri's vision of a global jihad. Ansar's goal is to disrupt civil society and create a Taliban-like regime in northern Iraq. To that end, it has already banned music, alcohol, photographs, and advertising in its stronghold. Girls are prevented from studying; men must grow beards and pray five times daily.

Originally published as *PolicyWatch* no. 699, January 15, 2003. Jonathan Schanzer is a Soref fellow at The Washington Institute.

Activities since 2001

Ansar first made headlines in September 2001 when it ambushed and killed forty-two Patriotic Union of Kurdistan (PUK) fighters. In February 2002, the group assassinated Franso Hariri, a Kurdish Christian politician. That spring, Ansar attempted to murder Barham Salih, a PUK leader; five bodyguards and two attackers were killed in the ensuing gunfight. In June, the group bombed a Kurdish restaurant, injuring scores and killing a child. In July, the group killed nine PUK fighters, and destroyed several Sufi shrines—a move reminiscent of the Taliban. In September, Dutch authorities arrested the group's leader, Najmuddin Faraj (a.k.a. Mullah Krekar), for suspected ties to al-Qaeda. In December, Ansar launched a surprise attack after the PUK sent 1,500 soldiers home to celebrate the end of Ramadan. According to the group's website, they killed 103 PUK fighters and wounded 117.

That same month, Jordan's prime minister announced that al-Qaeda operative Fazel Inzal al-Khalayleh (a.k.a. Abu Musab al-Zarqawi) had sought refuge with Ansar. Khalayleh had ordered the spring 2002 attack on Salih as well as the October 2002 murder of U.S. Agency for International Development officer Laurence Foley in Amman. Khalayleh's deputy, Nur al-Din al-Shami (a.k.a. Abu Abdullah), was killed in a battle with Kurdish fighters less than two weeks ago.

Currently, more than thirty Ansar militants (about twenty of whom are Arab) are incarcerated in Sulaymaniya. Their testimony has provided clues about the group's ties to Saddam Hussein, al-Qaeda, Iran, and weapons of mass destruction.

Chemical Weapons

Some Bush administration and PUK officials claim that Ansar has established chemical weapons facilities in Iraqi Kurdistan. Reports allege that Baghdad helped to smuggle these weapons from Afghanistan and that Ansar has tested substances such as cyanide gas and the poison ricin. Salih has cited "clear evidence" that such tests have been performed on animals. Moreover, the *Washington Post* reported that the group smuggled VX nerve gas through Turkey in fall 2001.

Links to Saddam

Bush administration and PUK officials have also speculated that Ansar may be working with Saddam through a man named Abu Wael, reportedly an al-Qaeda operative on Saddam's payroll. Kurdish explosives experts also claim that TNT seized from Ansar was produced by the Iraqi military, and that arms are sent to the group from areas controlled by Saddam. Iraqi officials deny all such ties, yet Saddam clearly profits from Ansar's activities, which keep Kurdish opposition forces tied up on the border and away from Saddam. Indeed, support for Ansar is not unlike the money Saddam gives to families of Palestinian suicide bombers; turning up the heat in Kurdistan and the Palestinian territories takes heat off Saddam as a crisis looms.

Currently, Kurdish and international sources are accumulating evidence they say could soon present a clearer picture of Saddam's cooperation with al-Qaeda.

Links to Iran

Iran supports Ansar by allowing it to operate along its borders. Iran may also provide logistical support by permitting the flow of goods and weapons and providing a safe area beyond the front. The Turkish daily *Milliyet* has noted that Ansar militants check cars leaving their stronghold en route to Iran, indicating coordination with the Islamic republic. Moreover, the recently apprehended Mullah Krekar spent many years in Iran and was arrested in Amsterdam after a flight from Tehran.

Iran has several possible reasons for supporting Ansar. For one, having a democratic protostate on its borders threatens the very nature of the Islamic Republic. Thus, continued guerrilla activity benefits Tehran, as does any movement designed to spread Islamism in Kurdistan. Furthermore, by supporting Ansar and other Islamist groups in Iraq, Tehran may attempt to gain influence among the various factions that could contribute to a new Iraqi government if Saddam's regime is overthrown.

Implications

More than one year after Ansar announced its formation, the State Department has yet to designate it a Foreign Terrorist Organization, nor has the Treasury Department listed it as a Specially Designated Global Terrorist (SDGT) entity. It would be interesting to know why. Other questions remain: Can Washington pressure Iran to cease cooperation with Ansar? Can it persuade Norway, where Mullah Krekar lived for several years, to examine his financial accounts? Can it verify ties between al-Qaeda and Saddam based on interviews with captured Ansar militants?

If such links are established, military force should be considered. Reports from the front indicate that Ansar could not withstand an aerial assault. Yet, Washington may be reticent to attack during this period of UN inspections for fear of international rebuke, particularly from Turkey. Ankara, already ambivalent about an Iraq war, may be sensitive to any measures that would potentially strengthen the Kurds. Still, Ansar al-Islam poses a threat to any future U.S. ground deployment. Moreover, dismantling the group would potentially weaken both Saddam and al-Qaeda—two primary targets in the war on terror.

Jonathan Schanzer

16
Foreign Irregulars in Iraq: The Next Jihad?

In light of the recent dramatic events in Baghdad, U.S. policymakers are eyeing the next phase of the war. U.S. forces will almost certainly encounter increased guerrilla fighting. Saddam Hussein's vice president, Taha Yassin Ramadan, recently stated that more than 6,000 Arab volunteer fighters are now in Iraq. With increasing numbers of such volunteers vowing to fight, could Iraq become the epicenter for the next global jihad?

Volunteer Fighters in Context

Although the entrance of foreign irregulars into Iraq is an alarming trend that necessitates continued monitoring, it is not a new phenomenon in the Muslim world. Arab volunteers, including Muslim Brotherhood fighters and elements of the Iraqi military, were known participants in the Arab-Israeli wars of 1948, 1967, and 1973. Nevertheless, each war ended in an Arab loss. In Iraq, an estimated 6,000 Arab volunteers joined Saddam's army in the early days of the Iran-Iraq War, increasing to 10,000 by 1985. Yet, their contribution only added to the number of casualties in a war that bloodied both sides, to no avail. During 1992-1995, approximately 1,000 fighters from a dozen Muslim countries fought the Serbs in Bosnia. The fundamentalist form of Islam that these fighters brought to the region was anathema to Bosnian Muslims, most of whom practiced a more liberal version of the religion. The volunteer fighters were accepted primarily because the Bosnians were in dire need of military assistance. This marriage of convenience ended when NATO forces intervened and the foreign fighters were marginalized.

One supposed exception in the ineffectual history of foreign Muslim irregulars is their role in the 1979-1989 war leading to the withdrawal of Soviet occupation forces from Afghanistan. Yet, the defeat of the Soviets was primarily due to the Afghans themselves, who constituted the vast majority of the fighters. Moreover, most of the weapons and funding for this resistance came from the U.S. and Saudi Arabian governments. The impact of foreign volunteer fighters became more significant after the Soviet withdrawal; their efforts played an important role in the Taliban regime's victories against the Northern Alliance, though both sides depended on extensive external assistance.

Originally published as *PolicyWatch* no. 747, April 10, 2003. Jonathan Schanzer is a Soref fellow at The Washington Institute.

Foreign volunteers have also had some impact on the current conflict in Chechnya. Chechen fighters are not looking to establish a strict Islamist regime in their territory, but they have been forced to rely on Islamist military aid and personnel in the absence of help from other sources. Although analyst Stephen Schwartz estimates that only "ten percent of people under arms in Chechnya are mercenaries from Muslim countries," volunteer fighters continue to arrive on the front. Regardless, Chechen forces have little chance of military success against the more powerful and organized Russian military.

Al-Qaeda Interrupted?

Many now fear that al-Qaeda elements might find a way to re-create their successes in Afghanistan (and to a lesser extent, Chechnya) by swarming to another area with weak central authority, where radicals can pool their resources and establish a formidable guerrilla fighting force. In the worst-case scenario, the terrorists dispersed from Afghanistan in early 2002 could reunite in Iraq. This is not likely, however, given the heavy presence of allied forces already in the country.

Still, Osama bin Laden recently released a message imploring Muslim fighters in Iraq not to be "afraid of their tanks and armored personnel carriers. These are artificial things. If you started suicide attacks you will see the fear of Americans all over the world. Those people who cannot join forces in jihad should give financial help to those Mujahedin who are fighting against U.S. aggression."

To date, however, U.S. officials have reported little activity on the part of al-Qaeda in Iraq. The most credible threat from the organization is the potential activity of Ansar al-Islam, an al-Qaeda affiliate based in northern Iraq. That group issued a statement on March 25 claiming that "300 jihad martyrs renewed their pledge to Allah, the strong and the sublime, in order to be suicide bombers in the victory of Allah's religion."

The Impact of Foreign Fighters in Iraq

The Associated Press reported Wednesday that thousands of foreign volunteers have been fighting allied forces in Iraq. Pockets of intense resistance by such volunteers continue to stymie coalition advances, despite significant gains in recent days. Indeed, volunteer fighters were out in force on the streets of Baghdad's Mansur district, close to the Iraqi intelligence service headquarters. They were also in control of streets in the Aadhamiya and Waziriya districts north of the city center. According to one government official, hundreds of these fighters have been captured. One officer with the 1st Marine Division reported that his troops fought a ten-hour battle with hundreds of fighters southeast of Baghdad yesterday, claiming to have killed several hundred. Some Iraqi citizens are now cooperating with allied forces, pointing out foreign fighters in their midst.

The foreign irregulars in Iraq hail from all over the region. Hizballah, Islamic Jihad, and Fatah have reportedly sent hundreds of trained fighters, while thousands of other volunteers—trained and untrained—have signed up to fight from Saudi Arabia, Sudan, Afghanistan, Morocco, Jordan, Algeria, Egypt, Somalia, and Lebanon.

Syria appears to pose the most serious threat. According to U.S. officials, the roads between Syria and Iraq, used by Saddam's arms smugglers in recent years, are now the main arteries for irregulars preparing to fight. According to the BBC, at least 2,000 fighters have left Syria in recent weeks to join the war. CNN reports that at least ten busloads of these volunteers from Syria have been stopped by coalition forces; one such bus, carrying Palestinians and other Arab volunteers, was struck by U.S. forces.

Implications

For the most part, the global jihad model has been unsuccessful; volunteer Muslim fighters have contributed relatively little to foreign military conflicts. Hence, it is unlikely that a jihad will bog down U.S. forces in Iraq so long as the foreign fighters remain limited in both number and training. In fact, this situation might even be in the best interests of the United States, since it presents an opportunity to fight several elements of the war on terror on the same front. Nevertheless, foreign irregulars may pose a threat beyond the war. In particular, they could impede or destabilize the new Iraqi administration by targeting both U.S. and Iraqi officials.

Jeffrey White

17
The Emergence of Resistance in Iraq

Whatever the long-term prospects for a stable and democratic Iraq, the potential exists for the development of resistance to that goal. This potential is rooted in both historical factors (e.g., Iraq's political culture; Iraqi distrust of the United States; enduring images of colonialism) and immediate circumstances (e.g., the collapse of Saddam Hussein's regime and the attendant destruction of governing systems and infrastructure; the legacy of regime crimes). Indeed, the latter circumstances have created precursors for resistance to coalition forces, the transitional government, and the eventual Iraqi government.

Sources of Resistance

Many of the regime's supporters have simply dissolved into the population; because there has been no formal surrender, a myth of defiance or resistance may emerge. Moreover, Iraqis have an extensive array of grievances that still need to be addressed. Baath Iraq has been wrecked, and the new state is barely conceived, much less born. Not all those looking for advancement in the new Iraq will be satisfied, and the war has created a new class of disenfranchised—the former rulers. Hence, the country is a fertile environment for the growth of violent political forces.

Potential sources of resistance can be readily identified, including former government officials, tribal elements, and ethnic and religious groups. Some of these elements may already be engaged in the beginnings of resistance. In Mosul, for example, much of the regime's presence simply disappeared. Many intelligence and security agents, Fedayeen Saddam fighters, and regular military personnel vanished rather than surrender, and they remain unaccounted for. In some cases, coalition forces have encountered residual opposition from an apparent combination of regime holdouts and local Sunnis.

In Tikrit, Saddam's home area and a center of regime loyalty, statues of the former dictator were not torn down when coalition forces arrived. The population was less welcoming toward the coalition than other Iraqis, and the locals organized themselves for self-defense against rival tribal elements. This sort of local self-organization on a tribal foundation could serve as a mobilization base for armed, organized resistance.

Initially, the Shiites in Baghdad and elsewhere seemed divided and uncertain as to how to respond to Saddam's defeat. Currently, however, some Shiite leaders are calling for the

Originally published as *PolicyWatch* no. 751, April 23, 2003.

rapid departure of coalition forces, and these demands could serve as a rallying cry. Indeed, both Sunnis and Shiites participated in demonstrations in Baghdad on April 18 against "occupation." The Sunnis are used to being in power, and the Shiites are used to resisting. Both have a built-in leadership structure in the form of senior or revered religious figures, some of whom are effective catalysts for mass mobilization. From this perspective, the mass Shiite religious demonstrations held recently in Karbala have clear political significance.

The Development of Resistance

Resistance often emerges as a result of one of three processes. The first is self-organization, wherein salient incidents, nascent leaders, and local conditions and grievances merge to form the basis for more extensive opposition. The second is conscious decisionmaking and planning by motivated individuals or groups. The third is spontaneous ignition in response to something specific: a violent clash, an arrest of a key leader, or the empowerment of an unpopular leader. Any one or more of these processes could already be at work in Iraq, which is why the developments in Mosul, Baghdad, and Karbala are troubling.

Resistance usually unfolds in stages. Initially, a populace may exhibit sullen acceptance of superior force, with only local displays of opposition. Later, opposition becomes organized and is manifested in more serious challenges to authority. Finally, organized groups with political objectives initiate armed resistance.

Certain indicators could help coalition forces identify growing resistance in Iraq. One sign would be the emergence of causes and leaders capable of mobilizing Iraqis at the local, regional, or national level. Another sign would be the emergence of overt opposition groups. Although such groups might not advocate violent opposition at first, they could turn to it eventually or serve as a recruitment base for those who do advocate it. A third sign would be the initiation of organized violence, including armed attacks on coalition forces or the interim government. Evidence of increasing cooperation among groups opposed to the new situation would be yet another sign. In any case, the coalition should not take too much comfort from the fractious nature of Iraqi society; history suggests that even highly divided resistance movements can cooperate to achieve major goals (e.g., the French under German occupation; the Jewish community in Palestine under the British).

Resistance can begin at the local level—in individual neighborhoods, villages, towns, or cities. The events in Mosul, Tikrit, and Baghdad, although different, could be early signs of emerging resistance. Moreover, problems at the local level can coalesce to pose challenges at the regional or national level. The country's ethnic, tribal, and religious divisions should serve to retard the formation of effective opposition at the regional level, but these divisions should not be counted on to prevent such resistance entirely. The largely Shiite south, with its extension into Baghdad, is the most probable candidate for organized regional resistance. National resistance—that is, resistance by one or more groups operating across the country and with similar objectives—seems less likely than regional resistance. Only the prolonged presence of coalition forces or extended political instability are liable to create an environment in which national resistance could become a real problem. Nevertheless, the potential for Sunni-Shiite cooperation needs to be monitored.

The wherewithal for opposition exists in Iraq, and manpower resources seem plentiful. The regime's survivors, foot soldiers and leaders alike, are just one source of such manpower. A number of non-Iraqi "volunteers" remain at large in the country, and more could arrive over time. Many elements of Iraqi society were armed and trained by the government, while others armed and trained themselves in order to resist the government. Moreover, the enormous amounts of cash in Iraq (some of which has disappeared during looting) suggest that financing resistance might not be a problem; the country is also awash in small arms, light crew-served weapons (e.g., mortars), and explosives, the ideal instruments of armed resistance. Finally, Iraq's neighbors could decide to provide support to resistance groups. Iran has a history of such activity, and Turkey, Syria, and Saudi Arabia could choose to become involved as well.

Countering Resistance

Some resistance is perhaps inevitable, but if it can be contained quickly, Iraq's future will be brighter. Several obvious measures will help to tamp opposition: repairing Iraq's damaged infrastructure, establishing the basis for stable self-governance, and withdrawing coalition forces. Although these measures are already in motion, they will have to outpace the growth of resistance. Suppressing resistance while rebuilding the Iraqi state will require other measures. First and foremost will be the creation of effective policing and intelligence services to identify and root out dangerous opposition groups: in other words, a political police force. This will be a delicate task in a country that has been terrorized by its police and security services for over thirty years, so the coalition must be prepared to take over these responsibilities for some time. In addition, the Iraqi authorities must develop the capability to intervene with whatever force is required to disrupt or eliminate armed resistance. Again, and for largely the same reasons, this responsibility will initially fall on coalition forces. Yet, it too will have to be passed to Iraqis themselves; whatever government eventually arises in Baghdad, it will need to be able to fight for itself.

Jeffrey White and Michael Schmidmayr

18
Patterns of Sunni Resistance in Iraq

Almost from the beginning of the occupation of Iraq, coalition forces have faced "resistance"—armed action against coalition forces, equipment, or facilities. Resistance is to be distinguished from violence by Iraqis against other Iraqis and from "opposition"—that is, anticoalition statements, demonstrations, or the organization of political activity—which appears to be more characteristic of the Shiites.

Situation

The U.S. Central Command's daily incident and security reports show that from the end of major combat operations in Iraq on April 14, 2003, until June 10, 2003, there were at least 112 incidents in which lethal force was employed against the coalition. Most of these incidents have occurred in Sunni areas of the country (53 incidents) or around Baghdad (39 incidents). Because incident reporting for Baghdad is usually not location specific, not all of the actions there can be attributed to Sunnis; at least 14 (of the 39), however, are very likely to have involved Sunnis. This supports the belief that "resistance" is primarily a Sunni phenomenon, whereas "opposition," or at least preparation for it, is characteristic of Shiite areas, including those in Baghdad. In the Sunni-associated incidents, coalition casualties have included 10 killed in action (KIA) and 37 wounded in action (WIA). Casualties among Iraqis have been much higher, with 54 KIA and 104 WIA as a direct result of the incidents.

Explanations

The number of incidents, the recent increased lethality of these incidents for U.S. forces, and the concentration of incidents in Sunni areas has provoked considerable analysis. There are four models that have either been used, or could be used, to explain Sunni resistance. The two most commonly used are the "locally organized" and "regime diehards" models (sometimes these two models are combined, as in "local resistance by Baathists"). A third model, "centrally directed," has generally been dismissed. U.S. military officials in Iraq maintain that there is, in fact, no central direction—that resistance is directed at the local level and based on remnants of Saddam Hussein's party and forces.

A fourth model, the one that seems to best fit the data, suggests that Sunni resistance is "self-organizing." That is, resistance elements are forming based on a combination of

Originally published as *PolicyWatch* no. 765, June 11, 2003. Michael Schmidmayr is a research intern at The Washington Institute.

factors: friction with the coalition; general discontent created by the loss by Sunnis of a relatively privileged position in Iraqi society; and overlapping local, family, tribal, and religious affinities. Baath diehards clearly comprise part of the resistance story, and at least some of the activity in Falluja has been attributed to "outsiders." The resistance also depends on political, economic, and social "microclimates," which can vary significantly from town to town or among city districts. Penetrating these affinities and microclimates is a difficult and time-consuming task for intelligence services. "Closing with and destroying" embedded resistance elements, as has been pledged by U.S. commanders, will be a challenge—perhaps more an intelligence- and security-service function than a combat-unit task.

Types

Attacks have ranged from simple roadside snipings to "quality attacks" featuring command and control; direction of fire; and a combination of weapons, including assault rifles, rocket-propelled grenades (RPGs), and light and heavy machine guns. The most common type of attack has consisted of firing at coalition targets (the "signature attack" consists of a small group armed with RPGs and automatic weapons); troops (thirty-eight attacks) and convoys (ten attacks) have been the most frequent targets in these attacks. Quality attacks have already taken place at Hawija, Haditha, Falluja, al-Qaim, and Tikrit; greater frequency, sophistication, and geographic spread of such attacks would be a cause for concern. There have also been a few cases in which anticoalition demonstrations or spontaneous events may have either been generated or exploited to produce clashes with coalition troops. This is one explanation for the bloody incidents that took place in Mosul and Falluja in April, and more recently in Hit. Whatever the cause, these events produce grievances against the coalition and contribute to the hostility that feeds resistance.

To some extent, the intimidation factor (large, armored vehicles; heavily armed, helmeted, and body-armored troops; helicopters overhead; disproportionate casualties) of U.S. forces has eroded. Resisters seem to be adapting and developing tactical responses to U.S. operations and activities. Some of these adaptations may include "RPG sniping" by individuals or small teams of three to four men, ambushes of soft vehicles on highways or in towns, and the targeted killing of individual U.S. soldiers manning guard posts or checkpoints. Resistance successes will contribute to further erosion in the deterrence value of coalition units, emboldening other, would-be resisters.

Baghdad is a special case. Western Baghdad appears to be the center of Sunni resistance, and, according to the *Wall Street Journal,* one district—Aadhamiya, in northwest Baghdad—has been identified as a particular problem area with its own potential resistance group, the so-called "Army of Muhammad." Opposition to the coalition is reportedly supported by the Abu Hanifa Mosque, and attacks are attributed by locals to both Baath cadres and Fedayeen Saddam still active in the district. Attacks in Baghdad have varied widely, with a range of weapons—from knives to mortars—employed.

Evolution

The nature and future growth of Sunni resistance will hinge on whether or not connectivity develops among so far geographically separate resistance elements. While resistance is occurring within a region roughly defined by Falluja-al-Qaim-Mosul-Baghdad, there is only indirect evidence that connections exist among resistance elements within this area. The existing road network supports movement and communication throughout the region. On May 24, a large shipment of gold was intercepted in the al-Qaim area of western Iraq. Numerous vehicles have been stopped transporting more weapons than needed for the self-defense of the occupants. Personnel, including Baath Party officials, have been captured on the road. And the June 8 checkpoint attack near al-Qaim is similar in method to attacks that have occurred in Baghdad. None of these incidents serve as strong evidence of a regional command and logistical structure, but they do suggest the potential for such a development.

The long-term outlook for Sunni-based resistance in Iraq is unclear. Occupation forces have begun to recognize the seriousness of the problem and are taking strong measures against resistance elements. Several resistance-type leaders have been arrested in Falluja and elsewhere; Baath Party officials are being actively pursued; and significant numbers of weapons have been seized. However, there is still much to be concerned about. Baghdad, Falluja, and Tikrit are the most active areas, but resistance incidents are occurring in more locations over time. Resistance also seems to be adapting—at least at the tactical level—and coalition deterrence, at least for some resisters, seems to be fading. While resistance may not yet be coalescing at the regional level, it may be doing so at the local level; that is, Baathist, religious, tribal, and family elements may be joining in support of armed action against the coalition. There is no fundamental reason that local affinities cannot naturally expand to the regional level, where family, tribal, and religious ties also exist. In some cases, resistance actions also appear to be more sophisticated; while the trend in the number of incidents per week has been decreasing, the incidents seem better organized and are more lethal.

Dealing effectively with emerging Sunni resistance will be one of the major tests of the occupation administration. At this point, relatively few Sunnis are likely involved actively in resistance. It needs to be kept that way.

Jeffrey White and Michael Schmidmayr

19
Resistance in Iraq

Armed resistance to occupation has emerged as a major problem in postwar Iraq. It has become a prime concern of the United States, and casts a shadow over its postwar plans for the country. The United States has set very high goals for its mission in Iraq; armed resistance, leading to U.S. casualties and a climate of insecurity, is one variable that could block the ultimate achievement of those goals.

While reporting on the resistance is extensive and sometimes insightful, much of the media coverage lacks context and perspective. It provides only names, places, and the immediate circumstances of attacks, or else personalizes the issue by focusing on the potential effects of the deaths of Saddam's sons. Coalition authorities have provided various, and sometimes conflicting, descriptions and explanations for resistance. For example, on July 16, 2003, the commander of U.S. Central Command, Gen. John Abizaid, invoked the concept of guerrilla war to describe resistance in Iraq. Eight days later Secretary of Defense Donald Rumsfeld denied that there was a guerrilla war in Iraq.[1] The Coalition Provisional Authority (CPA), the U.S.-administered temporary government of Iraq headed by Ambassador L. Paul Bremer III, largely avoids public speculation on the resistance, beyond generally attributing it to regime "dead-enders."

But dealing effectively with resistance—a long-term phenomenon—can only come from acquiring a clear understanding of the problem, and by eschewing oversimplified or politically motivated conceptions of the issue. History suggests that controlling resistance will be a difficult and time-consuming task, demanding commitment of significant resources and an effective long-term political, military, economic, and social strategy. Unless the coalition can thwart the armed resistance that it faces now, and may face in the future, the prospects for a stable and democratic Iraq will be dim.

This article attempts to go beyond the headlines and press briefings and provide an early perspective on the emergence of resistance in Iraq.

Fertile Ground

The situation in postwar Iraq has been fertile soil for the emergence of resistance. The nutrients include the survival of the regime's forces, the uncertain political future of the Sunnis, flagging reconstruction efforts, the growth and persistence of myths, and the widespread possession of weapons.

Originally published in *Middle East Quarterly* 10, no. 4 (Fall 2003). Reprinted with permission. Michael Schmidmayr is a research intern at The Washington Institute.

At the war's end, tens of thousands of the regime's security personnel simply disappeared. They include Ba'ath Party militiamen, special and regular Republican Guard troops, and whole divisions of the Iraqi army. These angry and bitter men, especially those most closely associated with the regime such as Saddam Fedayeen, are an abundant potential source of recruits for resistance. Most of the resistance to date has been attributed to them.

More generally, the Sunnis were the big losers in the war. They have been deprived of powers and privileges they have enjoyed for decades. The new governing council, with only five Sunnis, roughly reflects the diversity of Iraq, but it is also a good measure of the decline of Sunni political fortunes.[2] Sunni cooperation in building a new Iraq is likely to be grudging and limited in the best of circumstances for some time. To date, the CPA does not appear to have developed an approach for systematically engaging the Sunnis. Instead, there appears to be a reliance on select individuals, at least some of whom are former Iraqi military, to provide local leadership.[3] The Sunnis, resentful of their disenfranchisement, provide rich compost for resistance, and most resistance actions and operations have taken place in Sunni-populated areas.

Infrastructure repair and economic recovery have been slow. Many Iraqis expected that in the immediate aftermath of the war, the United States would lift the country out of its economic stupor. In fact, the coalition was slow off the mark in implementing plans for Iraq's postwar reconstruction, and in any case, Iraqi expectations were extremely high. The result has been a widespread sense of disappointment and frustration.

On the political side, false starts and apparent backtracking on promises have marred progress towards Iraqi self-rule. The CPA has shown weakness, making important decisions under pressure—first hiring and then firing Ba'athists, later giving into the demands of former Iraqi soldiers for pay. Decisions in June to postpone and modify steps toward self-government were interpreted as evidence of the coalition's bad faith.[4] The new Iraqi governing council established on July 12, 2003, has limited powers and has drawn sharp criticism from significant segments of the population, including Shi'ites and Sunnis.[5]

The Iraqi street is also rife with myths that nourish resentment, defiance, and resistance. Four of them are particularly salient:

- Saddam will return. The probability that he is still out there, that he may be leading resistance operations, and that he may return to power all create uncertainty about the future of Iraq.[6] Coalition authorities have gone from attributing little significance to him to considering him a major factor behind resistance.[7]
- "God liberated us, not Mr. Bush."[8] This myth is widespread in the Islamist community in Iraq, both Sunni and Shi'ite. It represents in part a refusal to accept the basic fact that the coalition delivered the Iraqi people from Saddam. Those who believe this maintain that they owe the coalition neither gratitude nor obedience and that the occupation authority is just another imposed regime.

- Americans covet our women. There are widespread rumors and beliefs revolving around sexual themes. The first of these is the belief that the night vision goggles employed by coalition troops can see through the clothes of Iraqi women. A variation of this was the rumor that coalition helicopters were flying low over Iraqi houses to observe women sleeping on the roofs. At least part of the story around the violent attack on British soldiers in Majar al-Kabir, in which six soldiers died, was the rumor that they were handling the underclothing of Iraqi women. And there have already been threats against women engaging in "horizontal collaboration."[9] While some of this may seem silly to Westerners, it reflects both cultural concerns and the sensitivity of Iraqis to the dominance of the coalition and their vulnerability to its actions.
- A fourth myth, surrounding the "heroic" deaths of Uday and Qusay Hussein, may well be in the making. Furthermore, Iraq already has a myth of national resistance based on opposition to the British occupation and the 1920 revolt.[10]

Iraq is also awash in weapons of the types that are most useful in a resistance situation: light to heavy automatic weapons, hand grenades and rocket-propelled grenades (RPGs), mines, military-class explosives, and mortars.[11] These weapons are effective for engaging most coalition units and are mobile and easy to hide. Saddam's numerous paramilitary and militia forces trained primarily in the use of these weapons. Coalition forces continue to seek out illegal arms, but these efforts are unlikely to limit drastically the availability of weapons to those who seek them. As one Iraqi put it, "We can hide artillery."[12] Measures to ban weapons from the street, while reducing lawlessness and random violence, leave true resistance operations largely unaffected.

To all this must be added the impact of escalating coalition operations. Resistance is occurring from within villages, towns, and cities; the responses of coalition forces deeply affect the civilian population.[13] Immediately after the end of major combat operations, coalition operations were largely limited to defensive actions (security checkpoints, police-type patrols). They were extended to limited-scope offensive actions (searches, raids). Coalition forces then shifted to large-scale intelligence-based offensive operations (e.g. Peninsula Strike, Soda Mountain).[14] As of the end of July, the coalition appears to be employing a "raiding strategy" against resistance leadership targets and supporting structures, making use of extensive human intelligence.[15] These operations, no matter how carefully pinpointed, still involve large-scale detentions, intrusions into homes, and the destruction of property. Civilians who have felt the brunt of occupation make for potential supporters of resistance.

Emerging Patterns

What is resistance? How is it different from opposition or dissent, which are also evident in Iraq? Resistance has usefully been defined as "organized attempts to work against the regime with the conscious aim of undermining it or planning for the moment of its demise."[16] Opposition and dissent are broader concepts that can include anything from armed resistance to solitary disgruntlement.[17] The essence of resistance is action, and for the purposes of this article, the action is armed and violent.

Because there was no formal end to the war (no surrender, no treaty), it is difficult to say precisely when conventional combat by the forces of the regime ended and resistance began. When major coalition operations ended April 14, 2003, Iraq was in a chaotic security situation. The grip of the regime was broken, its forces destroyed, dispersed, or vanished. But the coalition's forces had not asserted control. Coalition units were relatively thin on the ground, particularly in Baghdad and western Iraq, areas that would become important in the emergence of resistance. The coalition's inability to provide a stable security situation throughout the country helped to create an environment in which resistance elements could organize and act.

It is still unclear whether or not the regime planned for resistance and sabotage activities in advance of its defeat. Several reports have surfaced indicating that there was some preparation,[18] and the rapid onset of resistance following the end of major combat operations suggests that there may have been some pre-planning. In addition, the regime's wartime strategy of employing small elements of Saddam Fedayeen, Ba'ath Party militia, and other paramilitary forces would have served as a basis for an easy transition to resistance operations.

But even without any serious preparation, localized resistance, at least in Sunni areas, was predictable. These areas had been traumatized by the defeat of the regime. They absorbed large numbers of regime supporters with military skills, weaponry, and financial resources. It would have been remarkable if resistance had not developed.

And indeed, resistance emerged relatively swiftly after April 14. Between April 21 and April 27, there were ten reported incidents that can be classified as armed resistance.[19] Most of these were small-scale, but one of the attacks, in the Mosul area, involved 20-30 Iraqi paramilitaries. Between April 28 and May 4, the second week of resistance activity, reported incidents jumped sharply to 27. The incidents in the first two weeks already showed evolution. By the end of the second week, RPGs were being employed, and convoys had been targeted. Although the actions remained small, more towns became the sites of incidents.

There have been no dramatic changes in resistance from its beginning in the second half of April until the end of July. Rather the story has been one of evolution and adaptation. Resistance expanded geographically. Tactical adaptation and innovation were evident, and over time attacks have inflicted more casualties on coalition forces. The rate of change has been rapid, with new locations of incidents and new types of attacks being added on a weekly basis.

Data derived from U.S. Central Command and press reporting indicate that between April 14 and August 3, 2003, there were at least 202 serious incidents of armed resistance across Iraq. (Many incidents go unreported, but those involving coalition casualties are given coverage.) Most of these were in Baghdad or the surrounding area, and most were in Sunni-dominated areas of the country. Table 1 shows the number of reported incidents by location per week.

Table 1: Reported Incidents by Week and Location (W2=April 21-27, 2003)

Location	W2	W3	W4	W5	W6	W7	W8	W9	W10	W11	W12	W13	W14	W15	W16	Total Per Location
‘Amara					1					2						3
Baghdad	3	6	10	7	4	3	1	5	3	3	8	5		2	4	64
Baghdad, surroundings	1	1	1		1	1		3	2		1	2	3	1	1	18
Balad								2			2	1				5
Ba’quba			1		1						1	1		1	1	6
Basra					2											2
Bayji			1			1		1						1	1	5
Diwaniyya		1			1											2
Falluja		5				1	3			1		1				11
Falluja, surroundings	2	1	2										1			6
Habbaniyya				1												1
Haditha						1							1			2
Hawija					1											1
Hilla		1		1		1				1				1		5
Iskandariyya									1					2		3
Kirkuk												1				1
Kut		1	1		2											4

Table 1: Reported Incidents by Week and Location (W2=April 21-27, 2003) continued

Location	W2	W3	W4	W5	W6	W7	W8	W9	W10	W11	W12	W13	W14	W15	W16	Total Per Location
Miqdadiyya						1										1
Mosul	2			3				2			1		1	3		12
Najaf		1		1						1						3
Nasiriyya			1	1												2
Northern Iraq	1										1				1	3
Numaniyya				1												1
Qa'im							1								1	2
Ramadi										1	2			2		5
Rumayla Oilfield		1														1
Samarra		2	1			2		1	1							7
Samawa		2			1											3
Shatra			1													1
Southern Iraq		1														1
Taji				2						1						3
Tikrit	3	3	1				1	1								9
Western Iraq								1								1
Unspecified			2	2		1	1	1			1					8
TOTAL per week	10	27	20	22	14	12	7	17	7	10	17	11	6	13	9	202

The data also show that the number of reported incidents per week was higher earlier in the period than later. While the number of reported incidents per week declined after the first few weeks, the casualties inflicted on coalition forces per reported incident increased. Table 2 shows the coalition killed and wounded in action (KIA, WIA) per week per resistance incident.

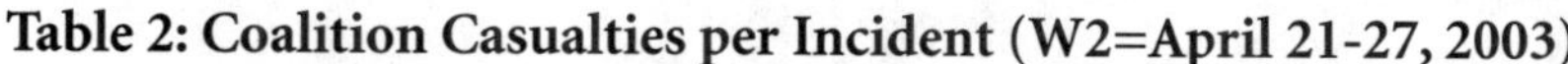

Table 2: Coalition Casualties per Incident (W2=April 21-27, 2003)

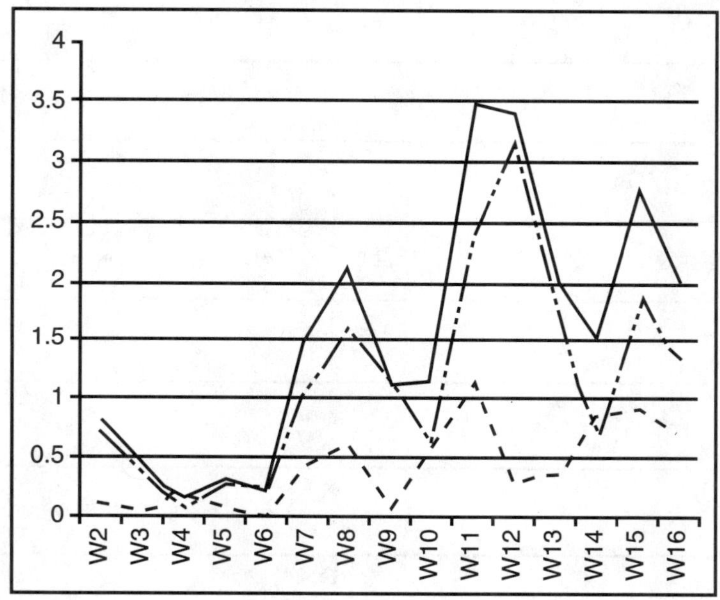

Weekly Coalition Casualties per incident
Weekly KIA Coalition per incident
Weekly WIA Coalition per incident

The Baghdad (25 KIA; 7 WIA), Mosul (6 KIA; 15 WIA), Ba'quba (5 KIA; 7 WIA), and Falluja (4 KIA; 18 WIA) areas have been the most dangerous locations.[20]

Resistance actions have become more dangerous to coalition forces as resistance tactics have become more diversified over time. This probably reflects the accumulation of experience by resistance elements, changes in coalition operations, and a decline in the deterrent profile of coalition forces. From relatively few types of attacks in the first several weeks, resisters progressed to more numerous attack techniques. Table 3 indicates the broadening range in types of attacks by resistance elements.

Attacks by fire (ABF) or shooting incidents were the most common type of action. In incidents where the types of weapons were reported (see Table 4), RPGs and light to heavy automatic weapons (assault rifles, machine guns) were employed most often.

Table 3: Type of Attack (W2=April 21-27, 2003)

Location	W2	W3	W4	W5	W6	W7	W8	W9	W10	W11	W12	W13	W14	W15	W16	Total
Attack by Fire (ABF)	7	21	16	15	6	6	6	10	3	4	4	3	1		1	103
Ambush	1			2	1	1		2		3	2	2	2	5	7	28
Attack					1			1			1	2				5
Encounter/ Engagement	1	3		1	1					2						8
Escape attempt								2								2
Explosion		1	1			1					2	3	1	2	1	12
Other		2			1	1				1						5
Raid			1	4	3	3		2			1			1		15
Sabotage									1		1			2		4
Sniper attack			2				1		3		5	1	2	3		17
Suicide Bombing					1						1					2
Unspecified	1															1

Table 4: Type of Weapons (W2=April 21-27, 2003)

Location	W2	W3	W4	W5	W6	W7	W8	W9	W10	W11	W12	W13	W14	W15	W16	Total
Explosive Device		1				1					4	5	1	7	5	24
Grenade			1	1	1				1	2				1		7
Grenade/ Small Arms		1														1
Heavy Machine Gun (HMG)	1															1
HMG/Small Arms					1											1
Machine Gun (MG)		3	1	2	1			2					1			10
Machine Gun/ Grenade		1														1
Machine Gun/ Small Arms			1	1												2
Mortar	1	1							1		1	1				5

Table 4: Type of Weapons (W2=April 21-27, 2003) continued

Location	W2	W3	W4	W5	W6	W7	W8	W9	W10	W11	W12	W13	W14	W15	W16	Total
None		2														2
Other		1			2	1		1	1		1					7
Rocket-Propelled Grenade (RPG)		2	3	4	1	1	1	3	1	1	5	4	1	1	2	30
RPG/Explosive Device								1							1	2
RPG/HMG/ Small Arms						1										1
RPG/MG			1				1									2
RPG/Small Arms			1			2	2				1	2	3			11
Surface to Air Missile (SAM)													1			1
Small Arms	1	4	3				2	1	1	1	1	1			1	16
Small Arms/ other		1							1							2
Unspecified	7	10	9	14	8	6	1	9	1	6	4			1		76

RPGs were involved in at least 39 incidents, making this antitank weapon the weapon of choice. Tactics have included both RPG-sniping (a single shot with an RPG) and RPG-strafing (firing from vehicles). RPGs are highly effective against light armored vehicles and soft vehicles such as trucks and the ubiquitous HUMVEEs. Resistance elements have also engaged in a type of targeted-killing action in which one or two Iraqis approach individual coalition troops at guard posts or check points and shoot them. At least 5 attacks of this kind have taken place in Baghdad and 1 in Qa'im. In Baghdad, there may be at least one resistance element that has specialized in these kinds of attacks. A developing trend has been the use of explosive devices in attacks. There were 24 such attacks reported, most of them occurring in July.

Other types of resistance actions include sabotage operations against key infrastructure targets (oil and economic), and attacks against Iraqi persons and facilities identified with coalition efforts. For example, the mayor of Haditha was assassinated along with his son on July 16, 2003, and there have been two reported cases of surface-to-air missiles fired at coalition aircraft. Generally speaking, resistance elements have chosen not to engage coalition forces conducting major sweeps (e.g., Peninsula Strike, Desert Scorpion, Sidewinder, Soda Mountain, and Ivy Serpent), probably preferring to avoid encounters where they do not have the initiative, surprise, or local superiority. Table 5 shows the range of targets attacked.

Although no trend has developed, there have been several "quality attacks," featuring organization, direction, and maneuver. While accounts are sketchy, quality attacks appear to have taken place at Hawija on May 25, Falluja on June 6, and near Balad on June 13 and July 4.

Geographically, resistance is taking place over a very wide area and on varied terrain. It has been encountered in relatively open areas in western Iraq and near the Syrian border, in agricultural and riverine zones, in villages and towns, and in major urban areas including Baghdad and Mosul. But most resistance incidents have occurred in or near built-up areas, probably because these afford resisters concealment, cover, and a civilian population into which to fade. Urban environments are difficult to penetrate; they provide both the anonymity of the large city and the closed atmosphere of a neighborhood. Table 1, last column, shows the geographic distribution of incidents.

Iraq's road system is also an arena of confrontation. There have been multiple incidents at checkpoints and roadblocks, including attempts to crash through them. Although there is only anecdotal evidence, some resistance elements appear to use the roads to move from place to place. Given the known ability of the coalition to intercept and track telephone conversations, it would be logical for resistance elements to use couriers operating on the road system for command and control purposes. The road system can also function as a vector for spreading resistance. People, weapons, money, and probably ideas are all moving over this network, and some of this is likely associated with resistance.

Table 5: Type of Target (W2=April 21-27, 2003)

Location	W2	W3	W4	W5	W6	W7	W8	W9	W10	W11	W12	W13	W14	W15	W16	Total
Aircraft													1			1
Car					1											1
Checkpoint		1			2	2	1	1			1					8
Civilian Infrastructure														2		2
Civilians				1								1	1	1		4
Convoy	1	5	5	2		2		2	1	1	3	4	1	7	5	39
Facility, military	2	3		1	3						1	2			1	13
Facility, non-military		1	1	1	1			1	1		2					8
Helicopter								1								1
HQ	2		1													3
Iraqi Police		1						2			1					4
Military Police				1	2			2	1	1						7
Observation Post			1													1
Pipeline									1		1					2
Police Station					1							1				2
Reconnaissance		1	1													2
Soldier		1	2								2					5
Soldiers	5	14	9	14	4	7	5	6	2	8	4	1	2	3	1	85
Soldiers and Iraqi Police						2										2
Tank								1								1
Vehicle				2				1	1		2	2	1		2	11

Level of Organization

Classifying resistance is not a simple task. Even the expression "the resistance" suggests some sort of overarching, centrally directed organization and structure. There is no evidence that such a structure was in place during the first three months of resistance. But the level of organization is something that should be monitored closely since the higher the level of organization, the more capability and operational flexibility a given group is likely to have.

Conceptually, resistance to the occupation can occur at four levels: individual, local, regional, and national.

The lone gunman exemplifies *individual* resistance. This is the Iraqi who takes up arms on an individual basis for his or her own reasons and strikes out at the occupation. To date, 26 attacks by individuals have been reported. A combination of weapons has been employed, including assault rifles, machine guns, and RPGs.

Most resistance appears to be at the *local* level by small groups of resisters (perhaps 2-10). Paul Bremer said as much in a statement of July 20, 2003: "What we're seeing is highly professional but very small, sort of squad-level attacks, five or six people at a time attacking us."[21] "Local" does not imply ineffective; even small groups can be highly effective.[22] Anecdotal evidence indicates that these resisters, once engaged, quickly disappear into the local community; coalition use of local informers makes resistance based on outsiders dangerous.[23]

Regional resistance would be the third level. Here there is only limited evidence, essentially involving Hizb al-'Awda (Party of the Return), which is said to be operating in multiple locales in Sunni areas. Limited reporting puts cells from this group in Baghdad, Basra, and Mosul and indicates it operates in Tikrit and Falluja. None of this can be confirmed, and coalition authorities have tended to dismiss the existence of resistance at this level.

There is no evidence of any *national*-level resistance movement, one that cuts broadly across Iraqi society. This is hardly surprising given the major fault lines in Iraqi society (Kurds, Sunnis, Shi'ites). Nevertheless, it is possible that at least Sunni resistance was organized at the national level before the regime's defeat and is now conducted on a decentralized basis.

How many Iraqis are involved in resistance? Estimating the number of active resisters-those who actually engage in attacks-is not easy. One estimate attributed to the Pentagon suggested several thousand.[24] Another estimate by senior U.S. military officials suggested 4 to 5 thousand.[25] And still another referred to the "gang of 9,000."[26] The coalition has estimated that each resistance element contains 5-10 persons, with some as large as 50.[27] If one estimates the size of the average resistance element as 10 and attributes a resistance element to each of the 34 localities and 10 Baghdad districts where incidents have been reported, that would yield a minimum number of 440 active resisters. Very likely there is an even larger number of individuals who support resistance elements by providing shelter, and other services.

Who Resists and Why

Coalition authorities attribute the great majority of resistance operations to "regime dead-enders."[28] These potentially include tens of thousands of members of the Saddam Fedayeen, Special Republican Guard, Republican Guard, security service, and Ba'ath party officials. It is indeed likely that these elements are providing the core of resistance. Whether any of them answer to Saddam is unknown, although some resistance elements have attempted to project the idea that he is alive and in command. The periodic messages attributed to him and rumors about his activities probably help to keep up Ba'athist morale and may aid in the recruitment of former regime associates.

But this does not exhaust the recruitment pool for resistance. Local Iraqis in villages and towns, angered by coalition operations (raids, searches, destruction of property, killing and wounding relatives, etc.) make for potential resisters.[29] Local Iraqis are also almost certainly providing assistance to active resistance elements, at a minimum by helping to conceal them from the coalition.

The resistance of some locals is apparently religiously motivated.[30] Several mosques have already emerged as centers of anti-coalition preaching and activities (e.g., the Abu Hanifa and Umm al-Qura mosques in Baghdad).[31] Mosques enjoy a large measure of protection from coalition operations because of their religious status, and they are logical locations for resistance activity, especially Islamist-based resistance. The July 1, 2003 explosion next to the Hasan mosque in Falluja, which may have involved a bomb-making class and killed the anti-coalition imam, is indicative of this.[32]

Tribesmen are also likely active in resistance, falling into a local category, but the tribes themselves do not appear to be resisting in a structured way.

Various types of outsiders make up another component of the recruiting pool. These are individuals who have entered Iraq to fight against the coalition for a variety of reasons. Some are apparently wartime volunteers who have remained.[33] Others are said to be terrorists seeking opportunities to strike at the United States.[34] Still others are mercenaries attracted by the payment of bounties for killing Americans.[35] These outsiders probably number in the tens rather than the hundreds since large groups of outsiders would not be able to blend into the Iraqi population and could be readily identified by coalition informers.

Why do they resist? In the very early stages, during the first two weeks or so after April 14, resistance is likely to have been primarily driven by isolated elements of the regime, and perhaps by the spontaneous hostile actions of individuals. After that, motivation probably became more complex: the regrouping of regime loyalists; the recognition by the Sunnis of their position as political losers; the emergence of Sunni religious-based resistance (the "Wahhabi factor"); a response to occupation actions seen as insensitive, provocative, or careless; monetary reward (the reported payment of bounties for killing Americans); and virulent anti-Americanism, inculcated over decades. Finally, some individuals are probably coerced by elements associated with the regime into either active resistance or providing support for it.

Beyond the desire to be rid of the occupation, some attacks may reflect a wish among their perpetrators to restore Iraqi honor. One regime-associated resistance element has proclaimed, "This is the time for you to prove to your people that you are men and for you to give your blood cheaply and wipe away your mark of shame."[36] The Iraqi forces lost virtually all the battles of the war, suffering disproportionate losses with no gain. They are not losing all the resistance actions. In some cases they are inflicting casualties without taking any, and in others, they are trading casualties with the coalition and then getting away. As of the end of July 2003, resistance elements were inflicting two casualties per reported incident on coalition forces. Such relatively successful actions restore pride and build confidence. Given the range of likely motives, simple one-cause explanations for resistance—e.g., "regime dead-enders"—are now questionable, and they will become increasingly so with the passage of time.

New resistance groups announce their existence almost weekly. By the end of July, nineteen or more groups had identified themselves. A number of their claims may be no more than disinformation intended to confuse coalition intelligence. Some of these groups may be little more than local gangs, and there may be some duplication. Claims of operational successes for any one group appear wildly exaggerated. At the present moment, only Hizb al-'Awda has pretensions of being a credible resistance group.

Iraqi Resistance Groups

Hizb al-'Awda
Nasserite Organization
Iraqi Liberation Army
Islamic Movement in Iraq
Muslim Brotherhood
Wakefulness and Holy War
Ansar al-Islam
Armed Islamic Movement for al-Qa'ida
Muslim Youth
Iraqi National Front of Fedayeen
Army of Muhammad
Saddam Fedayeen
"The Snake Party"
Iraqi Resistance Brigades
General Command of the Iraqi Armed Resistance
Salafist Jihad Group
Organization of Jihad Brigades in Iraq
Iraq's Revolutionaries-Al-Anbar's Armed Brigades
Black Banners Organization

The Shi'ite Question

This discussion so far has centered on resistance from within Sunni areas. Table 6 shows the incidents that have occurred in primarily Shi'ite areas, including districts of Baghdad.

Table 6: Incidents in Shi'ite Areas

Date	Location	Target (Coalition)	Type of Attack	Type of Weapons Used	Results Coalition
10-Apr-03	Baghdad	Soldiers	Suicide bombing	Unspecified	4 WIA
11-Apr-03	Southern Iraq	Checkpoint	Other attack	Other	No casualties
28-Apr-03	Kut	Soldiers	Other attack	Other	No casualties
30-Apr-03	Rumayla Oilfield	Facility (non-military)	Attack by fire	Unspecified	No casualties
30-Apr-03	Southern Iraq	Soldiers	Explosion	Explosive device	1 KIA
01-May-03	Baghdad	Soldiers	Attack by fire	Small arms	1 WIA
01-May-03	Samawa, vicinity	Convoy	Attack by fire	Small arms	No casualties
02-May-03	Najaf	Iraqi police	Encounter/ engagemt.	Mach. Gun/ Grenade	No casualties
03-May-03	Samawa, vicinity	Soldiers	Attack by fire	Small arms	No casualties
05-May-03	Nasiriyya	Soldiers	Attack by fire	Unspecified	No casualties
08-May-03	Baghdad	Soldier	Attack by fire	Unspecified	1 KIA
08-May-03	Kut	Facility (non-military)	Explosion	Grenade	No casualties
08-May-03	Baghdad	Soldier	Sniper attack	Unspecified	1 KIA
15-May-03	Nasiriyya	Soldiers	Attack by fire	Unspecified	No casualties
16-May-03	Najaf	Soldiers	Raid	Unspecified	1 WIA
18-May-03	Numaniyya	Soldiers	Attack by fire	Unspecified	No casualties
20-May-03	Kut	Soldiers	Encounter/ engagemt.	Unspecified	No casualties
20-May-03	Samawa	Facility	Raid	Unspecified	No casualties
20-May-03	Basra	Car	Raid	Unspecified	No casualties
22-May-03	'Amara	Facility (non-military)	Attack by fire	RPG	No casualties
24-May-03	Basra	Soldiers	Attack by fire	Unspecified	No casualties

Table 6: Incidents in Shi'ite Areas

24-May-03	Kut	Military police	Attack by fire	Unspecified	No casualties
24-Jun-03	'Amara	Soldiers	Attack by fire	Unspecified	6 KIA
24-Jun-03	'Amara	Soldiers	Ambush	Unspecified	8 WIA
26-Jun-03	Najaf	Soldiers	Ambush	Unspecified	1 KIA
27-Jun-03	Baghdad	Convoy	Attack by fire	Grenade	1 KIA/ 4 WIA
03-Jul-03	Baghdad	Soldiers	Attack by fire	Unspecified	1 WIA
07-Jul-03	Baghdad	Vehicle	Attack	Explosive device	1 KIA

There have been many fewer attacks associated with Shi'ite areas, and they are more isolated in time. As major political beneficiaries of the war, the Shi'ites had little reason to move early in the occupation to oppose the CPA. Their response so far has been one of watchful waiting, cooperating on some issues and withholding cooperation on others, while preparing for future political battles, both at the local level and within the Shi'ite community. Shi'ite politics are overwhelmingly religious in nature and led by clerics; no significant secular Shi'ite movement has emerged.

There are three Shi'ite movements or factions that have resistance potential: the Jama'at as-Sadr ath-Thani, or Sadr group; the Supreme Council for the Islamic Revolution in Iraq (SCIRI); and the Da'wa party. All three of these organizations are highly articulated, possess recognized leadership, and are actively competing for power within the Shi'ite community itself and on the national political stage.

The Sadr group is vehemently anti-occupation and has been very successful at gaining influence at the local level. Its leader, Muqtada as-Sadr, has denounced the Iraqi governing council, and called for the creation of an "Islamic army" answerable to Iraqi religious leaders.[37] The Sadr group was not given a place in the governing council.

SCIRI has aligned itself, at least to some degree, with one of the Sadr faction's powerful rivals, Grand Ayatollah 'Ali Sistani,[38] but has its own conspiratorial history and a background of Iran-supported armed resistance to Saddam's government. SCIRI was given a seat in the governing council. The third Shi'ite organization, the Da'wa party, also has a long history of underground resistance to Saddam. It, too, was given a place in the council.

Overall, the Shi'ites are probably a greater potential danger to the coalition and any transitional government than the Sunnis. Many of the Shi'ites already have the experience of professional resisters. If their political needs are not met, at least some Shi'ite elements are likely to move to resistance. If so, they would pose a major threat.

The Toll of Resistance

Resistance has taken a toll from both the coalition and Iraqi society. Most obvious has been the toll in terms of casualties. Table 7 shows the casualties reported for both sides from the beginning of resistance to the end of July 2003.

Table 7: Total Casualties (April 21-August 3, 2003)

Number of incidents	KIA Coalition	WIA Coalition	KIA Local	WIA Local
TOTAL 180	43	173	147	165

This is actually a low rate of attrition, with an average of 18 coalition troops killed or wounded per week in resistance incidents from a force of some 145,000 troops. Reporting on Iraqi casualties is fragmentary, and reports from coalition forces suggest significantly higher Iraqi casualties.[39] The publicity given to coalition casualties magnifies their importance. Every incident receives intense and repetitious media coverage.

Resistance sabotage actions have been directed against economic and infrastructure targets, including the oil industry, electric power transmission, and financial targets. The impression is that these have had some effect on the oil industry,[40] although there is no overall data on the economic effects of sabotage operations.

Finally, resistance delayed the redeployment home of the Third Infantry Division. The decision to retain this division in country was an explicit recognition of the security problems raised by resistance.

Resistance has driven up the human and material cost of occupation and reconstruction. So far this cost has not been prohibitive, but if the resistance adapts and escalates, so, too, will its impact on U.S. decision-making.

No End Soon

The long-term prospects of resistance in Iraq are uncertain, but there are already some immediate realities that the coalition must face.

Any ideas about a benign occupation and period of quiet reconstruction have been laid to rest. Even though the regime and the Sunnis lost the war, they are still in the struggle. Whether Saddam is alive or dead, elements of his regime are fighting against the occupation, and they are doing this with the support of at least some of the Sunni population. Resistance by forces of the former regime could not continue unless it had that support. Moreover, resistance is not confined to regime "dead-enders." There are Islamists, terrorists, mercenaries, and outsiders involved. These categories probably do not exhaust the persons and groups with a hand in resistance.

The resistance wins simply by surviving and staying active. Coalition operations, including the large-scale intelligence-based operations like Peninsula Strike, Desert Scorpion, Sidewinder, and Soda Mountain, will have temporary disruptive effects on resistance, but they will not end it. Resistance incidents recur after operations are concluded or move on. The coalition's shift to an intelligence-based raiding strategy, targeting the leadership of resistance elements, may prove more effective. But an unintended consequence of these operations may be to weed out the less capable resisters while providing the more capable ones with valuable experience in evading and adapting to coalition actions.

The emergence of resistance that combines, even if only tacitly, Sunnis and Shi'ites would be a very dangerous situation. This would have the makings of a true national revolt, perhaps something like that of 1920, and it would be difficult to control without significantly greater resources.

For the longer term, and assuming the CPA is able to create a legitimate Iraqi government, the danger is that elements of Sunni, and perhaps eventually Shi'ite, resistance groups will carry over into the transition and beyond. Armed, violent, and conspiratorial groups are a challenge for any political system, especially a nascent one. To some extent the coalition's use of informers and collaborators to support its goals is preparing the ground for internecine violence. Already resisters are attacking collaborators and eliminating informers. This kind of internal war is likely to carry over into a transition government and beyond.

During July 2003, coalition officials veered from describing the resistance as "regime dead-enders" to citing a mélange of Ba'athists, Islamists, terrorists, and mercenaries-all without central direction.[41] This is a step forward, but these same officials have not provided a credible model of resistance organization and operations. That would require facing up to the contradiction between the positive declared mission of "Iraqi freedom" and the negative missions inherent in occupation. The coalition's inability, or unwillingness, to fully characterize what it is up against suggests that it has not achieved the understanding necessary to defeat the resistance. The situation demands a realistic appreciation from the coalition and its supporters for the potential of violent opposition, both for the short and the long terms. Noble motives and millennial objectives will not spare the coalition a confrontation with an unpleasant and messy reality.

Notes

1. Associated Press, July 24, 2003.
2. BBC, July 14, 2003.
3. This is based on analysis of various mentions of former Iraqi military officers appointed to key positions such as mayors.
4. Associated Press, June 3, 2003.
5. Agence France-Presse, July 18, 2003.
6. *The New York Times,* June 22, 2003.
7. Associated Press, June 29, 2003.
8. "God Liberated Us, Not Mr. Bush," *The Economist,* May 31, 2003.
9. Agence France-Presse, May 17, 2003.
10. Judith Yaphe, "The Challenge of Nation Building in Iraq," in *U.S. Policy in Post-Saddam Iraq: Lessons from the British Experience,* Michael Eisenstadt and Eric Mathewson, eds. (Washington, D.C.: The Washington Institute for Near East Policy, 2003), p. 46.

11. *The Christian Science Monitor,* May 22, 2003.
12. *The Washington Post,* May 30, 2003.
13. Reuters, July 7, 2003.
14. Associated Press, July 13, 2003.
15. *The Washington Post,* July 28, 2003.
16. Ian Kershaw, *Popular Opinion and Political Dissent in the Third Reich,* new ed. (New York: Oxford University Press, 2002), p. 3.
17. Ian Kershaw, *The Nazi Dictatorship: Problems and Perspectives of Interpretation,* 4th ed. (New York: Oxford University Press, 2000), p. 207.
18. *The Washington Times,* June 9, 2003.
19. Counts are mainly based on reports from U.S. and British military sources. Serious incidents, those in which coalition forces take casualties, receive coverage. There are other, generally minor incidents without casualties, that go unreported. Neither the above-mentioned military sources nor the press reported any incidents in the first week after the end of major combat.
20. A single anomalous incident in the town of Majar al-Kabir in southern Iraq accounted for the most killed, 6, on any one day. This appears to have been a spontaneous incident and not true resistance.
21. Associated Press, July 20, 2003.
22. Julian Jackson, *France: The Dark Years, 1940-1944* (New York: Oxford University Press, 2001), pp. 496-7.
23. There has been one reported case from Falluja of resistance elements from outside moving into a town and conducting operations.
24. *Los Angeles Times,* July 21, 2003.
25. *The Wall Street Journal,* July 28, 2003.
26. *The Washington Post,* July 23, 2003.
27. *Los Angeles Times,* July 21, 2003.
28. Agence France-Presse, July 19, 2003.
29. Reuters, July 7, 2003.
30. Associated Press, July 18, 2003.
31. Agence France-Presse, June 6, July 18, 2003.
32. Reuters, July 2, 2003.
33. Gen. John Abizaid, press briefing, July 16, 2003, Department of Defense transcript, at http://www.defenselink.mil/transcripts/2003/tr20030716-0401.html.

34. Interpress Service, June 16, 2003.
35. Ibid.
36. *The Washington Post,* June 29, 2003.
37. *The New York Times,* July 19, 2003.
38. *The Washington Post,* June 30, 2003.
39. Ibid., July 28, 2003.
40. Associated Press, June 22, 2003.
41. Ibid., July 18 2003.

Jeffrey White

20
Resistance in Iraq: Emerging Capabilities and Threats

The increase in resistance attacks in Iraq is not simply a matter of a few spectacular successes, such as the five coordinated suicide bombings in Baghdad on October 27, the downing of a Chinook helicopter on November 2, or the suicide bombing of the Italian base in Nasariya on November 12. Since September, resistance elements have appeared to be better directed, better organized, and more capable, employing both new weapons and new tactics. Their capabilities are evolving, and even more serious threats may emerge over time. At the same time, it would be inaccurate to regard the current situation as a tipping point in which the resistance has gained the upper hand.

Changes in Fitness

The resistance has become more fit, or better adapted, to the environment in Iraq in several important ways.

Persistent. Despite frequent coalition raids, plentiful (though not perfect) intelligence, thousands of arrests and detentions, and the capture of tons of weapons, those areas that were troublesome from the beginning of the occupation—Baghdad, Falluja, Tikrit, Mosul, and other parts of the so-called Sunni Triangle—remain troublesome today. In fact, Falluja, Mosul, and the areas around them seem to be getting worse. The resistance is apparently making up for whatever losses the coalition inflicts upon it. In short, resistance elements have been persistent, continuing to operate despite the coalition's superior military technology and professionalism.

Embedded. The resistance also seems to have solidified its relationship with the Sunni community. Backing from radical Sunni Islamists, which emerged early on, has continued to foster generalized support for resistance, opposition to coalition authority, and recruitment of militant resisters. The mosque provides a moral and philosophical underpinning for resistance, a source of recruits, and a place for organizing, planning, and hiding. Although evidence is limited, at least some Sunni tribal leaders appear to be offering a measure of support to resistance elements. Clearly, they have not expressed meaningful opposition to the resistance. In a society where tribal relationships are important, even indirect or tacit support of the resistance can have a significant effect.

Originally published as *PolicyWatch* no. 804, November 14, 2003.

Gaining from backlash. The coalition's counterresistance actions often cause considerable distress within the Sunni communities in which they occur, frequently leaving dead or wounded Iraqis, damaged property, detained relatives, and humiliated citizens. Even with the best of intentions and efforts to minimize collateral damage, such actions generate recruits and support for resistance.

Growing Capabilities

In addition to adapting to its environment, the resistance appears to be expanding its capabilities in several important ways. At the most basic level, it is more active; coalition sources report an increase in anticoalition incidents from twelve to fifteen per day over the summer to thirty to thirty-five per day since then (there were 46 incidents on November 12 alone). This rise in activity is likely due to several factors: an increase in the number of resistance elements (currently estimated at 5,000 by coalition commanders), better command and control over resistance forces, and more aggressive operations by coalition forces.

The resistance also appears to be spreading geographically. In October, Kirkuk, previously regarded as quiet, became an active point of resistance. According to various press reports, this change reflected the movement of a small number of organizers and fighters (along with ample funds) to the area from the Sunni heartland.

Resistance elements are also employing an increased range of weapons in their attacks. Iraqi militants employed katyusha rockets for perhaps the first time in an October 28 attack in Kirkuk. Other relatively advanced weapons reportedly used by, or newly available to, the resistance include 160-millimeter mortars; shoulder-fired surface-to-air missiles (used to down the Chinook helicopter); an improvised, though not crude, multiple rocket launcher (used to attack the Rashid Hotel in Baghdad); as well as large improvised explosive devices (IEDs) and antitank mines (both used to damage several heavy-armored coalition vehicles). Resistance elements continue to attack with their original means-including rocket-propelled grenades (RPGs) and smaller IEDs—while adding new weapons, allowing them to engage more difficult coalition targets from longer ranges.

Resistance actions are also becoming more complex and well organized. Some resistance operations now feature combined attacks with IEDs, RPGs, and automatic weapons. Coordinated suicide bombings against nongovernmental organizations and police targets have been conducted in Baghdad, and the most visible symbols of the occupation—the coalition headquarters and facilities in the heart of the capital—have been repeatedly attacked with mortars and rockets. Moreover, the resistance has carried out a campaign of attacks on prominent Iraqis deemed to be collaborating with coalition authorities. Overall, the ability to attack in multiple places, identify and locate vulnerable targets, and conduct precisely timed operations suggests a greater degree of organization and improving command and control. Such improvements in resistance capability are a natural development given the passage of time.

In addition, one account states that a relatively large component of the Jaish Muhammad is operating in the Tikrit area with some 600 men organized into six divisions of 100, each with a commander. Although there is undoubtedly an element of exaggeration in this claim, it suggests that the resistance now has a degree of substructure, which gives it greater flexibility.

Finally, resistance operations have exhibited improved planning and targeting, largely due to an enhanced intelligence flow. Press accounts citing U.S. intelligence sources indicate that resistance forces obtain extensive human intelligence on coalition activities, allowing them to plan more effectively while protecting their own activities. Again, this is a natural development given that the coalition operates in close proximity to the Iraqi population and that remnants of Saddam Hussein's ubiquitous intelligence services are probably still active.

Implications

The resistance will not remain static; in fact, it may continue to improve its effectiveness. Changes that could occur in the future include:

- the rise of larger and more competent resistance units;
- the creation of areas of continuous resistance (i.e., the temporary liberation of some specific area);
- the emergence of more skilled resistance leaders; and
- the merging of popular opposition to the occupation with armed resistance.

The result of these changes could be larger, more frequent, and more skillfully conducted attacks, including attempts to isolate and destroy a coalition unit or outpost; more effective mortar attacks, including directed fire; increasing attacks on heavy-armored vehicles; and systematic efforts to restrict coalition air and road mobility.

Coalition commanders and officials are aware that the resistance is posing a growing challenge. On November 13, Gen. John Abizaid, the commander of U.S. forces in the Middle East, stated that armed opposition in Iraq was increasingly well organized and well financed, and that it was expanding geographically. The military challenge for coalition forces and the new Iraqi security forces will be to outpace the resistance, primarily through a better understanding of the opposition as well as adaptive tactical and operational methods.

Michael Eisenstadt, Jeffrey White, and Michael Knights

21 Insurgency in Iraq: Implications and Challenges

MICHAEL EISENSTADT

The War and the Resistance

Some have argued that the coalition might not be facing stiff resistance today if it had fought the war differently. To be sure, coalition forces would likely have killed more of the regime's Fedayeen Saddam cannon fodder if they had invaded from Turkey. Yet, those individuals most crucial to the current resistance (e.g., members of the Republican Guard and Special Security Organization; midlevel Baath officials) would most likely have gone to ground and escaped to fight another day. Coalition war planners made a deliberate, fundamental tradeoff, choosing "speed and shock" to promote a rapid collapse of Saddam's regime rather than pursuing a more thorough defeat of specific regime elements from the start. Although they made the correct choice, coalition planners are now dealing with the inevitable consequences of that decision as they face an armed opposition composed of former regime loyalists. Coalition forces should have been better prepared to move quickly into the Sunni Triangle after the fall of Baghdad, though it is unclear whether they would have known who to look for beyond the most senior adherents of the former regime.

Defining Victory

It is unrealistic to expect a halt to attacks on coalition forces and Iraqis working with the coalition any time soon. Because the insurgency's roots are deeply woven into the fabric of Iraqi society, simply limiting its impact will be a challenge. By their nature, even successful counterinsurgency campaigns take a decade or more to bear fruit, as was demonstrated by the British in Malaya in the 1950s and 1960s; by the Peruvians with the Sendero Luminoso in the 1980s and 1990s; and by the Turks with the Kurdistan Workers Party (PKK) during the same period. Therefore, the coalition must prepare for a long-term challenge. The two main criteria for success are: first, transferring power to a stable, legitimate Iraqi government capable of dealing with insurgents on its own; and second, integrating Sunni

On December 2, 2003, Michael Eisenstadt, Jeffrey White, and Michael Knights addressed The Washington Institute's Special Policy Forum. This rapporteur's summary (originally published as *PolicyWatch* no. 815, December 10, 2003) was prepared by Ryan Phillips.

Triangle residents into the nascent Iraqi administration and giving them a stake in the future of the country. The next six months will be crucial to meeting both of these criteria.

Long-Term Effects of the War

Every war sets loose social and political forces that have a greater impact on the ultimate outcome of the war than the actual result of combat itself. For example, Israel's invasion of Lebanon in 1982 led to the emergence of Hizballah, which played a central role in Israel's eventual withdrawal from the country two decades later. The U.S. war to liberate Kuwait in 1991 produced a dramatic military victory, but it was followed by sanctions fatigue, the rise of Osama bin Laden's movement, and U.S.-Saudi tensions. Many of the coalition's current actions will undoubtedly lead to political and social outcomes that, while only dimly perceptible at the moment, may have a dramatic long-term impact on Iraq and, quite probably, the region as a whole. Therefore, it is too early to judge the outcome and consequences of the war.

JEFFREY WHITE

Resistance attacks against the coalition have increased dramatically since late September, from around twenty attacks per day during the summer to a peak of fifty attacks per day in early November. Indeed, October and November accounted for approximately half of all coalition deaths since the end of major combat operations in May. Despite this evidence of increasing capabilities on the part of the opposition, there was no "tipping point" during which resistance elements achieved a strategic advantage over coalition forces, nor did these elements reach a "high-water mark" in their operations during this timeframe. The resistance has demonstrated that it will continue to adapt to the changing situation on the ground, even as coalition forces adjust their own operations in accordance with resistance activities.

How Have Resistance Forces Improved Their Capabilities?

- Resistance cells appear to be getting larger. The average size of cells has increased from an average of five to ten members during the summer to as large as twenty-five members today. As many as 100 highly organized insurgents participated in the intense battles that took place in Samara on November 30.
- Increased coordination and articulation of attacks. The resistance now seems able to conduct operations with a variety of capabilities rather than merely relying on simple attacks.
- Improved planning capabilities. Incidents such as the rocket attack on the Rashid Hotel on October 26 and the coordinated suicide bombings of Iraqi police stations on November 22 required serious logistical planning.
- Improved targeting of coalition forces. Resistance forces appear to know which targets are most vulnerable. They choose highly visible and symbolic targets and know when and where to strike them. For example, in the Samara incident, the insurgents were well aware that the convoy was escorting large amounts of Iraqi currency.

- Improved intelligence. Resistance forces have penetrated both coalition facilities and Iraqi security forces. There have been scattered reports that some members of the Iraqi police are cooperating with the resistance by providing information about the coalition's operations or location.
- Increasingly mobile. Resistance cells are moving from one area to another, mostly within the Sunni Triangle. These resistance elements are reportedly not executing attacks within their own communities, choosing instead to conduct their operations elsewhere.
- A variety of weapons. Many of the early resistance actions featured only one or two weapons systems. More recent attacks, however, have involved a variety of weapons employed in a concerted way (e.g., the Samara incident, in which insurgents used roadside explosives, rocket-propelled grenades, and automatic weapons, along with efficient means of transport).

Implications

- More mobile, deployable cells. Coalition forces may find resistance cells becoming even larger and more coordinated.
- Welding of resistance activities with popular opposition. Incidents such as the Samara battles, during which coalition forces unleashed massive firepower, can radicalize a local population against the coalition.
- Better resistance commanders. Resistance leaders are constantly learning more about the situation on the ground and becoming more efficient and elusive in commanding their cells.
- New weapons. Although antitank guided missiles have yet to be used against coalition forces, the former regime did have them in its inventory. The resistance may also eventually employ 160-millimeter mortar rounds, which are difficult to aim but extremely destructive.
- More quality attacks. Coalition forces should expect more attacks that feature careful organization, planning, and articulation. Resistance forces may also attempt to isolate and destroy a specific coalition element, as they may have been attempting to do in Samara.
- Attacks on senior and high-visibility coalition officials. As resistance tactics evolve, they may eventually target those officials most vital to the execution of the coalition activities.

MICHAEL KNIGHTS

One of the primary limitations on coalition operations in Iraq is actionable intelligence. The coalition is fighting an enemy whose own intelligence and reconnaissance capabilities are very good. One encouraging trend is the progression from current to predictive intelligence; coalition analysts are now attempting to predict resistance actions and generate early warnings.

Intelligence

Human intelligence is clearly the most important tool for defeating the resistance forces, but it takes a great deal of time to set up an effective human intelligence network. Every Iraqi policeman sent out on a patrol becomes a valuable sensor that reports information to the coalition's intelligence liaisons. Moreover, the coalition's increased number of raids and captures are bringing in quality intelligence that often leads to the foiling of attacks by resistance forces. Intelligence analysts are also beginning to use tribal connections to develop human intelligence, even recruiting new Iraqi security personnel from certain tribes.

In addition, coalition forces have been profiling and monitoring areas of resistance activity such as mortar launch sites, ambush sites, and safe houses. An intelligence picture is beginning to form that will expand exponentially over the next several months. One major concern for the coalition is ensuring that it does not lose this intelligence picture once the United States begins its upcoming troop rotation. It is essential to ensure that hard-fought expertise is not lost as intelligence analysts are replaced in Iraq.

Standoff Strikes

The increase of coalition operations that rely on artillery, helicopter, and air strikes is a logical development in the counterinsurgency campaign. The coalition is facing an increasingly elusive enemy that engages in a greater number of long-range attacks. In response, coalition forces have undertaken standoff strikes of their own. Such tactics enable the coalition to strike at enemy forces nearly instantaneously, regardless of whether they are operating from a great distance. These strikes have taken several forms:

- The killing of enemy personnel. Operations of this sort typically include helicopters or unmanned aerial vehicles that track insurgents and launch a precision strike at an opportune moment. Such strikes are nearly instantaneous and very lethal, as they are not preceded by a warning.
- Suppressing terrain with tactical value. Operations of this sort typically involve the coalition destroying suspected ambush sites, observation posts, or safe houses (which occasionally harbor resistance forces). The fact that resistance forces do not know if or when coalition forces will strike such areas often deters them from using these sites.
- Coercion and signaling to the enemy with military force. Operations of this sort involve using brute military force against targets that the coalition knows are empty and unused. Such targets include abandoned buildings that have previously been used as resistance safe houses.

The first two types of strikes are logical from a military perspective, as they deny the resistance a needed capability. The third type is more problematic, however, as it often sends Iraqi civilians mixed messages about the coalition's overall objective.

Jeffrey White

22
The Implications of Saddam's Capture for the Resistance in Iraq

The December 13 capture of Saddam Hussein is proving to be a compelling event, drawing massive media and official attention. Many commentators have been quick to offer profound conclusions regarding the impact that this development will have on the future of Iraq, the U.S. presidential elections, and the war on terrorism, among other things. Although the capture is indeed significant, its actual short- and long-term implications for Iraq generally, and for the resistance in particular, are likely to be complex and contingent, and not a matter for instant analysis.

Context of the Capture

Saddam's "end" came with a whimper, not a bang, a fact that is significant in its own right. He was captured as a result of coalition pursuit operations that were abetted by an informer. Moreover, his meek surrender—being pulled out of a hole in the ground, alone and looking for all the world like a vagrant—was both predictable and fitting. Unlike his sons, he chose not to die or be wounded in a "heroic" battle or suffer anything like martyrdom. Instead, he gave up without a fight, perhaps hoping for a better day. The coalition has thus eliminated an important loose end from the war and likely prevented any potential heroic "Saddam myth" from arising.

The military and political context in which Saddam was captured is also significant. Prior to this development, neither the resistance nor the coalition had a clear advantage in the Sunni areas of Iraq. Although no one views Saddam's capture as an indication that the end of active resistance is in sight, it could serve as a brake: slowing the momentum of the resistance; increasing doubts, especially among Baathist holdouts, regarding the future of the resistance; and discouraging more Sunnis from joining resistance elements. Some short-term deflation of Sunni opposition seems inevitable, even if it is only temporary.

Why It Matters

Saddam's capture is important for several reasons. The deposed leader was a symbol of an incomplete victory, of the triumph of Iraqi cunning over American technology, of the notion that the coalition could be successfully defied. His capture could serve the same

Originally published as *PolicyWatch* no. 817, December 15, 2003.

purpose as a formal surrender, which the coalition did not receive at the end of the war in May. More than anything else, it should bring home to the Sunnis that they lost the war and need to accept the new political and military reality in Iraq. Prior to his capture, Saddam was always lurking in the background, psychologically if not physically, casting a pall over Iraqis fearful of his return. Uncertainty over his location or fate allowed him to, in a sense, be everywhere. This supposed omnipresence was reinforced by rumors of his movements in Iraq (e.g., one rumor placed him in the town of Ramadi on the same day as Gen. John Abizaid, head of U.S. Central Command) and by the intermittent release of taped messages from him encouraging resistance. He was the personification of the old regime and a frequently employed icon of those Sunnis who rejected defeat and occupation. Even Iraqis who did not like Saddam may have rallied to him or his image in response to coalition actions. At the very least, perhaps fewer Iraqis will now stand over burning U.S. vehicles chanting, "O Hussein, we will die for you." His capture could also propel some Sunnis into supporting the coalition more actively, as a consequence of either reduced fear of the old regime or the natural tendency to bet on a winner. The coalition needs all the support it can garner from this sector.

Saddam's capture should also generate intelligence on a number of important issues. In particular, he should be able to provide details regarding the still obscure nature of the regime's planning for the postwar situation, including preparations for resistance, movement of funds, escape plans for senior officials and family members, and the participation of other countries and foreign officials in this activity. For example, even if he does not know the current location of senior officials such as Izzat Ibrahim al-Duri (who is suspected of playing a key role in the resistance), he may know something about their plans, assets, and activities since the fall of the regime. It has long seemed unlikely that Saddam himself directed the resistance. The circumstances of his capture suggest he was not active at the moment, but until more is known about where he has been and what he has been doing, it is inappropriate to draw firm conclusions on this issue. Even if he was providing only inspiration and funds, however, his capture should hurt the resistance. If he played a larger role, the damage will be correspondingly greater. For example, he may be able to help the coalition develop an increased understanding of current resistance operations, organization, leadership, methods, assets, and objectives. More broadly, his removal may make Iraqis more willing to provide intelligence on active resistance elements and their leaders.

Will It Matter to the Resistance?

Paradoxically, Saddam's capture may have only a limited impact on the resistance itself. Saddam was not leading the resistance in the sense of being its commander, so his removal does not strip resistance elements of their leadership. No resistance fighter will be looking over his shoulder or left waiting for orders from Saddam. In some ways, his capture may even allow a more robust leadership to emerge naturally from the struggle. The resistance has become somewhat of a popular phenomenon rather than simply a collection of regime diehards. This trend reflects the wide range of motivations underlying the opposition, including virulent and religiously infused anti-Americanism, antioccupation nationalism, Sunni discontent, revenge, and personal profit. The resistance has also proved to be persistent, finding a place within Sunni society and making itself difficult to root out. Adding to this persistence is the fact that the resistance has been a distributed phenomenon, emerging rapidly in a number of places. Resistance elements have also become better organized in recent months, further enhancing their durability and operational strength. Because of these characteristics, individual setbacks have not had a major effect on the opposition, thus endowing it with a degree of resilience.

Moreover, resistance elements do not seem to be running short of certain key assets. They do not need weapons in huge numbers, nor do they expend large amounts of ammunition as a field army would. In addition, they seem to have ample numbers of active personnel and supporters with the Sunni community. There are some signs, however, that money may soon become an issue of concern for them, particularly as the Iraqi currency exchange program progresses and coalition forces target their finances more deliberately.

Conclusion

Although Saddam's capture was an important victory for the coalition's fight against resistance in Iraq, it does not spell the end of the resistance. The positive effects of this development are likely to show up gradually rather than immediately, and they will be counterbalanced by certain well-established characteristics of the resistance itself. In the wake of Saddam's capture, the resistance will continue to evolve, perhaps in unanticipated ways.

Jeffrey White and Jonathan Schanzer

23
Eyewitness Perspectives Assessing Progress in Iraq: Security and Extremism

JEFFREY WHITE

The Resistance

Resistance activities in Iraq were at a high pitch in fall 2003. Attacks became better organized and more lethal, and several successful operations were mounted against the coalition. By the end of December, however, the hope was that the security situation was improving in the wake of several developments: the capture of Saddam Hussein; a series of U.S.-led offensive operations; an increased understanding of resistance forces; attrition within the resistance networks and their leadership; and the capture of significant amounts of money and arms.

Yet, the resistance appears to have rebounded somewhat from the losses of November and December. Resistance elements remain active, carrying out many of the same types of operations that they did prior to November. Reported incidents of attacks on coalition forces have increased recently from eighteen to twenty-four daily. The resistance has also begun to shift its objectives and targets in response to coalition operations. Militants are now attacking an increasingly broad range of Iraqis associated with the coalition. The list of "collaborators" now includes government officials, judges, police, intellectuals, informers, and translators.

The resistance seems to be focused on maneuvering itself into the best possible position for the imminent transition to Iraqi sovereignty. Resistance elements want to ensure that this transition is difficult and costly by making the situation on the ground as unstable as possible. Their goals include preventing the emergence of a Sunni leadership class associated with the coalition and penetrating the country's nascent political and security institutions. At the same time, the resistance wants to preserve its leadership and cadres, which probably accounts for its reluctance to engage coalition forces directly.

The resistance is more than simply the fighters who carry out the operations. The resistance operates from a base that includes command and control means, logistics,

---

On February 9, 2004, Jeffrey White and Jonathan Schanzer addressed The Washington Institute's Special Policy Forum. Both had participated in an Institute fact-finding delegation tasked with conducting an independent survey of local security conditions and emerging political currents in Iraq. Mr. Schanzer is a Soref fellow at The Washington Institute. This rapporteur's summary (originally published as *PolicyWatch* no. 830, February 11, 2004) was prepared by Jeff Cary and Ryan Phillips.

financial support, safe houses, and assistance in moving personnel and materials. It has apparently also developed an "outreach" component that recruits new members, conducts propaganda-related activities, and attempts to penetrate the institutions of the emerging government. In addition, some resistance elements appear to be heavily involved in countercollaboration activities, killing, harassing, and threatening those individuals who support the coalition.

The resistance may also be benefiting from popular discontent with certain aspects of the coalition presence. For example, hundreds of detainees swept up by coalition forces in past raids have not yet been released back into the Sunni community. Curfews are still being imposed in towns and cities, while damage and loss of life remain uncompensated in some cases. Divisive issues such as these have led to popular demonstrations against the coalition in the Sunni Triangle. Although the resistance is not yet popular among Iraqi society as a whole, it does appear to be gaining some measure of support.

Coalition Forces

The coalition's move from a proconsul-style arrangement to an ambassadorial relationship will likely have a significant impact on both the coalition and Iraqi society. At least one issue remains unclear: how the relationship between the U.S. embassy and the new Iraqi government will work out with respect to freedom of action for U.S. forces. The U.S. military posture in Iraq will undergo major changes, with a new corps headquarters being established in the country along with a four-star general position. This structure may allow for larger planning and intelligence staffs, which could in turn lead to improved overall management of coalition military operations. Some observers feel that the various U.S. divisions in Iraq have thus far waged more or less independent campaigns; this would likely change with the arrival of a new corps headquarters.

Coalition forces are in the midst of a massive troop rotation, during which a number of new divisions will be entering Iraq. This rotation will inevitably cause some loss in tactical experience and overall understanding of the situation, at least until the new divisions gain familiarity with current operational conditions. Coalition forces have proven highly adaptive as the character of the resistance has changed, and this dynamic will certainly continue with the introduction of new forces.

Although the multiple Iraqi security services currently being developed are making progress, they still have a long way to go before they can fulfill the mission requirements that are being thrust upon them. The new Iraqi army is making strides, but coalition and Iraqi authorities have yet to determine what role, if any, the army will have in providing internal security. The Iraqi Civil Defense Corps appears to be evolving as a regional and perhaps rural force that can be quickly deployed to trouble spots. The Iraqi Police Service appears to be an urban and local force that will represent the first line of defense against crime and insurgency. Each component of the new security forces is in need of basic resources, from uniforms to ethics training. Establishing these forces and bringing them to a mission-capable standard will be a time-consuming process.

The Emergence of Politics

Politics has reemerged with a vengeance in Iraq. One official claimed that there are currently 130 political parties and factions operating in the southern part of the country. Although this figure may be exaggerated, many Iraqi factions have armed militias or military wings that are in fact being employed for political advantage. The objective of such factions is to establish themselves as the dominant political force at the local or even regional level. Managing this political activity will be a major challenge for the coalition, especially when it turns violent.

Despite the negative elements inherent in the security situation, the new Iraq is showing several positive signs. Iraqis have high expectations that major improvements will commence once money begins to flow into the country and reconstruction projects begin. Coalition forces have a much better understanding of the resistance and how to fight it, while the Iraqi security forces are making progress and appear to be on the right track. The coalition is also beginning to see the stirrings of civil society in Iraq; individuals are gaining basic training in democracy, and grassroots democracy is emerging in some areas.

At the same time, it must be acknowledged that the security situation in Iraq has dangerous components that should not be downplayed. There is no assurance that all will turn out in accordance with the coalition's long-term desires.

JONATHAN SCHANZER

Ansar al-Islam

Prior to 2003, Ansar al-Islam was a small organization confined largely to the northern part of Iraq, in the Halabja area. The group was highly centralized with a clear command structure. Yet, after February 5, 2003, when Secretary of State Colin Powell announced that the group was a major U.S. concern, its leadership developed a dispersal plan. As a result of that plan, approximately 400 Ansar al-Islam fighters reportedly escaped to Iran. In the wake of Operation Iraqi Freedom, many fighters returned to Iraq, resuming their operations in the area of Falluja, Tikrit, and Ramadi. Similar to the current global structure of the al-Qaeda network, Ansar al-Islam has become quite decentralized, with members operating via small cells and informal groupings. According to one intelligence source, the average cell consists of about six operatives with one commander. These cells employ freelancers, outsiders, Baathists, and militants who do not fit the al-Qaeda mold to carry out operations.

Recent interviews with Ansar al-Islam prisoners in Sulaymaniya, as well as with other Iraqi and U.S. sources, indicate that the prewar cooperation between Baathists and Ansar may have been the result of one man's work: Col. Saadan Abd al-Latif Mahmoud al-Ani, also known as Abu Wael. Although he was not on the U.S. list of fifty-five most-wanted Iraqis, all of those interviewed stated that he was responsible for organizing some of al-Qaeda's activities inside Iraq. Apparently, he brought al-Qaeda to Iraq under a strategy not of winning war, but of foiling U.S. plans for the country. In the late 1990s, he invited several al-Qaeda groups to train at Salman Pak, a camp located twenty miles southeast of Baghdad, and helped to finance them as well.

In general, the majority of jihadists entering Iraq come across the Iranian border. Although Kurdish intelligence reports that three to ten such individuals are captured per week, they are unsure how many others are getting through. It is unclear whether the Iranian government is deliberately helping these individuals cross the border or simply turning a blind eye. Many foreign jihadists are using old smuggling routes that were employed during Saddam's time. After crossing the border they go to a safe house, receive weapons and orders, and then attack their targets.

Extremism

Although the coalition is doing a good job under difficult circumstances, some officials are overly optimistic about the prospects that Islamist extremism will not be popular in Iraq. Islamism is often a utopian crutch for people during uncertain times. It is usually popular among the young and unemployed, and Iraq has a young population with a high rate of under- or unemployment. Moreover, the Iraqi Ministry of Awqaf (religious endowment) is currently being restructured, leaving Iraqi mosques unmonitored in the meantime. For their part, Islamists are well positioned to provide social services that the coalition and the Iraqi government are still struggling to establish. Indeed, providing such services has been an effective recruiting aid in other countries, where Islamists take advantage of the vacuum left by other authorities in order to gain the support of the masses.

The potential for Islamist growth in Iraq is also evident in attitudes expressed by Iraqis in the Kurdistan region. For example, even though that region is less susceptible to Islamism than the rest of the country, an official in the Patriotic Union of Kurdistan (PUK) stated that Islamist factions would garner 10 to 15 percent of the vote in the PUK area if elections were held today.

Some have speculated that Iraq will come to resemble 1980s-era Afghanistan. To be sure, foreign jihadists have flocked to Iraq from Tunisia, Jordan, Turkey, Morocco, Syria, Egypt, Yemen, the Palestinian territories, and elsewhere. Nevertheless, Iraq is not the next Afghanistan, despite an upsurge in terrorism, porous borders, general confusion, and weak central authority. In the north, the Kurds have been fairly successful at counterterrorism (despite the recent bombings in Irbil). In the south, the Shiites keep the coalition informed about people who are new to the area and other suspicious individuals. In the central part of Iraq, however, the situation is likely to remain confusing. Fortunately, the foreign jihadist problem seems to be confined to that part of the country.

Jeffrey White

24
Faces of Resistance

The violent incidents that have occurred in Iraq since the beginning of this month illustrate the diverse faces of Iraqi resistance. The terrorist-style attacks in Iskandariya and Baghdad on February 10 and 11 drew much attention to the presumed links of terrorist organizations to antioccupation incidents. Although resistance elements do indeed employ terrorist tactics, the broad scope of resistance activity faced by the coalition has been reflected in several recent incidents, including a failed ambush on February 7, a series of military-style attacks in Falluja on February 12 and 14, and day-to-day attacks involving a range of explosive devices. Indeed, resistance elements seem to have rebounded from their losses of November-December 2003.

The transitional Iraqi government and its nascent security forces are likely to face a similar array of attacks once the coalition transfers authority to them. In fact, resistance elements are already beginning to shift their focus onto Iraqi "collaborators." As the United States withdraws its forces from high-threat areas, resistance actions will likely target Iraqi security forces with even greater frequency. These local forces are more vulnerable and are likely perceived to be more important targets in the long term, as they represent institutions critical to the future stability and security of the state.

A Variety of Tactics

The February 10-11 suicide bombings of Iraqi recruiting facilities were shocking, high-visibility events, killing as many as 100 army and police recruits and bystanders. These incidents reinforced widespread perceptions that the coalition is unable to prevent attacks on important Iraqi targets, a fact that may have a chilling effect on recruiting for the new security forces. From the perspective of resistance elements, the bombings were low-cost attacks in that they did not require exposure of cells and cadres to direct combat with coalition forces. Although the bombings served the goals of the resistance—that is, countering the threat represented by the new security services—they were probably carried out by terrorist cells associated with organizations such as Ansar al-Islam or al-Qaeda.

Iraqi resistance showed a different face during recent attacks in the Falluja area. Falluja lies thirty-five miles west of Baghdad, in the Sunni Triangle, and falls within the area of responsibility of the 82nd Airborne Division. The city has a long history of resistance activity, including attacks on U.S. forces and members of the Iraqi Police Service (IPS) and

Originally published as *PolicyWatch* no. 832, February 17, 2004.

Iraqi Civil Defense Corps (ICDC). U.S. forces had been withdrawn from the city in order to reduce friction with the population and the frequency of violent incidents.

Nevertheless, resistance elements launched what appeared to be a series of professional, military-style, small-unit raids in the area on February 12 and 14. First, militants attacked the ICDC compound in Falluja on February 12, a strike that may have served as either a probe of local defenses or a deliberate attack on a U.S. convoy arriving at the compound carrying the commanders of U.S. Central Command and the 82nd Airborne. Then, on February 14, two heavily armed groups struck separate targets, with one element attacking the ICDC compound (probably in order to pin down the forces stationed there) and the second assaulting the police station with the intention of killing as many Iraqi policemen as possible and freeing prisoners. Based on press accounts, as many as seventy attackers may have been involved. The February 14 incident had all the earmarks of an attack carried out not by a terrorist organization, but rather by resistance elements associated with the military and security services of the former regime. In terms of numbers, organization, preparation, and weaponry, it was similar to the major fight that occurred in Samara on November 30, 2003. Both the Falluja and Samara battles were highly visible clashes that will likely remain in the minds of local witnesses. Unlike in Samara, resistance forces won the fight in Falluja.

Resistance elements demonstrated additional capabilities on February 7 when they attempted to conduct a sophisticated night ambush near Muqdadiya, a town northeast of Baghdad. The attempt was broken up by troops from the 4th Infantry Division, who killed all ten of the insurgents involved. The troops found rocket-propelled grenades, machine guns, assault rifles, and night-vision goggles at the site.

These incidents demonstrate that resistance leaders remain willing to put armed, organized elements in the field despite the risks. In addition to these larger-scale military-style strikes, resistance elements have continued to mount near-daily attacks on Iraqi and coalition targets using mortars, rockets, and improvised explosive devices.

Troubling Questions

Although most experts acknowledge that it is difficult, if not impossible, to completely prevent suicide bombings, the military-style attacks in Falluja have raised several troubling questions. For example, who actually carried out the attacks? Rumors and reports of Islamic slogans, Shiite banners, foreign accents, and Iranian militants have emerged in the wake of the attack. Although Islamist resistance elements may well have been involved, organized Shiite and Iranian participation seems improbable.

Moreover, one press account indicated that, prior to the February 14 strike, warnings had been issued to the populace that an attack was imminent. Why were those warnings not brought to the attention of the intended targets? According to one U.S. commander, 95 percent of the population of Falluja supports the coalition. In light of this fact, how could the ICDC, IPS, and U.S. forces have been so completely surprised by both the timing and the sophisticated nature of the attack? Did the citizens of Falluja play any role in the incident? U.S. forces detained the city's mayor for questioning concerning the operation, and the raiders themselves and the prisoners they released melted into the population quickly following the attack, suggesting some measure of popular support.

Perhaps most important, how did fairly large and well-equipped resistance forces come to be in a position to conduct sophisticated attacks on the local and coalition forces that were supposedly providing security in the area? Did the attackers come from within Falluja itself, or were they "outsiders"? Accounts of the February 14 attacks indicate that the militants used vehicles for, at the very least, local mobility. If they came from outside the area, how were they able to get to, and then move into, Falluja undetected? Moreover, the use of separate but coordinated attacks on the fourteenth suggests a significant degree of organization. If these attacks are in fact related to the February 12 incident, this would suggest an even more substantial degree of planning and command and control capacity.

Implications

Despite the setbacks of November-December 2003, resistance elements have demonstrated the capacity to mount high-impact terrorist- and military-style operations while maintaining some level of more routine attacks. Their targeting and planning capabilities also seem to be improving. The incidents described above, far from being mere random attacks on vulnerable targets, are indicative of a concerted "countercollaboration" campaign. They reflect the work of dedicated and embedded organizations with substantial capabilities.

These resistance capabilities must be viewed in the context of changing U.S., coalition, and Iraqi capabilities. Although some of the changes that will accompany the ongoing rotation of U.S. and coalition forces will likely be beneficial, others will be detrimental. As fresh units are introduced, these forces will inevitably begin operations with less skill and knowledge regarding local environments. Even currently deployed units have not received advance intelligence on certain important incidents. As they withdraw to more secure locations outside towns and cities, U.S. forces will perhaps lose some awareness of, and sensitivity to, local conditions. Finally, it is unclear whether the new Iraqi security services will be able to compensate for these changes. In Falluja and Samara, at least, they could not.

Jonathan Schanzer

25
Al-Qaeda's Deadly Gamble

Tuesday's attacks against Shi'a targets in Baghdad and Karbala during Ashura, the holiest day in the Shi'a calendar, have all the markings of the simultaneous and co-ordinated attacks now associated with al-Qaeda. At first glance, it would appear that al-Qaeda is succeeding in its quest to destabilize Iraq. The attacks, however, may have been a dangerous gamble for the world's most dangerous terrorist network.

Tuesday's bloodshed was the first significant attack against a Shi'a target in Iraq's south since the August, 2003, car bombing in the holy city of Najaf. That attack killed Ayatollah Mohammed Baqir al-Hakim and more than 100 others as they emerged from Friday prayers. In retrospect, that bombing was likely not intended to spark internecine conflict. Rather, it was probably designed specifically to kill Mr. Hakim, whose co-operation with the United States labelled him a "collaborator" among those opposed to the U.S. occupation.

Tuesday's assault, by contrast, consisted of multiple suicide bombings designed to kill as many people as possible. The death toll from the attacks—yesterday the Iraqi Governing Council placed its estimate at 271 dead, although U.S. estimates are lower—marks the highest number of casualties in a single day since the start of the Iraq conflict. The fallout from this wanton bloodshed—among Iraqis and Muslims across the Arab world—is yet to be seen.

In recent history, al-Qaeda and its affiliates have alienated Middle East Muslims with grisly acts of violence. The carnage of the Luxor massacre of tourists in 1997, for example, pushed al-Qaeda affiliates to the fringes of Egyptian society.

Al-Qaeda cannot afford for this to happen in Iraq. Abu Musab al-Zarqawi, the man U.S. officials believe is co-ordinating much of Iraq's terrorist activity, recently admitted that attacking innocent Muslims could lead to a decline in tacit support for al-Qaeda, which is essential for the network's continued survival in the region. In a memo intercepted by U.S. intelligence last month, Mr. Zarqawi states that, "if we fight [the Shiites], that will be difficult because there will be a schism between us and the people of the region. How can we kill their cousins and sons and under what pretext?"

Even with the knowledge that this strategy could backfire, and in the absence of another viable strategy, Mr. Zarqawi and his associates appear to have settled on the Shiites as "the

Originally published in the *Globe and Mail* (Toronto), March 4, 2004. Jonathan Schanzer is a Soref fellow at The Washington Institute.

key to change. Targeting and striking their religious, political and military symbols will make them show their rage against the Sunnis and bear their inner vengeance."

Mr. Zarqawi's memo further details a plan to drag Iraq "into a sectarian war . . . because it is the only way to prolong the duration of the fight between the infidels [the United States] and us." Toward the end of his letter, the writer states flatly, "We have to get to the zero-hour in order to openly begin controlling the land by night and after that by day, god willing. The zero-hour needs to be at least four months before the new government gets in place." Approximately four months from now, of course, will mark the June 30 handover of sovereignty to the Iraqi people.

But even if Mr. Zarqawi's strategy is on schedule, it could backfire in other ways. While the attacks may have further soured Iraq's Shi'a population toward the Sunnis (playing upon a long-standing grudge), it is doubtful that even a significant minority of Shiites believes that violence against them stems from a monolithic Sunni offensive. Most Shi'a leaders, both religious and secular, understand that these attacks are largely perpetrated by outsiders wishing to foment unrest in a country that a Shi'a figure will likely soon lead.

The attackers also sought to drive a wedge between the U.S.-led Coalition Provisional Authority (CPA) and the Shi'a community, which responded by charging that CPA security is increasingly feckless and insufficient. Indeed, Shiites responded angrily to the attacks by chanting anti-American slogans and even throwing rocks at U.S. servicemen. However, Shi'a leaders recognize that the CPA will ultimately provide them the infrastructure for their new government. In short, Tuesday's attacks certainly reveal raw nerves, but are unlikely to have started a civil war.

In the end, the attacks certainly appear to adhere to the Zarqawi plan. But it is far from certain whether that strategy has the potential to succeed. In the highly unlikely event that Shi'a anger gives way to retribution against the Sunni population, the Shiites of Iraq will have played into the hands of Mr. Zarqawi and the al-Qaeda network. A more likely scenario is that Shi'a anger will give way to increased determination and tenacity, prompting al-Qaeda to push the envelope of violence and try again.

Jeffrey White and Ryan Phillips

26
The Battle for Falluja and Sunni Resistance

The battle for Falluja, in which U.S. forces have been fighting to break Sunni resistance elements in that city, has been one of the most sustained fights of the Iraq war and subsequent occupation. Significantly, Sunni insurgents are not only fighting in Falluja, but also across the Sunni heartland. Militarily, the battle suggests that the resistance maintains substantial capabilities despite a year of counterinsurgency operations, and that more tough fights lie ahead. Politically, it points to expanded Sunni opposition to the occupation.

The Resistance on the Eve of Falluja

By the time of the March 31, 2004, killing of the four U.S. contractors in Falluja, resistance elements had already become embedded in Sunni society. The resistance had rebounded from reverses inflicted by U.S. forces and extended itself into all areas of the Sunni Triangle. Persistent attempts by coalition leaders and commanders to portray the resistance as "a small minority" "on its knees" or "broken" were repeatedly frustrated by resistance actions.

Over time, resistance elements broadened their operational scope to include attacks on coalition forces, Iraqi "collaborators," the Shiite population, Sunni clerics, and Westerners and other foreigners assisting in reconstruction efforts. The resistance adapted its tactics to suit its targets, exhibited improved command and control, and recruited to replace losses inflicted by the coalition. It also proved adept at surprising coalition forces, especially in the context of the U.S. troop rotation which by April 2004 had replaced three seasoned divisions with three new ones.

Harbingers of Falluja

Several resistance incidents prior to the Falluja operation suggested that the resistance was capable of significant military action. On November 30, 2003, a three-and-a-half-hour fight in the city of Samara took place between U.S. troops of the 4th Infantry division and approximately 100 insurgents. This sustained battle indicated that resistance elements were capable of conducting complex actions and were willing to engage in close combat with coalition troops when necessary. In February 2004, several incidents in Falluja before the April battle itself pointed to the presence of substantial resistance capabilities in or

Originally published as *PolicyWatch* no. 856, April 13, 2004. Ryan Phillips is a research assistant at The Washington Institute.

around the city. These incidents also demonstrated the unreliability of Iraqi security forces, and suggested some degree of popular support for the resistance.

The Battle for Falluja

The timing of the operation in Falluja was driven by the need to react relatively quickly to the killing and mutilation of the four contractors. The fighting began on April 6. For three days, the Marines and insurgents slugged it out indecisively on the ground, with the resistance staying in the fight while its story was covered by the media as the "siege of Falluja." (Even U.S. commanders used the term "siege" to characterize the fighting.) Resistance tactics of closely engaging U.S. forces in an urban environment with automatic weapons, mortars, and rocket-propelled grenades; operating within the civilian population; and using mosques for cover maximized their tactical advantage while reducing the coalition's firepower advantage. It does not appear that the Marines expected significant sustained resistance, much less popular resistance. Statements suggest that they were anticipating a series of precise raids into the city to capture "high-value targets," while drawing out insurgents who could then be destroyed by coalition firepower. Lacking overwhelming force and unwilling to act too aggressively on the ground for fear of civilian and Marine casualties, U.S. forces got bogged down in inconclusive fighting.

Instead of a rapid and well-contained pacification action in Falluja, the coalition found itself facing active and aggressive resistance elements across Sunni areas. The slow pace of operations in Falluja allowed Sunni resistance elements in other areas to take action. The deadly April 6 ambush in Ramadi and the upsurge of incidents in other traditional trouble spots were subsequently accompanied by hostage taking and attacks on U.S. supply lines between Falluja and Baghdad. In fact, more than 80 percent of those U.S. personnel killed in action so far in April have been killed in Sunni areas.

Implications

The battle for Falluja and the widespread fighting have important military, political, and psychological implications for U.S. Iraq policy. Militarily, the fighting highlights several realities:

- The resistance is capable of conducting sustained operations against the coalition and inflicting significant casualties, despite coalition advantages in firepower and mobility. A bright spot for the coalition is the high number of casualties inflicted on resistance elements that came out of hiding to fight.
- Falluja, and, to a lesser extent, Ramadi, could be considered resistance "victories." In these places, insurgents stood and fought against the coalition, inflicting losses as well as taking them. Both battles will likely go down in resistance mythology as heroic stands.
- The resistance continues to surprise the coalition with innovative tactics, the latest examples being hostage taking and attacks on coalition supply lines.

- The resistance is capable of acting in a cooperative, if not coordinated, way across the Sunni Triangle. The battle for Falluja was indirectly supported by increased resistance activity in Baghdad, Mosul, Kirkuk, Tikrit, Baquba, Balad, Beiji, Abu Ghraib, Ramadi, and Samara. If these areas had not already witnessed recurrent clashes this would probably have been seen as a Sunni "uprising."

The fighting has also been important politically:

- The battle for Falluja may prove politically pyrrhic for the coalition. The casualties and damage to the city, the strain on the Governing Council, and the negotiations with the insurgents that the coalition set out to destroy make whatever tactical gains were achieved in battle seem minimal. The coalition is likely to continue to pay a price in more determined and deeper Sunni resistance and a more problematic Governing Council. Will any future "sovereign" Iraqi government acquiesce to another operation like that conducted in Falluja?
- The coalition also seems weakened with respect to Sunni resistance and opposition. It set out to pacify Falluja but has not done so. In all likelihood, the population of the city, and perhaps that of other areas, has been further radicalized by the fighting. The coalition is now entangled in a ceasefire brokered by politicians and tribal leaders, which will be seen as diminishing its prestige and power.

There are also potential psychological effects:

- The April fighting may represent a watershed or "defining moment" for the Sunnis—the moment when the Sunnis stood against the occupiers and began to shape their own future in the new Iraq. A clear set of Sunni political objectives has yet to develop, but Falluja is providing the kind of myth that every defeated people needs to begin retaking their destiny.
- Confidence in the new Iraqi security forces is likely at an all-time low, both from the coalition and Iraqi perspectives.

Conclusions

The outcome of the April fighting will be emergent, not linear. It will likely take weeks for some semblance of the uneasy pre-April order to return and for the real implications to emerge. All of this will occur against the backdrop of a highly unsettled political and military situation across Shiite Iraq. More surprises should be anticipated along the path to the June 30 power transition. The situation's complexity puts a premium on understanding and wisdom, at the same time making those qualities more difficult to achieve.

Jonathan Schanzer and Ryan Phillips

27
Iraqi Violence: Shiite-Sunni Collision or Collusion?

On April 5, Iraqi gunmen attacking U.S. forces in Baghdad's predominantly Sunni al-Azamiya neighborhood were joined by members of radical Shiite cleric Muqtada al-Sadr's militia, Mahdi Army. Soon thereafter, posters of al-Sadr, along with graffiti praising the cleric's "valiant uprising" appeared in the Sunni-dominated city of Ramadi. On April 8, as violence raged in Falluja, another Sunni city, announcements erupted from both Shiite and Sunni mosques in the Baghdad area, calling on all Iraqis to donate blood, money, and medical supplies for "your brothers and sons in Falluja." A donation tent in the Shiite-dominated Kadhimiya neighborhood urged individuals to "prevent the killing of innocents in Falluja by all means available." That night, thousands of Shiite and Sunni demonstrators marched to Falluja from Baghdad in a display of solidarity. On April 9, in the mixed town of Baquba, Shiites and Sunnis joined forces to attack a U.S. military base, damaging both government and police buildings.

The collusion between Iraqi Shiite and Sunni elements took many by surprise. After all, dominance by the minority Sunnis over the majority, downtrodden Shiite population has generated mistrust and hatred for almost a century. A recently intercepted memo from al-Qaeda associate Abu Musab al-Zarqawi even revealed plans to exploit this historical friction by prompting internecine conflict between the two communities. While the most recent example of Shiite-Sunni collusion against U.S. forces in Iraq was brief, the situation will require careful monitoring. A historical precedent of significant Shiite-Sunni cooperation does exist both in Iraq and in other parts of the region.

The Iraqi Precedent

Elements of Iraq's Shiite and Sunni religious communities have, in the past, joined forces to face a common enemy.

The Iraqi revolt. The April 1920 announcement of Britain's mandate in Iraq sparked a nationalist insurrection. As anti-British sentiment rose among Shiite religious leaders and disaffected mid-Euphrates tribal heads, Shiites and Sunnis sat together in mosques for anti-British gatherings. This symbolic cooperation in the name of Iraqi nationalism,

Originally published as *PolicyWatch* no. 860, April 20, 2004. Jonathan Schanzer is a Soref fellow, and Ryan Phillips is a research assistant, at The Washington Institute.

however, soon crumbled. The British used the predominantly Sunni military to crush the insurgent Shiites.

The Iran-Iraq war. Despite years of enmity between Iraq's minority Sunni and majority Shiite populations, both communities were able to temporarily set aside their differences in confronting a common enemy: Iran. During the 1980-1988 Iran-Iraq War, a temporarily strong nationalist sentiment among the Shiites overrode their shared sectarian identity with Iran, as well as their discontent with the oppressive Sunni Baath regime in Baghdad. Indeed, Shiites comprised the Iraqi infantry's majority rank and file, and the predominantly Shiite south sustained the most amount of damage from Iranian attacks. After the war, however, sectarian tensions reemerged.

Other Regional Precedents

Examples from other Middle East arenas demonstrate the willingness of Shiite and Sunni elements to cooperate in the face of a shared, nationalist threat.

Saudi Arabia and Yemen's Zaydi tribes. During Yemen's revolutionary phase, the country was host to a proxy war between republicans, backed by Egypt's Gamal Abdul Nasser, and royalists, backed by Saudi Arabia. The staunchly Sunni House of Saud provided a number of Zaydi (Shiite) tribes in Yemen with war materials and money to fight the Egyptians. The proxy battle lasted from 1962 to 1967, when the Six Day War with Israel drained Egypt's military resources. A defeated Nasser soon withdrew under cover of an Arab summit agreement, while Saudi Arabia agreed to halt support to the royalists.

Ansar al-Islam and Iran. Recently, Iran has provided significant logistical support to Ansar al-Islam, a radical Sunni Islamist faction based in northern Iraq, by facilitating the flow of goods and weapons from Iran proper, and by providing safe haven in Iranian territory just behind Ansar al-Islam's mountain enclave. After the U.S.-led assault on the group in March, Ansar's top leaders retreated to Iran, with the direct knowledge and facilitation of Iran's Revolutionary Guards. According to Ansar al-Islam prisoners held by the Patriotic Union of Kurdistan in Sulaymaniya, this Kurdish al-Qaeda affiliate still uses Iran as a base from which to plan operations against U.S. forces in Iraq. (Other reports allege that Iran is sheltering several senior al-Qaeda operatives, including al-Qaeda mastermind al-Zarqawi.)

Hizballah and the al-Aqsa Martyrs Brigades. According to Israeli intelligence sources and a flurry of media reports, Hizballah—a radical Shiite terrorist organization based in Lebanon—has assumed the role of financial patron for a large number of terrorist cells belonging to the al-Aqsa Martyrs Brigades, the radical arm of Yasser Arafat's predominantly Sunni Fatah movement. After Israel's May 2000 withdrawal from Lebanon, Hizballah moved some of its operations to the Palestinian territories, providing guidance and funding for the financially drained Brigades. Just before the March 14 bombing at the Israeli port of Ashdod that left ten dead, Hizballah transferred approximately $3,300 to a Brigade militant for the attack. In the inter-Arab alliance against Israel, Hizballah cooperation with the al-Aqsa Martyrs Brigades, as well as with Hamas and Palestinian Islamic Jihad, can be expected to continue.

Prospects and Policy

Despite strong differences in the interpretation of Islamic tradition that have led to historical inter-Muslim conflicts, Shiite and Sunni communities throughout the Middle East have cooperated in recent years in modern history when faced with a common enemy. The prospect of growing collusion between militant Iraqi Shiite and Sunni groups against U.S. forces, therefore, is a troubling prospect requiring the vigilance of U.S. decisionmakers.

Current fears of Shiite-Sunni collusion leading to a full-blown conflict in Iraq, however, have been drastically overstated. These Iraqi religious communities are far from monolithic. Rather, they are wrought with divisions. For example, on February 28, eight of the thirteen Shiite Iraqi Governing Council members walked out in protest after a majority voted to reject the institution of *sharia*, or Islamic religious law, in Iraq. In other words, five Shiite leaders took a staunchly secular position on this issue. More recently, al-Sadr's failure to ignite a broad-based Shiite revolt exposed fault lines among religious Shiites. The deployment of al-Sadr's militia was not well received in many Shiite towns, and was challenged by Iraq's top Shiite leader, Grand Ayatollah Ali Hussein al-Sistani. Other Shiite intellectuals, particularly in Najaf, have also staunchly opposed al-Sadr's dangerous confrontation with U.S. forces.

Similarly, Iraq's Sunni community is far from homogenous. While U.S. forces have come under fire from militants in the Sunni triangle, several Sunni municipal council members have served as crucial allies to the Coalition Provisional Authority. According to one former U.S. official, these local leaders may be the reason why some Sunni towns have remained cooperative with U.S. forces.

Getting a majority of Shiites or Sunnis to agree on anything within their respective communities can be difficult. Getting a majority of Shiites and Sunnis to work together against the U.S. occupation, while not impossible, would likely pose even greater challenges. Nevertheless, Shiite-Sunni cooperation is not unprecedented, and collusion between extremists could do great harm to Iraq's reconstruction and political transition. It will therefore be important to monitor Shiite-Sunni collaborative activity in the weeks and months to come. Meanwhile, success and stability on the ground in Iraq is likely the best way to prevent collusion. Indeed, the worse things appear on the ground in Iraq, the more inclined Iraqis may be to band together in an uprising against the coalition.

28
Crisis in Iraq: Assessments and Implications

JEFFREY WHITE

Fallout in Falluja

The insurgency in Falluja that began on April 6 (in response to the slaying and mutilation of four American contractors) was one of the most sustained fights of the Iraq war and ensuing occupation. A pinnacle in resistance activity, the siege of Falluja pitted U.S. and coalition forces against a multifaceted and highly complex enemy wielding such tactics as hit and run, sniping, rocket-propelled grenade (RPG) firing, and ambushes. Harbingers like the three-and-a-half-hour gun battle in Samarra on November 30 between 100 insurgents and the 4th Infantry division—as well as several other incidents around Falluja in February—demonstrated the prowess of the resistance and its growing capabilities. Coalition commanders planned for a short, precise operation in Falluja against limited resistance. Instead, the coalition and the Iraqi resistance fighters battled to a stalemate after three days of intense fighting in which the insurgents exhibited coordination, the ability to engage in an urban environment, and the willingness to utilize civilians and mosques for cover. In short, the battle in Falluja demonstrated that the resistance is neither on its knees nor broken.

Al-Sadr's Uprising

In conjunction with troubles in Falluja, U.S. and coalition forces face the challenge of Muqtada al-Sadr and his Mahdi Army. The simultaneous, coordinated attacks initiated by al-Sadr on April 4 in Baghdad, Kufa, Kut, Najaf, portions of Karbala, Nasariya, Hilla, Basra, and other locations indicate that the insurrection was clearly planned in advance. The myriad tactics in the militia's repertoire have included directing attacks with machine-gun and RPG fire against coalition headquarters and buildings, laying siege to local government buildings and police stations, liberating insurgents held in coalition detainment facilities, and taking hostages. The high tide of the Mahdi Army's activities was the April 7 fall of Kut and the humiliating retreat of Ukrainian forces stationed there,

On April 16, 2004, Jeffrey White and Michael Knights addressed The Washington Institute's Special Policy Forum. This rapporteur's summary (originally published as *PolicyWatch* no. 861, April 21, 2004) was prepared by Bjorn Delaney.

which resulted in the capture of Ukrainian armaments and facilities. However, al-Sadr's forces were not successful in either taking or holding positions when faced with a high-quality, aggressive coalition force opponent. The military sustainability of al-Sadr's militia—keeping the force active, operating, and firing in the absence of a sound logistical base—is also questionable.

MICHAEL KNIGHTS

New Iraqi Security Forces

Neither the new Iraqi security forces nor certain multinational forces are yet able to handle civil emergencies and resistance on the scale recently encountered—a reality clearly reflected by U.S. plans to increase force levels in Iraq. During recent fighting in Falluja and the Shiite south, Iraqi Police Service (IPS) and Iraqi Civil Defense Corps (ICDC) personnel were confronted by a dangerous operational environment and a severe test of loyalty. In the south the multinational forces did not attempt to deploy the ICDC, while the IPS was either passive or complicit in the fighting, allowing the Mahdi Army to capture police stations, weapons caches, and vehicles. These benchmarks indicate that the fledgling Iraqi forces need to be built over time; prematurely exposing them to serious fighting may stress their sectarian and religious loyalties before a more secure Iraqi national identity can be reestablished under a sovereign government. The coalition needs to increase the mentoring and training of Iraqi forces with the help of additional international police officers and foreign trainers, and speed up the disbursement of U.S. and Iraqi funding to provide equipment for these forces.

Multinational Division Forces

A rather mixed performance has been exhibited thus far by the two multinational divisions stationed in southeast and south-central Iraq, respectively. The British-commanded division in the southeast managed to weather Mahdi Army attacks well, using force and negotiation to quash insurgencies. The Polish-commanded division in south-central Iraq, however, failed to defend key points and respond to direct attacks on Coalition Provisional Authority (CPA) compounds. Incidents like the Ukrainian withdrawal from Kut will likely minimize Iraqi respect for some multinational division troops, making it difficult to continue using those troops in a security role—particularly in training new Iraqi security forces. Lack of troop cohesion was one source of weakness in the Polish-led division, where troops hail from twenty-three countries and speak seventeen languages. But the poorer performance of this division can also be attributed to contingent commanders phoning their own governments for tactical guidance instead of calling the Polish divisional commander. The restrictive guidance given by these national governments prevented troops from attempting to recover locations occupied by Mahdi Army militiamen, and even restrained them from defending themselves and the CPA compounds they inhabited. A new UN resolution and a larger role for NATO should allow multinational contributors to place their troops fully under coalition command and control, operating as part of a NATO-led division. The United States can also do more to share lessons learned with those international troops currently serving in Iraq or being pledged for future service there.

Jeffrey White and Ryan Phillips

29
Insurgent Operations Against the Highways in Iraq

The intensification of Sunni-based resistance operations and the onset of Muqtada al-Sadr's Shiite rebellion in early April confronted the coalition with a number of serious military and political challenges, few of which have been resolved. Coalition forces are facing new and increased operational demands, and among these demands is a substantially enlarged requirement for the coalition forces and reconstruction program to secure the main lines of communication (LOCs) connecting Baghdad to the outside world.

In situations of insurgency or rebellion, LOCs are almost always at risk, and Iraq is proving no different than cases extending from ancient warfare until today. The military problems inherent in protecting LOCs through hostile or potentially hostile territory are well known. The coalition must be able to move men and materiel with a high degree of assurance throughout Iraq. The April fighting has demonstrated that active measures and substantial resources are required to ensure such secure movement.

The Problem

Four highways are especially important to the coalition's logistical and reconstruction effort: Highway 10 from the Jordanian border to Baghdad, Highway 1 from the Turkish border to Baghdad, Highway 8 from Kuwait to Baghdad, and the road from Baghdad International Airport to the city. This represents over 1,000 miles of highway to secure. With numerous bridges, culverts, viaducts, and other chokepoints presenting targets for sabotage, these roads are vulnerable to interdiction throughout. Many highway segments pass through or near inhabited or agricultural areas, providing good locations from which insurgents can organize and conduct ambushes. Iraq's road system is relatively well developed and bypass routes exist, but these—usually in worse condition than the main highways and slower and more difficult (especially for civilian vehicles) to traverse—are no less vulnerable to attack.

Before April, the highways in Iraq provided relatively secure means of travel throughout the country. Attacks on coalition convoys and patrols were a routine feature of resistance operations in the Sunni Triangle, but until April no concerted resistance effort

Originally published as *PolicyWatch* no. 863, April 26, 2004. Ryan Phillips is a research assistant at The Washington Institute.

to interdict or seize control of highway segments had emerged. The events of April 2004 changed the situation dramatically. Resistance in Sunni areas intensified while the heretofore relatively quiet Shiite areas erupted in violence. Reporting from Baghdad indicates that as many as eighty convoys were struck in the first two weeks of April, while U.S. military sources reported that the rate of convoy attacks had doubled. The character of the attacks on convoys also changed. Relatively large resistance units, reportedly with as many as sixty personnel in some cases, were now involved. Resistance elements fought hard, actually contesting control of roads west and south of Baghdad with U.S. forces. The coalition military spokesman in Baghdad described this as "a concerted effort on the part of the enemy to try to interfere with our lines of communication, our main supply routes."

Determined and concerted attacks on highways represented a challenging new tactic on the part of the resistance. The size of forces and intensity of the fighting, coordination, and scope of attacks—on all four major LOCs, at multiple locations, and with multiple means—indicated new resistance capabilities. Resistance actions along the roads included:

- ambushing convoys, and firing on vehicles;
- hostage taking, at times combined with ambushes, primarily in the Ramadi-Falluja area;
- traditional attacks with improvised explosive devices, sometimes combined with direct fire attacks;
- and sabotage of bridges and overpasses, occasionally combined with ambushes, to disrupt convoy traffic and impede the redeployment of U.S. forces.

While the sustained fights along the roads between coalition forces and insurgent elements were more important in a military sense, hostage taking has had a dramatic psychological effect, personalizing the danger and insecurity along the highways and garnering massive press coverage. The theater of hostages in peril was an "information operations" victory for the insurgents.

Effects

Insurgent operations against the highways have had broad effects. Military operational effects included: some reduction in mobility for coalition forces, the requirement to allocate additional forces to convoy and route security, and increased difficulty in supplying forces. None of these represented insurmountable problems, but—coupled with the dramatic increase in insurgent actions in the Sunni Triangle and the Shiite south—they stretched coalition military capabilities.

Insurgent operations along the roads also affected reconstruction efforts and the Iraqi economy. Both reconstruction and Iraqi economic activity are dependent on the movement of massive amounts of material and large numbers of people. Road movement for both reconstruction and economic purposes was significantly disrupted. At the height of the ambushes and kidnappings, civilian contractors either stopped or substantially reduced movement within Iraq, reportedly bringing some reconstruction projects to a halt, and some reconstruction personnel were told by their governments to depart from

Iraq. Several major firms have decided to reduce or suspend reconstruction operations. Iraqi and other merchants have found it increasingly difficult to move within the country, adversely affecting what had been thriving commerce with its neighbors.

The attacks on the roads were also important psychologically. They reinforced the impression created by the uprisings of a loss of control by the coalition—a sense that the coalition was under siege.

Coalition Response

The coalition responded to insurgent operations against the roads with traditional military measures. Coalition forces attacked insurgent elements to open roads, leading in some cases to intense and sustained fighting. Brig. Gen. Mark Kimmitt, the deputy director of military operations in Baghdad, stated, "We've had to take extraordinary steps to get stuff to the [U.S. troops] fighting to open up some of the routes." Closures of segments of Highways 1, 8, and 10 were imposed to control road traffic and repair damage from sabotage. Convoys were provided with increased security in the form of more escort vehicles and troops and an increased number of armored Humvees and heavily armed patrol vehicles (the so-called "gun-trucks"). In addition, garrison commanders were given added responsibility to protect convoys moving through their areas. Logistical "work-arounds" were also implemented, such as flying in essential military supplies, delaying nonessential convoys, and using alternative routes.

Implications

The insurgents will have difficulty in mounting a sustained campaign against the highways at the level of intensity achieved in the first half of April. Serious LOC attacks already seem to have dropped off, much as the intensity of broader insurgent activity has fallen. Enhanced security measures instituted by coalition forces also have likely contributed to a reduction in successful attacks. Nevertheless, the insurgents have demonstrated that they can seriously impede road movement, and it is likely that intermittent attacks along the highways will continue to pose problems for military and civilian movement. In any future period of increased unrest, serious efforts to interdict the highway system can be anticipated. U.S. military action against either Falluja or Najaf would almost certainly trigger renewed fighting along the roads.

Even though the situation along the highways has steadied, the concerted attacks by insurgents have important implications for the U.S. mission in Iraq. The battle for the highways represents a "third front" in the struggle with the Sunni-based resistance and al-Sadr's supporters. Although coalition military forces can be supplied under such conditions—albeit with increased cost—the reconstruction program and Iraqi economic activity cannot be maintained if material and people cannot move relatively securely. The coalition is sustaining a society, not just an expeditionary force. Insurgent actions have shown that reconstruction can be seriously disrupted; and this will be of continuing concern, requiring the devotion of substantial military resources for the foreseeable future.

Jonathan Schanzer

30
Ansar al-Islam: Back in Iraq

Months before the Iraq war of 2003, *The New Yorker, Christian Science Monitor,* and *The New York Times* published reports about Ansar al-Islam ("Partisans of Islam"), a brutal band of al-Qa'ida guerrillas based in a Kurdish area of northern Iraq near the Iranian border. U.S. officials pointed to Ansar al-Islam as the "missing link" between al-Qa'ida and Saddam Hussein. When Secretary of State Colin Powell made the U.S. case for war against Saddam at the United Nations on February 5, 2003, he cited Ansar al-Islam as a key reason for invasion. Powell drew links among the group, al-Qa'ida, and Saddam, citing Central Intelligence Agency (CIA) documents declassified upon the request of the White House.[1]

As war approached, however, the Bush administration said less about Ansar al-Islam and al-Qa'ida. Rather, the administration focused on Saddam's attempts to develop weapons of mass destruction. After the war, it became a matter of common wisdom that Saddam had no links to al-Qa'ida. Carl Levin, chairman of the Senate Armed Services Committee, said that the case linking Saddam to al-Qa'ida was never "bullet-proof."[2] Former vice president Al Gore denied that such ties existed at all.[3]

But since the defeat and dispersal of Saddam's regime, U.S. officials have begun to talk of Ansar al-Islam once more. In July 2003, U.S. joint chiefs of staff chairman General Richard Myers stated "that group is still active in Iraq."[4] A week later, Myers revealed that some cadres from the group had been captured and were being interrogated.[5] The U.S. top administrator in Iraq, Paul Bremer III, reiterated Myers's message in August, saying that there were "quite a number of these Ansar al-Islam professional killers on the loose in the country," that they were staging attacks against U.S. servicemen, and that U.S. forces were trying to track them down.[6]

High-profile attacks against U.S. and international interests in Iraq in August also appeared to confirm suspicions that Ansar al-Islam was again operational. The attacks on the Jordanian embassy and the United Nations (U.N.) compound in Baghdad, followed later by a spate of suicide bombing attacks against foreign and U.S. targets, clearly fit the modus operandi of al-Qa'ida. However, Ansar al-Islam never claimed responsibility for these attacks. Thus, analysts are now wondering, who exactly in Iraq represents Ansar al-Islam? Has the group rebounded? Is it connected with other elements in the Iraqi

Originally published in *Middle East Quarterly* 11, no. 1 (Winter 2004). Jonathan Schanzer is a Soref fellow at The Washington Institute.

resistance, especially partisans of the old regime? If so, is it possible that it *did* have ties to Saddam even before the war?

These questions require careful analysis as U.S. forces prepare for more battles ahead.

The Rise of Ansar

The roots of Ansar al-Islam extend back to the mid-1990s. The group appears to be comprised of the various Islamist factions that splintered from the Islamic Movement of Kurdistan (IMK) in northern Iraq. As Iraq scholar Michael Rubin notes, they included groups called Hamas, Tawhid, and the Second Soran Unit, among others.[7]

On September 1, 2001, the Second Soran Unit and the Tawhid Islamic Front merged to form the Jund al-Islam. Jund al-Islam was soon renamed Ansar al-Islam. As the group grew, it bore the markings of other al-Qa'ida affiliates. Their cadres hailed from other Arab countries; some of them had experience in Afghanistan, and they based themselves in the part of Iraq under the weakest central authority: northern Iraq, also widely known as Iraqi Kurdistan.

Iraqi Kurdistan is an area of Iraq that until recently was protected in the northern "no-fly" zone by allied warplanes after the 1991 Kuwait war. The United States and Britain sought to defend the area from incursions by Saddam's regime (which was responsible for the brutal murder of hundreds and expulsion of hundreds of thousands after the 1991 war) but left the area to be governed by the Kurds themselves. The Kurds were successful in creating a semiautonomous region under an interim government.

But northern Iraq lacked overarching central control. Opposing political factions—namely the Kurdistan Democratic Party of Iraq (KDP) and Patriotic Union of Kurdistan (PUK)—held small hamlets of power, but they exercised no authority on the fringes of their zones. Those lawless fringes appeared to be the perfect spot to launch another jihad.

Ansar al-Islam announced its inception just days before the September 11 attacks on the United States. One month before, leaders of several Kurdish Islamist factions reportedly visited the al-Qa'ida leadership in Afghanistan[8] seeking to create a base for al-Qa'ida in northern Iraq.[9] Perhaps they knew that the base in Afghanistan would soon be targeted, following the impending terrorist attacks against U.S. targets.

There were other clear indications that al-Qa'ida was behind the group's creation. The authors of a document found in Kabul vowed to "expel those Jews and Christians from Kurdistan and join the way of jihad, [and] rule every piece of land ... with the Islamic Shari'a rule."[10] The *Los Angeles Times*, based upon interviews with an Ansar prisoner, also corroborates this, noting that in October 2000, Kurdish Islamist leaders:

> *sent a guerrilla with the alias Mala Namo and two bodyguards into Iran and then on to bin Laden's camps ... When teams began returning from the Afghan camps in 2001 ... they carried a message from bin Laden that Kurdish Islamic cells should unite. By that time, a number of al-Qaeda operatives had left Afghanistan and moved to northern Iraq ... militant leaders in Kurdistan were replicating al-Qaeda type camps on military training, terrorism, and suicide bombers.*[11]

According to several reports, Ansar al-Islam was started with $300,000 to $600,000 in al-Qa'ida seed money.[12] According to at least three journalistic sources, the group received money from a key cleric in the al-Qa'ida network, Abu Qatada, based in London.[13] In April 2003, the *Los Angeles Times* reported that Italian police had wiretapped conversations with an imam from Cremona, Italy, indicating that Syria was serving as a hub for recruits.[14] Some funds reportedly came from Saudi Arabia.[15]

While some thirty al-Qa'ida members reportedly joined Ansar al-Islam's Kurdish cadres in 2001,[16] the foreign fighter presence soon grew to between eighty and 120. The group's Arab members included Iraqi, Lebanese, Jordanian, Moroccan, Syrian, Palestinian, and Afghan fighters trained in a wide array of guerrilla tactics.[17] The fighters, armed with heavy machine guns, mortars, and antiaircraft weaponry, sought to create a Taliban-like regime. They banned music, alcohol, pictures, and advertising in their stronghold. Girls were prevented from studying; men were forced to grow beards and pray five times daily.

Ansar al-Islam operated in fortified mountain positions along theIran-Iraq border known as "Little Tora Bora" (after the Taliban stronghold in Afghanistan).[18] Colin Powell, in his February 5, 2003 statement to the U.N. Security Council, noted that the organization had established a "poison and explosive training center camp ... in northeastern Iraq."[19]

Prewar Violence

Ansar al-Islam made headlines in September 2001 when it ambushed and killed forty-two PUK fighters. This alarmed the Kurds, who quickly established a conventional defensive front. It was soon understood that the Kurds were the target of a new jihadist war.

A wave of violence erupted in spring 2002, beginning with a politically motivated plot. Ansar al-Islam attempted to murder Barham Salih, a PUK leader. Five bodyguards and two attackers were killed in the ensuing gunfight.[20] Ansar al-Islam's tactics became bloodier, with the aim of inflicting as much damage as possible. In June, Ansar bombed a restaurant, injuring scores and killing a child.[21] In July, the group killed nine PUK fighters.[22] In a move reminiscent of the Taliban, the group destroyed Sufi shrines.[23] In December, Ansar launched a surprise attack after the PUK sent 1,500 soldiers home to celebrate the end of Ramadan.[24] According to Ansar's website, they killed 103 PUK members and wounded 117.[25] Gruesome pictures of the group's victims were posted on the Internet.[26]

As Ansar al-Islam grew more violent, information began to surface about three worrisome aspects of Ansar al-Islam: (1) its interest in chemical weapons; (2) its possible links to Saddam's regime; and (3) its connections to Iran.

• *Chemical weapons.* By early 2003, more than thirty Ansar al-Islam militants (including fifteen to twenty Arab fighters) were incarcerated in the Kurdish "capital" of Sulaymaniyah.[27] *The International Herald Tribune* noted, "critical information about this network emerged from interrogations of captured cell members."[28] Based on this testimony and other intelligence, information was gleaned about Ansar al-Islam's nascent chemical facilities.

Specifically, it was reported that cyanide gas and the poison ricin were among the chemicals tested by Ansar al-Islam.[29] *The Washington Post* also reported that Ansar al-Islam smuggled VX nerve gas through Turkey in fall 2001.[30] PUK prime minister Barham Salih cited "clear evidence" of animal testing.[31] Other Kurdish leaders said they had "eyewitness accounts, prisoners confessions, and seized evidence" to support this.[32]

After Powell's U.N. speech on February 5, 2003, Ansar allowed a small group of reporters to visit their enclave to check for chemical weapons, "especially in the Khurmal and Sargat, areas where Ansar was believed to be developing ricin."[33] Neither Powell's claim nor the militants' denials could be verified.

• *Ties to Saddam.* Bush administration and PUK officials increasingly claimed that Ansar al-Islam was working directly with Saddam. Some reports indicated that Saddam's regime helped smuggle weapons to the group from Afghanistan.[34] Kurdish explosives experts also claimed that TNT seized from Ansar al-Islam was produced by Baghdad's military and that arms arrived from areas controlled by Saddam.[35] Another link was said to be a man named Abu Wa'il,[36] reportedly an al-Qa'ida operative on Saddam's payroll.[37]

It was also believed that Abu Musab az-Zarqawi, the al-Qa'ida operative who ordered the hit on Salih in spring 2002, had a relationship with Saddam. As war drew near, U.S. authorities announced that he had sought medical attention in Baghdad[38] where Saddam harbored what Powell called "Zarqawi and his subordinates"[39] for eight months. Intelligence revealed that he was also directly tied to Ansar; he reportedly ran a terrorist training camp in northern Iraq before the recent war.[40]

Zarqawi, by way of background, is thought to have coordinated the murder of USAID officer Laurence Foley in Amman, Jordan, in October 2002.[41] Former Federal Bureau of Investigation analyst Matthew Levitt notes that Zarqawi was the head of a 116-person global al-Qa'ida network and that "authorities have linked Zarqawi to recent attacks in Morocco, Turkey, and other plots in Europe."[42]

• *Links to Iran.* It was also suspected that Iran played a significant role in supporting Ansar al-Islam. Indeed, Iran openly allowed the group to operate along its borders despite the group's alleged affiliation with the al-Qa'ida network. Kurds further allege that Iran provided logistical support by allowing for the flow of goods and weapons and providing a safe area beyond the front.[43]

There were other connections; the group's spiritual leader, Mullah Krekar, spent many years in Iran and was arrested in Amsterdam after a flight from Tehran. The Turkish *Milliyet* also notes that Ansar al-Islam checked cars leaving their stronghold going into Iran, indicating coordination with the Islamic republic.[44] Tehran, for its part, predictably denied all ties to the group.

War Comes

By February, U.S. war preparations were nearly complete. Powell's U.N. speech made a plea to other governments to confront Saddam, and this was based in part on evidence concerning Ansar al-Islam.[45] In so doing, Powell also left no doubt that in addition to Saddam, Ansar would be a target in the imminent war.

Given this context, it might have made sense for the group to lower its profile. Instead it went on the offensive. Ansar al-Islam claimed responsibility for the February 8 assassination of Kurdish minister Shawkat Hajji Mushir, a founding member of the PUK. Ansar elements, posing as defectors, shot Mushir in the head. Four people were killed in the ensuing gunfight, including an eight-year-old girl; the Ansar gunmen escaped.[46] Later that month, a man thought to belong to Ansar al-Islam detonated a suicide bomb near a Kurdish checkpoint. The bomb, packed with metal shards, marked the first reported use of suicide bombings by the group.

On February 20, the U.S. Department of Treasury named Ansar al-Islam a Specially Designated Global Terrorist (SDGT) entity.[47] The designation effectively constituted a hunting license for U.S. forces. As the war neared, Ansar al-Islam braced itself for a combined U.S.-Kurdish assault. One Kurdish official noted that "nervousness" set into the group, which retreated to higher mountain peaks and dug into caves.[48]

On March 23, with the war fully underway, PUK fighters attacked Ansar al-Islam's stronghold, with backing from U.S. Special Forces, unmanned aerial vehicles, and aircraft strikes. Cruise missiles destroyed much of the enclave. Deserters left behind artillery, machine guns, mortars, and Katyusha rockets. On March 25, Ansar fighters made a desperate attack on PUK forces near Halabja but were repelled. Dozens of their forces were wounded or killed.[49] Within eight days, the entire Ansar enclave was decimated. At least 259 Ansar al-Islam fighters were killed in the fighting. According to the group's leader, some twenty-eight planes and 108 rockets destroyed the compound.[50]

During the fighting, PUK forces also took eight fighters into custody, including Jordanians, Syrians, Tunisians, and one Palestinian who stated that he came to Iraq to "kill Americans." Interestingly, many captured Arab fighters held passports with Iraqi visas, signaling that Iraq likely approved their presence.[51]

After rummaging through the debris, coalition officials found a multitude of intelligence leads, including a list of suspected militants living in the United States, the phone number of a Kuwaiti cleric, and a letter from Yemen's minister of religion. Evidence also reportedly showed that specific meetings took place between Ansar and al-Qa'ida activists.[52] German media reported that a three-volume manual was found listing chemical and biological experiments, including the use of ricin and cyanide.[53]

After U.S. forces began their March 23 assault on Ansar positions, wounded fighters hobbled across the border, seeking Iran's assistance. However, an official from the Kurdish Socialist Democratic Party noted that "they went inside one kilometer, but the Iranians made them go back."[54] On March 30, dozens more fighters escaped to Iran. However, Kurdish factions reported that on that occasion, Tehran detained them as prisoners.[55]

Hamid-Reza Asefi, a spokesman for Iran's foreign ministry, insisted that "there is no link between this group and Iran."[56] But, in subsequent months, Washington and Tehran were reportedly negotiating the transfer of several Ansar militants who were still in Iran. Among those sought by the United States were Abu Wa'il and a man named Ayub Afghani, an explosives expert trained in Afghanistan.[57]

It is still thought that Iran hosts several al-Qa'ida militants in its territory. In fact, some senior American officials believe that the orders to carry out the May 12, 2003 bombings in Riyadh came from Sayf al-'Adil, an al-Qa'ida operations chief based in Iran at the time of the bombing.[58] U.S. officials and Arab press reports have since indicated that al-Qa'ida spokesman Sulayman Abu Ghayth, Osama bin Laden's son Sa'd, and Zarqawi are among a number of al-Qa'ida operatives in Iran. Iranian president Muhammad Khatami, however, refused to allow U.S. investigators to question suspects detained there.[59]

Ansar Rebounds

Following the fall of Baghdad in early April 2003, some 140,000 U.S. forces occupied Iraq. Since then, relative calm has prevailed in the south under British control and in the north, still held by the Kurds. But U.S. forces in Iraq's center have become embroiled in a guerrilla war with unspecified numbers of irregular fighters who have inflicted a rising number of casualties.

For the first two months, Bush administration officials appeared certain that Saddam loyalists were the culprits behind sniper attacks and mine explosions that killed several soldiers per week. By July, however, after U.S. forces surrounded and killed Saddam's sons Uday and Qusay, officials began invoking the name Ansar al-Islam.

The resurgence of Ansar al-Islam was no surprise. After all, some 300-350 members fled the Ansar compound ahead of the Iraq war, meaning that the group was bound to survive.[60] And as one prisoner during the war stated, "I don't think the fight with Ansar will be over when America finishes its bombing."[61]

As if on cue, in late April, clashes took place between a band of Ansar militants and local Kurdish security forces 45 kilometers east of Sulaymaniya.[62] The following month, just after the war's end, a Kurdish spokesman stated that the group was trying to "regroup in the mountainous Iraqi-Iranian border region," and that "a number of Ansar members are trying to join another Islamic group" in the region.[63]

Soon after that, Kurdish officials cited an unconfirmed report that several thousand al-Qa'ida fighters could attempt to resuscitate Ansar's activities. Further, one Kurdish spokesman lamented that "if the strikes had occurred one year [before], we would have completely destroyed Ansar. They were half expecting the strikes, which gave them plenty of time to disperse, or for their leaders to relocate."[64] The official also noted that if the group had developed ricin or other chemical weapons, it likely moved them before the attacks. Thus, Ansar al-Islam could still carry out a chemical attack.

Finally, Kurdish officials also expressed fears that sleeper cells were waiting to be activated in the Kurdish enclave and that they could employ tactics such as suicide bombing. Evidence of this came in two wartime operations: the March 22 suicide bombing, carried out by a Saudi, killing an Australian cameraman at a checkpoint near Halabja,[65] and the thwarted suicide car-bombing on March 27 when security personnel shot an assailant before he reached the Zamaki checkpoint.[66]

Ansar's website, during the war and after, featured a "Letter from the Emir of Ansar al-Islam, Abu 'Abdullah ash-Shafi' to the Muslims of Kurdistan and Iraq and the World." The missive threatened that "300 jihad martyrs renewed their pledge to Allah, the strong and the sublime, in order to be suicide bombers in the victory of Allah's religion."[67]

Kurdish fears appeared to be vindicated in June when Ansar al-Islam announced that it had opened its doors to volunteers to fight the United States in Iraq. In a statement sent to *Ash-Sharq al-Awsat* newspaper, 'Abdullah ash-Shafi', the group's local leader, boasted (falsely) that his group had already destroyed ten U.S. tanks.[68]

When a car bomb rocked the Jordanian embassy in Iraq on August 7, 2003, and killed seventeen people, Ansar al-Islam was among the first suspected culprits. According to Lt. Gen. Norton Schwartz, no specific information about Ansar's involvement was available, but he still noted that Ansar had "infrastructure in Iraq, and some of that remains, and our effort is focused on eliminating that."[69] An *Al-Hayat* article on the same day iterated Schwartz's concerns, stating that Islamic militants from Pakistan had infiltrated northern Iraq with the help of bin Laden, and "it was suspected that the Ansar al-Islam group was in connection with the Islamists in Falluja, Tikrit, Bayali, and Baghdad" where attacks against U.S. forces were taking place.[70] Washington expressed fears that the number of fighters might have been in the hundreds.[71] Administration officials also expressed concerns that safe houses and other logistical operations in Iraq were being run by Ansar al-Islam.[72]

Meanwhile, the PUK reported in August that its forces had captured several Ansar militants among some fifty people caught infiltrating northern Iraq by way of Iran.[73] Among them were five Iraqis, a Palestinian, and a Tunisian.[74] Information gleaned from subsequent interrogations has not yet been made public by Kurdish officials.

Following the Jordanian embassy attack, there was fear that Ansar was still planning something bigger. Indeed, Bremer stated, "Intelligence suggests that Ansar al-Islam is planning large-scale terrorist attacks [in Iraq] ... I think we have to be pretty alert to the fact that we may see more of this."[75]

On August 13, a number of gunmen attacked U.S. troops in downtown Baghdad and then sped from the scene. Before they left, however, they dropped cards stating "Death to the Collaborators of America—al–Qa'ida." This may have been in reference to the Jordanian embassy bombing, or even to the forthcoming bombing at the U.N. compound in Baghdad on August 19, when a suicide bomber drove a cement mixer full of explosives that set off a blast killing seventeen and wounding more than 100 people. While two previously unknown groups claimed responsibility for the attack, The *New York Times* noted that "the immediate focus of attention was Ansar al-Islam, a militant Islamic group that American officials believe has been plotting attacks against Western targets in Baghdad."[76]

Ansar's Network

These operations, in the heart of Baghdad, raised the specter of cooperation between regime remnants and Ansar al-Islam. According to officials interviewed by The *Weekly Standard*, Ansar cadres were thought to be "joining with remnants of Saddam's regime to attack American and nongovernmental organizations working in Iraq."[77] There was much speculation that the Iraqi resistance was being coordinated by 'Izzat Ibrahim ad-Duri, a Saddam confidant and one of the most wanted Ba'athists. He was fingered by two captured members of Ansar al-Islam as an instigator of the recent campaign of violence against Americans in Iraq.[78] (However, subsequent reports indicated that ad-Duri was struggling for his life in a battle with leukemia and was probably incapable of coordinating attacks against Americans.)[79]

Meanwhile, a concurrent *Newsweek* report indicated that "Ansar fighters are joining forces with Ba'athists and members of al-Qaeda."[80] That report also indicated that Ansar's structure was morphing such that each "fighting force is said to be reorganized into small units of ten to fifteen members, each headed by an 'emir'."[81] According to this report, Ansar, through its use of cells and contract fighters, had become a microcosm of the larger al-Qa'ida network, which implements a similar structure worldwide.

Ansar al-Islam's Iranian connection also gave rise to speculation. In August, suspected Ansar militants and/or al-Qa'ida cadres continued to stream across the Iranian border. While Kurdish officials arrested some fifty militants in August 2003,[82] it is not known how many have made it across without incident.

Among the infiltrators, some came with fake passports while others had identification from Tunisia and even European countries. Once the infiltrators made it out of Iran, Saddam loyalists were thought to help smuggle them into central Iraq to fight U.S. forces.[83] In this way, it appears that the mullahs ensured continued fighting in Iraq.[84] Iran was also under increased scrutiny for its continued harboring of more senior al-Qa'ida operatives. Some of these operatives were expelled to their host countries. The whereabouts of others are unknown.[85]

Ansar al-Islam is not only back in Iraq; the group also appears to have gone global-at least, to some extent. *Ash-Sharq al-Awsat* reported in April that two Tunisians were arrested in Italy for ties to Ansar al-Islam.[86] In August, several suspected Ansar cadres were found with five Italian passports.[87] Italy appears to be a central jumping-off point for Ansar; wiretaps by Italian police confirm this to be true.[88] More recently, Italian intelligence revealed the existence of an extensive al-Qa'ida support network in northern Italy. The network, established in spring 2002 and based out of Milan, Varese, and Cremona, has reportedly provided funds and recruits to Ansar al-Islam and al-Qa'ida.[89]

But many questions remain about the extent of Ansar al-Islam's network. Lebanese, Jordanian, Moroccan, Syrian, Palestinian, and Afghan fighters have all fought among the ranks of Ansar. That could mean there is or was a recruiting infrastructure in each country to bring them to northern Iraq. Further, if the group did receive funds from Abu Qatada in London, then Ansar al-Islam also has at least some infrastructure there. If Syria is a staging ground for Ansar fighters, as the Italian wiretaps revealed, then Ansar is one more terrorist organization operating with a wink and a nod from Damascus. And finally, if some funding for the group came from Saudi Arabia, as Michael Rubin suggests, then one can assume that the Wahhabi infrastructure is supporting this group.[90]

Unfortunately, there are no definitive answers to these questions. Ansar al-Islam is a new terrorist group; information about it is still emerging. But one thing is clear: Ansar al-Islam is one of the most dangerous affiliates in al-Qa'ida's orbit, with the potential to strike at vital U.S. interests in Iraq. And given its broader links, the group could develop an even wider reach-like al-Qa'ida itself.

Notes

1. Colin Powell, remarks to the U.N. Security Council, Feb. 5, 2003, at http://www.state.gov/secretary/rm/2003/17300.htm; Stephen F. Hayes, "Saddam's al-Qaeda Connection," *The Weekly Standard*, Sept. 1-8, 2003.
2. *Congressional Record*, 108th Congress, 1st sess., "Iraq Intelligence," July 15, 2003, at http://levin.senate.gov/floor/071503fs1.htm
3. Al Gore, remarks at New York University, Aug. 7, 2003, at http://www.moveon.org/gore-speech.html
4. Agence France-Presse, July 30, 2003.
5. *The New York Times*, Aug. 7, 2003.
6. Paul Bremer news conference, Aug. 2, 2003, quoted at http://www.cnn.com/2003/US/08/08/nyt.gordon/
7. Michael Rubin, "The Islamist Threat in Iraqi Kurdistan," *Middle East Intelligence Bulletin*, Dec. 2001, at http://www.meib.org/articles/0112_ir1.htm
8. *The New York Times*, Jan. 13, 2002; author's interview with Barham Salih, Washington, D.C., Jan. 10, 2002.
9. *Los Angeles Times*, Dec. 9, 2002.
10. *The Kurdistan Observer*, Jan. 14, 2002, at http://home.cogeco.ca/~observer/14-1-03-memorandum-kurd-islam-qaeda.html
11. *Los Angeles Times*, Feb. 5, 2003.
12. NewsMax.com, Mar. 18, 2002, at http://www.newsmax.com/archives/articles/2002/3/18/74151.shtml; *The Christian Science Monitor*, Mar. 15, 2002.
13. *The Jerusalem Report*, Nov. 18, 2002; *The Christian Science Monitor*, Apr. 2, 2002; Le Monde, Nov. 13, 2002.
14. *Los Angeles Times*, Apr. 28, 2003.
15. Rubin, "The Islamist Threat in Iraqi Kurdistan."
16. Agence France-Presse, Dec. 4, 2002.
17. Author's interview with Barham Salih, Jan. 10, 2003; *The Christian Science Monitor*, Mar. 15, 2002.
18. Ibid.

19. Colin Powell, remarks to the U.N. Security Council, Feb. 5, 2003, at http://www.state.gov/secretary/rm/2003/17300.htm
20. *The Christian Science Monitor,* Apr. 9, 2002.
21. *Iraqi Kurdistan Dispatch,* July 5, 2002, at http://www.ikurd.info/news-05jul-p1.htm
22. *The Washington Post,* Sept. 5, 2002.
23. *Kurdistan Newsline,* July 23, 2002, at http://www.puk.org/web/htm/news/knwsline/nws/kurdlead.html
24. *Ash-Sharq al-Awsat* (London), Dec. 6, 2002.
25. Associated Press, Dec. 15, 2002.
26. At http://www.nawend.com/ansarislam.htm (site no longer available).
27. Author's interview with Barham Salih, Jan. 10, 2003.
28. *The New York Times,* Feb. 6, 2003.
29. *Al-Hayat* (London), Aug. 22, 2002; *Los Angeles Times,* Dec 9, 2002.
30. *The Washington Post,* Dec. 12, 2002.
31. Author's interview with Barham Salih, Jan. 10, 2003.
32. Author's interview with PUK representative, Washington, D.C., Mar. 2003.
33. Author's interview with PUK official, Washington, D.C., Apr. 1, 2003.
34. *The New Yorker,* Mar. 25, 2002.
35. *The Guardian,* Aug. 23, 2002.
36. "Ansar al-Islam," Iraq News Wire, no. 8, Middle East Media Research Institute (MEMRI), Sept. 1, 2002, at http://memri.org/bin/articles.cgi?Page=countries&Area=iraq&ID=INW802
37. *The Christian Science Monitor,* Apr. 2, 2002; *Los Angeles Times,* Dec. 9, 2002.
38. *The International Herald Tribune,* Feb. 7, 2003.
39. Powell, remarks to the U.N. Security Council, Feb. 5, 2003, at http://www.state.gov/secretary/rm/2003/17300.htm
40. *The Washington Times,* July 30, 2003.
41. Confirmed by source at the Pentagon.
42. Matthew Levitt, "Placing Iraq and Zarqawi in the Terror Web," PolicyWatch. no. 710, Washington Institute for Near East Policy, Feb. 13, 2003, at http://www.washingtoninstitute.org/watch/policywatch/policywatch2003/710.htm; author's interview, Dec. 10, 2003.
43. *The Washington Post,* Sept. 5, 2002.
44. *Milliyet* (Ankara), Jan. 7, 2003.

45. Powell, remarks to the U.N. Security Council, Feb. 5, 2003, at http://www.state.gov/secretary/rm/2003/17300.htm
46. *The New York Times,* Feb. 10, 2003.
47. Treasury Department statement regarding the designation of Ansar al-Islam, Feb. 20, 2003, at http://www.treas.gov/press/releases/js48.htm
48. Author's interview with PUK official, Washington, D.C., May 2003.
49. "USWAR/Ansar al-Islam Attacks PUK Positions," Islamic Republic News Agency (IRNA), Mar. 26, 2003, at http://www.irna.com/en/head/030326094847.ehe.shtml (site no longer available).
50. Associated Press, Aug. 12, 2003.
51. Author's interview with PUK official, May 2003.
52. Associated Press, Mar. 31, 2003.
53. Agence France-Presse, Apr. 9, 2003.
54. *The Washington Post,* Mar. 25, 2003.
55. Author's interview with PUK official, May 2003.
56. Agence France-Presse, Mar. 25, 2003.
57. United Press International, May 9, 2003.
58. *An-Nahar* (Beirut), May 21, 2003.
59. Agence France-Presse, Aug. 13, 2003
60. *The New York Times,* Aug. 13, 2003.
61. *The Boston Globe,* Mar. 19, 2003.
62. *Ash-Sharq al-Awsat,* Apr. 22, 2003.
63. Author's interview with Kurdish spokesman, Washington, D.C., May 20, 2003.
64. Author's interview with PUK official, Apr. 1, 2003.
65. Kurdish Media, Mar. 25, 2003, at http://www.kurdmedia.com/news.asp?id=3635
66. Author's interview with PUK official, Apr. 1, 2003.
67. At http://www.nawend.com/ansarislam.htm (site no longer available).
68. *Ash-Sharq al-Awsat,* June 13, 2003.
69. Associated Press, Aug. 8, 2003.
70. *Al-Hayat,* Aug. 7, 2003.
71. Agence France-Presse, Aug. 14, 2003.
72. *The New York Times,* Aug. 13, 2003.
73. Reuters, Aug. 12, 2003.

74. *The New York Times,* Aug. 13, 2003.
75. Ibid., Aug. 10, 2003.
76. Ibid., Aug. 20, 2003.
77. *The Weekly Standard,* Sept. 1-8, 2003.
78. Associated Press, Oct. 30, 2003.
79. *The Washington Times,* Oct. 31, 2003.
80. *Newsweek,* Oct. 13, 2003.
81. Ibid.
82. *Ash-Sharq al-Awsat,* Aug. 18, 2003.
83. Agence France-Presse, Aug. 17, 2003.
84. *Ash-Sharq al-Awsat,* Aug. 18, 2003.
85. *Middle East Newsline,* Aug. 21, 2003.
86. *Ash-Sharq al-Awsat,* Apr. 3, 2003.
87. *The New York Times,* Aug. 13, 2003.
88. *Los Angeles Times,* Apr. 28, 2003.
89. "Ansar Al-Islam's European Base," American Foreign Policy Council, Oct. 31, 2003, citing *Corriere della Serra* (Milan), Oct. 27, 2003.
90. Rubin, "The Islamist Threat in Iraqi Kurdistan."

Part Four

The Shiite Opposition

Jeffrey White

Introduction

The Sunni-based resistance movement became perhaps the primary driver of the postwar situation in Iraq. But the question of whether or not the Shiite community would support, or at least not actively oppose, the coalition and its objectives was a decisive determinant in allowing the coalition to operate in Iraq. The coalition could proceed in Iraq even with opposition from the Sunnis, but it would not have been possible to either occupy the country at acceptable cost or move forward with political reform and an effective transfer of sovereignty against wide Shiite opposition. That this was recognized and more or less successfully managed by coalition officials represents one of the major successes in the Iraq story.

Representing 55 to 60 percent of the Iraqi population, Shiites were well placed to take a leading, even dominant role in the new state. This was understood quickly by Shiite leaders, whose competition for power began as early as April 11, 2003, with the murder of moderate senior cleric Ayatollah Abdul Majid al-Khoei in Najaf by henchmen of Muqtada al-Sadr.

Unlike the Sunnis, the Shiites had historic and natural leadership groups to provide political direction, mobilize support or opposition to the coalition, and organize for the coming political struggle. Traditional Shiite religious leaders quickly emerged as political players, both competing and making alliances with other Shiite factions.

From the beginning, mainstream Shiites made a strategic decision to generally support the coalition. This was based on the recognition that they stood on "destiny's doorstep," with the potential for the coalition to deliver them a dominant political role in Iraq. This did not preclude disputes and tensions with the coalition, but the paramount objective of securing their "rightful" place in the new Iraq dictated a policy of compromise and restraint on the part of the mainstream Shiite leadership. This imperative was instrumental in delaying serious armed struggle with disaffected Shiites and, when such conflict became unavoidable, in managing it.

From summer 2003 on, Muqtada al-Sadr increasingly took on the role of the primary Shiite voice in opposition to the coalition and its political partners in Iraq. The son of the revered and martyred Grand Ayatollah Muhammad Baqr al-Sadr, he quickly emerged to challenge the coalition, first in Baghdad's Sadr City, Najaf, and Karbala, and later, as his organization spread, throughout southern Iraq. Parallel to his challenge to the coalition, al-Sadr confronted the established senior Shiite religious hierarchy. Given his youth and his lack of merit as either a scholar or speaker, it has never been clear whether al-Sadr led the movement with his name or served as the tool of those around him. Whatever the case, he became the "drummer" of the movement, the one man capable of mobilizing popular support and putting militiamen in the streets. Substantial numbers of Shiites were willing to act and die in his name.

Al-Sadr's movement began to extend its organizational structure and activities as early as summer 2003. By August it was in a position to challenge the coalition overtly with violent demonstrations in Baghdad. A more substantial challenge came in October 2003, featuring an ambush on U.S. forces in Sadr City by al-Sadr's newly formed militia, the Mahdi Army. This attack left two U.S. soldiers dead and four wounded. At the same time al-Sadr's supporters clashed with elements of the Iraqi police and supporters of Grand Ayatollah Ali Hussein al-Sistani, the de facto political leader of the Shiite community.

The October clashes and the tension raised by them brought the situation to the brink of full-scale armed confrontation. Both the coalition and al-Sadr backed away from this, choosing to avoid a potentially decisive test of strength and will. Al-Sadr used the relatively quiet period that followed to extend his organization further, to intimidate other Shiite political factions, and to increase the military capability of the Mahdi Army.

By March 2004 this lull was over, with al-Sadr's supporters again turning aggressive. The destruction by Mahdi Army elements of the village of Qawliya in southern Iraq during that month seemed to provoke the coalition into more aggressive action against al-Sadr. By late March events were moving swiftly. A Sadrist newspaper was closed for inciting anticoalition violence, precipitating popular demonstrations against the coalition. The arrest of a key al-Sadr lieutenant shortly thereafter sparked a widespread rebellion on April 4.

The April 4 rebellion was the first major armed test of the coalition by any Shiite element. As such it risked producing a general conflict between Shiites and the coalition, with the enormous consequences that implied. For the coalition, the Iraqi government, and the mainstream Shiite community, it was critical that the rebellion be put down without driving substantial numbers of Shiites into armed opposition. Occurring at the same time as the "siege of Falluja," the al-Sadr challenge was the more important.

The seriousness of the events of early April 2004 should not be underestimated. The coalition was chased out of Kut by the Mahdi Army, and other coalition outposts came close to falling. The Iraqi Police Service collapsed, Iraqi government offices were seized, and coalition lines of communication to Kuwait were threatened. Only rapid reaction by U.S. forces deploying from Baghdad and further north stabilized the situation.

Coalition efforts to manage the al-Sadr revolt do not appear to have represented a coherent policy implemented from the outset. It seems rather that coalition officials and commanders hit upon a successful approach to dealing with the crisis as it developed and after they had recovered from the initial surprise. Nevertheless, a combination of precise military action and political skill in working with moderate Shiite elements opposed to al-Sadr prevented the situation from escalating into a general conflict between the coalition and Shiites. Given the difficulties encountered in post-Saddam Iraq, this stands as a major success.

As of mid-August 2004, al-Sadr's prospects appear to be dimming, as coalition and Iraqi forces campaign to destroy the primary basis of his power, the Mahdi Army, and to reduce his hold on the city of Najaf. Having learned valuable lessons from the hostilities of April and May, his opponents seem more determined than ever to break his power and are willing to take significant risks to achieve their objectives. The August fighting could put paid to al-Sadr's political ambitions. Nevertheless, unless his militia is truly broken and his political organization dismantled, he could reemerge as a force to reckon with in the future, with a revived Mahdi Army to do his violent bidding.

Indeed, well before the beginning of Operation Iraqi Freedom, The Washington Institute recognized that Shiites would play a critical role in determining the future of the new Iraq. As the following analyses show, after the fall of the regime, Institute scholars identified the potential for opposition from elements of the Shiite community. In particular, they focused on al-Sadr as a real danger, tracking and projecting the course of his challenge and providing clear analysis of the nature, scope, and consequences of his rebellion and the coalition response to it.

Jeffrey White and Michael Schmidmayr

31
Shiite Opposition in Iraq: An Emerging Challenge

Riots last week in Baghdad and Basra raised questions about Shiite opposition to the Coalition Provisional Authority (CPA). While the Shiite community has been relatively quiet compared to the Sunni population, elements of the Shiite have adopted a consistent position against the CPA, occupation forces, and the appointed Governing Council. If they deem it necessary, those opposed to occupation have the means and motives to move to armed resistance, which would pose a substantial threat to the coalition.

Resistance in Shiite Areas

To date, most of the armed resistance activity in Iraq has come from within predominantly Sunni areas. However, in the first eighteen weeks of resistance activity there were some thirty reported incidents in principally Shiite areas, with fourteen coalition soldiers killed. Some of these incidents can probably be attributed to non-Shiites, including regime elements. The range of tactics and weapons used has been more limited than in Sunni areas. There have also been a number of anticoalition demonstrations, but it is evident that the Shiite community has been more accepting of occupation than the Sunnis.

While qualifying their support to the coalition and the Governing Council, the Supreme Council for Islamic Revolution in Iraq (SCIRI), led by Ayatollah Muhammad Baqr al-Hakim, and the Islamic Dawa Party—major Shiite political organizations—have both joined the new Governing Council. Nevertheless, Shiite acceptance of the occupation and transition process is conditional on progress toward self-rule, restoration of public services, and the expedited withdrawal of occupation forces. Ali Abdul Karim al-Madani, a prominent Shiite cleric associated with the moderate Grand Ayatollah Ali Hussein al-Sistani, was preaching anti-American violence and illegal arms activity, suggesting how precarious support for the coalition may even be among moderate Shiites; he was arrested in July.

There are at least five issues that could potentially mobilize Shiite opposition or that are already doing so: cultural clashes brought about by the everyday friction between coalition forces and volatile Shiites; religiously based opposition, often combined with anti-

Originally published as *PolicyWatch* no. 783, August 21, 2003. Michael Schmidmayr is a research intern at The Washington Institute.

American/anti-Western attitudes; problems related to reconstruction and the restoration of public services (security, water, power); spontaneous incidents; and political frustration, either for some Shiites now or the broader community later. These issues are resistant to easy solution, and some combination of them will likely pose problems as long as the occupation continues. These issues have already demonstrated the potential to rapidly merge, producing serious anticoalition outbursts. Serious incidents have the possibility to escalate further, and, in the wake of the inevitable casualties and damage, create conditions for further radicalization and armed resistance to emerge.

The most visibly dangerous Shiite political element at this time is the faction grouped around Muqtada al-Sadr, a radical but junior Shiite cleric who draws heavily on the memory of the regime's martyrdom of his father, revered senior cleric Mohammed Sadiq al-Sadr. Al-Sadr has proposed alternatives to the Governing Council, attempted to recruit an "Islamic Army" and a militia to defend holy sites, and called for the withdrawal of occupation forces and an end to the CPA. In addition, he has built an organization with substantial presence in Baghdad's Sadr City, Najaf, and Nasariya, and perhaps Basra, exploiting the need for social and other services and probably drawing at least in part on remaining elements of his father's extensive organization. His spiritual guide, Ayatollah Kadhim Husseini Haeri, is in Iran, where al-Sadr has visited and reportedly made contact with Iranian officials, including Expediency Council chief Hashemi Rafsanjani and an official of the Islamic Revolutionary Guard Corps Quds Force. Al-Sadr has also contacted Sunni Islamist elements opposed to the coalition, and may be receiving monetary and other support from them.

There is a sense of latent violence attached to al-Sadr and his faction. By all accounts his supporters were involved in the April 11, 2003, murder of Ayatollah Abdul Majid al-Khoei, a moderate senior Shiite cleric. His group is probably behind threats to Iraqis not observing Islamic law in Shiite areas of Baghdad. Given the history of Shiite resistance to authority in Iraq, it would be surprising if al-Sadr is not preparing for clandestine armed resistance. Statements by supporters indicate that they are already armed and prepared to act if given the order. So far al-Sadr and his associates have chosen not to give that order.

Spontaneous Combustion

One of the most disturbing aspects of the Shiite response to occupation is the potential for incidents to rapidly escalate into large encounters between Shiites and occupation troops. So far there have been three significant cases. The first, the deadly riots in the southern town of Majar al-Kabir on June 24, left six British military policemen and an unknown number of Iraqis dead. This incident seems to have been mostly caused by tension between the local population and British forces over weapons searches. The local community appears to have rapidly mobilized, deployed significant firepower (British accounts indicate rocket-propelled grenades [RPGs] and heavy machine guns were used), mounted multiple attacks on British troops in the town, and may have organized a deliberate ambush of a British reaction force moving to the troubled area.

The second spontaneous event occurred in the Basra area beginning on August 9. Here shortages in fuel and power, combined with severe temperatures, produced an outburst of anticoalition rioting. This rioting extended over several days but was not seriously exploited by those opposed to the occupation, although they supported the rioting. The events in Basra also demonstrated that average Iraqi citizens, not just members of opposition or resistance groups, could be quickly pulled into anticoalition disturbances.

This potential was confirmed by events in Baghdad's Sadr City Shiite district on August 13. It is unclear exactly what happened and why, but the Shiite population of this district was left with the clear impression that U.S. forces had deliberately blown down Islamist banners with helicopter rotor wash. Sadr City is substantially under Muqtada al-Sadr's sway. His cadre in the city was able to rapidly mobilize anticoalition demonstrations and generate demands by local clerics for the withdrawal of U.S. forces from Baghdad. Demonstrations turned violent and U.S. troops killed one Iraqi after receiving RPG fire. Coalition commanders subsequently apologized for the banner incident, and reportedly agreed to reduce patrolling and helicopter overflight activity.

From Opposition to Resistance

How large of a step would it take for some Shiites to move from opposition to resistance? Unfortunately not a large one. There are perhaps three mechanisms that could bring this about:

- A deliberate decision to organize violent actions against the coalition, most likely coming out of the al-Sadr faction. Muqtada al-Sadr has been very careful to avoid this step, skirting the edge of outright confrontation, but his willingness to challenge the coalition with demonstrations and demands is clear and appears to be growing; he also has the organization to move rapidly to armed resistance.
- Simple spontaneity. Coalition forces, by exercising tactical restraint, diplomacy, and operational flexibility, have been able to prevent serious incidents—such as those in Baghdad, Basra, and Majar al-Kabir—from escalating uncontrollably and constituting resistance. But the coalition's measured response, apologies, and withdrawals ultimately may encourage opponents. There will likely be more—and more serious—incidents in the future, and there is no certainty that they will always be contained.
- Some element decides to deliberately create or exploit an incident to generate violent resistance. Again, the most likely group is al-Sadr's.

Avoiding a serious break with the Shiites will be a complex and sustained challenge for the coalition.

Jeffrey White

32
To the Brink: Muqtada al-Sadr Challenges the United States

Shiite leader Muqtada al-Sadr, one of the most dangerous men in Iraq, has moved to the brink of a direct and violent confrontation with the Coalition Provisional Authority (CPA) and U.S. forces. This is neither an accident nor a surprise. He has prepared for this eventuality almost from the beginning of the occupation and is now on the verge of posing what could be one of the most serious challenges to the coalition. Specifically, al-Sadr may force the coalition to choose between enforcing its will on part of the Iraqi Shiite community (with the attendant risks of serious conflict) or acquiescing to the rise of a Shiite faction that is beyond its control and opposed to its aims.

Recent Developments

Last week, al-Sadr and his well-organized faction again challenged the coalition in the streets of Baghdad, and this week he began mounting an indirect challenge in Karbala. Tensions have been growing between al-Sadr supporters and U.S. troops since early October, with clashes, demonstrations, and the attempted arrest of the cleric Salah al-Obeidi in Baghdad's Sadr City, an area named after al-Sadr's late father.

On October 6, al-Sadr associate Moayed al-Khazraji was arrested, sparking a series of events whose consequences are still being played out. He was reportedly arrested for "criminal and anticoalition activities," which apparently included hiding weapons in a mosque. Soon after the arrest, al-Sadr once again demonstrated that he could exploit an opportunity presented by the coalition. His supporters quickly took to the streets in a well-established pattern: making demands on the coalition, declaring their intention to resist coalition actions within their areas, and issuing dire threats. Unlike in previous confrontations, however, al-Sadr's supporters deliberately employed armed violence against U.S. troops in an act of calculated resistance. (Past armed clashes between al-Sadr loyalists and coalition forces had been spontaneous in nature and relatively minor in terms of casualties.) On the night of October 9, an element of the 1st Armored Division conducting a routine patrol in Sadr City was lured into an ambush, reportedly by al-Sadr supporters. In the ensuing firefight, two U.S. soldiers were killed and four wounded; two Iraqi militants were killed as well. The fighting lasted for over an hour, with the Iraqis using rocket-propelled grenades, explosives, and automatic weapons.

Originally published as *PolicyWatch* no. 794, October 17, 2003.

The deaths of the two militants provided an opportunity for further demonstrations and challenges. On October 10, approximately 10,000 Shiites marched in the funerals for the two men. Prominent in the crowd were members of al-Sadr's militia, the Mahdi Army, who marched in formation, armed and openly wearing insignia. That same day, during his Friday sermon, al-Sadr announced the formation of an Iraqi government, including a cabinet, in defiance of the existing Iraqi Governing Council. One of al-Sadr's key followers in Baghdad, Abdul Hadi Daraji, described this new "government": "The imam's army [Mahdi Army] is the military side, and the cabinet is the political side." On October 13-14, al-Sadr loyalists, including Mahdi Army personnel, clashed with Iraqi police and supporters of Grand Ayatollah Ali Hussein al-Sistani (the most senior Iraqi Shiite cleric, who is tolerant of the occupation) in an attempt to assert control in Karbala. On October 16-17, Karbala was the site of serious clashes between coalition forces (U.S. and Polish troops, along with Iraqi police) and Shiite militiamen. Three U.S. soldiers and two Iraqi policemen were killed, along with a number of militiamen. Although al-Sadr's role, if any, in the latter incident is unclear, his actions in Karbala have been destabilizing. Moreover, around this same time U.S. troops had to move into Sadr City in order to force al-Sadr's men out of a government building they had seized.

Context

Al-Sadr's recent actions are part of a pattern of escalating opposition to the coalition. From the outset of the occupation, al-Sadr adopted a stance against the coalition and, after it was formed, the Governing Council. He moved rapidly into Sadr City, organizing his supporters there in the early weeks of occupation—a move that is now paying off in terms of influence and visibility. His creation of the Mahdi Army in August provided him with an overt military card, and it would be surprising if he did not command covert military forces as well (e.g., the suicide bombing of an Iraqi police station in Sadr City on October 8 cannot be positively laid at al-Sadr's feet, but his involvement is suspected). Al-Sadr also exploited the August incident in which a U.S. helicopter blew down Islamic flags on a mosque in Sadr City, using it to further establish his position in opposition to the CPA and the United States.

Until now, coalition officials have tended to downplay al-Sadr's significance, arguing that he represents only a fraction of Iraqi Shiites and that, according to polling data, the majority of Shiites are more or less satisfied with the coalition so far. Although both of these arguments are probably true, they miss the point: even with a limited following, al-Sadr poses serious problems. His supporters are disciplined, organized, energetic, and armed.

Indeed, Muqtada al-Sadr is a real presence in Iraq, in the spiritual, social, political, military, and physical sense. Spiritually, he wears his father's mantle, compensating to some extent for his own relatively minor religious stature. He uses his regular Friday sermons as a "bully pulpit" to inspire his followers and attack his enemies, and his clerical status ensures him a measure of protection from retaliation. Socially, his organization has provided needed services to Iraqis from the outset of the occupation. His political presence is evident both in terms of his well-organized cadres and his ability to rapidly muster supporters for demonstrations. His military presence is represented by the Mahdi Army and further suggested by the reports of arms stored in mosques. Finally, his physical presence is ensured by the visibility of his organization (both offices and individual supporters), the open activity of Mahdi Army, and al-Sadr's own public presence. While he is certainly not the most revered Iraqi Shiite cleric, nor the one with the largest following, he cannot be wished away.

Moreover, although al-Sadr does initiate some confrontational incidents, the coalition also provides him with numerous opportunities to exploit. The August flag incident is perhaps the best example of this, but U.S. patrols in Shiite areas of Baghdad and Karbala provide plenty of opportunity for other incidents, both spontaneous and planned. U.S. and local accounts of what happens in such incidents are usually quite different, disagreeing on both causes and results, with Iraqis tending to exaggerate events and believe the worst. As Lt. Gen. Ricardo Sanchez, the commander of the 1st Armored Division, has indicated, one of the problems for U.S. forces is an insufficient understanding of the political and social "microclimates" in which they are operating. This relative ignorance contributes to mistakes in dealing with the locals. Similarly, al-Sadr's selection of Karbala as the area in which to affirm his authority was likely intended to exploit, and test, the non-U.S. forces assigned to the area.

Implications

Muqtada al-Sadr seems bent on challenging the coalition. It is not clear how far he intends to take this challenge, but his provocations appear to be escalating, with several particularly dangerous moves going unpunished. Among the most troublesome developments are the assertiveness of his supporters, his creation of a militia, the October 9 ambush of the U.S. patrol, and his declaration of a new Iraqi government.

Already facing a significant persisting challenge from disaffected Sunnis, the coalition would hardly welcome the prospect of an emerging Shiite challenge, even if only from one segment of the Shiite community. As Gen. Sanchez stated on October 14, the coalition cannot allow any opposing political-military power in Iraq. If the coalition wants to enforce its writ, it will have to check al-Sadr's power. Al-Sadr's previous challenges have not been dealt with firmly, in part because the incidents in question have been complex and ambiguous, and also because al-Sadr has always drawn back from a full confrontation. Now, however, he seems to be edging closer to such a confrontation. Al-Sadr is capable of producing a crisis between the CPA and the Shiite community; in the event of a large-scale confrontation between al-Sadr and the coalition, Shiites would be forced to react, and some would probably opt to support him. The most immediate risk is a violent clash with a significant portion of the Shiite population. What is ultimately at stake is the coalition's ability to control the Shiite community at acceptable cost.

Jeffrey White

33
Over the Brink in Iraq: Muqtada al-Sadr Confronts the Coalition

Over the past week, Muqtada al-Sadr, a leading radical Shiite cleric in Iraq, has begun to launch direct, violent challenges to the coalition's authority. After a relatively quiet period of organization and preparation, al-Sadr and his faction have emerged as an even more dangerous factor in an already unstable security situation. His latest actions come at a difficult moment, as the coalition attempts to deal with an increasingly obdurate Sunni insurgency, a political challenge from Grand Ayatollah Ali Hussein al-Sistani (the most senior Iraqi Shiite cleric), and a general rise in political tensions before the approaching June 30 transfer of power. Coalition leaders may in fact have decided to provoke al-Sadr into an open challenge now rather than waiting for him to take action later. Yet, al-Sadr was ready, willing, and able to exploit this opportunity, inciting violent protests across much of southern Iraq and in his Baghdad stronghold.

Background

One of the great success stories in Iraq thus far has been the absence of any large-scale armed Shiite challenge. This success seemed on the verge of evaporating in October 2003, as al-Sadr's supporters became involved in a number of violent incidents with coalition forces, including a deliberate ambush of a U.S. military police element (see chapter 32, "To the Brink: Muqtada al-Sadr Challenges the United States"). In fact, al-Sadr went to the brink of armed conflict with the coalition, risking the suppression of his faction. He chose to draw back, however, and the coalition chose not to push further. These decisions postponed what was perhaps the inevitable, and the events of the past week have finally carried al-Sadr over the brink.

Al-Sadr used the period of quiet between October 2003 and the present to expand his capabilities. His Mahdi Army, which consists of some 6,000-10,000 militants, now seems better organized, better armed, and more capable. These improvements were highlighted on March 12 of this year, when al-Sadr's forces conducted a well-prepared and coordinated strike on the gypsy village of Qawliya, attacking it with mortars and infantry, occupying and razing it, and dispersing its population. Al-Sadr also expanded the nonmilitant portions of his faction, establishing new offices, religious courts, and prisons in southern Iraq.

Originally published as *PolicyWatch* no. 853, April 5, 2004.

Unlike Iraqi Sunni resistance elements, al-Sadr operates within a political framework, displaying overt leadership, an articulated organizational structure, and a unified militia force. He also has property, financial resources, and the name of his father (a prominent Shiite cleric killed by the Saddam regime in 1999) at his disposal. All of these factors make him a complex challenge that the coalition cannot take lightly.

Over the past week, al-Sadr became openly confrontational. After the coalition shut down a Sadr-linked newspaper on March 28 (see below), thousands of al-Sadr supporters took to the streets in protest. In an April 2 sermon in Kufa, al-Sadr crossed a line that he had carefully treaded since October by instructing his followers to fight "the occupiers" and to "strike them where you meet them." On April 3, the Mahdi Army marched in Baghdad and, the next day, al-Sadr's supporters initiated coordinated attacks on Iraqi police stations in that city while staging violent demonstrations in Najaf, Kufa, Nasariya, Amara, and Basra. In sum, the demonstrations resulted in 9 coalition soldiers killed (8 American and 1 Salvadoran) and 12 wounded, as well as more than 65 Iraqis dead and 250 wounded.

Context

The cause of al-Sadr's latest challenge appears to be a combination of two recent coalition-initiated events: the March 28 closing of the radical newspaper *al-Hawza* and the April 3 arrest of al-Sadr's senior aide, Mustafa al-Yaqubi, for his suspected involvement in the murder of a rival Shiite cleric in April 2003. Al-Sadr's challenge is also emerging in the context of other significant political and security developments in southern Iraq, where coalition military capabilities are limited, relative to those deployed against the Sunni resistance in central Iraq. Grand Ayatollah al-Sistani is posing a political challenge to the coalition with regard to the Transitional Administrative Law, the interim constitution recently approved by the Iraqi Governing Council. His supporters have indicated that they will use mass demonstrations to help fulfill their goals. Moreover, in addition to al-Sadr's forces, other armed Shiite factions and militias (e.g., forces associated with the Supreme Council for the Islamic Revolution in Iraq and the Islamic Dawa Party) are currently active in the south, competing for influence and position. Popular demonstrations against the coalition have already taken place in Basra and Najaf, while militants have conducted several attacks on police forces in the south and used bombs against British forces in the Basra area.

What Is to Come?

Unless the coalition takes strong action now, Muqtada al-Sadr and his faction will only become more dangerous over time. Although any such action will carry substantial risk, now may be the best time to suppress al-Sadr, while a strong U.S. military presence is in the country and with several weeks remaining before June 30. The coalition has a number of options from which to choose in confronting al-Sadr:

- Act on the warrant issued months ago by an Iraqi judge to arrest him and a number of his lieutenants in the hope of decisively weakening his faction. This approach could perhaps be combined with suppression efforts against the Mahdi Army.
- Attempt to avoid an escalation of the current conflict by seeking a truce.
- Solicit the aid of other Shiite elements in reducing the current hostilities and controlling al-Sadr's behavior.

All of these courses of action entail risk. Arresting al-Sadr or suppressing his militia would be seen as dramatic confirmation of his argument that the coalition is the enemy of Shiites. Direct action of this sort would eliminate any incentive to reduce the level of confrontation and would probably lead to sustained hostilities, including massive, violent demonstrations and armed resistance. Moreover, if given an opportunity, al-Sadr and his associates would attempt to mobilize support among other Shiite groups and leaders, al-Sadr's Sunni associates, and Iran. Specifically, they would attempt to portray a campaign against his faction as an attack on Islam and Shiites, comparing it to Saddam Hussein's brutal actions (including the killing of al-Sadr's father). Such efforts would appeal to at least some in the Shiite community. Al-Sadr would seek to adopt a strategy of long-term clandestine resistance, effectively opening a second armed front in Iraq.

If the coalition elects to avoid an escalating conflict at this time, al-Sadr and his faction would be emboldened to move even more aggressively to their political advantage. Increased defiance and risk taking would likely emerge. Moreover, other, weaker Shiite organizations would become more reluctant to oppose him, while Iraqi security forces would become more hesitant to challenge the Mahdi Army. In contrast, other powerful Shiite political organizations could well decide to move against him if the coalition chooses not to do so. Finally, al-Sadr's perceived success in confronting the coalition would likely attract adherents to his faction and recruits for his militia.

If the coalition were able to employ the aid of other Shiite political and religious elements in controlling al-Sadr, these elements would gain a distinct political advantage over other groups and would also likely feel that the coalition was in their debt. Armed action against al-Sadr by other Shiites would generate additional violence in both the south and Baghdad. In any case, controlling al-Sadr would unlikely curtail his ambitions permanently. He would continue to work toward his goals, eventually emerging again as a problem. Hence, whatever stance the coalition adopts, it will have to manage difficult challenges and unexpected consequences.

Implications

Al-Sadr's radicalism and willingness to violently oppose the coalition constitutes the first serious Shiite security challenge to the coalition. If he and his supporters are not dealt with effectively, the coalition's nightmare scenario of widespread armed Shiite resistance will become a reality. Such a development would stretch coalition military assets to the breaking point. Many of the coalition's multinational military contingents are neither prepared nor inclined to engage in the kinds of actions that U.S. forces conduct against the Sunni resistance, nor would their governments necessarily permit them to do so. Indeed, al-Sadr's response to coalition actions targeting his faction raises the specter of sustained hostilities between Shiite militants and coalition troops, along with the potential mobilization of portions of the Shiite population against the coalition. This dangerous mix of popular opposition and armed resistance has not yet been seen even in Sunni areas of Iraq.

Michael Knights

34
United States Should Choose Time, Place to Confront Radical Cleric

Since the beginning of Muqtada al-Sadr's uprising this month, the U.S. military has been uncompromising in its determination to bring the Iraqi Shiite cleric to justice. Brig. Gen. Mark Kimmitt, deputy head of U.S. military operations in Iraq, is on record as threatening, "We will hunt him down and destroy him."

More than two years into the global war on terror, "kill or capture" rolls fairly easily off the tongues of U.S. military commanders, who have used the phrase regularly with reference to Mr. al-Sadr since the uprising began. What General Kimmitt and other Coalition Provisional Authority figures might have added, however, is that Mr. al-Sadr should be dealt with—to borrow another well-worn military phrase—"at a time and place of our choosing."

If one lesson stands out from the recent flare-up of violence in the Sunni triangle and the Shiite south, it is that military force needs to be carefully calibrated and sparingly used in transitional Iraq.

It's heard often that Iraqis respected the strength of the Baathist regime, that the coalition needs to demonstrate similar resolve. But Saddam Hussein's routine use of violence against his internal opponents typically was patiently planned and precisely applied. The coalition can take this lesson from the former regime without having to adopt Baathist brutality.

Mr. al-Sadr was a security threat to the coalition before the Baathist defense of Baghdad had collapsed. His militia, the Mahdi Army, was strongly implicated in the April 10, 2003, killing of a senior Shiite cleric, prompting the coalition to issue an arrest warrant against him on charges of conspiracy to murder. Since October, when Mahdi militiamen killed two U.S. soldiers, the coalition and Mr. al-Sadr have been on a collision course.

Denied a position on the Iraq Governing Council, the cleric sought to control and tax a number of Shiite shrines and incited violence against coalition forces. After the coalition closed his newspaper, *Al-Hawza,* on March 28, Mr. al-Sadr instructed his militia to seize key areas in several southern cities, prompting the reinforcement of coalition forces in these previously quiet Shiite areas.

Originally published in the *Baltimore Sun,* April 16, 2004.

Faced by U.S. military mobilization, Mr. al-Sadr appears to have stepped back from the brink. In a situation reminiscent of the "cheat and retreat" tactics used by Mr. Hussein against the United States throughout the 1990s, Washington is caught in a dilemma: Should it pre-empt a demonstrated threat or hold fire until the threat has re-emerged?

Moving against Mr. al-Sadr could reignite the fighting and perhaps broaden it if the Americans are forced to enter the Shiite holy sites at Najaf to remove him. Capturing or killing Mr. al-Sadr would invite inevitable comparisons between the coalition and the Baathist regime, which imprisoned hundreds of Shiite clerics and killed Mr. al-Sadr's father in 1999.

But letting Mr. al-Sadr go free could strengthen him and bolster the confidence of other potential challengers. The pertinent question must now be: Does Mr. al-Sadr present such a clear and present danger that the United States is forced to move against him at a time and place of his choosing rather than that of the United States?

On all levels, the answer is no.

Mr. al-Sadr commands broad political sympathy but little actual support in Iraq's Shiite community, reducing the likelihood that he could instigate a national uprising. He is an upstart, threatening the tax revenues and challenging the status of other Shiite militias and clerics, and he has little support from other Shiite groups. His militia is neither tightly controlled nor well-trained.

Though it talked a good fight when faced by Iraqi police and coalition troops hampered by highly restrictive rules of engagement, the militia folded wherever it came into contact with determined security forces.

The coalition is now closely following its movements, limiting the potential for surprises. Mr. al-Sadr, as a coalition official told me, is a "spent force," and only the coalition can make him into a threat again, which it would do by seeking to kill or capture him at this sensitive time.

The lesson of Sunni Fallujah and the Shiite uprisings is that certain types of military operations—those that are protracted or subject to uncontrolled escalation—are highly counterproductive in Iraq, risking emblematic confrontations that can take on mythical status for Iraqi resisters. An incursion into Najaf to seize Mr. al-Sadr quickly would become just such a scenario.

Other types of military action—discrete, covert and brief—can be highly effective, and this is the type of action that the United States should reserve for Mr. al-Sadr and others like him. The young Shiite militia leader has pronounced his willingness "to sacrifice for the sake of the Iraqi people," and so he should, but only by disappearing from Iraq's political scene at a time and place of the United States' choosing.

Jeffrey White and Ryan Phillips

35
The Revolt of Muqtada al-Sadr: Characteristics and Implications

The challenge posed by Muqtada al-Sadr in the past several weeks remains unresolved, and its consequences are likely to be felt for some time to come. Al-Sadr's actions since March 28 present a complex challenge, one with both military and political implications. Eliminating al-Sadr and his organization as a political and military factor entails risk; but, if handled properly, the risks are worth taking.

Context

The clash with al-Sadr was long in development (see chapter 33, "Over the Brink in Iraq: Muqtada Al-Sadr Confronts the Coalition"). The coalition's decision to close one of al-Sadr's newspapers on March 28 precipitated a broad revolt by his followers in Baghdad and in the south. The scope of this rebellion surprised the coalition, leaving its forces and bases vulnerable to attack and isolated, thereby allowing al-Sadr to seize the military and political initiative across much of southern Iraq.

The near simultaneous outbreak of rebellion on April 4 at numerous locations in Baghdad and in the south indicates advance preparation. A combination of Mahdi Army assaults—including attacks on coalition posts and Iraqi government offices and police stations, violent demonstrations, and attacks on lines of communication—placed the coalition's southern position at risk. It also quickly became evident that a substantial portion of Iraqi security forces in the south were either actively or passively supporting al-Sadr.

Al-Sadr's supporters rapidly seized control of Kufa, Kut, Najaf, and portions of Karbala, and contested control of Nasariya, Hilla, Amara, Diwaniya, Basra, and other locations. The Mahdi Army displayed a willingness to directly engage coalition forces, despite the risk of casualties. The "high water mark" of the rebellion occurred on April 7 when Kut fell to Mahdi Army elements after the humiliating withdrawal of the Ukrainian contingent. In addition to attacking coalition footholds in urban areas, al-Sadr's supporters also began to seize foreign hostages and interdict the long coalition supply line from Kuwait to Baghdad.

Originally published as *PolicyWatch* no. 858, April 16, 2004. Ryan Phillips is a research assistant at The Washington Institute.

Military Challenge

The actions by the Mahdi Army and other armed supporters of al-Sadr represented a broad and decentralized threat to the coalition; indeed, the numerous attacks across a wide area served to confuse and dislocate any concerted coalition response. Coalition forces were put on the defensive in many locations, having to concentrate on holding their positions rather than regaining the initiative.

Still, despite substantial early successes, not everything went al-Sadr's way. Although some Shiites rallied to his cause, the majority did not. In part, this was due to al-Sadr's unpopularity in many areas and to the fact that no senior Shiite leadership figure overtly supported the revolt. Tribal leaders in the south urged calm and exercised a restraining hand, limiting the scope of the rebellion. Al-Sadr's forces also proved unwilling or unable to stand against determined and aggressive coalition military action. Where coalition forces stood and fought, they held. Where they acted aggressively, as the Italians did in Nasariya, al-Sadr lost, and lost heavily.

Coalition Response

From April 4 to April 7, al-Sadr held the initiative. In response, the coalition retook Iraqi police and government facilities in Baghdad, deployed U.S. combat elements from elsewhere into Iraq, reoccupied Kut (on April 9) against light resistance, and held on elsewhere. By April 9, U.S. forces had begun to concentrate on the outskirts of Najaf, awaiting a decision to clear the city of al-Sadr elements. By April 14, al-Sadr was speaking of a negotiated settlement, rather than repeating his previous declaration to fight to the death.

Other Shiite Actors

In addition to al-Sadr's supporters, other Shiite elements played, or could have played, a role in the course of the insurrection. Grand Ayatollah Ali Hussein al-Sistani played a cautious but essentially quieting part, attempting to calm the situation without openly supporting either the coalition or al-Sadr. This basically worked to the coalition's advantage by discouraging mass mobilization of the Shiite to al-Sadr's cause. The Supreme Council for Islamic Revolution in Iraq and the Islamic Dawa Party both played a limited role in discussions aimed at ending the U.S. standoff with al-Sadr. Overtly, the Iranians sent an envoy to Najaf in an attempt to diffuse the crisis, although their covert involvement remains unclear. All of these groups reacted cautiously to the situation, wanting neither to oppose al-Sadr directly, nor to express overt opposition to the coalition; they could afford to see how the situation developed before taking action.

Implications

The revolt of Muqtada al-Sadr will be a watershed event in the postwar history of Iraq. For the first time, the coalition faced organized and armed opposition from the Shiites. Even if al-Sadr's forces are brought under control, there are significant military implications:

- The limited, but not insignificant, ability of al-Sadr's militia to stand and fight against aggressive coalition forces, and their capability to inflict losses and damage on those forces.
- The ability of the militia to spontaneously draw strength in numbers from local Shiite populations. For example, some Shiites in Baghdad not normally supportive of al-Sadr proclaimed, "We are all Mahdi Army."
- The militia's ability to attack in many places simultaneously while combining different kinds of actions: indirect fire, assault, ambushes, and violent demonstrations.
- The exposure of coalition vulnerabilities, including uneven performances by some coalition military elements, long and vulnerable lines of communication from Kuwait to Baghdad, and the isolation of some coalition administrative and military elements.
- The unwarranted reliance on the new Iraqi Police Service (IPS), even for intelligence. IPS units appear to have either stood aside or joined al-Sadr's supporters. But the revolt is as much political as it is military.
- Al-Sadr's political organization is central to his strength and remains particularly active in Baghdad and the south. It operates comfortably on the violent edge of politics—murdering, intimidating, and suborning to achieve its objectives. Even in the unlikely event that al-Sadr actually disbands the militia, his political organization will remain intact.
- If al-Sistani and other clerics prove successful in resolving the crisis with al-Sadr, the coalition will pay a price. The power and prestige of these clerics will be enhanced relative to the Coalition Provisional Authority (CPA), and al-Sistani's role as the arbiter of Shiite politics will be confirmed. He is likely to feel that his influence has been enhanced by this role and will become even more difficult for the coalition to deal with.
- The revolt has demonstrated to the Shiites, and to the CPA, that force is an option if negotiations do not meet Shiite political objectives. Many Shiites—both organizations and individuals—stood on the sidelines in this crisis, but they could hardly fail to notice the difficulty the coalition had in meeting al-Sadr's challenge.

Prospects

Al-Sadr's revolt may well be settled "peacefully," through the intervention of al-Sistani and others. Such a scenario would represent a defeat for the coalition. Success for the coalition will only come, even if over time, through al-Sadr's elimination as a political and military factor in the Iraqi equation. There are various ways this could be accomplished, beyond the outright physical destruction of his faction, but political compromises and half measures will simply allow him to regroup and fight again another day.

Even if the coalition eliminates the al-Sadr factor, residual insecurity is likely to plague areas in the south. Remnants of al-Sadr's militia and organization would probably go underground and transition to armed resistance, targeting both coalition elements and Iraqis working with the coalition. Restoring the situation to its pre-March 28 state—or anything similar to it—will require a long-term effort.

Jeffrey White and Ryan Phillips

36
Muqtada al-Sadr's Continuing Challenge to the Coalition (Part I): The U.S. Military Response

Muqtada al-Sadr represents a serious long-term political and military challenge to the coalition and the new Iraqi government. Open warfare between al-Sadr and the coalition first emerged on April 4, 2004, with "uprisings" by his militia, the Mahdi Army, in Baghdad and across southern Iraq. Although al-Sadr has not achieved his objective of a broad-based Shiite rebellion, coalition forces have not been able to bring him to justice or dissolve his militia. Both sides are now playing a high-stakes game. The coalition is betting that it can eliminate or reduce al-Sadr as a political force without causing a serious breach with the larger Shiite community. Al-Sadr is gambling that he can persist, even prosper, in the face of the coalition. Indeed, he has long-term political goals and is positioning himself for the upcoming elections. The prospects that the coalition can bring him under control at acceptable cost and risk remain uncertain.

The Initial Revolt

Al-Sadr's April 4 uprising consisted of simultaneous small revolts in Baghdad and across southern Iraq. The seriousness of these actions varied from place to place, and coalition forces largely contained the revolt by mid-April. Nevertheless, the Mahdi Army remained entrenched in a number of critical areas, including Najaf, Kufa, Karbala, and Baghdad's Sadr City. Al-Sadr's cadres also remained active, if not in control, in other locations throughout southern Iraq.

When the rebellion broke out, the coalition moved almost immediately to improve its military posture in the south, deploying major combat elements from the experienced 1st Armored Division and 2nd Armored Cavalry Regiment. These forces gave the coalition an offensive capability that it had heretofore lacked in southern Iraq.

Politically, both sides sought an advantage in the confrontation by appealing to other Iraqi elements. The coalition looked to mainstream Shiite politicians, clerics, and tribal leaders to help bring al-Sadr and his militia under control. Al-Sadr directed his appeals to the broader Iraqi population (including Sunnis) and to Shiites in other countries. In any case, no Shiite political or militia element seemed willing to confront al-Sadr directly.

Originally published as *PolicyWatch* no. 873, June 7, 2004. Ryan Phillips is a research assistant at The Washington Institute.

The Coalition's Response

During the first two weeks following the containment of al-Sadr's initial revolt in mid-April, the coalition appeared to have developed a relatively effective but cautious approach to dealing with al-Sadr, at least from a military perspective. Recovering from the surprise and early setbacks of the initial phase of the revolt, the coalition initiated a campaign to isolate al-Sadr politically and neutralize his military power. Accordingly, U.S. forces launched offensive operations on April 26 intended to suppress and destroy his militia and remove its leadership, allowing the mainstream Shiite community to rein him in with a political solution. Maj. Gen. Martin Dempsey, commander of the 1st Armored Division, characterized the military component of this approach in a May 11 interview: "Essentially we want to eliminate Muqtada Sadr's ability to intimidate."

The coalition's military and political operations against al-Sadr have been mutually supporting. Reductions in his military capability have made him less of a threat to other Shiite political and religious elements. At the same time, these elements have exhibited increased opposition to al-Sadr, reducing his ability to mobilize support (especially armed support) among the broader Shiite and Iraqi communities. In general, the coalition's political efforts have consisted of two major elements:

- Winning over Shiite elements that have a stake in bringing order and security to southern Iraq. Efforts along this line appear to have spurred increased cooperation with tribal leaders.
- Encouraging moderate Shiite religious and political figures to limit al-Sadr's influence and press him to comply with coalition demands. At the same time, the coalition has avoided direct negotiations with al-Sadr himself.

The coalition has applied inducements along with military pressure in order to encourage religious and tribal support. Although the overt backing of mainstream Shiite leaders was not deemed absolutely necessary, mainstream Shiite clerics have reportedly been supportive of military action as long as the coalition does not attack shrines. This support has given U.S. forces significant freedom of action in the south that could not have been anticipated when the revolt first began in early April (e.g., to conduct operations even up to the very walls of shrines).

Military Measures

The U.S. military campaign against al-Sadr has thus far been waged with clear objectives, with forces that are highly experienced in the Iraqi insurgency milieu, and with a mixture of appropriate tactics. The objectives of this military action are to reduce or destroy militia elements and to dissolve al-Sadr's organization by demolishing its offices and removing its leaders. The coalition has also attempted to reinsert Iraqi security services into areas freed from al-Sadr's control. Key to the success of U.S. operations has been the deployment of appropriate personnel—namely, elements of the 1st Armored Division. This unit, which had already acquired a year's experience in the difficult urban security environment of Baghdad, including numerous brushes with al-Sadr militants in Sadr City, has been able to take the offensive in southern Iraq without inflicting large numbers of civilian casualties or putting key religious sites at unnecessary risk. The tactics employed by this division are varied and appropriate to its objectives. They include the following:

- A "war of posts" featuring the seizure of key positions in and around cities or areas held by the Mahdi Army, as well as the destruction of offices manned by al-Sadr's cadres. Actions of this sort have served to isolate Mahdi militia elements, reduce their hold on symbolically important facilities (e.g., government offices, police stations), and impede their freedom of action and movement.
- Precise small-unit actions based on specific intelligence and employing precision weapons, including airborne systems in close proximity to sensitive sites. Actions of this sort have been used to destroy militia elements, seize key terrain, and arrest leaders. They often involve devastating, though accurate, firepower at the point of attack, resulting in severe casualties for al-Sadr's forces.
- Mini "thunder runs" with heavy combat vehicles, intended to overawe the resistance and the population while drawing out militia forces in order to engage them.
- Aggressive patrolling intended to highlight the coalition's presence and draw out militia forces.

According to a senior source in Iraq, these relatively cautious tactics have upset senior Shiite clerics who were looking for the coalition to act more aggressively against al-Sadr's forces. Although coalition forces have killed many of al-Sadr's fighters (reportedly as many as 1,500 since the beginning of the revolt) and caused a great deal of localized destruction, military action has been employed in a precise, carefully orchestrated, even cautious way. This approach has helped the coalition avoid some potentially disastrous missteps (although the potential for such missteps will persist whenever military operations are underway).

Al-Sadr's Response

The campaign against al-Sadr has yet to run its course, and claims that his militia has been defeated are probably premature. Muqtada al-Sadr is not just a passive recipient of coalition blows. He is an adaptive opponent who is actively seeking to avoid complete military defeat while enhancing his political position.

Jeffrey White and Ryan Phillips

37
Muqtada al-Sadr's Continuing Challenge to the Coalition (Part II): An Adaptive Enemy

During late May and early June 2004, Muqtada al-Sadr's revolt was challenged by continuing coalition military action and mounting Shiite political and religious pressure. His militia was increasingly on the defensive, clinging tightly to defensive positions near key holy sites and disappearing from the streets whenever coalition military operations became too overwhelming. In response, al-Sadr initiated a combination of political and militant actions designed to deflect political pressure, expand his influence, and impede coalition military progress against his forces.

Political Warfare

Al-Sadr has played his hand rather well considering that his chances of military victory declined dramatically once the coalition began to deploy significant combat forces against him. As recently as late May, he remained politically active and still had a hold on Najaf and Kufa. Shiite politicians and religious figures were approaching him for negotiations, his personal popularity was rising, and his militia was far from defeated. He had also secured key support from tribal elements in southern Iraq, according to a senior source in Baghdad. Meanwhile, the threat of a wider Shiite rebellion continued to act as a restraint on coalition military action, and the strength of his militia both imposed caution on those Shiites opposed to him and insured that military action against him would be protracted.

In early June, however, al-Sadr's military situation—and, to some degree, his political standing—deteriorated. Although not prepared to challenge him openly, powerful Shiite religious and tribal forces were willing to limit his influence and apply pressure in order to constrain his actions. Perhaps most important, senior Shiite clerics reportedly pushed for aggressive coalition operations against the Mahdi Army up to the very boundaries of holy sites. Moreover, the increased offensive combat power available to the coalition after mid-April (in particular, the deployment of the U.S. 1st Armored Division to the south) tilted the military balance sharply against the Mahdi Army.

Originally published as *PolicyWatch* no. 874, June 7, 2004. Ryan Phillips is a research assistant at The Washington Institute.

In this context, al-Sadr has employed two key political tactics to frustrate the coalition and his political enemies. First, he has attempted to exploit the desires of certain mainstream Shiite political, religious, and tribal figures to achieve a negotiated settlement. In doing so, he hoped to escape coalition demands that his militia be dismantled and that he face Iraqi justice. These Shiite leaders were primarily interested in limiting the fighting as it approached key holy sites in Karbala and Najaf and wreaked havoc on the economy of southern Iraq. Many probably also fear al-Sadr's growing personal popularity; according to certain polls, he is the second most popular man in Iraq after Grand Ayatollah Ali Hussein al-Sistani (the most senior Iraqi Shiite cleric), making him a direct challenger to more senior Shiite clerics. Accordingly, al-Sadr has reportedly used as many as eleven different conduits in his efforts to open political talks with the coalition and others. He has also employed a well-conceived and responsive "information operations" campaign to spread his message across the Shiite community and the rest of Iraq. Moreover, the so-called ceasefire of May 27 was consistent with this tactical approach, as was his more recent "withdrawal" from the streets of Najaf and Kufa. From the beginning, al-Sadr has sought to avoid a decisive defeat by the coalition and to avoid firm agreements that would hold him accountable for what is done in his name. He has proposed or agreed to ceasefires and withdrawals only during moments of acute pressure from coalition forces or rising Shiite concerns about the risks to holy sites in Najaf.

Second, al-Sadr has used threats and bluffs in an effort to appear more formidable than his actual capabilities indicate he is. For example, he has threatened to unleash suicide bombers and to ignite violent resistance if coalition forces approach holy sites. Dressing in the robes of martyrdom and using his Friday sermons to disseminate anticoalition vitriol, al-Sadr has engaged in a sort of "theater of resistance" in order to buttress his supporters and deter his enemies. His most serious threat was to mobilize the Shiite community and Iraqis in general against the coalition. From the beginning of his revolt on April 4, he attempted to elicit active support from Iraqi Shiites, but with only limited success. Al-Sadr also appealed to the Iraqi Sunni community, again with limited success, and to Shiite communities in Iran and Lebanon. His attempt to reenergize his revolt in mid-May with mini-uprisings in Baghdad, Nasariya, and Amara failed to spread as well.

Irregular Warfare

Al-Sadr has not limited his actions to the political realm. The Mahdi Army has proven willing to stand and fight coalition forces, even at the risk of appalling loses, and to take the initiative whenever circumstances offer some prospect for success. The militia's irregular warfare has displayed five broad characteristics:

- Use of opportunistic attacks on exposed coalition elements, including ambushes of convoys and patrols, improvised explosive devices, and harassing fire against coalition and Iraqi government facilities.

- A geographically widespread "rebellion," with Mahdi Army elements fighting in many locations in the south, including Najaf, Kufa, Karbala, Nasariya, Amara, Kut, Basra, Samawa, and Diwaniya.
- The launch of mini-uprisings in Baghdad's Sadr City and other locations in the south in response to increasing coalition military pressure.
- A willingness to exploit Shiite shrines as cover from coalition attack.
- A tendency to disappear in the face of overwhelming coalition military pressure.

Because of their willingness to stand and fight, Mahdi Army elements have earned the grudging respect of U.S. forces engaged against them. Given that the militia is less than a year old, this tenacity suggests some type of outside assistance, probably from former Baath regime military personnel (including Sunnis, who reportedly have a considerable presence in the Mahdi Army).

Potential Outcomes of the Revolt

Neither the temporary, one-sided ceasefire of May 27 nor the Mahdi Army's withdrawal from the streets of Najaf and Kufa represent the end of his challenge to the coalition. In fact, al-Sadr surrendered little in exchange for a reduction of coalition military pressure against him. If fighting had continued at its previous level, his forces would have faced piecemeal destruction. In the current context, it has yet to be demonstrated that mainstream Shiite elements can bring him under control, much less hold him accountable for his criminal activity or dismantle his militia. The new Iraqi government's pledge that al-Sadr will be dealt with by the Iraqi justice system does not indicate that his movement will be dissolved anytime soon. Claims that his militia has been defeated across the south are also likely premature.

One potential outcome is that the coalition will eventually be able to contain al-Sadr without eliminating him as a serious political factor. For example, al-Sadr could reach a political arrangement whereby he simply takes his militia off the streets and curbs his rhetoric. Subsequently, he could remain politically active, with his organization largely intact and his militia awaiting orders to reemerge. This outcome seems quite likely under the current circumstances.

Another potential outcome is that al-Sadr will be enhanced as a political force, making him still more difficult to deal with in the future. According to one poll, nearly 68 percent of Iraqis supported him in May 2004, compared to only 1 percent in December 2003. Al-Sadr may be able to exploit this popularity as the political process unfolds.

Unfortunately, one near certain outcome will be some level of continuing violence in the south and in areas of Baghdad where al-Sadr has strong support. The coalition also faces the prospect of additional mini-uprisings, and a full-blown Shiite revolt remains a possibility under certain circumstances.

There appear to be at least two positive outcomes from the latest phase of the revolt, however. First, the coalition may have found a path toward winning the cooperation of mainstream Shiites instead of alienating them. Coalition military operations have benefited certain Shiite political and religious elements and encouraged them to rein in al-Sadr, showing that Shiites and the coalition can work together for mutual advantage. Second, the coalition appears to have learned a great deal about fighting in the complex religious and political environments of southern Iraq's urban areas—a lesson that has come none too soon.

Patrick Clawson

38
Security and Politics

The current fighting in Iraq was almost inevitable. The new political process we are putting in place is based on elections, and those who know that they are going to lose them have every reason to disrupt that process. The Sunni radicals and the Shiite rebel leader Moqtada al-Sadr realize that their only hope of achieving power is by resorting to force. It is hardly surprising that they are cooperating with each other, since a combined effort gives them their best shot at prevailing in a test of arms.

The more troubling confrontation is with al-Sadr, the 30-year-old son of the late, respected Grand Ayatollah Sayyid Muhammad Baqr al-Sadr. His followers are fanatical but few in number. Stymied politically, al-Sadr has built up his militia, the Jaysh al-Mahdi, or the Mahdi army. They are little more than thugs. In March, the Mahdi army drove out all the residents of Qawliya—a village rumored to be a red-light district—and used a bulldozer to knock down their homes. Another tactic of theirs is to throw acid in the faces of scarf-less women and to threaten those who open women's centers.

Sadr's group is hardly the only militia in Iraq. Many of the tribal leaders, religious figures, and local politicians maneuvering for power in the new civil structures have also been actively recruiting armed groups of supporters. Believing that force equals power and order, too many otherwise democratically minded Iraqis are tempted by totalitarianism. The problem we face was captured well in a recent Oxford Research International poll: Asked what Iraq needs at this time, 86 percent said "an Iraqi democracy," but 81 percent said "a single strong Iraqi leader."

Faced with the militia issue, the Governing Council inserted into the March interim constitution the provision, "Armed forces and militias not under the command structure of the Iraqi Transitional Government are prohibited except as provided by federal law." That did not go far enough for some. The *Washington Post* editors complained, "No plan has been announced . . . to disarm and dismantle" the militias. It thundered, "Only the United States has the means to force this vital step, and its time is running out."

So, it should have been obvious that in order to "disarm and dismantle" the Mahdi army, we would necessarily have to confront al-Sadr, as there was no way his forces could be co-opted into the new security services.

After threatening al-Sadr for weeks, the United States picked a fight with him. On March 28, in what al-Sadr's followers took as a provocation, we closed his newspaper.

Originally published in the *National Review*, May 3, 2004.

Then, when he reacted at Friday prayers the usual way—with incendiary rhetoric and some peaceful protests—we arrested his deputy, Mustafa al-Yaqubi. Not surprisingly, al-Sadr assumed this was the start of the confrontation we had long threatened, and so he reacted by pulling out all the stops. That is when the rebellion started.

One can make many arguments about whether it was a good idea to pick this fight now with al-Sadr. Maybe it would have been better to tolerate the Mahdi army so long as they confined itself to social issues. On the other hand, if a fight was inevitable, this is not a bad time to have it. Now, unlike after June 30, when Washington is scheduled to transfer power over to the Iraqis, we can at least control the process, and moreover, U.S. forces are at a peak.

But what is alarming is that it appears we were not ready for a clash: U.S. forces were not positioned to protect government installations; they showed little strength in the cities where al-Sadr has influence; and Iraqi security services were ill prepared to deal with the fighting.

We evidently assumed al-Sadr would simply fold when faced with our actions. U.S. Iraq policy has been characterized by extraordinary self-confidence, which served us well during the major combat operations but has been more of a problem since. In particular, we have not always paid as much attention as we should to what others may do to frustrate our plans. Before we take a hard line against a radical like al-Sadr, we should weigh carefully what he can do to us. For all the problems he has caused, we should try to find ways to draw him and his followers back into the political process.

We also need to bear in mind that the institutions of the new Iraq are weak and fragile. Yes, it is disappointing that the Iraqi security services have contributed little to the coalition effort, but on the whole, it would be inappropriate to ask them to do so. The largest components of those services are policemen and facilities guards, who are neither trained nor equipped to deal with combat.

We should not ask the new Iraqi security services to perform politically risky tasks, because they are of little use to us unless they enjoy public support. So far, the news on this front is good. The Oxford Research International poll showed 68 percent of people expressing confidence in the new police. In a similar vein, in the aftermath of a February attack on a police station in Fallujah, clerics representing more than 500 mosques in Anbar province—the heart of the Sunni rebellion, including Fallujah and Ramadi—signed a fatwa that may have been pointedly silent about attacks on Americans, but which stated firmly, "We condemn any act of violence against Iraqi state government workers, police, and soldiers, because it is aggression under Islamic law."

The strength of public support for the new Iraqi institutions is only part of the good news emerging from Iraq. Perhaps the most convincing evidence is that in the last year, more than a million refugees have returned to Iraq, despite being told not to by the U.N. High Commissioner for Refugees. And despite the constant complaining—a characteristic feature of Iraqi life—57 percent of Iraqis told Oxford Research International that their life is better now than before the war, compared with 19 percent who say it is worse and 23 percent who say it is about the same.

Still, all this progress will melt away if the security situation continues to deteriorate. The key to restoring security is to get the politics right. The Marines like to say, "You have no worse enemy and no better friend than a Marine." Today's task, when confronted with militiamen fighting us in Iraq, is to be that worst enemy, but we must be ready in the near future to make the transition to becoming the best friend of those who lay down their arms, no matter how much they criticize us.

Jeffrey White and Ryan Phillips

39
Sadrist Revolt Provides Lessons for Counterinsurgency in Iraq

The first serious challenge to Coalition forces in Iraq from Shi'ite elements began on 4 April 2004. Moqtada al-Sadr's organisation and its militia, the Mahdi Army, initiated demonstrations and attacks on Coalition forces and facilities in Baghdad's Sadr City and across southern Iraq.

Coinciding with the siege of Falluja and increased activity by Sunni resistance elements, US fears of a two-front insurgency materialised as al-Sadr's revolt posed a serious political and military challenge to the Coalition. At a tactical level, Coalition commanders had to defend threatened positions, respond to threats to the main supply routes through the south, and redeploy US forces from as far north as Mosul, to contain the challenge. At the strategic level, the Coalition faced the test of suppressing the rebellion without causing a serious breach with the Shi'ite community, or letting al-Sadr's political influence and military power expand dramatically. In particular, the Coalition had to weigh carefully the role of Grand Ayatollah Ali al-Sistani, the effective arbiter of Shi'ite politics and an uncertain ally, in any attempt to control al-Sadr. Without at least the tacit support of the Shi'ite community and al-Sistani there was, and there remains, no chance for the Coalition and the new Iraqi government to succeed.

Under the combined influence of Coalition military action and mainstream Shi'ite political pressure, al-Sadr has swung to a less confrontational stance, emphasising political co-operation and a reduced military profile. In doing so he has given up little, while working to convert the increased popularity he achieved as the leader of the revolt into political advantage. His militia and organisation, while damaged in the course of the revolt, are largely intact and will support whatever course he ultimately decides upon.

Background to the Revolt

The al-Sadr revolt appeared to break out suddenly, but in fact it had been long in the making. Almost immediately after the fall of Saddam Hussein's regime, al-Sadr, the son of revered Shi'ite cleric and victim of the regime, Mohammed Sadiq al-Sadr, emerged to challenge the occupation. By the summer of 2003, al-Sadr's organisation was politically active in Baghdad's Sadr City, Najaf, Basra, and elsewhere in southern Iraq.

Originally published in *Jane's Intelligence Review*, August 2004. Reprinted with permission from Jane's Information Group/*Jane's Intelligence Review*. Ryan Phillips is a research assistant at The Washington Institute.

In August 2003, al-Sadr's adherents clashed with US troops for the first time in Baghdad, and he announced the formation of the Mahdi Army, a militia ostensibly tasked with the mission of protecting Shi'ite religious shrines. In reality, the militia was formed to add a capacity for armed violence to al-Sadr's organisation. By late 2003, al-Sadr was in a position to begin challenging Coalition forces directly. In October 2003, armed al-Sadr elements clashed with US forces in Baghdad in what was described by US commanders as a deliberate ambush. In this incident, two soldiers of the US 1st Armored Division were killed and four wounded. Later that month, three US soldiers were killed in a clash probably involving Sadrist elements in Karbala. At this point the Coalition was, according to senior military officials, close to arresting al-Sadr, but deferred a decision because of appeals from Shi'ite political figures to let the community deal with al-Sadr in its own way.

Between October 2003 and March 2004, a surface quiet prevailed with no major clashes between al-Sadr and the Coalition. Al-Sadr's group used this period to organise, expand its reach, and develop the military capabilities of the Mahdi Army. On 12 March 2004, Mahdi Army elements razed Qawliya, a gypsy village near Diwaniyah in southern Iraq. In this action the Mahdi Army demonstrated a substantial increase in military proficiency. Witnesses described an infantry-style operation, supported by mortars, to drive the population out, followed by the systematic demolition of houses in the village with bulldozers.

The razing of the village was seen by Coalition officials as a direct challenge, and by late March the Coalition appeared to have decided to move against al-Sadr. On 28 March, *Al Hawza,* one of his newspapers, was closed for inciting violence. On 3 April, Mustapha al-Yacoubi, a key al-Sadr lieutenant, was arrested in Najaf. These actions, whether intended to provoke a major confrontation with al-Sadr or not, directly precipitated the 4 April rebellion.

The Sadrist Rebellion

Al-Sadr's organisation responded vigorously to the moves by the Coalition. The scope of his rebellion came as a surprise, allowing al-Sadr to seize the military and political initiative across much of southern Iraq.

The near simultaneous outbreak of the rebellion on 4 April in Baghdad and numerous places in the south indicated advance preparation. A combination of Mahdi Army assaults on Coalition posts, Iraqi government offices and police stations, violent demonstrations, and attacks on lines of communication placed the Coalition position in the south at risk. It also quickly became evident that a substantial portion of Iraqi security forces in the south were either actively or passively supporting al-Sadr, or were simply not up to the task of dealing with the Mahdi Army. Al-Sadr's supporters rapidly seized control of Kufa, Kut, portions of Najaf and Karbala, and contested control of key points in Nasiriyah, Hilla, Al-Amarah, Diwaniyah, Basra, and other locations.

The Mahdi Army displayed a willingness to directly engage Coalition forces, despite the risk of casualties. The 'high-water mark' of the rebellion occurred on 7 April when Kut fell to Mahdi Army elements after the withdrawal of the Ukrainian contingent. In addition to attacking Coalition footholds in urban areas, al-Sadr's supporters also began to harass the long Coalition supply line from Kuwait to Baghdad, seizing foreign hostages.

A Decentralised Threat

The actions by the Mahdi Army and other armed supporters of al-Sadr represented a broad and decentralised threat to the Coalition. The numerous attacks across a wide area served to confuse and dislocate any concerted response. Coalition forces were put on the defensive in some locations, trying to hold their positions rather than taking the offensive to regain the initiative.

Despite substantial early successes, not everything went al-Sadr's way. Although some sections of the Shi'ite community rallied to his cause, the majority did not. In part this was due to the unpopularity of his organisation in many areas, and to the fact that no senior Shi'ite leadership figure overtly supported him. Al-Sistani initially adopted a very cautious public position, neither supporting nor condemning either side in the confrontation, while watching carefully which direction the Shi'ite community was moving. Although al-Sadr was supported by some tribal elements, others urged calm and exercised a restraining hand, helping to limit the scope of the rebellion.

Al-Sadr's forces also proved unable to withstand determined and aggressive Coalition military action. Where Coalition forces stood and fought, they held. Where they acted aggressively, as the Italians did early in Nasiriyah, al-Sadr's militia lost, and lost heavily, or, in a pattern that was to become established over the course of the rebellion, simply disappeared.

From 4 April to 7 April, al-Sadr held the initiative. In response, the Coalition began to re-take Iraqi police and government facilities in Baghdad; deployed US combat elements from as far north as Mosul; reoccupied Kut with elements of the US 1st Armored Division on 9 April; and at least held on elsewhere. By 9 April US forces began concentrating on the outskirts of Najaf, awaiting a decision to clear the city of Mahdi Army elements. For his part, on 13 April al-Sadr began speaking of a negotiated settlement while continuing armed action; employing a political tactic that was to become standard.

The seriousness of the rebellion varied from place to place, but by mid-April Coalition forces had contained the revolt. The Mahdi Army remained entrenched at a number of critical points, including Najaf, Kufa, Karbala and Sadr City. In addition, al-Sadr's forces and organisation remained active, if not in control, in other locations in the south. The Mahdi Army, while taking substantial casualties, was able to remain in the field against the Coalition—reinforcing, digging in and re-supplying. Sadr's forces were contained and pushed back, but not suppressed.

The Coalition moved to improve its military posture in the south, particularly with the deployment of major combat elements of the experienced US 1st Armored Division and 2nd Armored Cavalry Regiment to stabilise or restore precarious situations at Kut, Karbala, Najaf and Kufa. The 3rd Brigade of the 1st Infantry Division also repositioned elements to the south. The arrival of these forces south of Baghdad gave the Coalition an offensive capability that it had heretofore lacked, with the 1st Armored Division playing the leading role in operations against the Sadr strongholds in Najaf, Kufa, and Karbala.

Politically, both sides sought advantage by appealing to other Iraqi elements. The Coalition looked to the involvement of mainstream Shi'ite clerics, politicians and tribal leaders to bring al-Sadr under control and draw the teeth of his militia. Al-Sadr appealed more broadly to the Iraqi population, including Sunnis, and to Shi'ites in other countries, especially Hizbullah in Lebanon, for support. For many Iraqi Shi'ites, and even some Sunnis, al-Sadr has the clearest message of opposition to the Coalition and occupation. No Shi'ite political or associated militia element was willing to confront al-Sadr directly. The relative weaknesses of both the Badr Brigades and the Dawa militia were exposed by their passivity in the face of the revolt. By late April the situation was essentially a stand-off, one which could not last.

While al-Sadr's objective of a broad-based Shi'ite rebellion had not been accomplished, Coalition forces had not been able to achieve their declared objectives of bringing him to justice and dismantling or destroying his militia. A new phase of the confrontation began on approximately 26/27 April, with Coalition forces launching a deliberate offensive against al-Sadr's organisation and militia. This offensive, undertaken with support from mainstream Shi'ite political, religious and tribal establishments, ground down al-Sadr's military capabilities and weakened the leadership cadre of his organisation. It is less clear that it has critically damaged his personal political strength and the long-term prospects for controlling him at acceptable cost and risk remain uncertain.

Coalition Strategy

In the period between containing al-Sadr's revolt in mid-April and the end of April, the Coalition appears to have developed a relatively effective, yet cautious, approach to dealing with al-Sadr, at least from a military perspective. Recovering from the surprise and early setbacks of the initial phase of the revolt, the Coalition acted to isolate him and neutralise his political and military power. This approach was based on recognition of the complex phenomenon al-Sadr embodies, including his strengths and weaknesses, and depended on combined political and military operations in the Shi'ite 'theatre'.

Coalition forces were to suppress and break up al-Sadr's militia and remove its leadership cadre, thereby providing the opportunity to wrap al-Sadr in a political solution supported and implemented by the mainstream Shi'ite community. Major General Martin Dempsey, the commander of the US 1st Armored Division, pointed to the military component of this approach in a 11 May interview, stating: "... essentially we want to eliminate [Moqtada] al-Sadr's ability to intimidate."

Coalition political and military operations against al-Sadr have been mutually supporting in that the reduction of his military capability makes him less of a threat to other Shi'ite political and religious elements. The increasing opposition of these elements to him reduces his ability to mobilise active support, especially armed support, from the broader Shi'ite and Iraqi communities. The Coalition's success, in conjunction with the mainstream Shi'ite community, in isolating al-Sadr's resistance stands in marked contrast to the situation in Falluja. The political operation against al-Sadr has had two major elements:

- Winning over Shi'ite elements with a stake in order and security in the south. This appears to have led to increased co-operation with tribal leadership, an emerging hallmark of the US military approach to establishing security in Iraq. Maj Gen Dempsey has referred to these people as "stakeholders".
- Encouraging moderate Shi'ite religious and political figures to limit al-Sadr's influence and press him to comply with Coalition demands.

The Coalition has applied inducements along with military pressure in order to promote religious and tribal support. Although the overt backing of mainstream Shi'ite leaders was not deemed absolutely necessary, mainstream Shi'ite clerics have reportedly been supportive of military action as long as the Coalition does not attack shrines. This combination gave US forces a degree of freedom of action in the south, including to the very walls of holy sites, that could not have been anticipated when the crisis in the south began in early April.

Military action has powered the Coalition's approach to dealing with al-Sadr. Importantly, while reportedly as many as 1,500 militia men have been killed since the beginning of the revolt, alongside localised destruction, military force has been employed in a precise, even cautious and carefully orchestrated way, avoiding potentially disastrous false steps.

Unlike Falluja, US forces operating against al-Sadr had clear objectives, used forces highly experienced in the Iraqi insurgency milieu, and employed a mix of appropriate tactics. The objectives of military action were to destroy or attrite militia elements and break up al-Sadr's organisation by physically demolishing its offices and removing its leaders while reinserting Iraqi security services into areas freed from al-Sadr's control.

US 1st Armored Division Tactics

A key to the success of US operations has been the employment of the right force. The US 1st Armored Division, with a year's experience in the difficult urban security environment in Baghdad, including numerous brushes with al-Sadr's supporters, and operating in the political and social warren of Sadr City, was able to take the offensive in the south without creating an irreparable breach with the Shi'ite population through inflicting large numbers of civilian casualties or putting key religious sites at unnecessary risk.

Tactics employed by the 1st Armored Division were varied and appropriate to its objectives:

- A 'war of posts' featuring the seizing and sometimes holding of key positions in and around cities or areas held by the Mahdi Army, as well as the destruction of Sadrist offices. These actions served to isolate and break up militia elements, reduce their hold on symbolically important facilities such as government offices and police stations, and reduce their freedom of action, including their ability to move forces from place to place.

- Precise small-unit actions based on intelligence and precision weapons, including the use of airborne systems in close proximity to sensitive sites, to destroy militia elements, seize key terrain and arrest leaders. While accurate, these actions employed devastating firepower at the point of attack, resulting in local destruction and severe casualties for the militia. Militia members killed in action have numbered in the tens of hundreds, in contrast to the relatively limited, although not trivial, Coalition deaths in action.
- Aggressive patrolling and mini 'thunder runs' with heavy combat vehicles to highlight the Coalition's presence, overawe the resistance and the population, and to draw militia forces out so they could be engaged.

According to a senior Coalition source in Iraq, these cautious tactics actually upset Shi'ite clerics who were looking for US forces to act more aggressively to destroy al-Sadr's militia. While offensive operations were largely a US show, British forces acted to eliminate militia elements that had seized government offices in the Multinational Division Southeast area of operations, and Italian forces fought to clear the main supply routes through Nasiriyah, and to destroy al-Sadr's offices there.

Al-Sadr's revolt posed a serious challenge to the Coalition, and almost any course of action aimed at suppressing it entailed risk. US forces faced substantial difficulties in fighting irregulars in urban environments and in developing and exploiting a clear understanding of the situation. The most obvious hazard faced by the Coalition was that, through accident, miscalculation, provocation, or a combination of these, Coalition forces would do something that resulted in an incident serious enough to mobilise widespread active support for al-Sadr. Such an action could include inflicting serious damage to one of the key religious sites, the death or injury through Coalition action of Grand Ayatollah Ali al-Sistani, or significant loss of civilian life in a single incident. The Coalition has conducted operations in such a way as to minimise the risk of such incidents; but the potential for a mobilising incident exists whenever military operations are underway in the complex military, religious and social environment of the Shi'ite theatre of operations.

Less obvious risks derived from the potential accretion of problems over time. The campaign against al-Sadr has been based on a limited political mandate from Shi'ite authorities and antipathy toward the Mahdi Army. The slow pace of Coalition operations, with mounting and disproportionate casualties suffered by militia elements and accumulating physical damage, risked shifting support away from the Coalition, and creating a basis for long-term hostility to the Coalition and its Iraqi allies.

Al-Sadr's *Modus Operandi*

During May, al-Sadr's revolt became increasingly problematic in the face of Coalition military operations and increasing political pressure from the mainstream Shi'ite community.

Although, based on polling data, his personal popularity increased, his military position deteriorated. His militia was on the defensive, clinging tightly to defensive positions near key holy sites or disappearing off the streets when Coalition military operations became overwhelming. Nevertheless, al-Sadr was far from a passive opponent, attempting both political manoeuvre and military action to at least maintain his position as a significant player in the Iraq situation.

By mid-May al-Sadr probably realised that he was not going to be able to generate widespread active support for his rebellion and that centrist Shi'ite political and religious forces were working to limit his influence. By this time al-Sadr had ample evidence that the Coalition was prepared to use sustained military force to destroy his militia and break up his organisation, even if that entailed taking risks. Al-Sadr responded to the rising pressure with a combination of political and military actions, designed to deflect political pressure and impede Coalition military progress against his forces. His actions demonstrated the ability to operate in a complex political/military setting, playing both political and military cards and avoiding any decisive action on the Coalition's part, such as his arrest, while conceding nothing of importance.

In this context al-Sadr employed a number of political tactics to thwart the Coalition and his political enemies. He attempted to exploit the desires of moderate Shi'ite political, religious and tribal figures to achieve a "peaceful" or negotiated settlement to escape Coalition demands that his militia be dismantled and that he face Iraqi justice. These Shi'ite figures were primarily interested in limiting the fighting as it approached key holy sites in Karbala and Najaf and wreaked havoc with the economy of the south. Many probably also feared al-Sadr's growing personal popularity which, according to some polling data, had made him the second-most popular man in Iraq, after Grand Ayatollah Ali al-Sistani. According to one senior source, al-Sadr employed as many as 11 different conduits to conduct political talks or try to open talks with the Coalition. Al-Sadr also employed a well-conceived and responsive 'information operations' campaign to get his message out across the Shi'ite theatre and Iraq. This aggressive use of many venues and means forced the Coalition into a reactive political stance. Al-Sadr's willingness to talk, even if cynical, served multiple purposes. It retarded Coalition military operations, which required some mandate from the Shi'ite mainstream. It also preserved his growing image as the one man in Iraq prepared to challenge the Coalition. Finally it allowed him to characterise failure or lack of progress in negotiations as principally the fault of Coalition intransigence. The success of his methods could be seen in his rising personal popularity.

All of al-Sadr's manoeuvring has been consistent with this tactical approach. From the beginning of his political activity with the fall of the Saddam regime, he has sought to avoid a decisive defeat by the Coalition and to avoid firm agreements that hold him accountable for what is done in his name. His willingness to propose a ceasefire, negotiate, or declare peaceful intentions—all on his terms—has tended to come at moments of acute pressure from Coalition forces, and rising Shi'ite concerns about the risks to the holy sites in Najaf.

Another of al-Sadr's political methods was to employ a threat-and-bluff strategy to appear more menacing than his real capabilities justified. This posturing took the form of threats to unleash suicide bombers, inciting violent resistance if Coalition forces approached holy sites and sparking still wider resistance in Iraq. Dressing in the robes of martyrdom and using his Friday sermons in Kufa as the occasion for vitriolic attacks on the Coalition, al-Sadr employed the resources of a 'theatre of resistance' to buttress his supporters and deter his enemies.

Al-Sadr's most serious potential threat was to mobilise the Shi'ite community and Iraqis more generally against the Coalition. From the start of his revolt on 4 April, he attempted to elicit active support from Iraqi Shi'ites, but with only limited success. He appealed to the Sunni community, also with limited success, and to external Shi'ite communities in Iran and Lebanon. Al-Sadr did not limit his actions to the Shi'ite theatre. An attempt to spread his influence to Kirkuk was blunted by a US forces and Iraqi police raid on one of his offices there and the arrest of supporters.

Irregular Warfare

The Mahdi Army proved willing to engage Coalition forces, even at the risk of appalling loses, and to take the initiative where circumstances offered some prospect for success.

The Mahdi Army's military actions displayed five broad characteristics:

- Opportunistic attacks on exposed Coalition elements, including ambushes of convoys and patrols; the use of improvised explosive devices; and harassing fire against Coalition and Iraqi government facilities. In addition to inflicting casualties, these actions were probably intended to show that the Mahdi Army was active and present in many areas; to keep the Coalition off balance; and to demonstrate the relative weakness of Iraqi security forces supporting the Coalition.
- A geographically widespread rebellion, one not confined to al-Sadr strongholds in Baghdad and Kufa. Mahdi Army elements turned up to fight in many locations in the south, including Najaf, Karbala, Nasiriyah, Amarah, Kut, Basrah, Samawah and Diwaniyah. While strengths and capabilities varied from place to place, the rebellion was not confined to a limited area or a few locations. Najaf, Karbala and, to a lesser extent Nasiriyah, proved especially difficult military problems. Najaf and Karbala required persistent hard fighting by US forces. In Nasiriyah, Italian forces were put on the defensive for a time, at one point even abandoning one of their facilities to the Mahdi Army.
- 'Mini-uprisings' in Baghdad's Sadr City and other cities in the south in response to increasing Coalition military pressure against the Mahdi Army and al-Sadr's organisation. These actions, while contained, demonstrated that al-Sadr's forces remained capable of taking the initiative, even in areas where they had previously suffered serious losses from the Coalition. While suffering attrition, the Mahdi Army has been able to avoid decisive defeat or annihilation. It remains to fight another day.

- Fighting from within the population, the Mahdi Army exploited the reluctance of Coalition commanders to inflict civilian casualties. Mahdi elements were able to use the cover of urban terrain and the presence of civilians to reduce the firepower advantage of Coalition forces. Coalition forces have yet to devise a military solution for this problem in Iraq.
- A willingness to utilise the shrines for cover from Coalition attack. This was especially evident in Karbala and Najaf where Coalition operations were constrained by the desire to avoid actions that could prove provocative to the mainstream Shi'ite community. As one Iraqi in Karbala said: "The Mahdi Army, they were using the shrines as shields." Suppressing armed opposition deployed close to religiously sensitive sites and within urban population centres without causing provocative damage was a major military and political challenge for the Coalition.

The Mahdi Army has proven adept at mounting organised attacks, exploiting urban terrain, employing the now standard Iraqi resistance tactic of mortar fire, patrol convoy ambushes and improvised explosive device attacks. For a militia force less than a year old, these capabilities suggest some type of expert assistance.

While the Mahdi Army did not seriously threaten the Coalition's military position in the south after the arrival of the US 1st Armored Division, it proved strong enough to prevent the Coalition from eliminating al-Sadr as a political force in Iraq. Mahdi Army elements earned the grudging respect of US forces engaged against them, if not for their military skill then for their willingness to stand and fight. In almost all the engagements of the rebellion, Coalition tactical skill and firepower overwhelmed militia forces and resulted in very heavy militia casualties while inflicting only light Coalition losses. Nevertheless, in the two months of the revolt the US 1st Armored Division lost 19 soldiers killed in action.

Two Faces of Resistance

The al-Sadr rebellion differs widely from the Sunni-based resistance that flared so dramatically in Falluja in April.

His movement itself began as a combined religious and social enterprise, only subsequently gaining a military component. From the beginning it had an organisation with material and financial resources, and leadership centred around al-Sadr, but with a number of other highly visible and active figures. Al-Sadr's rebellion may have been either a miscalculation forced upon him by Coalition moves or an over-reaction by some of his lieutenants to the same events, with al-Sadr essentially riding the spreading wave of rebellion. According to a senior source in Iraq, al-Sadr was being driven by the actions of his lieutenants, rather than directing the course of events. Nevertheless, al-Sadr is the symbol of the rebellion and the only man in his organisation capable of mobilising and motivating its members and supporters. In that sense alone he is the leader of the rebellion.

In contrast, the Sunni-based resistance has been more diffuse and more military in character from the beginning. Leadership of the Sunni resistance has been obscure, and its organisational structure shadowy. One senior source has indicated that Sunni resistance command and control is now excellent, with a 'board of directors'-type structure extending inside and outside of Iraq. Sunni-based resistance only now appears to be developing a political wing, involving associations of anti-Western Sunni clerics operating out of mosques, but with strong ties to the Baathists.

Al-Sadr's revolt also differed from the situation in Falluja in that the Sunni resistance achieved a degree of unity with the population and its religious and political leadership. The mainstream Shi'ite community either opposed al-Sadr or stood by, preventing a truly popular uprising from developing.

Potential Outcomes of the Revolt

Al-Sadr's challenge has yet to run its course although it seems to have entered a third round, characterised by political posturing and negotiations, punctuated by clashes between militiamen and reinserted Iraqi security services, and occasional Coalition operations.

As in all campaigns, there is a dynamic between the participants, and al-Sadr has not been just a passive recipient of Coalition blows. He is an adaptive and learning opponent, actively seeking to not only avoid defeat for himself and his army, but to enhance his political position.

Over the course of the rebellion, the situation has often appeared confusing, amid numerous small-scale military actions, ephemeral ceasefires and political agreements, and counter claims about specific incidents; but there is military and political logic to al-Sadr's rebellion. He is gambling that he can persist, even prosper, in the face of the Coalition. He has long-term political goals and is positioning himself for the upcoming elections.

Al-Sadr has given up little to reduce Coalition military pressure against him, and it has yet to be demonstrated that mainstream Shi'ite elements can bring him under control, much less to account for his activity or to dismantle his militia. His recent decisions to emphasise politics and to send his militiamen home probably do not reflect a fundamental change in his motivation or intentions.

The apparent emerging outcome is that al-Sadr will be allowed to enter the Iraqi political process. Al-Sadr appears to be taking his militia off the streets and has curbed his rhetoric, but he has gained an increasingly legitimate role in the new Iraqi politics with his organisation largely intact, and his militia awaiting orders to re-emerge. If events continue along this path, al-Sadr will be enhanced as a political force and probably become still more difficult to deal with in the future. According to one poll taken by an Iraqi research organisation, while only one per cent of Iraqis supported him in December, some 68 per cent supported him at least to some degree in May 2004. Over the long term, al-Sadr's organisation may be able to exploit this popularity as the political process in Iraq unfolds.

Many Iraqis clearly blame the Coalition for the loss of life and destruction incurred during the rebellion, even while acknowledging al-Sadr's involvement. With some hundreds of militia dead, localised destruction of property, damage to shrines, and repetitive images of relentless US use of firepower along with heavy combat vehicles and aircraft in urban fighting, it is hard to argue that hearts and minds were being won, at least by US elements of the Coalition.

One almost certain outcome of al-Sadr's rebellion will be further violence. As al-Sadr's forces cannot be completely eliminated and some elements may not be under his full control (perhaps as a convenience), violence is likely to persist; although its intensity and frequency is likely to vary from place to place and time to time, as al-Sadr variously emphasises talking or shooting to further his objectives.

It is very improbable that the south will return to the relative quiet of pre-April. The UK's decision to strengthen its contingent in Iraq with additional mechanised forces and engineers for fortification work suggests its view of the future in its area of responsibility. Yet more pessimistically, the Coalition still faces the prospect of further mini-uprisings, and a full-blown Shi'ite revolt remains a possibility under some circumstances.

There appear to be two positive outcomes from the rebellion. First, it seems that the Coalition has found a path that may allow it to win with the Shi'ite population instead of against them. Coalition military operations served the political advantage of some mainstream Shi'ite political and religious elements and encouraged them to rein in al-Sadr, in effect establishing that they could work together for mutual advantage. Secondly, the Coalition appeared to learn a great deal about fighting in the complex religious and political environments of the urban areas of the south. While unable to act with a free hand, US and other Coalition forces displayed the ability to conduct operations in built-up and densely populated areas without causing massive collateral damage. While limiting the risk to the sensitive holy sites, US forces were able to exploit the political mandate they had, to close with the Mahdi Army and inflict substantial attrition on it, contributing to al-Sadr's decision to ask for a ceasefire and reduce the visibility of the militia. These outcomes stand in marked contrast to the conclusion of the siege of Falluja. If Falluja taught the Coalition how not to conduct such operations, perhaps the campaign against al-Sadr is teaching the Coalition some more positive lessons.

Long-Term Implications

The revolt of Moqtada al-Sadr appears as an important moment in the post-war history of Iraq. For the first time, the Coalition faced organised and armed opposition from Shi'ite forces and, inevitably, there are significant long-term implications for the security and political situation in Iraq.

Al-Sadr's organisation is likely to develop as a political faction with an armed and violent component, a component that can be conjured up whenever it is necessary to resort to political violence. It operates comfortably on the violent edge of politics—murdering, intimidating, suborning, and, when deemed necessary, fighting to achieve its objectives. It is not at all clear that the new Iraqi government will have the means or the will to deal with such a group.

Increasingly, the new Iraqi security services will have the responsibility for coping with armed factions such as al-Sadr's, and here there is not much reason for optimism, especially in the short term. The April collapse of much of the security forces, including the successful intimidation or subversion of some Iraqi Police Service (IPS) elements by al-Sadr's organisation, and the apparent involvement of some IPS members and Iraqi Civil Defence Corps personnel in Sunni-based resistance activity, suggest that it will be some time before these can be counted on to control armed and dangerous militiamen.

The rebellion demonstrated, as did the siege of Falluja, that the US military still has problems in fighting insurgents in populated and sensitive urban environments. US operations, while precise and sensitive to collateral damage, were protracted and indecisive, giving al-Sadr time and opportunity to manoeuvre politically and wage his own campaign for public support. To an extent, the protracted and indecisive US challenge has energised him as a political power in Iraq.

More broadly, the revolt has demonstrated to the Shi'ites, the Coalition, the Kurds and the new Iraqi government that force is a real option if negotiations or the new politics do not meet Shi'ite political objectives. Many Shi'ites, both organisations and individuals, stood on the sidelines in this crisis; but they could hardly fail to note the difficulty the Coalition had in meeting al-Sadr's challenge, and this challenge represented only a fraction of the potential power of the Shi'ite community.

Part Five

Postwar Coalition Security Policy

Michael Knights

Introduction

Although the postwar Sunni resistance and Shiite uprisings spotlighted the security challenge facing the coalition, it was apparent even before Operation Iraqi Freedom that security-sector reform and security partnerships would be a major feature of any occupation. As war clouds were gathering in November 2002, The Washington Institute held a Policy Forum to discuss the potential challenges of rebuilding Iraq's security forces in a post-Saddam future. Even at this early stage, it was clear that manifold difficulties would need to be overcome. Michael Eisenstadt and Kenneth Pollack noted that while substantial portions of the Baath security architecture would need to be dismantled, careful thought would have to be given to the near-term political and security implications of such a step. Given that the Sunni community would be disproportionately affected by the dissolution of elements of the security apparatus, Eisenstadt argued that they would need to be reassured that the changes would not constitute "a vendetta against them." Specifically, he maintained that released regime security forces would need to be supervised and retrained to ensure their reintegration into the legitimate economy rather than into "organized crime or subversive activities against the new government."

Yet, as the November 2002 forum noted, this kind of sensitive de-Baathification would require in-depth knowledge of Iraqi political dynamics and deft political footwork. On May 23, 2003, the Coalition Provisional Authority (CPA) dissolved all Iraqi security institutions, releasing hundreds of thousands of men from government service and reversing previous policy, which would have retained selected elements of the regular military for labor and security duties. Postwar coalition security policy evolved in the shadow of this decision.

Aside from efforts to capture or kill resistance forces (covered substantially in parts 3 and 4 of this anthology), broader coalition security policy in postwar Iraq was primarily concerned with how quickly the new Iraqi security forces could be integrated into coalition security operations, and which Iraqi and multinational allies the coalition should adopt as security partners. The evolution of coalition policy can be split into three discernable phases, the first of which began with the June 25, 2003, decision to extend payments to released servicemen and announce the reestablishment of a range of new Iraqi security forces. This phase was characterized by an optimistic appraisal of the speed at which Iraqi security forces could be developed, which was in turn reflected in an emphasis on quantity over quality in the development of indigenous paramilitary forces such as the Iraqi Civil Defense Corps (ICDC) and the Iraqi Police Service (IPS).

Throughout summer and fall 2003, The Washington Institute highlighted concerns regarding the quality of the new Iraqi security forces and the late and incomplete payment of former soldiers. Further danger signals concerning the low disbursement rate of U.S. assistance to the security forces were evident in the months before the simultaneous Sunni and Shiite uprisings in April 2004. An Institute analysis in March 2004 noted that the ICDC and IPS were brittle—compromised in their provincial and municipal security roles due to their close ties to local factions, and ultimately threatened by strong regional militias.

The duration of the April-May uprisings by Sunni resistance groups and Shiite militias represented the second phase of coalition security policy in postwar Iraq, which witnessed a wide-ranging rationalization of what could realistically be accomplished by Iraqi security forces in the near term. The new security forces were prematurely exposed to intercommunal violence that strained their affiliations and limited training beyond the breaking point. Expectations concerning these forces were sharply scaled back, with a new emphasis on qualitative improvement through lengthier training schedules. As fighting raged in Falluja and the Shiite south, some coalition military commanders turned to local militias as new security partners. Yet, these arrangements were an expedient solution with easily apparent drawbacks, not a long-term alternative to the development of government-controlled security forces.

The April-May uprisings also showed that multinational forces had mixed levels of commitment and military capability. This fact reduced coalition expectations concerning the future replacement of U.S. forces with multinational contingents and served as a warning against any premature reduction in the U.S. military's profile. Accordingly, The Washington Institute advised its readership at an early stage that NATO did not represent a panacea for Iraq's problems. Although immediate postwar plans had sought to reduce U.S. forces in Iraq to 110,000 troops or less by summer 2004, the United States committed itself to maintaining 185,000 troops in Iraq throughout the rest of the year.

The third phase of postwar coalition security strategy emerged from the April-May uprisings, which were rich with operational and strategic lessons. On the operational level, it was clear that the so-called "Falluja model"—subcontracting local security to a nongovernmental militia—could not be applied elsewhere in Iraq outside of crisis conditions. It was also clear, however, that Iraqi security forces would fight effectively only under a sovereign Iraqi leadership. At the strategic level, it was evident by late May that the freedom of action enjoyed by coalition security forces up to that point had significantly eroded. Iraqis played major roles in crafting the political deals that reduced the level of violence in Falluja and undercut regional support for Muqtada al-Sadr.

Coalition military operations during the uprisings succeeded when they were integrated with Iraqi political initiatives (for example, against al-Sadr's militia) and failed when attempted in the face of Iraqi objections (as in Falluja). Moreover, Institute analysis in March 2004 noted that the training of Iraqi security forces needed to be regularized and centrally controlled. Indeed, as the Iraqi Interim Government took over an increasing amount of authority during a phased transition in June 2004, coalition security assistance was increasingly formalized. Ad hoc security training and partnerships devised by local coalition military commanders were replaced with the Office of Security Transition (OST), an integrated point of contact between multinational forces and Iraqi security forces. This office greatly facilitated the flow of U.S. security assistance. To extend political authorization and legal protection to multinational forces after the transition, the United States and Iraq opted to develop a temporary "status of forces arrangement" on June 8, 2004, a development that the Institute envisaged in an April 27, 2004, *PolicyWatch.*

The adoption of a political-military security strategy blending Iraqi political initiatives with the highly selective use of coalition military forces is emerging as a winning combination. The drive for political inclusiveness launched by the new Iraqi government will reduce the number of actors choosing to remain outside the political system and engaged in violent opposition. Thus far the new government has displayed the robustness that was hoped would emerge from self-governance. For example, when the coalition launched precision airstrikes against resistance and terrorist targets in Falluja in early July 2004, negative political reaction was minimal, and the interim government was quick to claim credit for providing the targeting intelligence.

An integrated approach to the development of Iraqi security forces is likewise generating results in delivering equipment and training. The interim government and the OST are concentrating on the near-term development of small numbers of highly capable Iraqi units, including some manned by troops who have specifically volunteered to serve in an internal security role, potentially pitting themselves against fellow Iraqis. Nine major militias have committed to disband and fold their fighters within government-controlled security forces, an option that has become more attractive and less threatening to factional leaders, and more feasible following the successful transition to an inclusive sovereign government. In partnership with multinational forces, the interim government and its successors face the difficult task of providing a secure environment for the winter 2004-2005 elections and the first constitutional elections in December 2005. The former occasion will mark the first major test of postoccupation coalition security policy.

Michael Eisenstadt and Kenneth Pollack

40
Envisioning a Post-Saddam Iraqi Military

Retraining and reorganizing the Iraqi military and eliminating weapons of mass destruction (WMD) will be vital tasks in the wake of any U.S.-led invasion of Iraq. Yet, political change is a prerequisite for military change, and neglecting the former could pose disastrous consequences for the latter. Specifically, the United States should assist in the creation of an apolitical, professional Iraqi military in concert with a new pluralist, federal, civilian-led Iraqi government with indigenous roots. Ultimately, these efforts would help to stabilize Iraq both internally and vis-à-vis its neighbors.

MICHAEL EISENSTADT

The political, economic, and military aspects of a post-Saddam Iraq are interconnected. Replacing Saddam Hussein with another autocracy would not serve U.S. interests. A broad-based, representative government that better reflects Iraq society is a precondition for successful military reform. That would entail creating a more representative military officer corps, reforming the security and armed services, and reorganizing the military along defensive lines. Moreover, a government organized along federal lines would rely on local law enforcement for internal security, alleviating the need for a large army or security apparatus. Such changes could foster a less aggressive Iraq that is less likely to assert a leadership role in the Arab world.

U.S. and allied forces will need to restructure Iraq's armed forces along several lines. First, Saddam's influence cannot be allowed to linger in the security and armed services. Given their repressive history, the bulk of Iraq's intelligence and security organizations should be scrapped, while those that can be reformed should be purged. These reforms may create political and security problems, though. Politically speaking, the United States must reassure the broader Sunni Arab community that such changes would not constitute a vendetta against them; to this end, it should promote Sunni tribes and individuals that have stood apart from Saddam's regime. From a security standpoint, individuals purged from the military would require retraining and supervision so that they could take part in the legitimate economy rather than organized crime or subversive activities against the new government.

On November 19, 2002, Michael Eisenstadt and Kenneth Pollack addressed The Washington Institute's Special Policy Forum. Mr. Pollack is a senior fellow and director of research at the Brookings Institution's Saban Center for Middle East Policy. His publications include *The Threatening Storm: The Case for Invading Iraq* (Random House, 2002). This rapporteur's summary (originally published as *PolicyWatch* no. 681, November 25, 2002) was prepared by Eran Benedek.

Although Iraq's new military must be able to support the country's real defensive needs, it must also be rendered incapable of posing a threat to Iraq's larger neighbors. The United States, not Iraq, will ensure regional stability and provide a counterbalance to Iran. Past wars and sanctions have dramatically decreased Iraq's military equipment and offensive capabilities. Given the inevitable postwar reconstruction, debt, and reparations obligations, a new Iraqi regime would lack the funds needed to pursue large-scale rearmament. In this context, U.S.-led forces should curtail Iraq's strategic mobility and its reliance on standing forces, which should eventually be replaced with a reserve system.

Even after Saddam is toppled, the Iraqi WMD threat will still present perhaps the greatest challenge to the United States. To manage this threat, the United States should adopt a number of measures: finding employment for former weapons scientists in Iraq's reconstructed economy; enhancing Iraq's missile/WMD defenses and incorporating the country into a Cooperative Defense Initiative program along the lines of that seen among the Gulf Cooperation Council (GCC) states; and providing U.S. security assurances to Iraq as a substitute for an independent WMD capability.

KENNETH POLLACK

In the immediate post-Saddam aftermath, Iraq's military needs will be minimal. U.S. troop presence will be large and prolonged (probably five to seven years) and should be sufficient to counter challenges to Iraq's territorial integrity. Moreover, three regional security arrangements could help to foster stability. First, a U.S.-Iraqi bilateral alliance could strengthen Iraq internally and ensure domestic cohesion. Second, a security condominium comprising Iraq, Iran, the GCC states, the United States, and other countries could agree to a series of arms-reduction and confidence-building measures. Third, the international community could encourage a security pact in the region with security guarantees for Iraq, which would obviate its need for a WMD program and generate regional economic benefits.

U.S. objectives do not include conquering Iraq and running the country. Hence, it would be useful to involve the UN in any political and military changes in Iraq, albeit with the United States at the core of any multinational force. In view of the quantity and nature of UN resolutions on Iraq, which already impose strict limitations regarding WMD production and military forces, the appropriate model for restructuring the country would be a UN-appointed "special representative of the secretary-general" rather than a U.S. military administration. Moreover, in the aftermath of a war, all Iraqis should be granted equal opportunity to contribute to the establishment of a new regime. Talented diaspora Iraqis should also be invited to participate in the reconstruction process. Yet, the United States should not privilege any particular groups or individuals by designating them as a provisional government or as the future leaders of Iraq. Iraqis must form a new government that derives its legitimacy from the citizenry.

The prospects for democracy in Iraq are better than for most Middle Eastern countries. Iraq still has a middle class and an urban society (albeit suffering from Saddam's repression and subsequent economic woes) that could ensure democratic viability. Many of the internal sociocultural problems that could impede democracy have been exaggerated. Still, democratization is not an instantaneous process. One essential ingredient is a national reeducation program that allows Iraqis to internalize the benefits of reconstruction.

GENERAL DISCUSSION

As long as the security services are intact (i.e., the Republican and Special Republican Guards), a coup against Saddam would likely be stifled. Were a coup to occur during the buildup to U.S. intervention, Washington could be forced to suspend its plans for military action pending confirmation that the new regime intended to comply with U.S. and UN demands (i.e., ending WMD production and domestic repression). Alternatively, if a coup occurred during an intervention, the United States would more likely continue its military efforts, particularly if operational momentum had already brought U.S.-led forces near Baghdad. In such a situation, Washington would need to evaluate whether to consider the new administration as a provisional government or replace it with a more democratically oriented transitional regime. In any case, once Saddam were unseated, the Special Republican Guard would lose its clout, and U.S.-led forces would need to dismantle its infrastructure and prevent its officers from participating in public life.

Ultimately, restructuring the Iraqi political system post-Saddam would be crucial for domestic cohesion and regional and international stability. Yet, this cannot be achieved through foreign imposition. Iraqis must create their own system in order to inculcate democratic values and build a better future.

Michael Knights

41
The Future Shape of Military Operations in Support of Postwar Stabilization in Iraq

Although military operations have passed the "tipping point" in Iraq, U.S. Central Command spokesmen continue to stress that their primary focus remains the completion of high-intensity operations against remaining pockets of resistance. Moreover, in contrast to previous statements that advocated allowing looting to burn itself out, recent statements suggest that the coalition will quickly reconstitute the Iraqi police force, actively preventing looting and imposing curfews on its own in the meantime. These are positive steps because accomplishing the mission—that is, neutralizing or apprehending leadership elements, uncovering weapons of mass destruction (WMD), and facilitating the humanitarian and economic recovery of Iraq—depends on closer engagement with the civilian population and robust policing activity. The coalition cannot afford to choose between fighting the high-intensity war or engaging in low-intensity civil affairs; both endeavors must be undertaken simultaneously, which will be a strain on both the limited numbers of coalition forces and relations with Iraqi civilians.

Securing Key Infrastructure and Individuals

Key infrastructure elements such as oil fields and dams have been secured throughout Operation Iraqi Freedom. Such efforts included the successful disruption of limited attempts to detonate southern oil wells. Yet, other lower-profile but nevertheless vital resources have not been secured as effectively. Widespread looting in major cities has greatly reduced the physical plant facilities available to Iraq's civilian ministries. In some instances, looting is causing actual infrastructure damage; for example, elements of the electrical grid in Basra have been dismantled and stolen. Generators, fuel, and medicines from hospitals are also under threat. In other cases, vital data is being lost, including regime security files in intelligence headquarters and records from Basra's central bank. These types of documentation are vital for the vetting of Iraqi officials, the pursuit of Iraqi war criminals, and the quantification of Iraqi debts.

Originally published as *PolicyWatch* no. 748, April 11, 2003.

Coalition forces have also had mixed success in securing key individuals. The coalition learned a major lesson when pro-American Iraqi Shiite leader Ayatollah Abdul Majid al-Khoei was murdered shortly after arriving in Najaf. The coalition must protect such figures, as well as interim authorities and other Iraqis who may be involved in internecine struggles or viewed as "collaborators" by regime loyalists. Even more significant, the United States has not captured as many key regime figures or military personnel as it had hoped to. The nature of the coalition's military advance and its supporting psychological operations has meant that few prisoners—currently estimated at less than 12,000—will be available for interrogation. Although this has eased the strain on coalition resources, it will also reduce the amount of intelligence that the coalition can obtain on Iraqi leaders and WMD and decrease the chances of capturing leaders and regime loyalists. It should be remembered that the process of lustration—purging loyalists from postwar political life—was made easier in post-World War Germany because so many members of the SS and Nazi Party were captured and identified, including leadership figures hiding among the masses. Because regime figures may choose not to fight a last stand in Baghdad or Tikrit, instead dispersing within Iraq or into neighboring states, the coalition must maximize the number of prisoners it takes during the campaign. If the coalition has to root such figures out of small villages, tension will undoubtedly increase between allied forces and tribal elements.

Engaging the Population

If securing prisoners is one key element in intelligence collection, engaging civilians is another. In Basra, where the static nature of operations meant that coalition forces closely engaged the population from an early stage, results have been encouraging. Intelligence from civilians allowed the coalition to identify Baath leaders and uncover arms caches. A similar pattern is emerging in central Iraq as coalition forces engage in closer contact with Iraqi citizens, resulting in the discovery of a suicide bomb factory.

Such engagement entails risks, particularly since placing troops in urban areas allows possible assailants and suicide bombers to get close to coalition forces. This is a major change from the previous level of interface between allied forces and Iraqis, who were initially warned to stay indoors and to avoid coalition units. House-to-house clearing operations along major roads were necessarily invasive; humiliating strip-searches of surrendering combatants and civilians were commonplace; and Iraqis moving in civilian vehicles continue to run a major risk of attracting coalition fire. In short, this messy fighting has likely left a major negative impression on many Iraqi citizens, requiring the coalition to create counterbalancing positive experiences as soon as possible in the postwar period.

The coalition is now taking steps to reassure Iraqis as to its intentions. Although close contact with Iraqis—including foot patrols—may pose extra force-protection risks, the use of such measures in Basra has helped many residents view the coalition presence as helpful rather than threatening. Moreover, so-called "quick wins" are being pursued in the "hearts and minds" field by providing time-sensitive military assistance to civilians, including desperately needed fuel supplies and medical assistance. More aloof, less manpower-intensive forms of interface may be less effective. Communications with broader Iraqi society are being established through coalition newspapers and television appearances, including regular messages from President George W. Bush. Yet, it remains to be seen how a population inured to government propaganda will receive these messages.

Invasive Policing versus 'Hearts and Minds'

Clearly, invasive policing operations must be undertaken simultaneously with high-intensity fighting and the effort to win "hearts and minds." This fact poses three key challenges:

- Force levels will be strained by the simultaneous, manpower-intensive requirements of displaying troop presence, enforcing curfews, preventing looting, defending key points, processing prisoners, and searching for WMD and regime leaders. Reestablishing the Iraqi police force will be problematic considering its recent history of corruption, ineffectiveness, and complicity in regime actions. In the meantime, the 4th U.S. Infantry Division is likely to be employed in a high-intensity role in Tikrit.
- The need for force protection both drives and complicates a broader civil affairs and policing role for coalition forces. On one hand, engagement with Iraqis will improve intelligence on regime remainders and WMD, thereby increasing security. On the other hand, closer contact and urban visibility will expose coalition forces to further attacks and suicide bombings.
- Iraqi reactions are difficult to predict. Balancing displays of authority and friendliness is a problem in these sorts of situations; it is difficult to gauge whether shows of force will engender respect or resentment among the population. In Basra, for example, British forces established their headquarters in a Baath Party office. What message did this send to the citizenry? Were they reassured or concerned? Such issues will likely require different solutions in different areas (e.g., Baghdad versus Tikrit).

Conclusion

The war has been fought with explicit focus on reducing the reconstruction burden and Iraqi resentment toward the coalition. Now, the coalition must enhance its visibility via closer engagement with the Iraqi people, both to accomplish its mission and to improve the postwar force protection environment. The need to maintain order and simultaneously win "hearts and minds" is an indication that the challenges of war and peace require the same blend of forethought, calculated risk, and determined execution.

Jeffrey White

42
The New Iraqi Army: Problems and Prospects

According to a June 23, 2003, coalition administration announcement, recruitment for the new Iraqi army is to begin shortly. This is a potentially momentous step with major long-term implications for the future of the state. It will not be easy to create a new army to support a democratic Iraq, and certain difficulties will have to be addressed from the very beginning of the process. Success or failure in establishing the basis for an Iraqi military with strong values as well as capabilities will have a significant impact on the future stability of Iraq.

The Future Force

The new Iraqi army will apparently consist of some 40,000 personnel organized into three infantry divisions of 12,000 troops each. At least one of these divisions is to be of the light infantry type. Presumably, the remaining 4,000 personnel would be used as headquarters and service-support staff. The new army's stated missions will include "guarding the borders" and "installation protection." Recruitment is said to be open to all former members of the Iraqi military except those of high rank, those of the regime security services, and those complicit in human rights abuses. Training for the new force is to be provided by contract staff, including former U.S. military personnel, under a $48 million deal with the Vinnell Corporation. According to one Coalition Provisional Authority official, the new army "will be professional, nonpolitical, militarily effective, and truly representative of the country." Establishing the force will take an estimated three years.

Missions

This is a very small force for a country the size of Iraq, given the state's history of internal and external warfare and its current domestic problems. From a military perspective, the missions designated for the army seem both too large and too small.

Guarding Iraq's borders with a field force of 36,000 infantrymen would be a very challenging mission in the current regional environment. As planned, the new army will be a minor force for a major state, a state that, historically, has played a key role in the region and will likely have to reassume such a role in the future. In addition to its small

Originally published as *PolicyWatch* no. 771, July 8, 2003.

size, the new army will have limited capabilities to carry out its proposed missions. It will be an infantry force in a region with extensive tank and mechanized infantry units. Most of Iraq's neighbors will possess significantly larger militaries: Iran with some 520,000 military personnel, Turkey with 515,000, Syria with 380,000, and Jordan with 100,000. Although none of these states is likely to initiate a military confrontation with the new Baghdad, a militarily weak Iraq is a distortion in the regional situation, one bound to have unforeseen consequences for stability.

Added to these problems is the fact that the new Iraqi army will have to do more than protect the borders. Protecting government installations will require diverting troops, further weakening border defense capabilities. Other potentially important missions such as national integration and nation building have not been addressed. Similarly, no mention has been made of internal security, a task that will need to be undertaken by some organization in Iraq if a new democratic state is to survive. The new army will almost certainly be a factor in the internal situation, even if only by default. Yet, the projected size and character of the force is unlikely to deter serious dissident elements; after all, the Kurds and the Shiites were willing to take on even Saddam Hussein's heavy formations and air power. The Kurds already deploy relatively high-quality, experienced, and numerous light infantry personnel of their own (the *peshmerga*). The new Iraqi army will have to define relationships with both the overtly and covertly armed elements in Iraq; the national army cannot afford to be intimidated by such elements.

Capabilities

The announced plans for the new army appear to be missing some potentially important pieces. There is no mention of long-range mobility assets (potentially critical in a country with Iraq's size and borders), no planned air component (at the very least, helicopters and transports should be included), and no provision for an intelligence service. With a small army, it is all the more important to know what and where the threats are, and to be able to reach them relatively quickly.

Recruitment issues will also be crucial. There is an old saying that every army reflects the society it is drawn from, and Iraq is, in many respects, a shattered society. The timing of the announcement of the new army suggests that one of its goals is to get some of the thousands of former soldiers off the streets. This should relieve some of the real and potential problems caused by unemployed soldiers, but it cannot be the basis for a long-term recruitment policy. With an army of only 40,000, the emphasis should be on recruiting the best troops and officers possible—those without the baggage of the old regime and its pronounced antidemocratic traditions, but with a high degree of experience and professionalism. Issues of religion, ethnicity, tribalism, and regime complicity will have to be faced as well. For example, will the new battalions be recruited on a national, regional, or local basis? Will religiously and ethnically differentiated personnel be kept together, or will integrated units be established? These questions will be critical to the new army's future cohesiveness, discipline, and responsiveness to democratic institutions. Especially important will be the recruitment and selection of the officer class. Saddam's military had a core of capable soldiers, and, assuming they are not complicit in the crimes of the regime, some of them could serve as the foundation of a new officer corps. Careful vetting will be necessary to prevent regime diehards from infiltrating the new military. There are no easy answers to these recruiting issues, but the choices that are made now will affect the army and the state well into the future.

Implications

Unless peace descends suddenly on the Middle East, Iraq will require protection. If the new Iraqi army is too small or ill equipped to protect the country's borders, then an effective regional security arrangement will have to be put in place in order to meet the security needs of Iraq and its neighbors. Alternatively, U.S. or coalition forces will have to protect Iraq in some manner for the foreseeable future.

Iraq will also need an internal security force, since the most salient threats to the new government will likely emanate from within. Unless parallel measures are taken to create effective internal security apparatuses (police, intelligence, and security services), the coalition will have to remain involved in this role indefinitely. Although a long-term coalition presence would help to guarantee Iraqi security, it would also raise questions concerning Iraqi sovereignty and become a target for political opposition and armed attack.

For the long term, then, Iraq will likely need a military that is strong enough to accomplish both its initial missions and other important national tasks. Although an infantry-based force of 40,000 is a good start, it should be viewed as the basis for building, over time, a larger and more capable Iraqi military, one that reflects the values of the new democratic state and can protect it from enemies both foreign and domestic.

Michael Knights

43
Economics of Iraqi Security: Assessing the Value of Security Spending

Expanding the size of Iraqi government security forces will be key to reducing the amount of international troops in the country, including U.S. forces. On October 19, the *Washington Post* reported a U.S. plan to reduce its military presence in Iraq from the current level of 130,000 troops to 100,000 by summer 2004, and to as little as 50,000 by mid-2005. Whether such reductions are possible will depend in large part on how quickly Iraqi security forces fill the gap, especially in light of uncertainty over the number of international peacekeepers that will replace U.S. forces.

Increasing the size and scope of Iraqi security forces will require extra funding. In 2004, various Iraqi security sectors will be allocated a total of $4.8 billion from several different sources. In cost-benefit terms, such expenditures could reap major savings for the United States in terms of both blood and treasure (assuming that the Iraqi forces in question are loyal and efficient). Moreover, the development of security structures such as police forces will have beneficial effects on Iraqi society, reducing the endemic levels of crime that impede economic recovery and complicate the process of reconstruction.

Direct or Hard Security Spending

The 2004 Coalition Provisional Authority (CPA) budget for Iraq, financed by Iraqi resources such as oil exports, allocates funds for a variety of hard security items (i.e., items directly related to security):

- $146 million has been budgeted for the new Iraqi army and the Ministry of the Interior. The army is scheduled to receive $23 million in 2004 for a projected 26,500 soldiers, increasing to $72 million in 2005. The Interior Ministry is to receive $123 million for 65,105 personnel. According to CPA administrator L. Paul Bremer, over 58,000 of the ministry's staff are currently deployed in security roles, including 37,000 police officers, 2,500 Civil Defense Corps paramilitary troops, approximately 14,500 Facilities Protection Service (FPS) guards, and 4,700 U.S.-trained border guards. The start-up costs for these forces have been paid by the current half-year 2003 budget; their recurring costs will be covered by $103 million in salary payments allocated by the 2004 budget.

Originally published as *PolicyWatch* no. 796, October 21, 2003.

- $138 million has been budgeted for the Ministry of Justice, including $42 million for rebuilding courthouses and prisons.
- Additional funds have been budgeted for other items, such as $14 million for airport security guards. Some security forces may be included within the $745 million budgeted for regional and local governments. Yet, the $45 million allocated to the Ministry of Oil in 2003 may not be available for security once pipeline protection is taken over by the FPS. Most of the hard security spending in Iraq will be financed by off-budget infusions from the $18.6 billion U.S. supplemental funding request. That request allocates over $4.6 billion to various security, law enforcement, justice, public safety, and security-related civil society programs:
- $2.1 billion has been budgeted for the new Iraqi army and the paramilitary Iraqi Civil Defense Corps (ICDC). According to the CPA, the army recently turned out its first infantry battalion and is aiming to field a 12,000-man division by January 2004 and a 30,000-man corps by December 2004. The army is also negotiating a deal to obtain small arms, night-vision equipment, and trucks. The 2,500-strong ICDC will be expanded to an eighteen-battalion force totaling 9,000 troops.
- $950 million has been budgeted for the Iraqi police force, which will double the number of officers to 75,000 and fund the establishment of a police training college.
- $284 million has been budgeted for other security forces. The FPS will receive $67 million, which will expand it to 20,000 guards and pay for training and vehicles. Iraq's border guard training program will be maintained throughout 2004 at a cost of $217 million.
- $1.3 billion has been budgeted for justice, public safety, and civil society infrastructure, including $209 million for prisons, $509 million for hardening and securing public buildings, and $100 million for a witness protection program that will directly benefit intelligence collection and law enforcement efforts.

Indirect or Soft Security Spending

Under the 2004 CPA budget, the Iraqi Ministry of Finance is slated to pay $250 million in stipends to demobilized soldiers. The stipends will reportedly be distributed to 320,000 former soldiers, giving them an average of $780 for the year; in contrast, the average government workers salary in 2004 will be $2,000. Although the stipend will provide demobilized soldiers with money, it will not occupy their time, giving them ample opportunity to get into trouble (e.g., join the resistance). Former soldiers will need real jobs as well as short-term social safety-net support. Expanding local security forces may help absorb some of the disgruntled former military personnel who could prove troublesome to the CPA if left unemployed.

Even so, there is a troubling gap between the reported 320,000 scheduled to receive stipends and the 440,000 soldiers and security personnel that were demobilized on May 23, 2003. The 120,000 presumably unsuccessful claimants may become doubly aggrieved once the new budget takes effect. On October 11, an estimated 14,000 former soldiers and security personnel took part in violent demonstrations in Baghdad, with one protestor killed.

Extensive government employment may also help ease social tension. As many as 2 million government jobs have been budgeted for 2004 (although many of these jobs will be disguised unemployment, giving employees a wage but little actual work to do). Central government salary expenditures will be $2.8 billion, not including the salary component of the $500 million allocated for state enterprises and the $745 million allocated for local and regional governments. The CPA will also continue the public distribution system begun under the UN oil-for-food program, allocating $3.5 billion to it for 2004, or $130 per Iraqi. The CPA projects that it will increase funding for the system to $4.9 billion in 2005, with no plans to phase it out until after 2006.

Implications

The United States is serving its own interests by investing in Iraq's security forces. By the end of 2004, the CPA plans to have nearly 140,000 Iraqi police, military, and paramilitary forces under arms at a cost of around $2.2 billion (including a variety of start-up costs). These forces will thereafter be relatively cheap to maintain in the field. Even the initial annual cost of $2.2 billion will seem like a bargain, averaging out to about $43 per day per Iraqi soldier/policeman. In comparison, maintaining U.S. forces in Iraq currently costs $3.9 billion per month for 130,000 troops, which works out to $1,000 per day per soldier, not including salaries. To be sure, the CPA need not choose between Iraqi and U.S. forces. Ideally, the two would be mixed: Iraqis would undertake law enforcement as well as static and border defense, with smaller U.S. forces responsible for proactive counterinsurgency operations.

Small financial sacrifices now could well reap big rewards in the long term. For example, if 120,000 former soldiers are not in fact given demobilization stipends, the maximum savings will be relatively small (less than $100 million per year). Moreover, these savings could be more than offset if a considerable number of these soldiers cooperate with the resistance. Counterinsurgency is very expensive, and much of it is directed against active resistance elements that may number fewer than 5,000 fighters. The CPA would be well advised to use such cost-benefit analyses to determine how economic and employment issues affect its security program.

Michael Knights

44
Militias and the Monopoly of Force in Transitional Iraq

One year after Operation Iraqi Freedom began, Iraqi security forces are beginning to take greater responsibility for the security of the country. Nevertheless, questions remain concerning the diffusion of military power within Iraq. The Iraqi Fundamental Law drafted earlier this month stated that militias will be considered illegal entities after the Coalition Provisional Authority (CPA) transfers power to local authorities on June 30, 2004. In practice, however, many militiamen will likely be absorbed into existing security organizations such as the Iraqi Civil Defense Corps (ICDC), where their loyalties will continue to be divided between their Baghdad paymasters and local or sectarian affiliations. The challenge for the CPA is to find practical ways of balancing these sometimes contending pressures on local militias in order to prevent them from diluting the CPA's—and, eventually, the Iraqi central government's—power.

Background

Currently, U.S. forces are pulling back from major Iraqi cities and stationing themselves in fewer and more remote bases. In central Baghdad, for example, the U.S. presence will be reduced from twenty-four bases to two by May 2004, and only six bases will remain immediately outside the city; the troops in these eight bases will serve as a quick reaction force. Moreover, the CPA is steadily handing over the bulk of checkpoint security, patrolling, and law enforcement responsibilities to Iraqi security forces, and the forthcoming transitional government will depend on these forces as threats to stability intensify.

New Security Forces

The new Iraqi security forces consist of the New Iraqi Army (NIA), the ICDC, the Iraqi Police Service (IPS), and the Facilities Protection Service (FPS). The NIA's Development has been accelerated in order to establish twenty-seven battalions (of approximately 800 soldiers each) by September 2004. A special 400-strong NIA counterterrorism battalion will also be trained by the end of 2004. In addition to these relatively small numbers, the NIA may be constrained in its efforts to play an internal security role in the provinces due

Originally published as *PolicyWatch* no. 842, March 16, 2004.

to lingering mistrust of government security forces, a legacy of the Baath era. Indeed, the Kurdistan Regional Government will resist central governmental efforts to deploy the NIA to the north, and regions in the south could follow suit. Moreover, the CPA directive establishing the post-Saddam military stated that the NIA "shall not have or exercise domestic law enforcement functions, nor interfere in domestic political affairs." More likely than not, existing provincial and multiprovince governments in Iraq will supplement IPS forces with locally recruited, trained, and equipped ICDC forces.

The ICDC is currently 19,000 strong (twelve battalions), and CPA plans may call for it to triple in size. For now, the ICDC is employed by provincial governors to man checkpoints and provide interpreters and representatives during coalition raids. From the corps's inception, many local leaders feared it would become a new tool of central government oppression. Consequently, they have heavily seeded the ICDC with their own constituents. Like the majority of IPS and FPS forces, particularly outside Baghdad, the loyalties of regional ICDC units are divided between their central government paymasters and the local communities from which they are drawn. Unlike the NIA—where each unit has been carefully balanced to reflect the proportional ethnic makeup of Iraq—the other three main security organizations recruit locally and do not deploy outside their base area. Another important indication of their local character is that their personnel sleep at home, not in barracks. In theory, IPS, FPS, and ICDC personnel are under a chain of command reporting to the Ministry of Interior in Baghdad. Yet, provincial governors have hired and fired local IPS and ICDC personnel on numerous occasions, reinforcing their status as patrons. These local leaders will resist the centralization of FPS, IPS, and ICDC training at facilities designated by Baghdad.

In practice, many of those who apply and are accepted into these security forces were previously members of existing militia movements such as the Kurdish *peshmerga*, the Badr Brigades (run by the Shiite Supreme Council for Islamic Revolution in Iraq [SCIRI]), or various tribal confederations. After all, these individuals are the most likely to have paramilitary experience. Hence, ICDC forces in the Iraqi Kurdish region would likely pay as much attention to instructions from their former *peshmerga* colleagues and other Kurdish officials as they would to orders from their superiors in Baghdad. Similarly, SCIRI is likely to influence the ICDC in the south given the large number of defense corps personnel there who once served in the Badr Brigades. Although the ICDC may eventually absorb old militias, it will take vigilance and time to ensure that the old chains of command do not remain in place. Realistically, the ICDC will remain largely under the control of the same local leaders as the old militias for some time to come.

Smaller Local and Unofficial Militias

Iraq is a heavily armed country (e.g., CPA directives permit each Iraqi household to keep an AK-47 rifle), and its citizens are unlikely to be disarmed even in the long term, let alone while insecurity reigns. Moreover, junior coalition military commanders established a number of militias immediately after the war to assist with local security (although many

U.S. and British divisions have adopted different approaches to the issue of militias). Hence, in addition to the above-named forces, a plethora of local militias exist in every major area of the country, where they are used by various groups to influence local politics. In the jockeying for power that will inevitably accompany the transition period, these militias may be used to influence elections. For example, in southern Iraq—where factionalism is at its most diffuse and complex—over 130 Shiite militias have been identified by the CPA, and a number of them have already influenced the results of small local polls carried out by factional leaders seeking to fabricate a democratic mandate. Small groups of Shiite militants have also been used in other ways to advance a political agenda (e.g., carrying out attacks against alcohol merchants). Although coalition and Iraqi security forces have attempted to halt illegal activities by smaller militias, they cannot formally disband such groups while Iraqis retain the legal right to bear arms.

Policy Implications

If current trends continue, the future Iraqi central government will not hold a monopoly on the use of force, but will instead be challenged by strong regional militias and a broad base of smaller local militias operating without any government mandate. The coalition should take steps to reverse these trends while it still retains influence over Iraqi affairs in the transitional period. Specifically, the CPA should first ensure that the ICDC and other legitimate security forces absorb existing militias, and then increase central government control over these forces (i.e., centralize selection and training, strengthen command and control, increase professionalism, etc.). Much can be done in this respect. For example, the CPA could send Iraqis to the United States for training programs; increase the number of Iraqi personnel undergoing lengthy training courses in neighboring countries such as Jordan; and enlist the assistance of countries that have more experience than the United States with paramilitary law enforcement forces. Although the ICDC and other Iraqi security forces will effectively resemble and act like local militias for the time being, the above steps offer the best chance of slowly bringing them under centralized political control.

Michael Knights

45
Setting Realistic Expectations for Iraq's Security Forces

Faced with both the Muqtada al-Sadr uprising and intense fighting in Ramadi and Falluja, Washington announced that it will hold the number of U.S. forces in Iraq at the current level of 134,000 by delaying plans to withdraw some troops during the current rotation. The announcement is a recognition that Iraqi security forces are not yet able to handle civil emergencies and armed resistance on the scale being seen in central and southern Iraq. These forces have been sorely tested in recent incidents; the Iraqi Police Service (IPS) failed to warn about the attack on U.S. contractors in Falluja, and it surrendered control of its police stations and vehicles to al-Sadr's Mahdi Army in cities from Baghdad to Basra. The Iraqi Civil Defense Corps (ICDC), designed by the Coalition Provisional Authority (CPA) to provide paramilitary support to IPS and coalition forces, underperformed in its first major deployment in the Falluja fighting and failed to prevent the collapse of IPS forces in the face of Mahdi Army pressure in the south.

These incidents should prompt new analysis of what can be done to support the continued development of Iraqi security forces, and a realistic reevaluation of expectations regarding the role of these forces before, during, and after the upcoming transition period. Most important, these fragile forces should not be prematurely exposed to serious fighting or other situations that are likely to strain their loyalties.

Background

Currently, more than 220,000 Iraqi security personnel are active throughout the country. These forces include the following: 3,000 soldiers in the new Iraqi army (a slowly building force that has been designed for external defense); nearly 140,000 Facilities Protection Service (FPS) and border guard forces charged with static defense of critical infrastructure, government ministries, and borders; 66,800 IPS personnel; and 15,000 locally recruited and trained members of the ICDC.

The IPS is a fledgling law enforcement organization under severe strain because of the postwar collapse of the rule of law in Iraq, which spurred a rise in serious and organized crime while fostering the extreme militarization of Iraq's factional politics. Perhaps understandably, the IPS has failed on most occasions to stand up to well-armed militias,

Originally published as *PolicyWatch* no. 854, April 8, 2004.

from which many of its members are drawn at a local level. Most recently, the IPS ceded its police stations and vehicles to al-Sadr's Mahdi Army. In part, the failure to resist aggressive militia activity is caused by a lack of confidence, partly derived from the historically low status accorded to the Iraqi police, but also because the IPS has not yet received sufficient amounts of equipment (e.g., heavily armored vehicles, body armor, communications gear) that could help it feel like part of a stronger network of well-protected coalition security forces. Over the past year, more than 350 Iraqi police have been killed by insurgents and criminals (many died in five major bomb attacks on police stations between November and February).

The ICDC is similarly crosscut by local and sectarian affiliations, reducing its usefulness in local security crises while simultaneously hampering its ability to provide the paramilitary support needed by the IPS and the coalition. As shown in Falluja, where two battalions of ICDC forces dissolved after refusing to take part in serious fighting, the organization does not yet have the confidence to operate alongside, let alone take the place of, coalition forces in such contingencies.

Realistic Expectations

Iraq's security forces are still fragile; they operate best when they are closely supported by coalition troops, but even then, they lack the ability to undertake offensive operations against strong resistance. Most of these forces—particularly in the Shiite community—are also hesitant to fight their sectarian brethren, as witnessed at the Majar al-Kabir police station, where six British soldiers were killed on June 24, 2003, and more recently during al-Sadr's uprising. Like a number of Iraqi security forces, the loyalties of the IPS remain divided between local, sectarian, and national affiliations, and a considerable number of IPS personnel in the south appear to have assisted the Mahdi Army in consolidating its control over southern police stations and government buildings. Until Iraqi security forces can identify more closely with a sovereign Iraqi state and absorb the training and equipment needed to bolster their confidence, they should not be exposed to heavy fighting or to sectarian dilemmas that will strain their loyalties.

The ICDC and IPS should continue in the roles they have succeeded at so far: supporting and guiding coalition raids and performing the vital service of reducing normal crime. The CPA should also integrate both bodies into the broader interagency intelligence system. Though it may be unfair to demand that the IPS fight resistance forces or militias, it is perfectly reasonable to expect that Iraqi security forces provide warning of attacks or disturbances before or as they develop. There are strong indications that local communities were warned of certain attacks on the coalition beforehand (e.g., the November 2003 ambush at Samara; the February 2003 police station attack in Falluja; the recent killing of four Blackwater security personnel in the same town; the occupation of the governor's palace in Basra). The CPA originally considered stationing military intelligence officers at local police stations and building each post into a sensor that would feed into the broader intelligence system. Indeed, one must question why the IPS failed to generate useful warnings regarding attacks such as those listed above. In developing the newly established National Intelligence Service, the CPA needs to develop incentives for Iraqi security forces to provide early warning data—perhaps based on the model used to encourage tribes to protect pipelines, where coalition forces have employed a strict performance-based system. Considering the large number of Iraqis attracted to security jobs by the relatively generous payments package, the CPA could afford to hire and fire according to performance. The coalition would then need to ensure that a communications network is created to support this flow of information.

Policy Implications

With the crucial transition period less than ninety days away, the lessons of Falluja and southern Iraq must be absorbed and acted upon. Coalition forces may indeed need to be fixed at the current level in the coming months, and the process of withdrawal from city centers may need to be reversed. As CPA administrator L. Paul Bremer noted, the numbers of Iraqi security forces have already been successfully boosted; attention must now be turned to training these personnel. Special attention should be accorded to the integration of Iraqi security forces into an early warning network, so that even if Iraqi forces cannot or will not directly confront illegal activity or militia pressure, they are made to understand that their job security relies on reporting such activity to the coalition. Lacking regular channels of communication, isolated Iraqi security forces currently suffer from low morale and cannot add to the coalition intelligence picture.

Therefore, all efforts should be extended to the development of local security forces. In practice, this means speeding up the flow of resources to IPS and ICDC forces before the transition. In Diyala province, for example, the local coalition police trainer recently complained that $2.1 million worth of purchases of weapons, body armor, and communications equipment were trapped in bureaucratic logjams (specifically, these funds are being withheld until the CPA transitions into the new embassy in early July). Even without considerations of risk, it is surely cheaper to speed up the development of Iraqi forces than to retain far more expensive U.S. military forces in country.

46
Lessons of the Iraq War and Its Aftermath

The 101st Airborne Division returned to the United States in February after spending most of the previous year stationed throughout Iraq's four northernmost provinces. Although the division was engaged in daily combat with insurgent forces in its mission to provide security, it was also heavily involved in the reconstruction effort, particularly in rebuilding vital infrastructure and establishing government institutions. The 101st Airborne functioned under two critical operating procedures: first, to foster, create, and underwrite as many beneficial programs and policies as possible in order to give the maximum number of Iraqis a stake in the success of the new country; and second, to conduct operations in such a way as to remove insurgents from the streets while avoiding tactics and incidents that motivated more Iraqis to join the resistance.

The division was confronted with three different types of insurgents in northern Iraq:

- *Former regime elements (FREs).* These fighters are former Baath insiders who have no hope of playing a role in the new Iraq. Their well-funded leadership structure has been gradually destroyed, most significantly with the deaths of Uday and Qusay Hussein.
- *Criminals freed by Saddam Hussein.* Well before the war, insurgents of this type had demonstrated a willingness to kill. Since the war, they have been dedicated to ensuring that law and order do not prevail in Iraq because they know that it would mean a return to jail. Most of these individuals are unemployed, which made them dangerous candidates for recruitment by FREs.
- *Extremist groups.* Some insurgents of this type originated from organizations based outside Iraq (e.g., al-Qaeda), while others were homegrown (e.g., Ansar al-Islam). These extremists have a vision for the new Iraq that is far beyond what is acceptable to the vast majority of Iraqis.

From the beginning, the strategy of the 101st was to achieve early victories in the "hearts and minds" of the Iraqi population and then to continue building on that momentum. Accordingly, the division became heavily involved in several reconstruction missions, including the following: holding early provincial elections, repairing the main

On April 7, 2004, Maj. Gen. David Petraeus addressed The Washington Institute's Special Policy Forum. General Petraeus commanded the 101st Airborne Division during Operation Iraqi Freedom. Previously, he served as assistant chief of staff for operations in the NATO Stabilization Force in Bosnia, and as deputy commander of the U.S. Joint Interagency Counter-Terrorism Task Force there. This rapporteur's summary (originally published as *PolicyWatch* no. 855, April 9, 2004) was prepared by Ryan Phillips.

bridge spanning from Irbil to Mosul, solving severe fuel shortages, paying civil servants, reopening the Syrian border, and rebuilding the badly looted Mosul University and other educational facilities.

Many of these projects were funded through the Commanders Emergency Reconstruction Program. This funding, which originated from captured Iraqi funds, was disbursed to commanders throughout Iraq in order to finance various reconstruction efforts. Over a period of seven months, the 101st underwrote approximately 5,000 projects with these funds, including clean-up efforts, infrastructure repair, and information projects (e.g., the establishment of Mosul TV).

The 101st Airborne also played a role in developing innovative methods of reducing violence in northern Iraq. In one case, an ammunition dump became the site of frequent infiltration, leading to several firefights in which Iraqis were killed. Inquiries with local leaders determined that the infiltrators were after the brass used to make the ammunition, not the ammunition itself. Accordingly, a commercial firm was established to extract and sell the brass. Some of the proceeds were then used for hiring local security forces to guard the ammunition dump.

The Iraqi Security Services

The newly recruited Iraqi police have all undergone at least three weeks of special training. Although that does not sound like much, most of these individuals already had some experience in policing. To be sure, even veteran Iraqi police had no experience with the sort of police work done in the West. Under Saddam Hussein, Iraqi police basically directed traffic and handled minor criminal cases, while regime elements (e.g., special security services personnel) handled the major cases. Still, veteran Iraqi police came equipped with several key skills and a modicum of knowledge regarding weapons. Moreover, recruits who had not previously served as policemen were placed in an eight-week training course. Much of this training was conducted by a U.S. military police unit whose primary function is to train both policemen and police trainers.

The process of establishing the new Iraqi police force has been challenging. Finding uniforms, communication gear, and weapons proved daunting. Moreover, in mid-July 2003, former Iraqi military personnel who were uncertain about their wages staged a large riot in Mosul. The Iraqi police killed some of the demonstrators, and the structure of the police force itself collapsed. U.S. forces had to reenter the area and establish order, at a cost of seventeen soldiers wounded and three destroyed vehicles. A new police chief was appointed, however, and over time, the police have performed quite well. They have taken serious casualties, though; they remain primary targets because they are easier to hit than coalition forces.

Similarly, members of the Iraqi Civil Defense Corps received three weeks of training before they were put in uniform and sent out to begin their guard duties. Their training continued as they performed missions; the guiding principle was to start them out with basic tasks and then upgrade these duties as part of on-the-job training. Finally, members of the new Iraqi army are receiving much more extensive training because they will be expected to do more than other security personnel (including collective tasks such as offensive operations).

Challenging Times Ahead

Iraq appears much more manageable on the ground than it does from afar. That said, the recent escalation of violence is troubling. Overall, there are several key lessons to be learned from the past year:

- Every area of Iraq is different, so there is no one tactic or approach that will work across the entire country. In fact, an approach that works in a given area today may not even work there tomorrow. The enemy has been adapting constantly, and U.S. forces must do so as well.
- Great restraint is needed when operating near large crowds of Iraqis. A major concern is that crowds can easily turn into mobs that could pose a serious threat to coalition forces. In the past week especially, large gatherings of Iraqis have become a key source of concern in several predominantly Shiite areas of the country.
- Iraqi security forces need continuous training and sufficient equipment. In partnership with local Iraqi officials, the coalition must also work to instill a sense of pride and trust into the various security organizations, something that was nonexistent under the reign of Saddam.
- Once military operations in a given area are substantively complete, all parties must show the local population that they have a stake in the success of the new Iraq. This will be a great challenge in the Falluja and Ramadi area, which was a military industrial center that remains home to many former military personnel.
- Local initiative is crucial to the future of Iraq, but it is a substantial challenge in a country that has traditionally been subject to widespread centralization efforts originating from Baghdad.
- Efforts to keep the country's leadership free from the yoke of Baath loyalists must be coupled with reconciliation. It is not possible to fire all former Baathists and expect them to become anything other than enemies. The coalition must reconcile with a number of the thousands of former Baath officials and bring them into the new system, giving them a direct stake in the success of the new Iraq.

Michael Knights

47 The Multinational Divisions in Iraq: Lessons Learned

Madrid's determination to withdraw Spanish troops from Iraq, combined with the collapse of some multinational forces during recent fighting, poses serious questions about the contribution that such forces can make to security during the period leading up to the June 30 transfer of power.

Background

The performance of the two coalition multinational divisions (MND) varied widely during the recent Muqtada al-Sadr uprising. The British-commanded MND South-East proved effective in weathering Mahdi Army attacks, defending key points, and acting quickly to recover lost terrain. When al-Sadr's militiamen occupied the Basra governor's headquarters, British forces compelled them to leave, while Italian troops undertook a series of assaults to recover control of strategic bridges in Nasariya. In sharp contrast, the Polish-led MND South-Center failed to defend many key points or to respond to direct attacks on Coalition Provisional Authority (CPA) compounds. Instead, U.S. troops from the Sunni Triangle were required to drive out militia forces throughout the south-central sector, even though these troops were needed to secure areas around Baghdad.

Causes of Failure in the South-Central Sector

MND South-Center did not fail in its mission due to lack of support from NATO, which has provided logistical, communications, and intelligence support since the division's establishment. Although the entire coalition military structure was surprised by the speed at which the threat posed by al-Sadr escalated, the CPA and the U.S.-led Combined Joint Task Force 7 headquarters arguably blindsided the Polish-led division by stepping up actions against al-Sadr without fully consulting the division.

Still, MND South-Center did display a number of intrinsic weaknesses. Comprised of twenty-three national contingents—communicating in seventeen languages and fusing units with little experience working together—the division lacked the cohesion needed to respond quickly to the uprising. Moreover, the division leadership does not appear to have maintained effective control over its forces, with some contingents phoning their native

Originally published as *PolicyWatch* no. 859, April 19, 2004.

countries for guidance. Many MND South-Center forces were consequently limited to noncombat roles that did not include either aggressive patrolling or holding and recapturing terrain claimed by militias. Most concerning, however, was the failure of multinational forces to defend CPA compounds, forcing the CPA to withdraw from all but one of its provincial outreach stations (Najaf) in south-central Iraq. Individual contingents refused to fire on mortars targeting CPA compounds and to target militiamen firing rocket-propelled grenades at CPA buildings, other than those that they were personally defending. Indeed, the rules of engagement used by MND South-Center forces appear to have been so narrow that they restricted the ability of coalition soldiers to fire unless they were personally targeted. In some cases, the response of MND South-Center troops was limited to calling for assistance from the Iraqi Police Service.

Multinational Forces in the Transitional Period

Along with the development of the new Iraqi security forces, which also suffered major setbacks in recent fighting (see chapter 45, "Setting Realistic Expectations for Iraq's Security Forces"), multinational forces are key to the speed at which the number and profile of U.S. forces in Iraq can be reduced. The Sunni Triangle area will require U.S. forces for the foreseeable future, but multinational divisions can replace U.S. divisions elsewhere in the country. Spanish and Bulgarian forces—deployed in south-central Iraq—may withdraw in the coming months. In the southeast, the British-led division is largely self-sufficient, and key force providers such as Britain, Italy, and Japan have shown resolve in the face of recent kidnappings aimed at forcing the withdrawal of their troops. In the meantime, a new multinational division may materialize in northern Iraq. On April 15, the newly elected South Korean government quickly reaffirmed the country's commitment to send 3,600 troops to join other multinational forces taking over the U.S. 101st Air Assault division sector there; however, these forces will principally assist with reconstruction and not engage in offensive security roles. The Korean government backed away from the deployment of its troops in the dangerous environment of Kirkuk, where multinational troops are badly needed.

As the June 30 transition approaches, both northern and south-central multinational units may lack contingents capable of acting robustly against security challenges, suggesting that U.S. forces may again be drawn in to handle the periodic crises likely to punctuate the transition period. A new UN Security Council Resolution may attract more capable troops from advanced military nations, but unless these contingents adopt more aggressive and committed rules of engagement, their utility will be strictly limited to noncrisis situations. Each major city or densely populated province in Iraq is typically controlled by a 2,000- to 3,000-strong coalition brigade combat team. It is imperative that in the MND areas, each of these teams has at least one unit capable of performing a quick reaction force (QRF) role, reinforcing threatened areas or counterattacking to recover occupied locales. Such a capability was present in British- and Italian-controlled areas, but not in south-central Iraq, where coalition control quickly disintegrated. To reduce the need to regularly engage in QRF operations to recover lost ground, other coalition forces need to adopt standardized rules of engagement that allow them to carry out broader self-defense.

Policy Implications

U.S. and coalition support provided to multinational forces should be enhanced. For example, outgoing U.S. forces have been careful to transfer lessons learned to incoming U.S. troops during the current rotation; this kind of support should be expanded to current and future multinational partners. Ultimately, however, the strengthening of multinational forces in Iraq needs to be discussed within both the NATO and UN contexts. NATO could provide much of the command and control structure for multinational divisions and the training support for contributor nations, beginning with a formalization of its role in MND South-Center; this should be discussed at the alliance's Istanbul summit on June 28-29.

A new and robust UN resolution would undoubtedly help attract new or maintain existing multinational force contributions to Iraq, which would be useful as the six-month tours undertaken by most multinational forces expires in June. A relatively modest resolution—one that does not add much to UN Security Council Resolution 1511 (which authorizes a multinational force under unified command to use "all necessary means" to achieve stability)—might attract new and better trained forces to Iraq from advanced military nations (e.g., France, India) as well as from other countries. It could also make force providers more comfortable with placing troops fully under divisional control, where each state would have a national representative as opposed to merely retaining a veto option on actions through direct communication with field units.

Finally, the coalition needs to ensure that each multinational brigade combat team has a unit that can serve as a reliable QRF, one that is willing to broadly interpret its self-defense mandate and is capable of offensive operations. Until Iraqi security forces can undertake extremely sensitive missions—against local militia leaders, for example—the United States should maintain its ability to dispatch small strike groups to each MND that will act in this capacity, remaining mindful of the need to avoid blindsiding coalition allies during future crisis periods.

48
Crisis in Iraq: Military Lessons for the Coalition

Recent U.S. confrontations with insurgents in Falluja and with Muqtada al-Sadr's Mahdi Army in the south have exposed a number of U.S. misconceptions regarding the Iraqi political-military environment. These two militant challenges to the long-term stability of Iraq have necessitated a change in approach on the part of the coalition. The fighting has also provided early indications of unanticipated complexity in the operating environment leading up to (and following) the June 30 transfer of sovereignty.

Lessons Learned

The United States underestimated the troublemaking potential of its enemies in Iraq, the constraints on its military freedom of action, and the dangers—potential and actual—of resorting to force under the current circumstances. These dangers include strengthening al-Sadr's popular standing, further discrediting members of the Iraqi Governing Council, and, most important, alienating large parts of the Iraqi population. Such consequences point to a failure by U.S. officials to fully comprehend either Iraqi political dynamics or the mood on the street.

This lack of understanding may be due to the relative isolation of coalition officials and their lack of interaction with broad segments of Iraqi society, but it may also be attributable to the bifurcation of the political and military arms of the occupation: the Coalition Provisional Authority (CPA) and the Combined Joint Task Force 7 (CJTF-7), respectively. Communication and coordination between the CPA and CJTF-7 has never been substantial. It sometimes seems as if subordinate units of CJTF-7 work without a solid grasp of the broader political context in which they are operating, or of the limits of military power under the current circumstances. CJTF-7's response to the challenges posed by Falluja and al-Sadr's militia are cases in point (see chapter 28, "Crisis in Iraq: Assessments and Implications").

Neither the unrest in the Sunni Triangle nor the challenge posed by al-Sadr is amenable to a military solution, nor is the coalition free to use force as it wishes. Addressing both challenges will require patience, perseverance, and the adroit use of political, economic,

On April 16, 2004, Michael Eisenstadt addressed The Washington Institute's Special Policy Forum. This summary (originally published as *PolicyWatch* no. 862, April 22, 2004) was prepared by Mr. Eisenstadt.

and military levers by the coalition and by the Iraqi interim authority that takes over on June 30. The key to success is ensuring that the maximum number of Iraqis have a stake in the new political order, while marginalizing political and religious extremists by peaceful means whenever possible—using force only when necessary.

Falluja is an extreme manifestation of the problem the coalition faces in dealing with former regime elements and religious extremists (local and foreign) throughout much of the Sunni Triangle. Capturing, disarming, or killing identifiable insurgents, while offering generous financial inducements to the general population in order to win their cooperation are necessary components of the counterinsurgency effort, but they will not expunge the attitudes, ideologies, or political conditions that gave rise to the insurgency. This problem requires a political solution, which the U.S. military cannot deliver.

Likewise, capturing or killing al-Sadr (the declared U.S. objective) will not halt the activities of the clerical network he inherited from his late father—a network that fulfills a variety of communal and social-welfare functions. Nor will these measures put an end to the phenomenon of "Sadrism," which taps into Shiite grievances against the United States (including its failure to protect them after encouraging the Shiites to revolt in 1991, and its failure to provide personal and economic security after the fall of Saddam Hussein), as well as a tradition of religious activism that appeals to a segment of the Shiite community. Disarming al-Sadr's Mahdi Army is not a viable option at this time, although the coalition—or better yet, Iraqis—can at least insist that militia members not bear arms in public.

Al-Sadr can, however, be marginalized. His following is relatively small, and he is reviled by broad sectors of the Shiite public and the community's clerical leadership. It should be possible to discredit him by emphasizing his reliance on funding from clerical networks in Iran (exposing the lie of al-Sadr's own nativist rhetoric and appealing to the Iraqi nationalism of many Shiites). His role in the April 2003 murder of moderate Shiite cleric Abdul Majid al-Khoei and the thuggish exploits of al-Sadr's followers should also be publicized. All of this would best be done by Iraqis.

Toward the Transition

In the period leading up to and following the June 30 power transfer, coalition military forces will likely face increasingly difficult circumstances:

- *A push by the Iraqi interim authority for a significant decisionmaking role in security matters, further curbing the coalition's military freedom of action.* Average Iraqis are likely to bridle against what looks like an open-ended occupation and heavy-handed coalition tactics. Populist Iraqi politicians will likely exploit this discontent for political gain.
- *An increase in insurgent activity.* Insurgent groups and radical populist politicians want to underscore the fact that the occupation continues by keeping coalition forces involved in providing security, thereby fomenting an anticoalition backlash and enhancing the ability to recruit new adherents.

- *Reduced economic activity caused by the deteriorating security situation.* Businesses shut down following outbreaks of violence, reconstruction projects are slowed or halted, foreign contractors quit or are withdrawn by their employers, and foreign lenders and investors shun Iraq. This progression is likely to feed anticoalition sentiment and further discourage cooperation with coalition forces.
- *Difficulty in obtaining accurate, timely intelligence.* The security environment and uncertainty about the future is liable to discourage many Iraqis, including security personnel, from cooperating with the coalition. The Iraqi interim authority and the subsequent elected government will likely inherit the Sunni Triangle insurgency, the al-Sadr problem, and the challenge of disarming the country's various militias. These challenges will stress the fragile institutions of the nascent government, test the new Iraqi security forces, and complicate the transition from dictatorship to democracy in Iraq. On the other hand, the very weakness of the new government may compel it to eschew the use of force and seek political solutions to the country's problems whenever feasible. This would be a novel and welcome development for Iraq.

Implications

Successfully rebuilding Iraq will ultimately require the creation of a legitimate, representative, and effective new government. This is a necessary condition for the achievement of several key objectives: successfully dealing with insurgents and political extremists, who will no longer be able to claim that they are fighting foreign occupiers and infidels; rebuilding Iraq's security forces, which are more likely to hold together if ordered into action by a legitimate Iraqi government (instead of by foreigners); and attracting foreign lenders and investors, who are awaiting the restoration of security and the formation of a new Iraqi government before putting their money on the line. Coalition military actions should be evaluated by how they will affect these overriding objectives. While the use of force against insurgents and extremists will remain necessary for the foreseeable future, the resort to force must be selective, implemented with great care and precision and with an eye toward minimizing political collateral damage.

49
Short-term Stabilisation in Iraq Could Have Long-term Costs

The Coalition security policy in Iraq has evolved in important ways since the major public diplomacy setback of the Abu Ghraib prison abuse scandal and the dual security challenges in the Falluja-Ramadi area and the Shi'ite south during April and May.

The actions taken by the Coalition Provisional Authority (CPA) and its military counterpart, Combined Joint Task Force 7 (CJTF-7), will shape the security environment as Iraq passes through a series of transitional steps-from the handover to the Iraqi Interim Government (IIG) on 30 June to the fully constitutional Iraqi government that is scheduled to take office on 31 December 2005.

In close co-operation with Iraqi mediators and local non-governmental security forces, Coalition military actions have improved the security environment in Falluja and reduced the threat from radical Shi'ite cleric Moqtada al-Sadr. However, in the long term these actions may make the task of re-unifying Iraq even harder by reinforcing the strength of local actors at the expense of weak central government in Baghdad.

Solving the Dual Security Crises

The stand-off between US 1st Marine Division forces and armed Falluja residents ended when local military figures offered to form the Falluja Protection Army (FPA) to police the city, allowing the US Marines to pull back to a series of forward operating bases on the city's outskirts. The FPA, which took over security in the city on 1 May, is led by a committee of former Ba'athist military and intelligence officers. Its nominal head is Major-General Mohammed Abdel Latif, a former military intelligence officer, but the FPA appears to be operationally controlled by Major-General Jassim Saleh, the former commander of the Iraqi Regular Army 38th Infantry Division and chief-of-staff of a Republican Guard division.

Although barred from formal command of the FPA due to his controversial record in Saddam's service, Falluja-born Gen Saleh has proven central to the success of the militia because of his ability to draw local men to the unit. As CPA sources have commented, the FPA is primarily staffed by men who were fighting the Coalition forces only a week

Originally published in *Jane's Intelligence Review*, June 1, 2004. Reprinted with permission from Jane's Information Group/*Jane's Intelligence Review.*

beforehand. By doing this, the Coalition has effectively driven a wedge between what might be termed the 'popular resistance' (the many hundreds of Falluja residents who joined the resistance during Marine offensive operations in early April) and the 'professional resistance' (including long-term insurgents and foreign fighters). Although the FPA's capability to prevent insurgent attacks will be tested throughout the coming months and any failure could lead to an explosive US re-entry into central Falluja, the delegation of inner-city security to local former military figures is a model that may be adopted elsewhere in Iraq if it is successful.

In the Shi'ite cities of southern Iraq, the Coalition set about neutralising al-Sadr's Jaish al-Mahdi militia in order to shape a favourable climate for local Shi'a factions to politically marginalise the cleric. By the end of April, Jaish al-Mahdi controlled key religious shrines in Najaf, Kufa and Karbala, plus the Baghdad neighbourhood of Sadr City. A range of military and non-military means were used to degrade the threat posed by the militia and CPA provincial outreach personnel struck deals with a number of less militant Jaish al-Mahdi cells. For example, in Samawah, a Jaish al-Mahdi cell leader broke with al-Sadr and declared his allegiance to Ayatollah Ali Sistani.

In addition to political persuasion, the Coalition launched a series of military operations intended to reduce the intimidating presence of Jaish al-Mahdi forces in order to allow Shi'ite leaders to bring pressure to bear directly on al-Sadr. In Diwaniyah, US 1st Armoured Division operations since 29 April identified ammunition caches in schools; created a presence on city streets; and seized Jaish al-Mahdi offices.

In Karbala, US troops undertook a similar series of 'cordon and search' operations, seizing three Jaish al-Mahdi gathering places away from the key religious shrines, including a tribal democracy centre that burned fiercely after its capture due to the large amounts of ordnance stored within it. When US 1st Armoured Division troops seized the Mukhaiyam mosque, a key Sadr stronghold in central Karbala, the Jaish al-Mahdi fell back to positions around the Shrines of Abbas and Hussein, from which they continued to direct small-arms and rocket-propelled grenade (RPG) fire onto the mosque. In the absence of widespread local opposition to the US presence in central Karbala, the USA is taking increasingly daring steps to lever Jaish al-Mahdi out of its holy sanctuary. In the early hours of 17 May, the USA directed an AC-130 gunship strike against a gathering of militiamen collecting on a street corner only 49m from the Shrine of Abbas, killing 16 Jaish al-Mahdi fighters.

In Najaf and Kufa, the Coalition spent over two weeks preparing intelligence before the US 2nd Armoured Cavalry Regiment directed a series of targeted air strikes and raids to reduce Jaish al-Mahdi's control over the city. This included an air strike at Kufa on 29 April that killed an estimated 40 Sadr militiamen, daily armoured 'thunder runs' into central Najaf followed by withdrawal before dusk, as well as the recapture of the governor's palace and the instalment of Adnan al-Zurufi as the new governor. By the middle of May, Jaish al-Mahdi fighters were operating from the holy cemeteries abutting the Imam Ali shrine in Najaf, having been slowly driven from the streets of the city.

When Sadr sought to broaden the conflict to offset these losses, he suffered similar setbacks in Basra, Amarah and Sadr City. In Sadr City between 8 and 10 May, US 1st Cavalry Division forces took control of a number of weapons caches and destroyed a major Sadr office with air strikes, bypassing determined attempts by Jaish al-Mahdi to barricade the inner reaches of the town.

Although they have gained in tactical sophistication due to recent combat experience, Jaish al-Mahdi remains a less formidable foe than the Sunni resistance. Its attacks have largely involved the use of unsophisticated small-arms and RPG fire against Coalition military patrols or convoys, or long-range mortar fire against CPA compounds. CPA personnel in southern Iraq told *JIR* that Jaish al-Mahdi militiamen became used to acting with impunity when faced by multinational forces in south-central Iraq. They set up mortar tubes in plain sight of Coalition checkpoints and failed to use cover when firing small arms—knowing that they would not be targeted due to the restrictive rules of engagement of those international units.

Against US troops, however, Jaish al-Mahdi forces employing these tactics have suffered heavily, losing every tactical firefight they have engaged in and melting away when faced by aggressive US action. Since US and multinational troops began occupying the schools and even mosques used by Jaish al-Mahdi as headquarters and arms caches, Sadr's militiamen have been forced to seek the shelter of religious shrines as firing positions and operating bases—steps that have reduced popular support for Sadr's uprising.

Although Sadr appeared at Friday sermons in a white cloak in early May, signifying his willingness to die as a martyr, the Coalition actually stepped back from the provocative step of killing or capturing him as early as the first week of April and is unlikely to enter the inner sanctum of the Shi'a shrines that the Jaish al-Mahdi has occupied. The Coalition's patient and focused use of military force successfully set the conditions for a range of local Shi'ite actors to bring pressure to bear on Sadr, who has consistently failed to incite broad public participation in his planned coups in October 2003 and April 2004. At the same time Sadr has antagonised the Iraq Shi'ite religious, political and mercantile elites with his disruptive activities. Iraq's Shi'a neither wanted Sadr to emerge victorious in his stand-off with the Coalition, nor did they wish the US military to wade into Sadr's refuge near the Imam Ali shrine in Najaf to remove the militia leader. The Supreme Council for Islamic Revolution in Iraq (SCIRI) moved to undercut Sadr in Karbala, using its influence in the Iraqi Ministry of Awqaf (religious endowments) to reduce the status of a number of Sadr's mosques in the city.

In Najaf, negotiations involving 20 Shi'a tribal, professional, and religious leaders failed to secure Sadr's voluntary withdrawal the city, even after Sistani ally, Ayatollah Sheikh Sadreddin Kubanji, delivered sermons on 8 and 11 May calling for Sadr to leave. Demonstrations against Sadr's militia and organised by Kubanji were called off when Jaish al-Mahdi militias threatened to break them up. Following the failure of indirect influence, Ayatollah Sistani directly weighed in on 18 May, calling for Sadr's militia and Coalition forces to leave Najaf. This pressure could culminate in the negotiation of a compromise solution, leading to Sadr's detention under tribal-administered house arrest and the lowering of the Jaish al-Mahdi's street presence, replacing them with tribal and political militias.

Tactical Success, Strategic Costs

The reduction of insurgent or anti-Coalition militia activity in Falluja and across the Shi'ite south is a necessity as Iraq's transition approaches: the prominent role that Iraqis played in the process reflects the Bush administration's increasing willingness to hand real power over the Iraqis. However, in what constitutes a revolution in Coalition security strategy, the US government has essentially sidelined the incoming IIG as a major security player in the coming months. Among the many changes resulting from the recent uprisings, Coalition decision-makers have written off the prospect that effective central government-controlled Iraqi security forces can be forged until Iraqis have rallied around what White House decision-makers have described as "an Iraqi standard"—a new sovereign Iraqi government. Following the widespread failure of Iraqi Civil Defence Corps (ICDC), New Iraqi Army (NIA), and Iraqi Police Service (IPS) forces in the uprisings, the Coalition is not going to rely on Iraq's government forces to provide national or 'top-down' security to Iraq's regions. Instead, these forces are going to be slowly built up over a period of two years by Ali Abdul Allawi, Iraq's Minister of Defence and Major-General David Petraeus, the head of the new US Office of Security Transition and former commander of the 101st Air Assault Division. The Pentagon's decision to maintain as many as 135,000 US troops in Iraq until the end of 2005 is an indicator that Iraq's forces are going to be slowly grown through the generation of a strong non-commissioned and commissioned officer cadre and the development of a military education system. A US Central Command planner told *JIR* that Petraeus would use these institutions to "reinforce the positive aspects of Iraqi military heritage", as well as to reintegrate select individuals drawn to the 36,000 "tier IV" Ba'athists previously banned from government service. While commanding the 101st Armoured Division, Petraeus experienced the most success of any US divisional commander in training Iraqi security forces, some of whom fought with distinction during early May attacks on provincial government buildings in Mosul.

According to a range of US Central Command and Pentagon sources canvassed by *JIR*, until central government-controlled Iraqi forces are ready to take on serious security roles, Iraq's security system will comprise occasional intervention by top-down national armed forces provided primarily by the Coalition, alongside local paramilitaries providing more routine security assistance to municipal and provincial governments. Iraqi militias and political factions may also be the principal providers of intelligence as the Iraqi National Intelligence Service (INIS) is slowly developed under its minister, Mohammed Abdullah Shehwani. This 'bottom-up' model of security may have a significant impact on Iraq's political development during the transition period as the dual security crises created a significant class of new political actors, ranging from newly sanctioned militia commanders, to religious or tribal intermediaries and other new 'securocrats'. These figures will intermingle with and exist alongside the body politic that UN special representative Lakhdar Brahimi will develop at Iraq's National Assembly in July 2004, representing a parallel network that may complicate Iraq's transition to democratic rule.

Apparent political winners from the recent security crises include the range of Islamist groups that secured the release of foreign hostages and negotiated with both Falluja residents and al-Sadr. The most well known example is the Muslim Scholars Council, which is based at the 'Mother of All Battles' mosque in Baghdad, but other Sufi and Salafist Islamist groups based at the Gailani and Ibn Toubal mosques in Baghdad also increased their influence during this period. Imam Sheikh Jamal Shaker Nazzal, a radical Sunni cleric detained by the Coalition in October 2003, was released on 30 April in order to negotiate with Falluja residents. Political and tribal intermediaries have also etched new roles and higher profiles for themselves by brokering deals and issuing demands to the Coalition—most notably Ahmed Hardan, the chief Iraqi negotiator at Falluja, who secured US$50m worth of reconstruction aid for the town from US coffers. The leaders of a number of southern tribes have been installed as new replacement governors and police chiefs in areas where they assisted the Coalition in opposing Sadr's uprising. Iraq's tribal networks were a key tool for the Coalition in influencing Jaish al-Mahdi actions in some areas and the Iraqi National Council of Tribes (representing 25 key tribes comprising an estimated two million Iraqis) was a key player in negotiations with al-Sadr.

Sanctioned delegation of local security to militias remains the most dangerous trend, as it threatens to systematise the imbalance that already exists between weak central government security forces and numerous powerful local and regional militias. Initial experience of the FPA at Falluja suggests some future drawbacks to the "bottom-up" security model. Although it successfully deactivated popular discontent over the security environment and the presence of foreign troops, the approach risks creating 'no-go' zones for Coalition troops, complicating the task of carrying out targeted operations against dedicated insurgents and foreign fighters. FPA Gen Latif stated: "There are no foreign fighters in Falluja ... maybe there were some a month ago, but now they are gone." This may well be the case considering the close focus on their activities and the disruption their presence could bring to the city. Yet, as long as US forces stay outside central Falluja neighbourhoods, Iraqi insurgent activity in the city cannot be effectively monitored and it remains difficult to escort Coalition or reconstruction convoys transiting through the city. Once no-go zones have been agreed, they may ossify into permanent arrangements. Gen Latif and the rank-and-file of the FPA have issued multiple statements warning the US Marines to stay outside the city limits or face the unit's reversion into a popular resistance faction.

A Model for the South?

There are signs that the Falluja model may be used in the Shi'ite south. Previously, some multinational forces—notably the British and the Spanish—had forged local alliances with SCIRI Badr Organisation armed forces and other local militias; US Secretary of Defence Paul Wolfowitz told Congress on 18 May that if US tactical commanders requested permission to use local militias such as the Badr Organisation, their requests would be considered. Meanwhile, 1st US Armoured Division commander Major General Martin Dempsey called on five Shi'a factions to provide a total of 2,000 troops for special IPS and ICDC units that could take over control of sensitive sites from Sadr's Jaish al-Mahdi, deploying where the US troops cannot enter. Even if under nominal IPS or ICDC command, these forces would essentially revert to their factional affiliations if their loyalties were strained. A potential downside to such agreements is that they formalise no-go zones in which resistance or terrorist activity can germinate, while Coalition and perhaps even Iraqi government forces are not allowed to enter. Such restrictions could complicate the extremely challenging task that Coalition forces will face in securing Iraqi elections in December 2004, January 2005 and December 2005, when thousands of polling stations will need to be secured as millions of Iraqis travel around the country to vote in their home constituencies.

Following the episodes of the siege of Falluja and the Abu Ghraib abuse scandal, Iraqi public opinion is also likely to strongly influence Coalition military operations in Iraq, even outside such sensitive areas. Steve Hadley, US Deputy National Security Advisor, stated that the Coalition already closely consults with the outgoing Iraqi Governing Council and local leaders before undertaking sensitive operations. For example, in Falluja the Coalition tested FPA capabilities by driving a convoy of US commanders to a meeting in the city on 11 May, but the route taken by the convoy was dictated by the FPA and the force protection detail's armoured escort was pared down according to FPA directions. At the national level, it will be hard for the Iraqi Interim Government to resist the opportunity to bolster its credibility and distance itself from the Coalition by taking populist steps to restrict US military freedom of action. At local and national levels, the Coalition will increasingly have to either plan carefully interlocking military-political actions (such as those aimed at al-Sadr) or suffer the same frustrations as those experienced by the Marines at Falluja.

The UN Role

If the USA cannot secure a fresh and clearly-worded UN mandate to undertake security operations in Iraq, operating there will be even more complicated matter, and multinational forces are likely to continue to play a minor role. Coalition forces are currently legally authorised and offered legal protection by UN Security Council Resolution 1511, plus elements of Iraq's Transitional Administrative Law and a number of CPA directives. Although a new UN resolution containing fresh authorisation will be tabled by the US "well before the June 30 transition", according to Hadley, it remains unclear whether this draft will be delayed or blocked at the UN. US Central Command negotiators have told *JIR* that a temporary and potentially controversial security agreement is being drafted to act as back-up and to supplement the existing resolution. A fresh UN resolution is vital to the prospect of building effective multinational divisions in Iraq. When Spanish, Dominican, Honduran, and Ukrainian elements of Multinational

Division South-Centre (MND/SC) failed to defend CPA compounds during the Sadr uprising, it was largely because these contingents had extremely restrictive rules of engagement or were banned from any combat role due to the unclear international mandate for the operation. Under a new and clear resolution, the Coalition might not only attract new members, but would also allow national governments to equip their troops with more robust and synchronised rules of engagement. Increased NATO involvement in Iraq would also help to structure better multinational contributions, but appears unlikely until its difficulties in meeting new alliance commitments in Afghanistan can be resolved and until a North Atlantic Council meeting addresses the issue of Iraq in the context of a new and clear resolution.

An Unstable Future

Uncertainties about US freedom of manoeuvre are particularly unsettling because there is likely to be a high demand for 'top-down' intervention by Coalition forces in the next two years. A cyclical pattern of violence is anticipated, with continuing serious unrest throughout June and July, again during Ramadan in October/November and once again during December 2004/January 2005 as anti-Coalition forces seek to disrupt elections. As the elected Iraqi Transitional Government develops Iraq's permanent constitution in January and October 2005, Iraq is likely to see a resurgence of the major sectarian tensions and resultant outbreaks of serious violence that threatened to attend the negotiation of the transitional administrative law in early 2004. This could continue until Iraq's first constitutional elections, currently scheduled for 15 December 2005.

US forces may be required to provide heavy security for key Iraqi locations during any of these periods to prevent a repeat of earlier looting, collapse of basic government services, sectarian violence and putsch attempts. There are obvious drawbacks to using locally organised militias to oversee local elections or to prevent sectarian violence, suggesting a major continuing role for US and multinational security forces as the ultimate guarantors of stability in Iraq.

Although essential for near term security and convenient in terms of quickly providing ready-made local forces that are governed by a chain of command; the adoption of the Falluja Protection Army model across Iraq would be a further blow to its prospects of functioning as a recognisable state when its first constitutional government takes office. It can be argued that Iraq is not a state in danger of breaking up, but is already a cluster of semi-autonomous regions that need to be re-unified. Current trends suggest that it will be governed by a very strong form of federalism, with central government playing a minimal role. With the traditional central government role of security devolved to the regions, Iraq's oil revenues could become the only real element of the Iraqi state holding the nation together—the only feature with sufficient gravity to stop the centrifugal forces of sectarianism from pulling the country apart.

Michael Eisenstadt and Michael Knights

50
The Transfer of Sovereignty in Iraq: Prospects for a Security Agreement

In congressional hearings on Iraq last week, legislators repeatedly asked testifying administration officials whether the United States would negotiate a formal security agreement with the post-June 30 Iraqi Interim Government. The officials explained that following the planned transfer of sovereignty to Iraq, U.S. and coalition forces would operate in accordance with current arrangements or a new UN resolution, pending the conclusion of a formal agreement. This solution has some advantages as the eventual negotiation of a security agreement is liable to be a contentious affair. It also has drawbacks, as the continued presence of coalition forces will almost certainly cause political controversy in Iraq, leading to the imposition of constraints on the coalition's military freedom of action.

Background

In accordance with the November 15 agreement, which outlined an accelerated timetable for transferring sovereignty to Iraq, the United States was to conclude a security agreement with the Iraqi Governing Council (IGC) by the end of March 2004 in order to formalize the terms of the U.S. or coalition military presence in Iraq. These plans were scrapped due to the objections of Grand Ayatollah Ali Hussein al-Sistani and members of the IGC, who insisted that an agreement be negotiated and signed only by an elected Iraqi government. It is therefore likely that an agreement will again be deferred until after Iraqi elections, currently expected to be held by January 31, 2005.

Post-June 30

In the meantime, U.S. forces will continue to operate under the authority provided by UN Security Council Resolution 1511, paragraph 13, which "authorizes a multinational force under unified command to take all necessary measures to contribute to the maintenance of security and stability in Iraq"; Coalition Provisional Authority (CPA) Order Number 17, which grants coalition forces "immun(ity) from Iraqi Legal Process"; and Article 59 of the Transitional Administrative Law (TAL), which defines the Iraqi armed forces as "a principal partner in the multi-national force operating in Iraq under unified command"

Originally published as *PolicyWatch* no. 864, April 27, 2004.

pursuant to UN Security Council Resolution 1511. The TAL also states that the Iraqi armed forces will ultimately answer to the prime minister of Iraq. It is not clear how the efforts of UN Special Representative Lakhdar Brahimi might alter this framework. The United States is seeking a new UN Security Council Resolution on Iraq, but any provision about the status of a multinational force could be a divisive issue in the UN Security Council.

How such an arrangement would work in practice is not clear, since the Iraqi interim government will likely seek to exert control over Iraqi security forces and demand a say in all coalition decisions concerning the use of force. Likewise, with the emergence of domestic politics in Iraq, the role of coalition forces is likely to become a matter of political debate, as they continue to intrude into peoples' lives, impose inconveniences, and cause the death of civilians through accidents and military action. In such an environment, populist politicians and extremists are likely to try to limit the coalition's military freedom of action, and use incidents involving coalition forces as justification for the creation and maintenance of militias to provide security and keep coalition forces from entering "liberated" neighborhoods. This would further complicate efforts to disarm and demobilize tribal and party militias.

The Security Agreement

Once an elected Iraqi government is on its feet, the United States is likely to seek a formal bilateral security agreement covering a variety of matters, as President George W. Bush stated in his news conference on April 13. These might include a Status of Forces Agreement (SOFA) to define the legal status of U.S. military personnel, building on the broad legal immunity of U.S. forces established in CPA Order Number 17. The United States may also negotiate basing access agreements (perhaps for use of Iraqi air bases) and an Acquisition and Cross-Servicing Agreement (ACSA) for the local purchase, for instance, of food, fuel, or transportation.

The negotiation of a security agreement is likely to be a contentious matter, for historical reasons. Under the monarchy (1921-1958), British influence in Iraq was formalized through two treaties of alliance. The first (concluded in 1922), provided for the appointment of British advisors to the Iraqi government. The second (concluded in 1930, shortly before independence), allowed Britain to use the air bases at Shuaiba and Habbaniya and to station troops there, permitted British forces to transit Iraqi territory, and made Iraq dependent on Britain for weapons and training. Britain's enduring influence and the privileges awarded it under these treaties was a matter of controversy in Iraqi domestic politics and a perennial source of tension between the crown and nationalist politicians. An attempt in 1948 to extend the 1930 treaty another twenty-five years led to widespread riots, the resignation of the cabinet, and the repudiation of the so-called Portsmouth Treaty by the new Iraqi government.

There are cautionary lessons to be learned from elsewhere in the region. In 1964, the signing of a SOFA agreement between the United States and Iran granting legal immunity to U.S. personnel and (unusually) their dependents, produced a harsh anti-American backlash. Incensed, Ayatollah Ruhollah Khomeini condemned the agreement—acidly noting that the SOFA granted an American dog in Iran more rights than an Iranian citizen—and attacked the shah and the United States, leading to his exile to Iraq. This was a key event in Khomeini's rise to prominence and power, which he frequently recalled following his return to Iran in 1979, and it is not hard to imagine some Iraqi ayatollah or populist politician likewise using the issue of immunities granted in a standard SOFA to discredit establishment politicians and gain political advantage.

More recently, SOFA agreements have become a source of tension with even friendly and allied governments. The involvement in the past decade of U.S. military personnel in automobile accidents, or criminal acts (e.g., rape or assault) against host-country nationals in Japan, South Korea, and the United Arab Emirates have led to calls for the local prosecution of U.S. personnel, and have stoked anti-American sentiment in these countries. In short, the United States should expect the path to a security agreement to be difficult and possibly protracted; its signing will not necessary put an end to problems and controversies.

The Way Ahead

The U.S. government will do well to downplay the need for such an agreement with the Iraqi Interim Government. Until Iraq has an elected government, Iraqi leaders will lack the legal or popular legitimacy to make such a decision. Furthermore, the controversial nature of a security agreement could discredit an interim government, and could tempt populist politicians to score political points by opposing such an agreement.

Nonetheless, there are issues that need to be addressed in the near term. CPA Directive Number 17 shields U.S. personnel from prosecution in Iraqi courts, but with the CPA dissolving on June 30, the post-transition status of this agreement—and other CPA directives—is unclear. Under these circumstances, the IGC or the Iraqi Interim Government may need to sign an Article 98 agreement with the United States that would prevent the handing over of U.S. personnel to the International Criminal Court. Failure to sign would preclude the United States from providing assistance via the Defense Department's International Military Education and Training, and Foreign Military Financing programs. The United States will likewise need to ensure that there is clarity about the legal status and rules of engagement of U.S. and foreign private security companies who currently have 2,000 armed employees in Iraq. Finally, a new UN Security Council Resolution should replicate or expand on the language used in UN Security Council Resolution 1511 to give coalition forces full authorization under chapter seven of the UN charter to use force in support of the broad mission of restoring stability to Iraq.

Part Six

Post-Saddam Economics and Politics

Patrick Clawson

Introduction

The most important question about the post-Saddam Iraqi political and economic scene has been how far-reaching a transformation will be attained. Washington Institute scholars examined from many angles the realistic prospects for moving Iraq, over the short term, toward a more democratic, liberal society. While the answers differ depending on the author and on what aspect of social change one is considering, the general theme of the Institute's work has been to caution against establishing overly ambitious goals for the near term. Creating exaggerated expectations can lead to a crippling perception of failure even when what is achieved is in fact quite impressive. There is a natural temptation to forecast that much can be done if only the United States would make a sufficient commitment to the task at hand. As the Institute's scholars have warned, however, progress could be slow no matter how much effort the United States puts forth.

Institute scholars often concluded that the situation was going rather well in view of the great challenges to Iraqi reconstruction. At the same time, they recognized that this progress still might not be good enough, as continuing problems could overwhelm many of the successes. And, in any case, the actual progress was nowhere near the inflated expectations fed by rosy forecasts and blind faith (offered by Iraqis as much as, if not more than, Americans) that the United States has the power to do anything it puts its mind to. Whether the question was that of restoring the economy, disbanding the militias, or handing sovereignty to Iraqis, Institute scholars generally emphasized ways to make measured progress while warning that overreaching would risk setting back the process. Most Americans endorse the vision of Iraq as a democratic and liberal example for the Arab world. At the same time, however, there should be no illusions that the road to that goal will be short or easy.

Indeed, the situation in Iraq has repeatedly turned out to be even more difficult than Institute scholars had foreseen. Iraq's physical infrastructure was in poorer shape than expected. More important, the human infrastructure was also falling apart, with Saddam Hussein's government functioning poorly and the once-proud Iraqi middle class unable to quickly take control of society. The Iraqi state is fragile and will remain so for years; civil society will reestablish itself but slowly. Accordingly, the tenor of Institute analysis has changed over time, as more information has emerged about how thoroughly Saddam decimated the middle class.

Getting a handle on the dynamics and divisions of Iraqi society has not been easy, either for Americans or for Iraqis themselves. Iraq was a closed book for decades, with serious research forbidden and Iraqis too wary of repression to speak freely. The Kurdish north was the exception, and so the Institute was able to offer more analysis of the situation there. Although several essays explore Iraq's Shiite radicals, of whom the most famous is Muqtada al-Sadr, the Institute would be the first to admit the limitations to its understanding of Shiite political dynamics. Al-Sadr's strong rhetoric clearly resonates among many, but it is not clear how that rhetoric interacts with the strong desire among Shiites to build a new Iraqi government in which they play the prominent role their demographic weight would suggest.

The greatest mystery, however, has been the Sunni Arab community. This is reflected in the striking absence of commentary from Iraqi Sunnis willing to speak publicly about matters such as the U.S. military presence or the country's political future. (On these questions, as on many political issues in Iraq, the Institute has held several off-the-record briefings and workshops involving such individuals. Unfortunately, their comments cannot be reflected here.) The grave risk is that the resistance to the U.S. presence may come to be seen as the authentic voice of the Sunnis. Certainly, it is difficult to identify many Sunni leaders who accept a temporary U.S. presence. Institute scholars warned how difficult it would be to offer Sunnis a vision of their role in the new Iraq. Unfortunately, the problem has turned out to be at least as great as we forecast.

51
What Next after Saddam?

Patrick Clawson: I want to say a few words about the standards of success by which we should judge progress in Iraq after Saddam Hussein's regime is deposed. In the immediate aftermath of Saddam's fall, the institutions necessary to holding a free election simply will not exist: no robust, independent press with respected commentators and journalists who can accurately report the positions of the various candidates; no political parties through which tested leaders can emerge who are used to the ideas of compromise and cooperation; and none of the other things necessary to make democracy operate. We will need to help the Iraqis rebuild the institutions of civil society gradually, starting with local elections, other semirepresentative institutions, and a free press. Then Iraqis will begin to gain the experience they need to make democracy work. We will also need to help create a consultative council similar to the Loya Jirga held in Afghanistan. There, people who are not used to compromise—not used to the idea that they can differ with someone on an issue without declaring a blood feud that lasts until the end of days—can begin getting accustomed to cooperation. That kind of intermediate situation might last for several years. This would be the lesson of other countries that are going through democratization: the best way to produce a stable, working democracy is to build representative institutions gradually. If the standard being held out is the creation of democracy, people will complain, "But we haven't had elections yet." That's precisely as it should be, though; elections should be held well down the road in the process of democratization, not immediately after liberation from tyranny.

The United States can deem itself successful if, five years from now, there is a government in Iraq that looks rather like the government in Jordan, which is to say, a regime that is reasonably representative and reasonably respectful of human rights, with a reasonably free press. I would even settle for an Iraqi government that resembles Egypt's, which offers fewer such freedoms but is nevertheless not so bad. If we achieve anything more than another Jordan, that would be wonderful. Yet, it is overly optimistic to think that we can take a country that has emerged from under a totalitarian regime with its institutions of civil society in total disarray and create a beacon of democracy within five years. We could run into serious trouble if we operate under that notion.

Excerpted from an edited transcript originally published in *Bush Administration Middle East Policy: A Mid-Term Assessment*, proceedings of The Washington Institute's 2002 Weinberg Founders Conference, October 4-6, 2002.

Amatzia Baram: Iraq has been characterized by a great deal of divisiveness—revolutionary zeal, religious schisms, protests, violence, and various tribal, regional, and class divisions—since the Umayyad times [in the eighth century]. As a result, after the Abbasid era, no Iraqi-based regime was truly representative of its population. This is the first lesson of Iraqi history. Although the Sunni Arabs and Sunni Kurds in Iraq accepted the Ottoman sultan as a legitimate ruler by the end of the nineteenth century, the Shiites—who already constituted a clear majority in the area now called Iraq—did not. This lack of representative government persisted with the establishment of modern Iraq. Since 1921, when King Faysal I came to the throne, Iraqis have lived under minority rule by Sunni Arabs, who compose 15 to 20 percent of the population. This is one of the reasons why the Iraqi monarchy had such difficulty establishing its legitimacy among the Iraqi people.

Rather than become more representative, Iraqi governments—including the benign, partly democratic monarchy, which lasted until 1958—have instead chosen to destabilize the regional order. Adventurism became a means of winning domestic legitimacy. Some Iraqi Jewish friends of mine who grew up in Amara told me how their geography teacher would say to them, "Iraq will conquer the Gulf and flatten the Fertile Crescent," whereupon all students were allowed to stand and dance on their desks. They were speaking of the early 1940s, under the monarchy. Iraq has never conquered the Gulf or flattened the Fertile Crescent, but Iraqis were taught to work toward a change in the regional status quo. More recently, the Palestinian issue has become a mechanism for the unpopular and illegitimate Iraqi regime to appeal to the passions of its people.

Some have spoken about the possibility of appointing another Sunni Arab military man—a good-looking army general riding a white horse—to rule Iraq after Saddam. This man would handle all of Iraq's postwar problems, and the Americans could quickly fulfill their admirable promise of leaving Iraq. Yet, this is not a good solution for the simple reason that such a regime would be unpopular and would lack legitimacy. As soon as it freed itself from American tutelage, this regime would resort to the proven strategy of destabilizing the region in order to divert domestic dissent. As George Orwell suggested in *1984*, hate works; Kanan Makiya titled his book on Baath Iraq *Republic of Fear*, but he could just as easily have called it *Republic of Hate*.

The Republican Guard must be dismantled completely. Because it has long been the private army of Saddam Hussein, you cannot simply place its more apolitical officers in the general army; they will have to go through a vetting committee. You must also remove all politicized officers from the general army, with some severance pay. Eventually, you will have to start releasing Tikriti and Baath prisoners. The first to be released should be those who surrendered; in fact, you should advertise this fact during psychological warfare operations as an incentive to surrender. Eventually, however, you will have to release the rest of the prisoners. Rest assured that they will have weapons and money stashed away. Saddam's three options are to try to wage Armageddon, to seek political asylum, or to establish an underground. He is already prepared for the last option, and you may have great difficulty finding him.

You have to be ready for the possibility that Saddam will slip away to lead an underground resistance. That is why you cannot release Tikriti or Baath prisoners of war until you have each one in check.

What about the Iraqi political elite? Some of them will need to be jailed immediately and put on trial, but many will not. In addition to protecting them in well-defended Baghdad compounds, Saddam has long monitored them, and you will need to do the same. Although many are not necessarily criminals, they are Baath elites, and there is a very good chance that some Iraqis will attempt revenge killings against Saddam's supporters. Such bloodshed must be prevented at all costs.

Alina Romanowski: I have been asked to talk about the specific challenges that the U.S. military will face in a post-Saddam situation. I want to raise our awareness of the range of such challenges and examine how we can mitigate some of the worst-case scenarios that might emerge. If the United States invades Iraq, it will have two key objectives: toppling the regime and eliminating weapons of mass destruction. The U.S. military will then have the responsibility of setting up a new regime, and Machiavelli's first rule will come into play: he who has power must rule. The burden will fall, first and foremost, on General Tommy Franks and his troops. They will have to administer Iraq and facilitate the transition to whatever authority will follow them. U.S. forces will be responsible for establishing and maintaining law and order and for giving a new regime legitimacy, even if it is only an interim government. They will also need to ensure the personal security of the new leadership.

The U.S. military will be stepping into a morass. Iraq presents as unpromising a breeding ground for democracy as any in the world. It has never really known democracy or even legitimate, centralized rule for any great duration.

The country is riven between mutually hostile ethnic groups that are themselves divided into a multiplicity of contending tribes. Iraq's politics have, historically, been brutally violent. Whichever American or Iraqi leader sits in the presidential palace in Baghdad after Saddam's demise will face immediate and enormous problems. Iraq has long been rich in vendettas, and never more so than now; hence, a small U.S. force sufficient to bring about Saddam's demise might not be sufficient to stop the subsequent bloodletting. Even if one believes those pundits who assert with utmost confidence that the Iraqis will welcome us with open arms, our troops cannot go into Iraq without at least planning for a string of revenge killings. Moreover, how will U.S. troops deal with the aspirations of those ethnic groups who want to assert their control over areas that Saddam has long deprived of political influence?

We must face the possibility that whatever government we foster or impose may be considered illegitimate from the start and may survive only as long as we are prepared to exercise the force necessary to suppress opposition. Alternatively, we may be far better off if the burden of administering Iraq is a multinational effort, under some regime with international legitimacy. So, how do we get there? Thus far, few in the international community are clamoring to join the United States in identifying an alternative regime or even a political process. Ultimately, the only stable and legitimate government will be the one Iraqis impose on themselves. Is the U.S. military prepared to take on the longer-term job of providing the security and control across Iraq that will allow the Iraqi people, with or without international monitoring, to hold elections? What about the task of helping Iraqi security leaders develop a new strategy and design and equip a new Iraqi defense force? This task calls for new strategic concepts, new doctrine, new training, and new organization. Will we take on that burden? Unless we have an international consensus to intervene in Iraq, we will look like a unilateral force that is trying to reshape an entire country on its own. In that case, we had better have the answers up front. We cannot wait for the situation to deteriorate and then say, "Gosh, we didn't think about that."

Participant: Professor Baram, in Afghanistan we were able to use some of the local institutions, along with the Loya Jirga, to try to organize politics, even though one could argue that we have not done a great job so far. Is there any comparable institution in Iraqi history that would provide some sort of legitimacy to regime change? Would you recommend trying to get one Kurd, one Shiite, and one Sunni into some sort of troika to run the country provisionally? How would you recommend that Iraq's administration be organized in the immediate aftermath of U.S. action?

Baram: The Iraqi army will still be necessary, though you can reduce its size. Most Iraqis regard it as a legitimate institution, even one that they can be proud of, despite the various atrocities it has committed. I have met Shiites who fought against the army in what they used to call *intifadat Shaban,* the March 1991 Shiite uprising against the regime. The army decimated these opposition forces. But when I asked them a few questions about relations between officers and soldiers in the army during the Iran-Iraq War, they looked at me and said, quite genuinely, "But Professor Baram, these are national secrets. The army is the property of the people."

Then there is the Iraqi police force. Although all institutions in Iraq are completely penetrated by Saddam loyalists and by the Baath Party, the police are less troublesome than most. They focus on actual crime rather than political matters. Perhaps the General Security Service (al-Amn al-'Amm) can be retained—it is a state institution, not a party institution. It will need reform, however; unlike the regular police, it does deal with political crimes, and that mandate must be taken away. Nevertheless, those of its personnel who have not engaged in torture and other abuses can retain their posts, and the organization itself can be modeled on the Federal Bureau of Investigation.

Representative Howard Berman: I would like the panelists to elaborate on what they have said in the context of two things. First is the Republican Party's rhetorical position over the last ten years (and particularly since George W. Bush campaigned for president in 2000) against the United States assuming the role of nation builder. Second is Bernard Lewis's comment earlier in these proceedings about Israel's experience in Lebanon, where Israelis came as liberators and stayed to become occupiers. All of our key interests in Iraq—eliminating weapons of mass destruction, safeguarding the country's territorial integrity, and so forth—seem to require us to remain there for a while in the wake of an invasion.

Clawson: One of the arguments I was trying to make in saying that we should set our standards of success in Iraq relatively low is that I am a fan of the idea that we should liberate Iraq and then get out of there as quickly as possible. We should confine our presence primarily to upholding our security guarantee against external aggression. We should allow the Iraqis to make their own mistakes, and we should have a light role after the initial period. Alina was talking about U.S. responsibilities over several months. I think we may end up having to play the principal role in Iraq for the first year; after that, we should hand control over to the Iraqis and get out of there. Even if the result is less than optimal, it would be a whole lot better than facing the situation that the Israelis did in Lebanon.

Iraqis were one of the very few people who rebelled—in the form of a major revolt in 1920—when the British showed up to run a mandate. The Iraqis have a long history of strongly nationalistic, almost xenophobic reactions that makes me extraordinarily nervous about our sticking around there. If we are unsure about how we will be greeted when we first arrive, I strongly suspect that we will face serious problems if we overstay our welcome. So, I would argue that we should set relatively low standards for what we expect to accomplish there; then, if things go better than we had hoped, then all to the better.

In his book *The Threatening Storm: The Case for Invading Iraq*, Kenneth Pollack argues that if we do anything other than achieve a perfect democracy in Iraq, we will have failed. He also contends that such a failure could only be attributed to a lack of will. He does not once suggest that if we stick around, we will face the threat of engendering a nationalistic revolt against us, and that such an event might make the question of U.S. political will moot. That is a profound misreading of Iraqi society and history. If we try to transform Iraq into a democracy, we will need more and more troops over time because we will have to quell nationalistic revolts.

Romanowski: We need to decide what the mission is. What are we really after: regime change or weapons of mass destruction? If the latter, there are many other ways we can accomplish this mission without an invasion. If we do not want to get tied into nation building to the extent that we may have to in Afghanistan, or to the extent that we had to in Germany and Japan, then we should think very carefully about which comes first: regime change or weapons of mass destruction.

Baram: Establishing a democracy in Iraq would be a longer and more difficult process than that seen in postwar Germany (I do not know enough about Japan to offer a comparison to it). Before the war, Germany went through the same social and political developments that, say, Britain and France did, only in a much shorter period. These included the development of capitalism, industry, a middle class, and even a limited African empire. So, Germany had some notion of liberalism and a middle class that could carry a democracy. Iraq does not yet have those assets, so building democracy there will take longer. I agree with Patrick that you can settle for less than a perfect democracy. In fact, you can settle for a regime that is simply benevolent and representative of the main groups in Iraqi society. Anything less than that, however, would not hold water. The United States will have to remain in Iraq at least long enough to achieve those conditions.

One way of reaching this goal without garrisoning a huge number of forces in Iraq would be to control the money. Corruption has always been a big problem in Iraq, and whoever takes over the country after Saddam will attempt to pocket its oil revenues. If the United States (or, alternatively, the UN) pays Iraqi officers, teachers, intelligence and internal security personnel, and so forth, it will be able to build a pyramid of dependence and keep its own hand on the big tap.

As for ameliorating Iraqi resentment and nationalism during a military occupation, the United States must live up to its promises and show Iraqis that conditions are improving rapidly. In the event of a total disruption of Iraqi society (e.g., if, after an invasion, Iraqis stop showing up for work), the U.S. military will have to take over the country entirely. That would not be a good thing, but you must prepare for it.

A better and more likely approach would be to employ Iraqis in every possible vacancy. Iraqis are hard-working, and they really would like to do what needs to be done. Yet, you must be prepared to call on them to report for duty and to pay them good salaries, as opposed to the symbolic salaries they currently receive. You must also begin to improve their lives relatively quickly, not necessarily in dramatic fashion, but in readily discernible ways. If the people see such improvements within six months, they will feel a sense of stability.

Fighting crime will be a particular challenge. Although the crime rate in Iraq is fairly low at the moment, it was very high only a year and a half ago. Once the various militia groups and special forces are forced to return to their homes, they will still have ready access to weapons. Weapons are not in short supply in Iraq, and the Tikritis and others might use them to form some kind of mafia. It would be a dangerous mafia indeed; the Tikritis are well trained in both tactics and the use of weapons, and they are capable of penetrating Baghdad and destroying post-Saddam society. Yet, if you prove, even in a limited fashion, that stability and respect for property are possible with little crime or bloodshed, then the general Iraqi hatred of foreign control will be ameliorated, and you can stay there for a while.

What reception can U.S. soldiers expect in Iraq in general, and in Baghdad in particular? The Kurds will certainly welcome an invasion, but they will not fight for you outside of Kurdistan. At the same time, they are unlikely to pose a problem unless you need to keep them out of Kirkuk. Nine out of ten Shiites will accept you, not with great joy, but with a sigh of relief. Yet, in the Sunni area of Tikrit, Beiji-Dur, they will fight you. In Baghdad, most citizens—the majority of whom are Shiite—will not fight you. Yet, they will not be at all happy to see you, because you will bring devastation and hardship with you. You will need to win Baghdadis over quickly. They do not like any foreigners except those who come as tourists and spend a lot of money. They will accept an invading force only reluctantly, and only for a while. But you can win them over, especially by helping them, setting attainable goals, and telling them that you will leave as quickly as you can once those goals are achieved.

Ze'ev Schiff, *Ha'aretz:* Listening to the long list of responsibilities that the panel is giving to the U.S. government and its military, I am a bit amazed, particularly when I hear you say, "Don't stay too long, but stay as long as is necessary to bring prosperity to the Iraqis."

Let us assume that, just after an invasion, President Bush calls the three of you and tells you that Saddam has disappeared and that some Republican Guard units are fighting a terrorist campaign. What is the maximum amount of time that each of you thinks the U.S. military must stay in Iraq in order to fulfill the goals you have proposed?

Clawson: The U.S. Army will have to stay one year, the U.S. Air Force probably five to ten years. This long list of responsibilities you mention could be completed fairly quickly, and U.S. forces could then help the Iraqi military become strong enough to take over. Afterward, the U.S. Air Force could effectively guarantee Iraq's external security, even while based in a remote area out of the way of the Iraqi people, similar to Prince Sultan Air Force Base in Saudi Arabia. We could still work with the Iraqi military in the meantime, selling them arms and working to build up their conventional forces.

Romanowski: I would give it a bit longer than one year. The U.S. Army will have to stay about eighteen months. I would not keep the U.S. Air Force in Iraq in the same capacity that Patrick described, but I would maintain a U.S. presence throughout the region as a security umbrella. The U.S. presence in Iraq would be accepted as a means of helping the region provide for its own security; it is already viewed as such in Saudi Arabia, Qatar, Jordan, and elsewhere. If you decide that you will occupy Iraq for eighteen months and then leave, you will either have to leave the entire region or build a different framework for staying there. Currently, regional states are pretty bad at providing for their own defense, so the United States would do well to help them become more self-reliant. As for Iraq, U.S. forces will need to work with a post-Saddam military before determining whether it can be modernized to the point of providing for Iraq's security on its own.

Baram: If you dismantle the Republican Guard and send its equipment and its less politicized officers and troops to the regular army, Iraq would have a reasonably capable military that could be modernized within a few years. Of far greater concern is the possibility of domestic bloodletting, particularly the emergence of a mafia or other underground organization. Even a relatively small underground (e.g., a few hundred people) could rob banks, arm itself, interfere with politics, and kill U.S. soldiers. You have to remember that Saddam and his lieutenants have repeatedly mentioned Mogadishu and Beirut. They remember U.S. experiences in both cities and have drawn all sorts of conclusions from them. Without a legitimate post-Saddam government and reasonable progress toward stability, nationalist resentment would build up among Iraqis and make the U.S. position there difficult. Hence, I am a little more pessimistic than my fellow panelists; U.S. forces will need to remain in Iraq for up to two years, and they will not have an easy time there.

Occupying Iraq without unnecessarily arousing Iraqi sensitivities is not a simple matter. U.S. forces must be careful; if they behave in Iraq as they sometimes have in Afghanistan, they will run into trouble. For example, some U.S. special forces operatives in Afghanistan walked around half-naked with their guns, looking like Rambo. In an Islamic country, such behavior is received quite badly. People do not like it; it is not respectable. So, U.S. soldiers will have to behave themselves in Iraq, as they did in Germany and Japan. If the United States maintains a minimal and respectful presence, then Iraqi irritation will be less problematic. If I am wrong, however, and conditions are more adverse, then U.S. forces could be in Iraq for as long as five years. If I were advising the president, then, I would be honest with him. Still, under normal circumstances, the military presence will last a year or two at most.

Clawson: Amatzia, your five-year option makes me very nervous. If things go badly, the United States should withdraw immediately.

Baram: That is another option, yes. You can say "forget it" and go home, but you would leave behind chaos—a vacuum that Iran may be happy to fill.

52
Building a New Iraq

With the fall of Saddam Hussein's regime, the top priority for the United States should be ensuring security so that Iraq can be reconstructed and then transformed. Unless Iraq becomes a stable, responsible, and friendly country, it could reemerge as a threat to the international order, conceivably reconstituting its weapons-of-mass-destruction (WMD) programs. The United States cannot skimp on its commitment to building a new Iraq.

The best means to ensure a stable and friendly Iraq is to ensure it has a broad-based government that respects the dignity of Iraqis, launched on a sustainable process of democratization. Replacing Saddam Hussein with another strongman is not a reliable way to achieve stability; after all, rule by generals and domination by one ethnic minority (the Sunni Arabs) has brought Iraq decades of instability and war. The surest way to break from this pattern is for Iraqis to have a government that rests on the consent of the governed, not on the force of arms.

The process of creating such a government will have three stages: stabilization, transition, and a new government. How long each lasts should depend on accomplishing specified goals, rather than being dictated by a preannounced timetable.

Stabilization

During the stabilization period that will follow immediately upon the demise of Saddam's regime, sufficient U.S. forces will need to be committed to provide security and to respond to any remnants of the old order who continue resistance. A U.S.-led military administration will need to govern Iraq, though even at this early stage, participation by international partners will enhance acceptability. To the extent practical, the U.S.-led force should work with the Iraqi government bureaucracy, once Iraq's totalitarian political leaders, secret police agents, and those who stand accused of war crimes and crimes against humanity have been removed. Iraq is not a failed state in which the government has collapsed; it has many highly skilled technocrats ready to assume administrative responsibility. As some of the two million Iraqis abroad return, they too should play an important role, especially those from the community of Iraqis abroad who have labored

Edited excerpt from *Winning the Peace in the Middle East: A Bipartisan Blueprint for Postwar U.S. Policy* (The Washington Institute, March 2003), a report prepared by Institute staff members Dennis Ross, Robert Satloff, Patrick Clawson, David Makovsky, and Matthew Levitt, and endorsed by Lawrence Eagleburger, Newt Gingrich, Alexander Haig, Robert Kerrey, William Perry, Fred Thompson, and R. James Woolsey.

so hard to keep alive the ideal of a free, open, more tolerant Iraq. Throughout, the U.S.-led military administration should reach out to Iraqis who espouse a democratic vision for their country; while all groups within the country must be represented, the role of tribal and religious leaders should be kept to a minimum.

After thirty years of brutal dictatorship and twenty years of nearly continuous war, Iraqis want to begin the process of building their lives anew. In this effort, the United States should be a full partner. In order to demonstrate its commitment to Iraq's reconstruction, the United States should adopt the principle that it will rebuild whatever civilian assets are destroyed during a war.

Transition

As soon as practicable, the U.S.-led military administration should give way to an international administration that will be characterized by these components:

Security. Once stabilization has been achieved, the security situation may remain fragile; there is a risk of unsettled conditions in parts of the country. Peace can be ensured only if there is a security force with enough muscle to put down challenges to the central authority. This force, established within an international or UN-authorized framework, should include an active role by the advanced industrial countries, with participation by Muslim countries but a minimal role for Iraq's immediate neighbors. Meanwhile, most Iraqi soldiers should be demobilized and provided assistance for reintegration into civilian life.

Political. With stabilization of the security situation, authority over Iraq's civilian affairs should pass to an interim international administration charged with launching Iraq on a path toward more broad-based, representative government. In addition to Iraqis, this should include participation from representatives of a broad range of countries rather than just the wartime allies. Any role for regional states will have to balance Iraqi national pride and suspicions about its neighbors' intentions with the need to give regional states a stake in the success of the transitional process.

Building a more broad-based, representative Iraqi government is not only what U.S. and world public opinion will expect, but it is also the best way to ensure the legitimacy of the new government in the eyes of Iraqis, rebutting charges that post-Saddam Iraq is only an American puppet. Throughout, the United States should support a vision of a democratic future for Iraq, while maintaining realistic, achievable expectations of what can be accomplished in the short run. Democratization is a process, not a one-time event; Washington's early focus should be on helping Iraqis build those institutions (such as a free press and responsible political parties) and on advocating those principles (such as free speech, minority rights, and the rule of law) that are essential elements of democratic development and have been denied to Iraqis during a generation of Baath tyranny.

In the interval before free elections can be held at the national level, political authority should be spread widely rather than concentrated in the hands of a new powerful national leader. An executive council and a consultative council should be chosen from those with strong support on the ground. Initially to avoid a premature focus on who will serve as its leader, the executive council should have a rotating head. The selection of members for these bodies should openly favor modern-minded forces committed to democratic values rather than automatically relying on traditional ethnic and religious leaders. To a considerable extent, power should be devolved away from Baghdad to local officials, encouraging the emergence of new leaders. Those local officials would include the two Kurdish regional governments run by the Patriotic Union of Kurdistan (PUK) and the Kurdish Democratic Party (KDP), whose support for the new government will be critical to its success. The role of Shiites in public life will need to be increased in such a way as to minimize apprehensions among Sunni Arabs that they are being marginalized.

Economic. Given that Iraq has the financial and human resources of a middle-income country, the United States should encourage Iraqis to take charge of the reconstruction process, with aid organizations playing a limited role. That Iraqis themselves are leading the reconstruction effort will also counter the myth that the war was fought for foreigners to gain control of Iraqi oil. Questions of whether U.S. and other international oil companies should play a prominent role in expanding oil output, and if so which oil companies, should be left up to Iraqis and to the workings of market forces rather than dictated by foreigners.

Iraq can pay its own way in the world if relieved of the heavy burden of Saddam-era debt. The new government should be given immediate access to the several billion dollars in Iraqi cash in the oil-for-food escrow account held by the UN. Setting an example for others, the United States should forgive all the debt Iraq owes it and should urge the Gulf monarchies and industrial countries to do the same, so that what debt payments Iraq can make go to middle-income creditors such as Russia. In addition, the United States should ask Kuwait to contribute to Iraq's post-Saddam reconstruction by dropping its remaining claims for compensation, which would allow a quick end to the UN-mandated deduction of 25 percent of Iraqi oil exports for compensation payments.

Formation of a New Government. While the United States and its allies must commit to the transitional administration the time and effort needed, they should not stay longer than needed to develop a new constitution and the civil society institutions necessary for national elections and to supervise the peaceful transfer of power to full Iraqi authority. Experience suggests it may be difficult to produce in short order the fully democratic and prosperous Iraq for which Iraqis and Americans both yearn. The U.S.-led coalition would be well advised to set achievable objectives for postwar Iraq, while also working toward a grander vision to be realized over time. It would be a serious error for the U.S.-influenced international administration and security force to overstay their welcome; both the cause of democracy in Iraq and America's own national interests would be hurt were the United States perceived to be a colonial power erecting an empire in Iraq. What can be accomplished in a few years depends crucially on how ready the Iraqis themselves are to break with the past political patterns and build a new political community.

One key area in which the United States and its allies are likely to stay involved for years is security. They should ensure that the new government has domestic security forces adequate to face any internal challenges. Washington should make every effort to build a close security relationship with Iraq's new government, including the reconstruction of its armed forces with Western expertise and equipment. Such steps provide the best guarantee that post-Saddam Iraq adopts responsible policies that contribute to regional security. They also provide the most effective way to prevent a new Iraqi leadership from deciding to resume its WMD programs with the technical knowledge and expertise that will still be available, even with the intrusive monitoring system that will remain in place for the indefinite future following the complete postwar destruction of Iraq's WMD program.

Furthermore, a rebuilt Iraqi military in a close relationship with the United States and its allies could take on an active role at protecting the Gulf, allowing reduction of the U.S. military profile in the Gulf and less Western dependence on Saudi Arabia, which might sit well in both Riyadh and Washington. At the same time, the U.S.-led coalition should seek to take advantage of Saddam's downfall to seek new security arrangements with Iraq's neighbors, especially Iran. Tehran needs to know that threats it poses to regional stability, especially its pursuit of weapons of mass destruction, will be a key factor in determining the size and power of Iraq's reconstituted armed forces.

Conclusion

Investing in a new Iraq must be viewed as the logical continuation of any war effort. Victory in war will be squandered if it is not followed by a similarly determined effort to help Iraqis rebuild their country. After freeing Iraq from tyranny, the guiding principle governing U.S. policy in post-Saddam Iraq should be to help the Iraqi people regain control over their country so they can define their own national destiny in peace and security. America's endeavor in Iraq will ultimately fail if the United States attempts to remake Iraq in its own image; America's endeavor will succeed—with beneficial impact on U.S. interests throughout the Middle East—should U.S. efforts culminate in providing the free people of Iraq their long-denied opportunity to build their future for themselves.

Yitzhak Nakash

53
The Shiites and the Future of Iraq

The prospect of American military action in Iraq has raised concerns that dismantling the Baath regime will weaken the state and spur the defection of its Shiite majority under the influence of Iran. Yet, much of the pessimism surrounding this assessment obscures the historical role that the Shiite community has played in supporting the Iraqi state, not to mention the vital interest it has in preserving the country's territorial integrity. If war in Iraq leads to a more representative government that is willing to address Shiite political aspirations, the likely result would be stability and the establishment of a more moderate religious leadership quite different from that seen in Iran.

The Shiite Stake in Iraq

With shrines throughout the country and religious centers at Najaf and Karbala, Iraq has long been a locus of Shiite learning and history. Yet, Shiites did not constitute the majority of Iraq's indigenous population until the beginning of the nineteenth century. As nomadic Arab tribes abandoned their itinerant lifestyle in favor of agriculture, a large number of them became Shiites. They did not attain political power, however. Since the creation of modern Iraq in 1921, the country's Sunni minority has wielded disproportionate influence over the Shiite majority (which constitutes some 65 percent of the population) and the Kurdish minority. Sunni dominance has been bolstered by both the preponderance of Sunni governments in the Arab world and by the West, which until recently viewed Saddam Hussein's regime as a bulwark against the influence of revolutionary Shia Islam.

Although Iraqi Shiites had long been politically marginalized, sectarian confrontation did not become salient until the 1970s, when conflict emerged between the Sunni-dominated Baath Party and the Shiite Islamic Dawa Party. Despite the apparent influence of Iran's Islamic Revolution, however, Iraqi Shiites harbored no aspirations to replicate the political theology of the Islamic Republic. The vitality of the Islamic Dawa Party was the product of Shiite frustration with the exclusivity of state politics rather than any desire to follow the Iranian model. The bulk of Islamic Dawa Party supporters were inhabitants of Baghdad slums and university students who had become disillusioned with the Iraqi Communist Party's failure to bring about political change.

On February 21, 2003, Yitzhak Nakash addressed The Washington Institute's Special Policy Forum. Dr. Nakash, a professor of Middle East history at Brandeis University, is author of *The Shiis of Iraq* (Princeton University Press, 1994). This rapporteur's summary (originally published as *PolicyWatch* no. 719, March 4, 2003) was prepared by Evan Langenhahn.

Differences between Iraqi and Iranian Shiites increased during the 1980-1988 Iran-Iraq War and the Shiite uprising that followed the Gulf War in 1991. In the former case, Iraqi Shiites constituted the majority of the Iraqi infantry and fought against their Iranian coreligionists despite Saddam's systematic repression. In the latter case, Iraqi ayatollahs failed to exploit the Shiite rebellion, offering little in the way of guidance, much less open advocacy for the formation of a separatist Islamic government. Historically, the vast majority of Iraqi Shiites have rejected calls to implement a political system favoring the rule of the Islamic jurist (*velayet y-faqih*), instead choosing to reaffirm their commitment to Iraqi nationalism.

Iraqi Shiites also have a vested interest in preserving the country's territorial integrity. If Iraq were divided into separate statelets following a war, the Shiites would likely lose Baghdad (where they constitute nearly half the population), the shrine cities of Kazamin and Samarra, and any share in the revenues from northern oil wells. Given that they already compose the core of the country's middle class and secular intelligentsia, the Shiites would much prefer to seek power within a unified postwar Iraq. Moreover, the states that would emerge from a divided Iraq would be too weak to influence regional affairs, whereas a united Iraq might allow Iraqi Shiites to become a strong regional voice.

Possibilities for a Post-Saddam Iraq

The Iraqi nationalism long favored by the Shiite majority would likely prevail over a revitalized pan-Arab ideology as the foundation for a post-Saddam Iraq. Building on the political thought of literary ideologues such as Ali al-Sharqi, the country could well develop a nationalist ideology grounded in both the Arab and tribal character of Iraqi society. The Iraqi military would be pivotal in this transition; once purged of its pro-Saddam elements, the army could be transformed into a symbol of national unity with a specific mission closely tied to the aims of the new state.

Under such conditions, the emergence of an influential Shiite presence in the new Iraqi government would probably not cause internecine strife. Moreover, the Baathists would be unlikely to resurrect themselves as a vociferous political force. Although the United States would probably engage in some level of de-Baathification, Washington would also strive to avoid alienating Iraqi Sunnis, primarily by maintaining the technocratic elements of the Baath system and by mitigating any threat of Shiite reprisals.

The most positive scenario would be the destruction of the Baath regime and its replacement by a pluralistic state in which the Shiite majority can gain access to power and the Kurds can enjoy a degree of autonomy. For its part, Washington should encourage Iraqis to adopt a representative system based on a written constitution, with parliamentary seats distributed proportionally among the country's ethnic and religious groups. In lieu of a single national leader, a triumvirate representing Iraq's major constituencies (e.g., a Shiite president, a Sunni prime minister, and a Kurdish parliamentary speaker) could share interim political power.

Toward an Arab Alternative

Should political conditions in post-Saddam Iraq allow for the revitalization of Iraqi Shiite clerical training schools, a reinvigorated Iraqi Shia Islam based in Najaf could rival Qom as a center of influence in the Shiite world. Historically, Shia has been a somewhat laissez-faire sect, emphasizing competitiveness rather than conformity in its ideology. The rise of an alternative power center in Iraq could therefore encourage the defection of dissident clerics in Iran. In fact, if Najaf were to produce moderate clerics who became well integrated with the new Iraqi state, the positive repercussions would likely be felt throughout the Middle East. A moderate Najaf would present an alternative to the ideology of Hizballah spiritual leader Sheikh Muhammad Hussein Fadlallah and other extremist elements. Similarly, Iraqi Shia could function as an important counterweight to the predominant radical force in the region, Sunni Wahhabism, which is as vitriolic toward Shia as it is toward the United States.

Washington can and should help to create a post-Saddam Iraq in which Shiites can prosper. Iraq has many resources that could facilitate this process and ease the political transition: oil reserves, a tradition of market economics, a talented bureaucracy, and a strong agricultural sector. Should the United States repeat its post-Gulf War failure to address Shiite aspirations, opposition to U.S. efforts will grow.

Soner Cagaptay

54
Turkmens, the Soft Underbelly of the War in Northern Iraq

With the northern front in Iraq being officially launched today, coalition forces may soon move toward the city of Kirkuk, which they began bombing on March 21. Kirkuk, claimed by Kurds as the prospective capital of a Kurdish region in postwar Iraq, is the bastion of the Turkmens, a Turkish-speaking community that shares close historical, social, and cultural ties with the Anatolian Turks in neighboring Turkey. Their fortunes will be closely scrutinized in Turkey during and after Operation Iraqi Freedom. If Turks feel that the Turkmen community is being discriminated against or threatened, they could force Ankara to take action, perhaps undermining what remains of U.S.-Turkish cooperation in Iraq.

Background

No reliable contemporary data are available on the size of the Turkmen population. The 1957 Iraqi census—the last in which the Turkmens were permitted to register—counted 567,000 Turkmens (9 percent of the population) among Iraq's population of 6,300,000. The census also counted 819,000 Kurds (13 percent of the population).

The Turkmens' ratio in the Iraqi population may have dropped since then. The Turkmens are more urban and middle-class than Iraq's other Muslim communities, so they are likely to have experienced slower population growth. Moreover, the Baath regime's forced Arabization policies—including a ban on non-Arabic education, broadcast, and associations as well as expulsion of non-Arabs from the major cities of northern Iraq—seem to have had some impact on the Turkmens. Even so, given the growth of the Iraqi population as a whole (currently estimated at 23 to 25 million people), the Turkmens are likely more than 1 million strong today, perhaps as many as 1.5 million.

The Turkmens live in a rather compact section of northern Iraq. While the Kurds dominate the mountainous northern and eastern portions of the region—much of which they control as autonomous zones run by the Patriotic Union of Kurdistan (PUK) and the Kurdish Democratic Party (KDP)—an overwhelming majority of the Turkmens inhabit the foothills and plains in the southern portion currently ruled by Saddam Hussein. (Baghdad is home to a large Turkmen community as well.) The traditional Turkmen

Originally published as *PolicyWatch* no. 735, March 27, 2003. Soner Cagaptay is coordinator of The Washington Institute's Turkish Research Program.

homeland is a band of territory stretching over 150 miles from Telafar in the northwest through Mosul and Kirkuk to Tuz in the southeast. In this area, the Turkmens constitute pluralities in many towns, while in cities such as Irbil and Kirkuk, large Turkmen communities enjoy preponderance due to the fact that they are better educated and wealthier than other Muslim communities.

Political Organization among the Turkmens

Despite their advantages, the Turkmens have been overshadowed by the Kurds in recent decades:

- the Turkmens are almost equally divided between Shia and Sunni Islam, unlike the more tribal and feudal Kurds, who are overwhelmingly Sunni;
- the Turkmens did not take up arms against Saddam until recently;
- since the end of the Gulf War, the majority of the Kurds have lived in their autonomous areas, developing significant cultural and political institutions, while the Turkmens have remained oppressed under the regime in Baghdad, which has shut down most of their own such institutions.

In the late 1990s, the Turkmens took steps to redress their political weakness. In 1995, twenty-six Turkmen groups merged under an umbrella organization, the Iraqi Turkmen Front (ITC), in order to facilitate united political action. Only a few groups remained outside this organization, most notably the Turkmen Islam Union (TIB), composed of Shiite Turkmens. The ITC has served a useful purpose, rallying most Turkmens around a common political platform for the first time in modern history. The Turkmens also gained leverage in the aftermath of the 1992-1996 civil war between the KDP and the PUK. An American-Turkish-brokered ceasefire assigned Turkey responsibility for maintaining peace between the Kurdish factions. The agreement also created a Peace Monitoring Force (PMF) headquartered in Irbil and composed of non-Kurds, namely Turkmens and Assyrian Christians. Since its inception in April 1997, the PMF has served as a training school for the Turkmens; more than 2,000 of them have participated in the force, receiving professional military instruction from the Turkish army.

Turkmen Welfare during and after the War

Despite achieving enhanced military and political organization over the past few years, the Turkmens may still be vulnerable to the vicissitudes of war. First, most of them live in the large cities of northern Iraq, such as Kirkuk, which have yet to be captured by coalition forces. If close combat becomes necessary to secure these cities, the Turkmens could be caught in the crossfire. Second, tens of thousands of refugees—mostly Kurdish, but also Turkmen and Assyrian—were driven away from their homes in Kirkuk and other northern cities during the Arabization campaigns of the 1980s and 1990s, and most of them are eager to return home after a coalition victory. If not monitored properly, the return of these refugees could result in reverse ethnic cleansing; in particular, the Kurdification of Kirkuk and other cities could put the Turkmens already living in these areas in jeopardy.

Turkish Perceptions

In general, the Turks care greatly for the welfare of Turkish communities in neighboring countries. Until recently, however, the Turkish public paid little attention to the plight of the Turkmens, despite their persistent subjection to Baath Arabization policies over the past few decades. This lack of interest seemed to be rooted in the fact that the Turks have traditionally paid little attention to Iraqi politics, including the nature of Saddam's regime, his actions against the Turkmens, and his efforts to manufacture weapons of mass destruction. Nevertheless, Turkey's attitude toward the Turkmens seems to have changed lately, with the Turkish media following their fate closely. Much of the Turkish public suspects that, after the war, the Turkmens will be forced to live under Kurdish factions such as the KDP and the PUK.

Although huge political demonstrations are rare in Turkey, the plight of Turks in other countries is perhaps the one issue most likely to attract masses to the streets. For example, during the late 1980s, when the communist regime in Bulgaria began a campaign of forced assimilation among the country's Turks, millions demonstrated in Turkey, compelling Ankara to take action. In 1989, then prime minister Turgut Ozal amassed troops along the Bulgarian border and successfully persuaded Sofia to reverse its assimilation policy. Hence, if the Turkmens are placed in harm's way during the current war or disregarded in its aftermath, Turkish public opinion may become inflamed once again, perhaps spurring Ankara to intervene in northern Iraq.

In order to avoid such a situation, the coalition must find ways to incorporate Turkmens in any new Iraqi government. Structuring the postwar government explicitly along ethnic lines would run the risk of exacerbating ethnic tensions. That said, Iraqis and outsiders will inevitably scrutinize the ethnic composition of any new Iraqi leadership, so it will be important that Turkmens feel they have a fair share in running Iraq.

Michael Knights

55
Iraq's Ruptured Pipeline to Peace

The attacks against the United Nations headquarters yesterday and against Iraq's oil pipeline to Turkey last weekend illustrate how political and economic security are closely entwined. Ba'athist diehards know that the continuing hardships stemming from economic collapse is what will raise the political temperature among ordinary Iraqis. The lack of basic services, poverty and unemployment angers even the least restive Iraqis and further provokes the tribes of the Sunni triangle. Iraqis expected their economic situation to improve rapidly after a coalition victory. Who can blame them when coalition psychological operations told them that, like the Afghans liberated from Taliban rule, their standard of living would "drastically improve" after the fall of Saddam Hussein?

Iraqis were not the only ones to have unrealistic expectations about the country's economic recovery. Dick Cheney, the US vice-president, suggested that Iraqi oil production could be quickly increased to 3m barrels per day by December 2003. Production is currently just over 1m b/d and is unlikely to rise any time soon because of war damage, looting, and technical problems. The Coalition Provisional Authority has been forced to revise its oil production forecasts with dizzying regularity and at some cost to the credibility of the organisation.

In it latest six-month budget, the CPA should have warned that the Iraqi economy was probably not going to revive as quickly as expected, owing to stubborn bottlenecks in the oil industry and the limited capacity of the country to absorb reconstruction funds. Instead, it once again over-estimated oil production levels, which account for 88 per cent of Iraqi government revenues. According to the plan developed by the Restore Iraqi Oil group at the CPA, the country will have to raise sustainable production to 2m b/d by December 2003, and rapidly increase it to 2.8m b/d by April 2004.

Maintaining this level of production will be challenging. Even if serious acts of sabotage cease, it is not certain that the important oilfields in the south can maintain, let alone expand production. Lengthy pauses in extraction may be required later this year to undertake vital above-ground repairs. Furthermore, even if production levels were to increase beyond the current 1m b/d, there are many limitations on export capacity. The southern fields export oil via the northern Gulf port of Mina Al Bakr, which will not be easy to expand. Northern oilfields largely service the domestic market. The 180,000 b/d

Originally published in the *Financial Times* (London), August 20, 2003.

Syrian pipeline remains closed following damage in the war and because Washington has no desire to reward Syria with the return of oil transit revenues. Iraq could not start to export from the north without much higher pipeline security.

According to the US Army Corps of Engineers and industry estimates, increasing Iraq's oil export potential would require $1.6 billion investment by December 2003, up to $2.5 billion in 2004 and a further $4.5 billion by December 2005. But foreign direct investment on this scale is unlikely to come until a new constitution and investment laws are enacted in 2005.

Beyond these technical and legal limitations, the mechanisms of supply and demand dictate that increases in Iraqi production may be offset by a fall in oil prices. Iraq is unlikely, therefore, to generate either the $3.4 billion in oil revenues projected for July-December 2003, or the $14 billion that the CPA tentatively forecast for 2004. The CPA's budget deficits will probably exceed its projected $2.2 billion for 2003 and $4 billion for 2004.

While Iraq could earn income by securitising future oil production or from contributions at the UN donor conference this autumn, the country will not begin to show signs of economic recovery until well into next year. The lack of security throughout the country, and the need to keep a large number of paramilitaries on the payroll, have imposed unforeseen costs on the interim administration. Furthermore, the experience of recent post-conflict situations, particularly Afghanistan, suggests that even pledges of immediate aid cannot kick-start a rapid economic recovery. Development agencies will not disburse funds quickly while security is poor. Investors will wait or go elsewhere.

As long as attacks against US forces and international facilities continue, there is little prospect of economic recovery in the short term. But many Iraqis still harbour unrealistically high expectations of an economic recovery. So to avoid building further resentment, the CPA must bring expectations in line with reality. It should amend its budget and growth forecasts to reflect the bottlenecks that limit Iraq's ability to generate and absorb funding. Its 2004 budget must be more prudent in its projections about oil exports and more cautious about Iraq's ability to use oil revenues for reconstruction.

The US-led coalition cannot deliver an economic recovery while guerrilla activity, looting, sabotage and the tapping of oil pipelines continue. As part of a broader communications strategy the coalition needs to persuade ordinary Iraqis that it is self-inflicted damage and not the failures of the occupying powers that is holding back the country's recovery.

Michael Eisenstadt

56
Give the Sunnis a Break—and a Stake

Expressions of hope by US officials that the demise of Uday and Qusay, the sons of former Iraqi President Saddam Hussein, and indeed of Saddam himself, would undercut the Sunni Arab resistance in Iraq betrays a fundamental misunderstanding of the opposition in the so-called "Sunni triangle" north and west of Baghdad. While the departure of Saddam would reassure Iraqis who fear the *ancien regime's* return, the elimination of Iraq's former rulers or the dismantling of their political and security structures would be insufficient to end the low-level insurgency simmering in the region.

The resistance, prosecuted by varied elements acting out of diverse motives (including former regime dead-enders, local Islamists, foreign jihadists, and criminal elements), draws considerable strength from political and religious attitudes, tribal values and communal solidarities deeply ingrained in the population of the provincial villages and towns of Iraq's Sunni triangle.

Among the factors driving the resistance are the deeply felt humiliation engendered by the Anglo-American coalition's military victory and occupation; the sense of entitlement still felt by members of the Sunni Arab tribal minority that until recently ruled Iraq; the anxieties of the larger Sunni Arab community (some 20 percent of Iraq's population) that fears political and economic marginalization in a democratic Iraq; a potent brand of Iraqi-Arab nationalism well entrenched among sections of Iraq's Sunni Arab population; and the increasing popularity of political Islam among sectors of the rural Sunni population.

Capturing or killing members of the old regime engaged in violence against the coalition, accompanied by civil-military operations to create goodwill, remain the key to success for the Anglo-American effort. But military action and civil-military operations are not enough. Defeating the insurgents will require parallel steps to alter the larger political and economic context in the Sunni triangle in order to build bridges to residents of the region and isolate those who have taken up arms against the coalition.

Thus, as the coalition mercilessly pursues the insurgents, it must reassure the residents of the triangle that it is not pursuing an anti-Sunni Arab vendetta; and that although the Sunni Arab minority no longer enjoys a monopoly on power, those who embrace change have a crucial role to play in the new Iraq.

Originally published in the *Daily Star* (Beirut), September 6, 2003.

To this end, the coalition must ensure that the residents of the triangle have an identifiable voice in the new political order. At present, only one of the five Sunni Arabs on the 25-member Iraqi governing council is from the triangle (and he only recently returned from exile), and it is not clear whether any of the newly appointed interim cabinet members hail from the region. A special effort should be made to involve more individuals from this region in the drafting of a new Iraqi constitution in the coming months, and in the new Iraqi government established thereafter.

The coalition thus needs to cultivate individuals and tribes from the triangle region that suffered under the old regime (there are many) and who would rue its return. Many of these are also hostile to the coalition out of distrust for US intentions or because of nationalistic or religious conviction. Bringing these people around to work with the new order and eliminating the ideology of entitlement that makes many hostile to the idea of sharing power is essential to building post-war Iraq. While it may not be possible to win "hearts and minds" in the Sunni triangle, it may be possible to demonstrate that the coalition and residents of the region have a shared interest in cooperating.

To deal with Sunni Arab fears of marginalization, the US should encourage Iraqis to adopt a form of decentralized administrative federalism (versus ethnic federalism) as the basis for a new government in Baghdad. In Iraq, federalism has generally been cast as a means of dealing with Kurdish demands for autonomy within the framework of a unitary Iraqi state. It can, however, also be thought of as a way to ensure that the residents of each region in Iraq—including the Sunni triangle—retain the final word on how they run their lives at the local and regional levels, within constitutional parameters, as a means of guaranteeing minority rights.

Finally, the coalition must address the plight of those who have lost their jobs as a result of de-Baathification and the dismantling of the military, knowing that a disproportionate number lived in the Sunni triangle. While many of these individuals deserve little sympathy, it is in the coalition's interest to make sure they are not just receiving handouts (as in the case of former members of the armed forces), but that they find stable employment, perhaps in public works projects, where they can be watched—partly to ensure that they do not participate in anti-coalition violence—and be made to feel that they have a stake in the new order.

By taking these steps, the coalition will not only enhance the prospects for success in dealing with the low-level insurgency it is now fighting in the Sunni triangle and in Baghdad itself; it will also improve the prospects for the eventual emergence of a stable, and democratic Iraq.

Patrick Clawson

57
How Iraqis View U.S. Role Is Key to Evaluating Progress in Iraq

Reports about U.S. casualties inevitably take top billing in media coverage of postwar Iraq. Yet, assessing how Iraqis themselves view the current situation is, arguably, just as important for evaluating progress in Iraq. Two recent public opinion polls have provided systematic data about Iraqi views, and this data in turn complements mounting anecdotal evidence regarding daily life in post-Saddam Iraq.

Polls: Growing Optimism, Lingering Suspicions

Recent Gallup and Zogby International polls show consistent results: most Iraqis are optimistic, but they do not welcome a long-term U.S. role in Iraq. Gallup surveyed 1,178 Baghdad residents in late August and early September. Asked whether the ousting of Saddam Hussein was worth any hardships they have suffered since the coalition intervention, 62% answered yes and 30% no. Among the million residents of Sadr City, the poor Shiite district of the capital, 78% of respondents answered yes, a figure that lends perspective to accounts of anti-American agitation in the area by radical Shiite Islamists (e.g., firebrand cleric Muqtada al-Sadr). In contrast, respondents from the relatively affluent mixed-sect district of al-Karkh were evenly divided, with 47% answering yes and 47% no. Similar differences emerged when those polled were asked whether the Coalition Provisional Authority (CPA) is doing a good job: Sadr City respondents largely answered yes (37% positive, 13% negative) while al-Karkh respondents largely answered no (38% negative, 20% positive; the remaining respondents were neutral).

In August, Zogby International polled 598 residents of Basra, Mosul, Kirkuk, and al-Ramadi, the latter a center of Sunni Arab resistance to coalition forces. The poll did not ask whether the overthrow of Saddam was worthwhile. Asked how long coalition troops should remain in Iraq, 25% of respondents answered two or more years, compared to 32% who said that coalition forces should leave in six months. The latter group included some individuals who, while friendly to the United States (e.g., Ahmed Chalabi), are optimistic that Iraqis can take over within a short time.

All of these polls indicate that Iraqis are optimistic about the future. According to 67% of Baghdadis and 69% of those in the four regional cities, Iraq will be better off in five

Originally published as *PolicyWatch* no. 787, September 29, 2003.

years, compared to 8% and 20%, respectively, who think the country will be worse off. When asked whether the CPA was doing a better job than it had been two months earlier, 50% of Baghdadis answered yes, only 14% said no, and 33% saw no difference. Moreover, 61% of Baghdad respondents expressed favorable views of the Iraqi Governing Council, compared to only 13% with negative views.

Although they are optimistic about improvements, Baghdadis have mixed views about the present. Asked whether Iraq is better or worse off than it was before the invasion, 29% answered "somewhat better" while 32% answered "somewhat worse," with 15% saying "much worse" and only 4% "much better" (the remaining respondents were neutral). These attitudes are no doubt related to the fact that 94% of the respondents feel that the capital is more dangerous than it was before the invasion.

One continuing problem is Iraqi suspicion toward the United States. Among Baghdadis, 44% expressed a negative view of the United States compared to only 29% offering a favorable view. In the four regional cities, 50% think the United States will hurt Iraq over the next five years while 35% think the United States will help; among Sunni Arabs in the Zogby sample, the split is 70% hurt, 13% help. (Sunni Arabs constituted roughly 27% of the Zogby sample. Although the poll results do not list Sunni Arabs separately, they do differentiate between Sunnis and Kurds; subtracting Kurds from Sunnis produces a good approximation for Sunni Arabs).

The Zogby poll also asked respondents whether Iraq should have an Islamic regime or a government that allows citizens to practice their own religion. Overall, 33% favored an Islamic government. Yet, 62% of Sunni Arab respondents called for an Islamic government, compared to only 27% of Shiite respondents; this finding lends perspective to reports of Shiitesupport for Iranian-style clerical rule.

Anecdotal Evidence: Daily Life Goes On Despite Problems

The polling data above is fully consistent with anecdotal observations regarding the nature of post-Saddam life in Iraq, some appearing in numerous press accounts and others gained during the author's own recent 700-mile trip across southern and central Iraq riding in taxis and various beat-up cars and hitchhiking. These observations show that daily life goes on with ups and downs relative to the prewar period.

One striking development has been the CPA's abolition of taxes. Iraq has become one huge duty-free zone, with imports flooding in at much lower prices than in the past. For example, a used Chevrolet Caprice that cost 18 million dinars ($9,000) before the war now sells for 8 million. As a result, some 300,000 imported vehicles have reportedly been sold in Iraq since the war, with midprice used cars disappearing from the car lots of countries as far away as the United Arab Emirates. Similarly, the bazaars are full of inexpensive clothing from Southeast Asia, while the sidewalks in front of shops in Baghdad and Basra are stacked high with every type of consumer durable, especially air conditioners, freezers, washing machines, and televisions. Major importers talk of excellent sales, while industrialists complain vociferously about the flood of what they claim are unfair imports, which force them to close factories (Saddam-era controls and UN sanctions created hothouse conditions for local factories, which are now facing a cold blast due to imports).

Current income levels are difficult to judge. Teachers are no doubt happy: although they have not received all of their paychecks on time, their salaries have been raised from $5-7 per month to $120 per month. Unemployment has risen dramatically, however, despite growth in the informal trade sector (small traders and service providers abound) and the creation of numerous street-sweeping and irrigation canal-cleaning crews funded by the CPA. As for reported economic discontent among Sunni tribes, some individuals who were close to Saddam's regime say that these tribes reacted in such a manner in the past when they did not get the large cash payoffs they demanded.

Security remains a concern, but Iraqis are more worried about thieves than about anticoalition resistance. From rich businessmen to taxi drivers, the primary fear in Baghdad is of being carjacked or murdered during a robbery, particularly given the fact that Saddam released all criminals from prison before his regime fell. More troops or a broader coalition would not necessarily solve this problem. Indeed, many Iraqis commented favorably on the low profile of coalition forces—the author's own 700-mile trip was interrupted by only five checkpoints, all manned by Iraqis. The Iraqi police are beginning to make their presence felt. For the first time ever, they are patrolling in cars (Saddam's police simply sat in their stationhouses), and Baghdad traffic officers are fitfully helping at the most clogged intersections. Outside the capital, security is vastly improved; for instance, on one Thursday night in Basra, men and women could be seen strolling in and out of the fanciest hotel with no security in sight.

Noticeable progress has been made on other problems as well. Gasoline stations in central urban areas had only short lines, while those in suburbs and villages had none. Besides encouraging rampant smuggling, the low gasoline price (seven cents per gallon) cuts the cost of running the ubiquitous generators that have made the electricity situation much better than that suggested by data on central power plant output (for ninety dollars, Iraqis can buy a quiet, 1,200-watt generator capable of running a television and numerous lights).

Conclusion

Life in post-Saddam Iraq is neither chaotic nor a disaster; rather, it is a mixture of pluses and minuses. The polling data suggests that Iraqis are, on balance, optimistic. So long as that remains the case, the United States has reasonably hopeful conditions for the difficult task of transferring power to a new Iraqi-run government. Moreover, both the Zogby and Gallup polls suggest that Shiites are much more aligned with the U.S. position than are Sunni Arabs. Shiites and Kurds—who were not well represented in either poll—together constitute at least 75% of the population. So long as they remain sympathetic to U.S. goals, it will be difficult for resistance elements to become active in most of the country.

Michael Knights

58
Economics of Iraqi Security: Employment

A recent series of violent riots has underlined the close relationship between employment and security in Iraq. On October 12, riots broke out at a Baghdad recruiting station for the new Facilities Protection Service and at a Mosul employment office. Other protests have been launched by those demanding government severance pay. On October 4, demobilized soldiers rioted in Basra, resulting in the killing of two protestors. On October 11, an estimated 14,000 former soldiers and security personnel took part in violent demonstrations in Baghdad that ended with the killing of one protester. Without real jobs that provide both work and a salary, the Iraqi population will have little else to do but protest, highlighting the need to develop long-term employment opportunities as well as short-term social safety-net measures.

Background

July 2003 CIA data shows that Iraq's working-age population is 13.8 million. Not every Iraqi of working age is seeking employment, however; some men are outside the labor force (e.g., students and the disabled), and a lower proportion of women have traditionally sought work outside the home. The potential labor force is therefore in the range of 8 million.

There is no reliable data on private-sector employment. The October 9 joint UN-World Bank Needs Assessment estimated that a majority of working Iraqis are employed in the informal economy. Many Iraqis work in the nongovernment service industries (e.g., wholesale and retail trade; construction). According to the U.S. Agency for International Development (USAID), at least 500,000 Iraqis are self-employed farmers, and another 250,000 small farming businesses are in operation. An unknown number of Iraqis work in the country's private manufacturing sector (e.g., industries such as food processing and packaging).

A number of factors continue to impede the rapid expansion of private employment. The most obvious problem is the lack of stability and rule of law (e.g., police protection; a legal code; functioning courts to enforce contracts). Another problem for Iraqi industries is that the Coalition Provisional Authority (CPA) drastically reduced all import duties. On September 21, Finance Minister Kamil Mubdir al-Gailani announced a flat 5 percent duty on all imports, meaning that Iraq will be a virtual free-trade zone. This policy forces local

Originally published as *PolicyWatch* no. 795, October 20, 2003.

manufacturing industries to compete with imports—not an easy task after years of protection and subsidies. Meanwhile, Iraq faces many daunting problems in its attempts to attract foreign direct investment, such as uncertainty over the security situation and over the future government's long-term commitment to current investment measures.

Government Jobs

The 2004 CPA budget allows for 1,047,718 government jobs next year at a total cost of $2.1 billion—that is, at an average salary of $2,000 per year. The budget also includes $500 million in government subsidies for state-owned enterprises, which employed nearly 500,000 people in 2003. In addition, the budget provides $745 million in grants to local and regional governments, which presumably will use some of this money to hire local staff. (If half of the funds went for staff at the same average salary as central government employees, that would be another 185,000 personnel.) Another $250 million is allocated for stipends to demobilized military personnel, which would be sufficient to cover payments to approximately 300,000. (The budget mentions $450 million in other transfer payments, most of which are presumably earmarked for Iraq's 350,000 pensioners). Overall, the CPA budget covers at least 1.8 million people of working age. Although the CPA has placed a freeze on government ministry recruitment, it has also forbidden reductions of ministry staffing by more than 5 percent in 2004 without permission.

It is not clear whether the budget includes certain other categories of government employees. For instance, it allocates $2.5 billion for the "public distribution system" (the former oil-for-food program), but it is unclear whether that amount includes an estimated 46,000 former oil-for-food program employees. It is also unclear whether the government will employ any off-budget security personnel.

Aid-funded Jobs

As with government employment, aid-funded jobs will increase short-term employment opportunities and give the private-sector service industries a boost. In addition to existing USAID capital construction, the $18.6 billion U.S. funding supplemental will include $5.6 billion for the electrical grid, $2.1 billion for the oil industry, $4.3 billion for other utilities, and $1.8 billion for other urgent capital construction projects. In particular, the USAID school rehabilitation program is already employing sixty Iraqi firms and may receive a further $415 million in contracts in 2004. The UN-World Bank Needs Assessment may draw some donor funding specifically for employment creation, which is given a prominent place in the list of social safety-net priorities. The assessment calls for $357 million toward employment creation in 2004, highlighting the need to create "make work" projects in order to reduce short-term unemployment. General reconstruction-related spending will also inject large quantities of cash into the Iraqi economy, indirectly spurring employment in the labor-intensive service sector.

The employment potential from aid-funded jobs can be overstated, however, and a number of obstacles will reduce the impact of such programs on the overall job market. For example, many of the construction programs outlined in the U.S. supplemental funding request, particularly in the oil industry, are not labor-intensive and will primarily benefit foreign contractors and consultants. Even those that are labor-intensive have proved disappointing to Iraqis, as the foreign contractors implementing them have used large proportions of imported third-country nationals (TCNs), notably from Asia. These TCNs require lower wages and are considered to be less of a security risk, and their use has become standard operating procedure for many companies operating in the other Arab Gulf states. It would be unfortunate if Iraq became like Jordan, which suffers a high unemployment rate but supports a large TCN population.

Aid-funded projects are also likely to take some time to mature. The UN-World Bank Needs Assessment states that only around 14 percent of pledged funds will be disbursed in the first year, meaning that large pledges for the social safety net will not necessarily translate into greatly increased employment in the near term. The immediate impact of U.S. aid may be similarly limited.

Implications

On June 10, Paul Bremer estimated Iraqi unemployment at 50 percent and stated that reducing this figure would be among his highest priorities. Implementation of the 2004 CPA budget and the proposed U.S. supplemental spending for Iraq is sure to help considerably. If they are implemented as planned—a big "if"—CPA and foreign aid funds could directly and indirectly finance over 2.5 million jobs, and spending by these employees would give a further boost to private employment. More can be done, however. In particular, if the U.S. government wants to use economic and employment issues to justify its security measures, it should take the risk of employing more Iraqis in place of TCNs. Further thought should also be devoted to the impact of free-trade liberalization on Iraqi domestic manufacturing, with reconsideration of some form of limited relief for private industry similar to the support that the unprofitable state-owned industries are still receiving. Moreover, the security problem represented by underemployment should be considered alongside that of unemployment. Providing severance pay to soldiers may give them an income, but it will not meet their expectations or get them off the streets. Payments must be replaced with jobs (particularly security-related jobs) for demobilized soldiers as soon as possible.

Patrick Clawson

59
Economics of Iraqi Security: Financing Reconstruction

Although economics is not the driving force behind Iraqi resistance to the U.S.-led coalition, restoring vital public services and improving the standard of living will improve security. The key question asked about the economy has been reconstruction costs: how high will they be and who will pay them? The good news is that these costs can be met without large additional injections of U.S. funds. The bad news is that economic recovery will take years, and the Iraqi public may become disenchanted about the gap between their high hopes and the reality of slow progress.

How Much?

Calculating the amount of money Iraq needs for reconstruction is not easy. This amount will depend to a large extent on the expected outcome of reconstruction; for instance, bringing Iraq up to U.S. standards in all areas would require as much as $1 trillion in investment over the next decade. It is unlikely that the international community would take on the task of making Iraq as wealthy as the United States. Other estimates of Iraqi "needs" argue that hundreds of billions of dollars must be spent in Iraq within a few years—an argument that holds true only if the goal is to transform Iraq into a fully developed country within that timeframe, which would be a herculean task. After all, according to the UN-World Bank Needs Assessment (hereinafter Assessment), Iraq's prewar income levels were $600-700 per person per year—only two-thirds the average income in the West Bank and Gaza at the height of the intifada. Indeed, the Assessment seems to point to a more modest goal of making Iraq's annual per capita income levels on par with those of some of Iraq's neighbors: somewhere between Turkey (about $3,000) and Jordan or Iran (both at slightly more than $1,500), and certainly better than Syria (about $1,000).

There are several different estimates of Iraqi needs, each covering a variety of time periods and sectors. The Assessment estimates Iraqi needs at $36 billion for 2004-2007. Yet, the UN-World Bank looked at only a limited set of sectors (e.g., electricity, water, transport, education, health, housing, agriculture, employment creation). This set did not include certain sectors for which the Coalition Provisional Authority (CPA) has provided

Originally published as *PolicyWatch* no. 798, October 22, 2003.

needs estimates (e.g., oil, foreign affairs, religious affairs, environmental issues). The Assessment does, however, include estimates of required commitments in many of the areas covered by the U.S. supplemental budget request (which calls for $20 billion for 2004). For instance, the Assessment estimates needs of $12.1 billion for electricity generation, transmission, and distribution, whereas the U.S. budget supplemental commits $5.7 billion to this same sector. In general, there is much overlap between the UN-World Bank Assessment and the U.S. budget supplemental.

It would seem, then, that the best way to estimate Iraq's overall needs is to combine the Assessment's estimates for the sectors it looked at (again, $36 billion for 2004-2007) with the CPA's estimates for the sectors it looked at ($19.4 billion for the same period). This results in a total estimate of $55.4 billion for 2004-2007. Indeed, according to the October 21 *New York Times*, $55 billion is what "senior Defense Department officials are using as a rough estimate of the amount required to rebuild Iraq through 2007." For 2004, the combined Assessment-CPA estimate is $17.5 billion: $9.3 billion for the Assessment's sectors plus $8.2 billion for the CPA's (including $5 billion for security and $2 billion for oil).

The above figures represent the amount that needs to be committed in 2004-2007-that is, how much money must be pledged over four years. That is by no means the same as amount disbursed, or actual cash spent. As the Assessment explains, "[World] Bank experience with projects in postconflict and other emergency environments would indicate that if donors make commitments against all the needs identified in the Assessment, i.e., US$36 billion, disbursement in the first year might be in the range of US$5 billion." In some of the sectors for which the CPA made estimates, disbursements may be more rapid (e.g., funds for imported refined oil to meet demand that local refineries cannot supply). Nevertheless, disbursements in 2004 would still be far below commitments.

Some confusion may arise in light of the fact that the Assessment is not entirely consistent in its estimates. In certain sectors, the Assessment does not include needs for which financing has already been promised, even though such needs are included in other areas. In particular, the Assessment does not include $1.5 billion of electricity investment (including $1 billion in 2004) in its $36 billion total because the former amount has been pledged by the UN oil-for-food program and other unspecified "identified donors." And in the health sector, the Assessment leaves out $1 billion in 2004 needs for which it was assumed funding had already been secured (no such estimate is provided regarding already-secured funding for later years). The justification for this procedure is unclear. Nevertheless, it does not pose a big problem for those looking to estimate Iraq's needs; although it requires an adjustment in focus, it does not change the overall picture.

Where From?

The UN-World Bank's peculiar procedure regarding electricity and health highlights the manner in which needed funding can come from a wide variety of sources, not just the pledges made at Madrid. A significant amount of the money could come from Iraqi resources or from private funding. As the Assessment puts it, "Not all of the identified reconstruction needs will need to be financed externally. It is expected over time [that] an increasing share of these expenditures could be covered by [Iraqi] government revenues or private sector financing, thus diminishing the need for external financial support." Indeed, the CPA budget provides $11.3 billion in capital financing for 2004-2006 (of which $700 million is for 2004). Assuming that the level of CPA capital financing in 2007 would be the same as in 2006 ($5.4 billion), the total funding provided by the Iraqi government from 2004 to 2007 could be as high as $16.7 billion. This would constitute 30 percent of the previously described total needs assessment of $55.4 billion over the same period, leaving $38.7 billion to be raised from other sources.

The U.S. budget supplemental would provide $18-20 billion, depending on final congressional action. There is good reason to expect that the remaining half of the $38.7 billion could be readily secured without any additional U.S. funding required, even on the conservative assumption of no private financing for oil reconstruction, electricity generation, or other potentially profitable activities. Possible sources for the remaining $1921 billion include:

- The World Bank is considering a $5 billion loan program over 2004-2007.
- Japan is considering a $5 billion program of loans and grants for 2004-2007, though at Madrid it may only make a firm commitment of $1.5 billion for the first year.
- European Union members are on track to commit as much as $1 billion for 2004, led by Britain, Spain, and the union as an institution. That could translate into $4 billion over 2004-2007, although the amount might be higher if more is committed as the U.S. role shrinks and Iraq assumes a greater degree of self-governance.
- The UN oil-for-food program's September 17, 2003, report lists $2.6 billion in "unencumbered funds." The program is due to shut down on November 21; in light of the withdrawal of most UN personnel from Iraq, the plan is to hand over responsibility to the CPA. The report's opaque language also seems to indicate that an additional $7.8 billion was committed but not yet disbursed: $5.6 billion "prioritized for shipment" (much of which had not yet been delivered) and another $2.3 billion whose priority had not yet been reviewed.
- Other contributions can be expected from countries such as Canada (which is considering $260 million) and members of the Gulf Cooperation Council, led by Saudi Arabia and Kuwait.

How Quickly?

If the good news is that considerable funding should be readily available, the bad news is that reconstruction projects will be seriously constrained by implementation problems. To quote the Assessment, "Experience by the [World] Bank in other post-conflict countries shows that constraints to reconstruction are often due not to a lack of funds, but rather to difficulties in developing and implementing time-bound investment programs according to established international procedures."

Dedicating even more money to Iraq would not make much difference in how quickly reconstruction takes place. A rule of thumb in the development business is that a country can efficiently handle foreign aid only up to about 20 percent of its national income. The Assessment estimates Iraq's gross domestic product in 2002 and 2004 at $15-20 billion, which translates to a maximum efficient aid level of $3-4 billion per year. In this light, the projected aid levels detailed above are already so high that some funds may be not be well used. Moreover, additional aid money could drive wages up to an unsustainable level and divert resources from productive activities into aid-financed boondoggles.

It would be very difficult to speed up the implementation of reconstruction projects. One way to do so is to award contracts more quickly, but that requires short-circuiting established procedures, which could create the perception of cronyism (as has already been seen in charges that Halliburton unfairly benefited from good political connections). Another way to accelerate projects would be to charge ahead in the absence of personnel trained in the usual reporting and accounting procedures (skills in which few Iraqis are qualified); however, this could lead to charges of fraud and abuse. Another method, much used in the Persian Gulf states, is to bring an entire team from abroad to implement the project in question (e.g., using South Asian laborers and American supervisors); yet, this could raise costs and create resentment among Iraqis at how few jobs are being created for them. Another approach is to make decisions quickly by having a narrow group of experts decide what to build; yet, that could create ill will among Iraqis who expect their local politicians to have an important voice in decisionmaking.

The most likely scenario is that reconstruction will proceed at a measured pace. That means the standard of living for most Iraqis will improve only slowly. That could be a problem in the battle for hearts and minds, especially if Iraqis have been given the impression that their lots would be improved quickly.

Conclusion

To date, much of the focus on the reconstruction problem has been about how to secure sufficient funding to meet Iraq's needs. In fact, the available funding may be well in excess of what can be spent in the short term—indeed, the effective constraint on the pace of reconstruction may be the country's absorptive capacity rather than the amount of money pledged. Despite the fact that funding will not be as much of a problem as is often thought, the standard of living in Iraq may be slow to improve, which could become a real political problem.

Ruth Wedgwood and Neil Kritz

60
Trying a Tyrant: Should the Iraqis Alone Sit in Judgment of Saddam?

RUTH WEDGWOOD

The question of whether Saddam Hussein should be tried by an international tribunal or by an Iraqi court has been widely discussed lately. The International Criminal Court (ICC), to which the United States has long objected, does not have jurisdiction for such a trial; it can only consider crimes that occurred after July 1, 2002. Moreover, since neither Iraq nor the United States was party to the treaty that created the ICC, they would need to convince the UN Security Council to draft a resolution referring the matter to that court. In addition, the ICC treaty demands that trials be held locally if the country in question is capable of carrying out the necessary legal procedures.

Some have suggested that Saddam be tried by the ad hoc International Criminal Tribunal for the Former Yugoslavia (ICTY), based in The Hague. Although that body has a structure and a prosecutor, the latter can barely handle his current caseload; adding more responsibilities would probably not be a good idea. Also, as with the ICC, using ICTY to try Saddam would require a Security Council resolution.

In short, any international trial for Saddam would require a Security Council resolution, even if a special international court were set up for just this purpose. The five permanent members of the council would have to agree on the jurisdictional scope of any such court, which would be tricky. The French, Germans, and Russians would be unwilling to legitimize the occupation of Iraq and the transfer of power to the new U.S.-anointed authorities, and their opposition could hinder the pretrial process significantly. The death penalty is another problematic issue; most European countries hold that the death penalty is against international law, so they may insist that this penalty be withheld from any new international court. Differences could also emerge regarding the process of appointing a prosecutor.

Even if a Security Council resolution were passed, the UN is infamous for having many mechanisms that permit delay and complications. In particular, the Advisory Committee

On December 19, 2003, Ruth Wedgwood and Neil Kritz addressed The Washington Institute's Special Policy Forum. Dr. Wedgwood is the Burling Professor of International Law and Diplomacy at Johns Hopkins University's Paul H. Nitze School of Advanced International Studies. Dr. Kritz directs the U.S. Institute of Peace's Rule of Law Program. This rapporteur's summary (originally published as *PolicyWatch* no. 821, December 30, 2003) was prepared by Joyce Karam.

on Administrative and Budgetary Questions has many ways to impede a resolution if it does not agree with the final objective toward which that resolution aims. In short, bringing the Saddam issue to the UN would mean long delays.

Another lesson that the UN is reluctant to learn is that it does not carry much legitimacy in some parts of the world; the bombing of the UN headquarters in Baghdad served as solid proof of this fact. The history of UN sanctions in Iraq would not make it any easier for the organization to gain legitimacy in the eyes of Iraqis.

Two other factors that work against the international tribunal option are cost and distance. For example, ICTY proceedings in The Hague are conducted in both French and English, with the French translations costing a great deal of money. Moreover, a trial in The Hague would seem very distant to the Iraqi people and to potential witnesses.

Saddam's trial could most readily be conducted by a local court. Trying Saddam would not require constructing an entire legal system in Iraq; all that would be needed is approximately five trial court judges, nine appellate court judges, and some number of investigating magistrates. The court could follow the model used in Cambodia and Sierra Leone, namely, the so-called mixed tribunal, which combines both local and international elements. Indeed, international judges appointed by the governing authority of an Arab or Muslim judge would give credibility to the court and might make its decision more acceptable to Iraqis who would otherwise worry about political influence on the judges. The court could also employ international experts and observers at every stage in the process.

As for the level of proof that is needed to convict Saddam, using the "command responsibility doctrine" of criminal negligence would greatly ease any evidentiary problems. Under this doctrine, if the troops under a given military commander's control commit atrocities, then that commander can be held responsible as if he had committed the atrocities himself, even if it cannot be proven that he ordered the crimes in question.

Trouble may arise if Saddam is permitted to choose his own lawyer. In particular, he might misuse the trial as a stage from which to revive his political movement and foment a Baath uprising. Alternatively, the trial could be a spectacular didactic event, as the Nuremberg trials were.

NEIL KRITZ

The international community spent enormous time and effort creating the ICC, without the participation of the United States. The court's fundamental principle is complementarity; hence, in the case of Saddam Hussein, the local option takes priority and internationalizing his trial is the least desirable option. Trying Saddam locally could be a difficult and lengthy process—much more so than a trial in The Hague—because it would require rebuilding the local justice system in a post-conflict environment.

Even so, a local court would make the Iraqi people, who had no control over their fate for decades, feel empowered. No new government in Baghdad can achieve legitimacy until it exhibits complete Iraqi ownership in a country free of occupation. Thus, the process of achieving justice and accountability for three decades of regime abuses should be based on that goal.

During summer 2003, Physicians for Human Rights surveyed approximately 2,000 households in southern Iraq, generating several interesting results. For example, although an overwhelming majority of the respondents held that war crimes trials would be essential to preventing future problems in Iraq, only 12 percent were supportive of international trials. In other words, Iraqis have expressed a surprising level of trust in their judiciary system.

Whatever its form, an Iraqi war crimes court would need to work out many issues. It would need to find a way to review millions of relevant documents (over 300 million, according to some estimates). It would also need to establish a security system, a witness protection system, and a proper defense mechanism. The Iraqi judicial system before Saddam was greatly influenced by the Egyptian system, where the role of prosecutor has traditionally been extremely weak. For all of these reasons, any Iraqi war crimes court should prove its effectiveness before trying Saddam. Toward that end, it should try somewhere between 50 and 150 defendants before him.

The recent Iraqi Governing Council statute establishing a war crimes tribunal has created a new model that combines many of the lessons learned from postconflict situations over the past several decades (e.g., regarding local ownership and judicial effectiveness). The statute requires the appointment of international observers and advisors to bolster the local process. This measure is wise because the court will need broad international support in order to reverse widespread distrust regarding Iraqi justice.

Barham Salih

61
Iraqi Kurdistan and the Transition, Post–Coalition Provisional Authority

The current situation in Iraq constitutes a unique moment in the history of the Islamic Middle East. For the first time, Arabs, Kurds, Turkmens, and Assyrians of the same nation have an opportunity to cooperatively evaluate the task of shaping their shared future. The challenge between now and June 30, 2004—when the Coalition Provisional Authority in Iraq is scheduled to hand over power to the local authorities—is to articulate a transitional law through which a sovereign provisional government can be elected. Naturally, there is significant debate as to how this goal can be achieved. Although significant challenges lie ahead, the progress made following the liberation of Iraq has been incredible, particularly in light of the country's numerous complicating factors. Iraq's leaders now have the opportunity to build on this unique situation by creating a viable state.

Future of the Iraqi Nation

Nature of the Iraqi government. All parties understand that the current debate is not a zero-sum game, and they are making efforts to arbitrate their differences of opinion. Such dialogue is new in the Islamic world, and its success has been illustrated most visibly by the use of street demonstrations rather than violence as a mode of resolving differences.

Notably, all of the major parties have endorsed federal democracy as a basis for the future political system of Iraq. Iraqi Kurds envision this system as a balance of power between the regions and the center. Accordingly, any transitional law must permit all regions to establish governing institutions that will eventually have a place in the permanent constitution of Iraq.

Holding direct elections would be extremely challenging in the current environment. The eventual solution to the challenge of achieving a full transition of power must be reached through debate between Iraqis and with help from the United States and the UN. Additionally, all parties must recognize the legitimate Shiite grievance over having been unjustly barred from power for so long. At the same time, they must ensure that Iraqis of

On January 23, 2004, Barham Salih addressed The Washington Institute's Special Policy Forum. In January 2001, Dr. Salih became prime minister of the Kurdish regional government in Sulaymaniya, Iraq. Having joined the Patriotic Union of Kurdistan (PUK) in Iraq while it was an underground movement, he left for the United Kingdom and served as the movement's spokesman from 1985 to 1991. From 1991 to 2001, he served as the PUK representative to North America. This rapporteur's summary (originally published as *PolicyWatch* no. 829, January 29, 2004) was prepared by Brock Dahl.

different backgrounds understand the political process and perceive the new provisional government as representative and legitimate.

Religious influence. A democracy must reflect the values of its constituents. Rather than allowing groups such as the Wahhabis or other radical elements to build mosques in Iraq, the government should take responsibility for this effort. At the same time, however, clergy should not be given a role in day-to-day politics. Islamic parties can be part of the political process, but religion and politics should be kept as far apart as possible. The reality of religious parties can be countered only by contending secular parties that do a more effective job of meeting the needs of their constituents.

UN participation. Iraqis are apprehensive about the UN. They have had an unfortunate experience with UN bureaucracy, and many have criticized its management of the oil-for-food program. They are also disappointed that the UN and other international organizations did not do much to save the people of Iraq from the previous regime's atrocities. Nevertheless, it is imperative to involve the international community in the transition. Although international organizations and foreign ministries are accustomed to dealing with the status quo and with accepted norms of politics, all parties must avoid arrangements that salvage the old political systems of Iraq. A fundamentally different system is necessary to achieve lasting success.

Security. Those responsible for continuing terrorist activities in Iraq consist of Islamic fundamentalists, domestic Wahhabis, Baath remnants, and operatives from al-Qaeda and Ansar al-Islam. Kurdish intelligence shows that terrorist attacks involving tactical weapons (e.g., rocket-propelled grenades) were carried out primarily by former regime loyalists; such attacks have declined since the capture of Saddam Hussein. Large car bombs and similar attacks have been perpetrated by al-Qaeda and Salafi fundamentalist elements.

Future of the Kurdish North

Although the Kurdish community has been in a state of conflict with Iraq for decades, it has come to accept that it is part of Iraq. Indeed, Iraqi Kurds seek a unified, Iraqi solution to the current quandaries. At the same time, Iraqi Kurdish leaders must reassure their constituents that they are not returning to the tyranny of the past. Some Kurds argue that they should worry about Kurdistan alone, disregarding Baghdad and the Iraqi nation. Ultimately, however, the dominant view among Kurds is that they must be represented in Baghdad if they are to avoid the genocidal horrors of the past. Any new arrangement must give the Kurds and other peoples of Iraq tangible assurances that recentralization will satisfy the security and political requirements of all involved. In any case, Iraqi Kurds regard Baghdad as their capital, and they will be working with other Iraqis to create a system that will ensure safety, security, and prosperity for all.

Kurdish regional governments in Iraq. Past divisions within the Kurdish community in northern Iraq resulted from the conflict between the PUK and the Kurdish Democratic Party (KDP). In light of improving relations between these organizations, many hope that regionwide elections will be held in March 2005. Whoever wins those elections should be given the responsibility of forming the region's next government. A unified Iraqi Kurdish region could provide an element of stability for other regions of the country to emulate. Moreover, a unified regional government would facilitate the reintegration of Iraq's Kurdish region back into the Iraqi state, as part of a new federal arrangement. It is important to note, however, that no Iraqi governmental institution should be based on ethnicity or religion. In fact, this principle should be integrated into the new Iraqi constitution, and the Kurdish region of Iraq should not be excepted from it. In addition to Kurds, this region is home to Turkmens, Arabs, and Assyrians. Accordingly, members of these ethnic groups would have to be given equal opportunity to vie for leadership positions in the regional government alongside Kurds.

Kirkuk. There will not be a Kurdish claim on Kirkuk to the neglect of other claims. One Kurdish demand is nonnegotiable, however: the eradication of the area's ethnic cleansing and forced Arabization policies. The effects of such activity must be reversed through a legal and political process, after which the people can then decide the fate of Kirkuk. Moreover, the area's oil revenues must never again come under the control of the central government, which has historically used them as a pillar of tyranny. A revenue-sharing scheme will need to be devised in order to resolve the oil issue.

Turkish concerns. In conversations with Iraqi Kurdish officials, Turkey has stressed that Iraq's future is something for the people of Iraq to decide. Iraqi Kurds value that view and are urging neighboring countries to refrain from any interference in Iraqi domestic politics. The Kurdish region of Iraq has been a valued partner of Turkey over the past twelve years, particularly on security issues. Moreover, Turkish companies are performing significant amounts of work in northern Iraq, soon to reach $60 million worth in the Sulaymaniya region alone. As for the Kurdistan Workers Party (PKK), that is a matter for the state of Iraq and the state of Turkey to decide. Iraq cannot be a safe haven or launching pad for military organizations that are hostile to neighboring countries. By the same token, Iraq expects its neighbors to respect its own territorial integrity and security.

62
Eyewitness Perspectives Assessing Progress in Iraq: Politics, Transition, and the Kurds

PATRICK CLAWSON

The New Iraqi Politics

The character of Iraqi politics has completely and irreversibly changed in recent months. The prevailing sense among Iraqis is that Saddam Hussein is not coming back; they are now focused on the question of what new power arrangements will emerge.

Because Saddam prevented the formation of civil society institutions, Iraqis are beginning their new political life with few social connections outside the family. When they do look outside the family, Iraqis will initially have few places to turn. As a result, they may well fall back on their primordial links—that is, their ties to ethnic, religious, and tribal groups. Because such groups often define politics in zero-sum terms, it should come as no surprise that ethnic, religious, and tribal tensions have increased since the war's end.

Nevertheless, the nascent Iraqi government is beginning to mature as the new ministries take responsibility for making decisions (e.g., regarding government pay) that were previously under the purview of the Coalition Provisional Authority (CPA). The progress of the new government in addressing daily life issues seems to be as important to ordinary Iraqis as any national political issue. In fact, CPA polling in the Basra province found that repairing roads and sewers were among the respondents' top concerns, while national political issues barely registered.

The Iraqi police force serves as a good example of the new government's progress. Five months ago, only a few Baghdad intersections were allotted police officers to direct traffic, and those few officers appeared dispirited at their lack of success in getting drivers to pay attention to them. Now, however, almost every major intersection has a police officer standing confidently in the middle of the street, able to halt multiple lanes of traffic with a simple hand gesture. The police are also beginning to experience some success in investigating crimes, something they never did under Saddam. The fact that Iraqis are now

---

On February 9, 2004, Patrick Clawson and Soner Cagaptay addressed The Washington Institute's Special Policy Forum. Both had participated in an Institute fact-finding delegation tasked with conducting an independent survey of local security conditions and emerging political currents in Iraq. Mr. Cagaptay is coordinator of The Washington Institute's Turkish Research Program. This rapporteur's summary (originally published as *PolicyWatch* no. 831, February 12, 2004) was prepared by Jeff Cary and by Ryan Phillips.

reporting crimes illustrates the increased level of public confidence in the police, as does the high demand for police jobs. For example, Basra already has more policemen than it needs, and tribal leaders there have gathered long lists of men seeking police jobs.

Despite the steady progress it has made, the new government faces an uphill climb before it can be considered adequate to all of the tasks that will be thrust upon it. In particular, it has not yet been able to deliver personal security to all Iraqis, for whom the main danger is ordinary daily crimes rather than political attacks. Equally troubling is the fact that many Iraqis are still swayed by the old paradigm of force. For example, one tribal leader argued that the local governor should have an armed contingent at his disposal because political power is based on force.

The U.S. Role in the New Politics Is Unclear

In the old Iraqi politics, the exclusive role of the United States was to depose Saddam. In the new politics, however, the U.S. role has yet to crystallize. Many of the relevant issues are quite complicated, and the CPA lacks detailed knowledge of Iraqi society. To be fair to the CPA, reliable information on Iraqi society is difficult to come by; as two Iraqi sociology professors aptly explained, Saddam strongly discouraged studying the subject because it was too politically sensitive.

This problem of inadequate information is most pressing with regard to the Shiite community. Although Washington is placing all of its bets on Shiite cooperation, U.S. officials have only the vaguest sense of the diverse dynamics inherent in Shiite politics. For example, Shiite leaders who proclaim their undying respect for Grand Ayatollah Ali Hussein al-Sistani (the most senior Iraqi Shiite cleric and a potentially powerful political candidate) will often qualify these sentiments by arguing that elections should not be held for at least two years, in part because they are far too complicated, but also because Iraqis do not understand what democracy entails. Indeed, many Iraqis may give different information to coalition officials than they do to others with whom they speak, a problem to which CPA officials do not seem fully sensitive.

Another disturbing trend is that the United States continues to receive full blame for the CPA's shortcomings but no credit for its successes. Iraqis rarely say anything positive about what the United States has accomplished other than offering praise for deposing Saddam. Although many Iraqi criticisms are exaggerated, it is fair to blame the United States for the slow pace in delivering aid. The $18.6 billion supplemental budget has yet to be implemented, and few expect the aid program to make a noticeable difference on the ground until at least six months from now. The U.S. reconstruction effort is drowning in red tape, and the situation is likely to become much more complicated after June 30, 2004, when the CPA is scheduled to hand over power to the Iraqi authorities.

At the same time, the Iraqi economy is recovering, mainly due to the Iraqi people's new freedoms and growing confidence about the future. Iraqis are spending more money, and expatriates are sending more funds back into the country. One particularly striking example of this economic improvement occurred following the removal of international sanctions and the subsequent lifting of Iraq's 300 percent tax on automobiles. As result of these measures, the number of vehicles registered in Basra province has increased from 21,000 before the war to 50,000 today, and many more vehicles are not yet registered. Iraq has also experienced a construction boom. For example, Sulaymaniya has so many building projects in progress that there is a shortage of construction workers. In the south, numerous small brick factories have sprung up in response to the tenfold increase in brick prices (unfortunately, this brick boom has created a serious pollution problem).

The Transition Will Pose a Great Challenge

It is perhaps overly optimistic to expect that the new Iraqi institutions will be ready to assume full power by June 30. The most obvious reasons for concern lie in the security realm. Clearly, Iraq will still depend on U.S. forces to carry out large-scale operations against the resistance long after the deadline passes. In fact, the new Iraqi government is unlikely to have even a functioning Ministry of Defense to provide informed guidance to U.S. forces.

Another daunting challenge for the CPA will be the task of managing changes in its own structure. After June 30, the CPA's authority will be curtailed to an advisory role. The plan is to shift jurisdiction over the CPA from the Defense Department to the State Department, in the manner of an embassy. The difficulties in changing from one set of bureaucratic procedures to another can paralyze an office for weeks.

On the Iraqi political front, the CPA is currently devoting much of its attention to the question of whether the country's Transitional National Assembly should be selected by election or by caucus. Yet, the coalition may be better served by putting this issue aside for now and seriously reconsidering its deadline for transferring authority to the Iraqis. If the CPA insists on a June 30 handover, the new Iraqi government may lack legitimacy: the new assembly would likely be unelected, the government would not be prepared to take on many important functions, and U.S. influence would remain so pervasive that it would be viewed as still in control. Indeed, such an arrangement might remind Iraqis of the early-twentieth-century British mandate: indirect imperial control behind a façade of local democratic government.

In general, Iraq is on the road to sovereignty. The main question that remains is which Iraqi constituencies will wind up holding the primary reins of power. June 30 is not a magical date on which everything in Iraq will suddenly change. Rather, Iraqis are slowly taking on more responsibility and working out power arrangements. After June 30, the new Iraqi government will still be on training wheels and heavily reliant on the United States.

SONER CAGAPTAY

Northern Iraq

The Kurdish Regional Government in northern Iraq already has the trappings of independent statehood, and the Kurds will look to maintain as many of them as possible. Among the most important of these trappings are control over borders, militia forces, and finances. For example, the Kirkuk area alone holds about 40 percent of Iraq's oil. If the Kurds have control over this oil, they will effectively become the holders of the world's ninth largest oil reserves.

In general, Kurdish officials are prepared to accept federal status for Iraqi Kurds with two caveats. The first is that laws passed in Baghdad cannot contradict Kurdish laws or secularism. Some Kurdish officials have been adamant on that position. The second caveat is that Iraq should be organized as a binational state of Kurds and Arabs. Over the next year, Kurdish authorities will likely pursue two strategies in order to ensure that these conditions are met. First, they may resist calls for holding Iraqi elections soon, preferring that national elections be held one or two years down the road. Kurdish authorities already have a large sphere of influence, and elections could undermine some of their control, given that they represent a minority in Iraq.

Second, they will try to maintain de facto control over as much of the north-central region as they can during the transitional period. This region stretches from the Syrian border to the Iranian border and includes the cities of Mosul, Irbil, and Kirkuk. It is the only area (other than Baghdad) where all of Iraq's various ethnic groups coexist in significant numbers (the south is 90 percent Shiite, if not more; the far north and northeast are heavily Kurdish; the central region and the western desert are overwhelmingly Sunni). North-central Iraq contains ethnic enclaves within enclaves and is the only area where no group enjoys plurality across the board. Despite its diversity, much of the area is currently controlled by the Kurds, whose checkpoints stretch as far south as an hour's drive north of Baghdad. Hence, if Iraq does fracture, it will do so because of developments in the north-central region.

Despite their currently extensive reach, it is uncertain whether the Kurds will retain this level of influence in the long term. The Kurds have maintained a maximalist agenda in part to ensure that they have a strong hand when they begin bargaining with the rest of the country. Afterward, they may in due course give up some of their gains. In particular, they may be willing to give Baghdad control over their borders and integrate the *peshmerga* militias into the Iraqi army.

Turkey and the Kurds: Natural Political Allies

Iraqi Kurds and Turks can become close political allies if they can overcome their political differences in the short run. Given the large Kurdish population in Turkey, Turks view the Kurds as a part of the Turkish family. Moreover, as a country on the brink of European Union membership, Turkey is a natural passageway to the Western world for the Kurds, whose largely secular political culture mirrors Turkey's own. In fact, the Kurds are the most potent secular force in Iraq, which fact will put them squarely in Ankara's camp when it comes to maintaining a secular Iraqi political culture. Water will be another key issue binding Turks and Kurds. Turkey has long held the most favorable upstream position with regard to water rights in the Tigris and Euphrates Rivers. In the new Iraq, however, the Kurds will join Turkey as another upstream power, given their control over the mountainous north. Hence, if negotiations on regional water issues are held in the near future, Syria and Iraq, the two downstream countries, will be sitting on one side of the table, with Turkey and the Iraqi Kurds on the other side.

63
The Iraqi Bill of Rights in Regional Perspective

The Iraqi Transitional Administrative Law (TAL)—to be officially published tomorrow, when the mourning period for the victims of the March 3 Ashura bombings ends—includes an extensive bill of rights. Yet, several of the Arab countries whose constitutions offer similar rights have a decidedly unsatisfactory record on human rights. Indeed, the region's poor track record with regard to actually implementing constitutional guarantees may make the TAL appear less impressive to Arabs than it does to Americans. At least as important as what the TAL says is whether the legislation will be respected in practice.

The TAL's Provisions

According to the Coalition Provisional Authority website, "An important function of the TAL will be to guarantee the basic, inalienable rights of all Iraqis." It explains, "The rights that the TAL will protect will include, but not be limited to: the right to think, speak, and publish freely; the right to peaceable assembly; the right to free association and organization; the right to vote; the right to freedom of religion; the right to privacy; the right to a fair, speedy, and public trial in accordance with the law; the right to be presumed innocent of a crime until proven guilty; [and] the absolute prohibition of torture and of other cruel and inhuman treatment." The website also asserts that "the TAL will make a break with the past in ensuring that Iraqis can enjoy with confidence the rights that they naturally share with citizens in democracies throughout the world."

When the TAL was finalized by the Iraqi Governing Council on March 1, Secretary of Defense Donald Rumsfeld stated, "This interim constitution includes as its cornerstone a bill of rights that provides protection of individual rights that are unprecedented in the history of Iraq, and indeed the region." He was echoing the words of Adnan Pachachi, the council member who was most involved in preparing the TAL and who described its bill of rights as "something that is unheard of, unprecedented in this part of the world."

Comparable Arab Constitutional Provisions

In fact, the majority of the rights guaranteed in the TAL are also guaranteed in the constitutions of most Arab states. Nearly every Arab state has a constitution; even Saudi

Originally published as *PolicyWatch* no. 840, March 4, 2004.

Arabia has a Basic Law of Government that closely resembles a constitution. Each of these documents includes provisions regarding the rights of citizens. Some of the key areas generally covered by these provisions are outlined below.

Freedom of speech. Libya's 1969 constitution is one of the few that spell out what is the practice in so many other Arab countries, namely, that free speech is tolerated only insofar as it eschews criticism of the government. As Article 13 of that document puts it, "Freedom of opinion is guaranteed within the limits of public interest and the principles of the Revolution." Most Arab constitutions include more permissive speech-related provisions that do not necessarily reflect the reality within the countries in question. For example, according to Article 38 of the Syrian constitution, "The state guarantees the freedom of the press, of printing, and publication in accordance with law." (To be fair, the relevant U.S. constitutional provision—"Congress shall make no law . . . abridging the freedom of speech"—has been interpreted in practice to permit laws banning obscene speech and penalizing slander.) Several Arab constitutions offer absolute guarantees of free speech, as seen in Article 48 of Egypt's 1980 constitution: "Freedom of the press, printing, publication, and mass media shall be guaranteed. Censorship on newspapers is forbidden as well as notifying, suspending, or canceling them by administrative methods." Similarly, Article 41 of Algeria's 1976 constitution reads, "Freedom of expression, association, and meeting are guaranteed to the citizen."

Freedom of religion. In many Arab countries, the basic laws regarding religious rights are similar to Article 46 of the Egyptian constitution: "The state shall guarantee the freedom of belief and the freedom of practice of religious rites." Other countries qualify the right to practice religion in public; for example, Article 35 of the 1962 Kuwaiti constitution "protects the freedom of practicing religion in accordance with established customs, provided that it does not conflict with public policy or morals" (for the record, Kuwait has several Christian churches and a Jewish cemetery). The exception to these relatively liberal provisions is Saudi Arabia's 1992 Basic Law, Article 34 of which states, "The defense of the Islamic religion, society, and country is a duty for each citizen."

Judicial rights. Many Arab constitutions include all of the basic principles considered essential to guaranteeing full judicial rights. Article 28 of the 1973 Syrian constitution states, "Every defendant is presumed innocent until he is proved guilty by a final judicial decision. No one may be kept under surveillance or detained except in accordance with the law. No one may be tortured physically or mentally or treated in a humiliating manner." The 1991 Yemeni constitution is the most specific and comprehensive regarding such rights. For example, Article 32 states, "Anyone whose freedom is restricted has the right to remain silent and to speak only in the presence of an attorney.... Whoever is temporarily arrested for suspicion of committing a crime shall be arraigned within twenty-four hours. The judge shall inform him of the reasons for his arrest, question him, and give him the opportunity to plead his defense. The judge shall immediately issue a reasoned order for his release or continued detention."

Women's rights. Interestingly, Arab constitutional provisions regarding women's rights are more in line with what their governments actually strive to achieve (albeit not always successfully) than provisions regarding other rights. For example, Article 11 of the Egyptian constitution reads, "The state shall guarantee the proper coordination between the duties of woman toward the family and her work in society, considering her equal with man in the fields of political, social, cultural, and economic life without violation of the rules of Islamic jurisprudence."

Iraq's Past Constitutions

Iraq's longest-lasting constitution occurred under the monarchy; it was adopted in 1925 and replaced in 1958. Under Baath rule, Iraq adopted several interim constitutions, most recently in 1990. Those constitutions included a variety of provisions that sounded wonderful but remained dead letters. For example, the 1990 constitution stated that "it is inadmissible to arrest a person, to stop him, to imprison him, or to search him, except in accordance with the rules of law.... The dignity of man is safeguarded. It is inadmissible to cause any physical or psychological harm." The 1925 constitution went further: Article 7 stated, "There shall be no violation of, or interference with, the personal liberty of any of the inhabitants of Iraq.... Torture and the deportation of Iraqis from the Kingdom of Iraq are absolutely forbidden." It will be interesting to compare the bill of rights in the final version of the new TAL with the 1925 and 1990 Iraqi constitutions; they may in fact have many features in common.

Implementation Is What Counts

Constitutions are not necessarily accurate predictors of an Arab country's actual track record on human rights. Those regimes with reasonably good records in practice (e.g., Kuwait) sometimes have constitutions that contain the most qualifications and limitations to human rights, while those regimes with poor records (e.g., Syria, Algeria) sometimes have the most liberal constitutional provisions. The Yemeni constitution contains the most potent bill of rights, but it is by no means clear that Yemen has the best human rights record in practice.

The Iraqi people remember all too well that the rights spelled out in their 1925 and 1990 constitutions were not enforced. Hence, it would be unrealistic to expect them to have much faith in the new interim constitution simply because of the wording of the text. Much more important than the phrasing will be the implementation. In particular, Iraqis must be shown that all parties will be bound by the provisions of the new constitution. That will not be easy to do during the current emergency period, with its continued insurgent and foreign terrorist activity. The U.S. military now faces the challenge of adopting and implementing procedures that are fully consistent with the TAL. If U.S. practice falls short of the TAL's principles, Iraqis may lose confidence that the political procedures spelled out in that document will determine the actual distribution of power.

Michael Knights

64
Kurds Aim to Secure Continued Regional Control

When, on 22 December 2003, the Kurdistan Regional Government (KRG) called for its autonomous status to be permanently enshrined in Iraq's new Fundamental Law, Kurdistan Democratic Party (KDP) leader Massoud Barzani warned that "after 12 years of self-rule, the Kurds will not accept less than the current situation".

In response to the KRG proposal, an estimated 2,000 protestors from the Arab and Turkmen communities descended on government buildings in Kirkuk on 31 December, sparking violent clashes in which four protestors were killed by *peshmerga* from the Patriotic Union of Kurdistan (PUK). Tit-for-tat killings and small bombings have continued since then, and on 5 January a rocket-propelled grenade was fired at a PUK headquarters.

However, the suicide bombings that took place at the KDP and PUK headquarters in Arbil on 1 February are less easy to integrate into this pattern of attacks. Simultaneously targeting both KRG offices, the suicide attacks killed 56 people and injured up to 200—a modus operandi suggestive of Ansar al-Islam involvement.

Ansar al-Islam had previously assassinated Kurdish politician Franso Hariri in February 2002 and attempted to kill Barham Salih, Prime Minister of the PUK wing of the KRG, in April 2002. Other Ansar al-Islam attacks, including restaurant bombings and ambushes, have killed 155 constituents of the PUK since the first major Ansar al-Islam attack in September 2001. That said, the attacks mark a deviation in the organisation's targeting strategy. Previous Ansar al-Islam attacks have concentrated exclusively on the PUK, whose territory abutted the Ansar al-Islam enclave and whose forces destroyed that settlement in March 2003. The PUK hold around 30 Ansar al-Islam prisoners in As Sulaymaniyah. The targeting of both the KDP and PUK offices of the KRG in the Kurdish zone's capital of Arbil suggests that Ansar al-Islam symbolically struck the KRG as a whole.

The spectrum of factions opposed to KRG proposals for northern Iraq is already coalescing. The 2,000-person Kirkuk protests were carefully organised events, bringing together Sunni, Turkmen, and Shi'ite protestors. According to local police forces, the Arab protestors came from villages outside the city including Kharmatu, Tuz, Tarjil, and

Originally published in *Jane's Intelligence Review,* March 1, 2004. Reprinted with permission from Jane's Information Group/*Jane's Intelligence Review.*

Hawija—the latter having been a hotbed of Sunni resistance since the war ended—suggesting that they were trucked into the city by Sunni community figures, some of which may maintain relations with Ansar al-Islam. Other attacks appear to have been carried out by Turkmen activists. Moqtada al-Sadr's Shi'ite faction, which has organised anti-Kurdish demonstrations in Najaf and Karbala, was present at the protest.

On the international front, with the USA effectively backing away from the issue, Iraq's allies remain concerned that a federal Iraq could threaten the existence of the Kurdish state and result in overspill or mimicking by regional minorities within their own states.

A Modest Proposal?

KRG policies during and since the war have confounded many of the pre-war analyses of Kurdish intentions. The KRG has remained committed to semi-autonomy within Iraq, rather than the creation of a Kurdish state, and both the KDP and PUK restrained the activities of their *peshmerga* militias and the extent of "reverse ethnic-cleansing" in areas of the north affected by Saddam Hussein's 'Arabisation' programme.

Salih told *JIR* that the Kurdish parties recognise prominent participation in the Baghdad government as the only way to consolidate and buttress KRG gains to date. Salih said: "It would be easy for us to forget that whatever we have today in Sulaymaniyah or Arbil, if there isn't a decent government in Baghdad, these gains are easily reversed."

In line with this policy, the KDP and PUK were the first opposition forces to move their leaderships into post-war Baghdad, where they played a major role in convening early political meetings, even as the Ba'athist leadership fell. There are now five Kurdish representatives on the Iraqi Governing Council (IGC) and Kurdish bureaucrats run five of the 13 key ministries. Salih noted: "Baghdad is our capital." The challenge now is to establish the exact nature of the relationship between the KRG and the Baghdad government, which had no interaction and has established many parallel institutions and laws since the early 1990s—requiring some degree of "reunification", in the words of Kurdish political figures.

The 22 December proposal sought to influence the way that the Fundamental Law will describe the relationship between the KRG and the Baghdad government. The Kurdish proposal suggests that Iraq should remain split into 18 provinces, albeit with some adjustments to increase the areas of the predominantly Kurdish provinces of Dahuk, Arbil and As Sulaymaniyah. The suggested changes would attach the oil-rich areas of Kirkuk in the At Ta'mim province and oilfields in Khanaqin to the KRG, and add other Kurdish enclaves in Nineveh and Diyala provinces. In each of these areas a referendum would be held in which voters could demonstrate their willingness to join the KRG zone, and full legal protection for local minorities would be enshrined in the Fundamental Law.

Salih told *JIR* that the centrepiece of the proposal is the development of "a legal modality for provinces to merge", after which they would form regional governments to communally deal with the Baghdad federal government. They would have legislative and executive powers in all fields apart from defence, foreign affairs and fiscal policy. If these structures were adopted into the Fundamental Law, the KRG would emerge as the first such multi-province regional government in Iraq and would be formalised and protected by law. Other multi-province regional governments are likely to emerge in the governates containing Iraq's southern oilfields, or around the twin Shi'ite centres of Najaf and Karbala. As any Iraqi constitution is likely to ban sectarian or religious discrimination, each multi-province government could theoretically be led by a Shi'ite or Sunni Arab, Kurd, or other minority. However, regional governments are likely to have a strongly sectarian or religious composition.

Territorial challenges

The status of Kirkuk and other Kurdish territorial claims threaten to inflame the situation in northern Iraq. Salih said: "We have all the ingredients here for a major failure. Kirkuk is a powder keg that could turn into a Bosnia or a Kosovo."

In spite of de facto Kurdish control of Kirkuk, the KRG is still seeking to cement its historical claim on Kirkuk through the formal mechanisms of a future federal government in Baghdad. In March 2003, Salih told *JIR* that the Kurds believed the route to Kirkuk lay through Baghdad, and this remains the KRG position, even though Kurdish militias have taken effective physical control of the region.

Following the liberation of Kirkuk, in which the *peshmerga* played a major role, the Kurdish groups have successfully taken control of the city's key instruments of power as well as the school system. Former *peshmerga* dominate the police force and the bodyguard of Abdul Rahman Mustafa, the Kurdish mayor of Kirkuk, and up to 35,000 Kurdish returnees, have camped out in commandeered government and military buildings.

The KRG will seek a government position on Saddam-era Arabisation in the north, and any central government judgement on the future of Kirkuk would have major implications for the stalled process of permanent settlement of Kurdish returnees. When Kirkuk fell to US and *peshmerga* forces, the KRG captured very complete files detailing the process of Arabisation. The regional government hopes to use these as a means to verify individual land claims by returnees. Having prevented massive reverse ethnic-cleansing during and immediately after the war, the KRG will now pursue a legal process through which many Kurdish citizens can return to their original homes, while Arab settlers will be compensated for their move through central government funds. With IGC backing, property claims have been heard in local courts in the KRG zone since December 2003.

Paying for It

Although the KRG can boast of its fait accompli in establishing a parallel government infrastructure and maintaining physical control of its territory, the Kurdish zone remains reliant on external funding, suggesting one of the dimensions in which a future Baghdad government could exert pressure.

In the near-term, the KRG is comfortably meeting its operating costs. The KRG previously received 13% of Iraq's annual oil revenues from the Oil-for-Food Programme (OFP), although only around half of this total ended up being dispensed by the UN system operating in northern Iraq. Under US guidance, the IGC is providing a US$500m emergency operating budget to the KRG, as well as a proportion of unspent funds from the now suspended OFP. The KRG relies on outside agencies to fund major capital investment, using a combination of the last $750m transferred from the OFP to the regional government for previously UN-administered schemes, plus US Agency for International Development (USAID) and CPA-budgeted reconstruction projects.

Longer-term economic security is less certain, as a future Baghdad government could suspend the special payments that provide the operating costs of the regional bureaucracy. Consequently, the KRG is seeking a formalised arrangement for sharing the income from the northern oilfields at Kirkuk and Khanaqin.

Kurdish leaders are quick to point out that oil has traditionally been a curse to Iraqi Kurds, providing massive resources to oppressive regimes in Baghdad and imbuing the north with a strategic value that has deterred the central government from considering Kurdish autonomy. With Kirkuk firmly in Kurdish hands, the KRG now proposes that Iraq's provinces should enjoy some control over their sub-soil natural resources, in a similar manner to Canadian provinces. The KRG would like to have the final say in how local hydrocarbon resources are exploited, perhaps going as far as allowing foreign ownership of these assets—which Iraqi national law and the outgoing Ba'athist constitution currently bans. The KRG has said it would send "a significant share of oil revenue to the central government". However, these proposals, which would also allow the southern Iraqi governates to take control of their resources, are likely to be highly controversial and will require serious amendment of existing constitutional principles when a new constitution is written.

In the interim, the KRG is promoting its reputation as a pro-Western, technocratic and investment-friendly region in order to attract Western investment to the northern hydrocarbon sector. With neither cross-border trade nor central government funding a reliable source, the KRG has established the London-based Kurdistan Development Corporation (KDC) to attract direct foreign investment, and it has partnered with Kuwait's K-International Aircraft Leasing to run daily commercial flights directly to Arbil. The success of KDC will be strongly influenced by the Kurdish parties' ability to legitimise the Kurdish unit in Iraq as a legally recognised entity, as well as to ensure security in the KRG zone. Before the 2 February 2004 bombings, the KDC had stressed the KRG's status as a low-risk, business-friendly portal to Iraq, Turkey, and Iran. Following these high-profile attacks, the KRG will have to demonstrate that it can restore security to the region.

Security Issues

Despite the urgent need to improve security, the Kurdish political parties are unlikely to fully entrust a Baghdad government with the security of Kurdish areas. Although the KRG has signalled its willingness to leave national defence in the hands of a federal government, definite limits to the extent of security co-operation will remain. Kurdish leaders have said that central government troops will not be allowed to enter the Kurdish multi-province zone unless the KRG parliament has authorised the deployment. Central government deployment to certain sensitive areas, such as Halabja, will be permanently off-limits. Neither the KDP nor PUK will disband their *peshmerga* militias; instead they will likely to be headquartered at Arbil and incorporated into the permanent network of provincial civil defence forces that the CPA is establishing to perform a National Guard role. The KRG will also retain the effective intelligence organisations built up by both the KDP and PUK.

The KRG is also likely to maintain close direct links with Washington through Iraq's Kurdish Foreign Minister Hoshyar Zebari and Salih, who currently acts as the KRG's unofficial Washington point man and is tipped to become Iraq's next ambassador to the UN.

Preparing for Deadlock

The Fundamental Law will be the first major test of whether the IGC is going to accept a formalised KRG role in Iraq. Kurdish leaders are expected to work closely with veteran Sunni diplomat and IGC member Adnan Pachachi and his legal advisor Feisal Istrabadi, who head the IGC's subcommittee on the issue.

Early indications suggest that most non-Kurdish IGC members will seek to keep the Fundamental Law as vague as possible. However, even if vague, the law will set an important precedent on the road map linking the current status quo to the future constitution. Salih told *JIR*: "We are not expecting final settlement issues to be in the law; it will set the parameters to allow the development of federalism." Among the IGC there is broad support for some form of federal government.

While these developments unfold, the KRG will continue to strengthen its institutions. Should the KRG transition into a formal Iraqi regional entity, Kurdish sources confirmed that Nechirvan Barzani, the Prime Minister of the KDP wing of the KRG, is likely to become the KRG president. Former PUK Prime Minister Kosrat Rasool is frontrunner to head the local parliament.

The KRG continues to run parallel ministries to each of the CPA-run ministries in Baghdad—and remains ready to maintain this parallel structure in perpetuity and even evacuate it from the key cities to ensure continuity of government in the face of central government or foreign moves against it.

The Path to (In)Stability

With tensions running high in the KRG, and likely to be raised yet further as federalism is discussed, Kurdish leaders are nervous about the prospects of instability attending the parliamentary elections it must hold in August 2005. Student elections in the KRG during December were marred by poor organisation and outbreaks of violence, and saw Islamic parties register an unprecedented 18% of the vote.

Kurdish and Shi'ite interests are diverging on the issue of elections. While IGC figures, including Chalabi, have moved to a position of support for early elections before or on the 30 June transition deadline, Kurdish leaders have repeatedly cast doubt on the advisability of an early transition. Officially, the KRG opposes elections on the grounds that they cannot be organised in time, yet KRG elections in the early 1990s were sometimes arranged in only three months and were widely applauded for their fairness and efficiency. It is more likely that the KRG recognises the advantages it enjoys while the CPA runs Iraq, especially since the CPA accepted on 7 January that the KRG position would not change until a sovereign Iraqi government rules on the matter. This effectively handed the problem to a future Iraqi government and the longer it takes for that government to emerge, the more time the KRG will have to establish itself in its new post-war territories.

Though the scale of the 1 February bombings has eclipsed previous terrorist actions in the northern Iraq, Kurdish leaders have long accepted that some instability in the KRG areas was inevitable during the political reunification of Iraq. Salih recently told a Washington policy audience: "There will be some chaos and turbulence, and why not? Why should Iraq be an exception amongst nations?" The key difference since Operation 'Iraqi Freedom' is that while before the war, federalism was seen as a threat to Iraq's survival as a state, since the war, federalism is increasingly emerging as the only viable way of reunifying it. KDP leader Massoud Barzani recently outlined the new environment, stating: "The situation is different now from the past. The Kurds have been successful in running their affairs, establishing several civil society institutes like [such as] the regional parliament and regional government, and they are willing to make great sacrifices to preserve them."

Nevertheless, the obvious semi-autonomy of the KRG has alarmed foreign states, forcing Kurdish spokesmen to subtly change their message in recent months. Instead of downplaying the likelihood that a Kurdish unit will emerge in Iraq, the KRG now highlights the benefits that co-operation with the Kurdish bloc can offer.

The wartime and post-war survival of the KRG owed much to the Turkish parliament decision to prevent a US-Turkish ground invasion of northern Iraq, and to the KRG's success in maintaining relative peace and security in the north compared to the rest of Iraq. The KRG is actively engaged in security co-operation with Turkey to curtail Kurdistan Worker's Party (PKK, now known as the Kurdistan People's Congress or KONGRA-GEL) activity from its territory, and has also interested Turkish commercial concerns with partnership deals in airfield construction at Arbil and As Sulaymaniyah, as well as other ventures. Furthermore, while key states such as Turkey have seen some of their worst fears gradually come to pass, there appears to be little appetite for the international censure that a direct intervention in Iraqi politics would entail. The Turkish government, for instance, remains fixated on the issue of EU entry, and will not compromise that goal with military adventurism in Iraq. Furthermore, Turkey has said it would respect any decision that the Iraqi people made about their future system of government.

Patrick Clawson

65
Iraq for the Iraqis: How and When

Regardless of the government that assumes sovereign authority on June 30, it will remain fragile and weak at first, and heavily reliant on the United States. Indeed, the U.S. influence may remain so pervasive that it could look like indirect imperial control, which is how the British ran Iraq for decades. If the handover goes ahead as scheduled, Iraqis, Middle Easterners, or the world at large may not accept the government as legitimate. In that case, resistance attacks, which have already reached the dimensions of uprisings in Fallujah and Najaf, could spread and intensify.

The administration seems determined to make the handover on June 30. But the mood in Iraq among responsible people is this: get it right, even if it takes longer.

These conclusions emerged from a ten-day trip to Iraq in February by a six-person team from The Washington Institute for Near East Policy. Our team traveled 1,000 miles by car from Turkey across all of Iraq to Kuwait. Ours was one of the few groups—if not the only one—to have done this complete tour. We arranged our trip ourselves and controlled our itinerary rather than relying on the Coalition Provisional Authority (CPA). We stayed in Iraqi hotels and traveled by ordinary cars. We were often on the road by 5:00 a.m., with meetings all day until dinner sessions that stretched well into the night.

We were in Irbil and Sulaymaniya in Iraqi Kurdistan for discussions with leaders of the Kurdistan Democratic Party (KDP) and Patriotic Union of Kurdistan (PUK). Members of our group went to Halabja to interview Ansar al-Islam prisoners; to Kirkuk to meet with the Turkmen community; and to the Iranian mujahideens' camp Ashraf. In Baghdad, we spent three days meeting with senior CPA and coalition military officials. We also spent many hours with Governing Council (GC) members, Iraqi intellectuals, and senior Shi'ite clerics. From Baghdad, we went to Hilla where we met with a senior reformist cleric and a large group of tribal leaders. We then proceeded to Basra where we met British military and civilian officials, as well as another group of tribal leaders and the provincial governor.

From our top-to-bottom passage through Iraq, we reached the same conclusion as many of our Iraqi interlocutors: it would be a mistake to rush the political process in Iraq.

Originally published in *Middle East Quarterly* 11, no. 2 (Spring 2004). Reprinted with permission.

Government and Economy

The new Iraqi government is starting to take hold. Salaries are being paid promptly, and the new 11-grade salary schedule is generous. On January 1, the lowest government salary rose to 150,000 Iraqi dinars (ID) ($100) per month, compared to ID3,000 prewar. Additionally, food rations continue, so that a family gets a basket with more than 2,500 calories per person per day for a cost of less than ID1,000 per month. The government heavily subsidizes many other services such as electricity, kerosene for cooking and heating, and gasoline. There are no taxes. So the standard of living compares favorably to the recent past. At the upper level, salaries have also gone up but less so: the maximum is ID1,500,000 compared to ID300,000 prewar.

The traffic police provide an example of how the new government is working. Five months earlier, during a previous trip to Iraq, I found that some (but not all) of Baghdad's major intersections had a few bedraggled and dispirited traffic police struggling to get people's attention. Now almost every major intersection has a policeman confidently standing in the middle of the street, able to bring three lanes of traffic to a halt by just pointing his hand.

Harder to evaluate are the police charged with investigating crimes. We heard many plausible stories of how the police are beginning to have some successes investigating crimes—something they never did under Saddam Hussein. And we heard many stories about how people now report crimes, which shows a growing confidence in the police. This has an effect on police morale. We saw firsthand evidence of how highly prized police jobs are in the south: the very first action of the tribal leaders meeting with Basra's governor was to hand over a petition asking that a long list of their tribe members be hired for the force. CPA officials told us that they are besieged by such requests in Basra.

The situation with the police also shows how far the new government has to go. The police are poorly equipped and barely trained, and they are no match for the resistance. Indeed, given how little vetting was done, it is no surprise that some of the police have turned out to be sympathizers of the resistance—police by day and insurgents by night. Not only are the police of little use in combating political violence, they have not been able to make Iraqis secure from crime. The main danger for Iraqis remains ordinary criminals, not political attacks. There continues to be much fear about kidnappings and carjackings.

The police are also an example of how uncertainty causes everyone to hedge bets. We often heard how the same policemen who take orders from the coalition also take orders from one or more political parties (and that the same tribal leaders who work closely with the coalition are also actively protesting coalition policies). Some CPA officials had a tendency to minimize these dual loyalties and assume that the new Iraqi government institutions had taken root. In fact, these institutions have shallow roots; were there a storm, they would be badly shaken and might not survive.

Just as troubling as the crime situation, is the fact that Iraqis are still much influenced by the view that power proceeds from armed force. The long-standing Iraqi tradition is to keep an impressive amount of arms at home. (We heard about people celebrating

Hussein's capture by firing rocket-propelled grenades into the air.) Many social groups are armed and organized, including new political parties, militias, and tribes. Iraqis are uncertain whether future power will derive from the ballot box or the gun barrel. Radical elements are already testing whether they can seize and hold local power by force of arms. If they succeed, many Iraqis may decide that force still is the way to power, and violence could spread and multiply.

Meanwhile, the economy is recovering, mostly because the new freedoms and confidence about the future are leading Iraqis to spend more and persuading Iraqi expatriates to send back cash. For example, the flood of Iranian pilgrims—15,000 a day through official crossing points was the estimate of one knowledgeable official—has so stimulated the Najaf economy that real estate prices are up ten-fold from before the war. The removal of sanctions and the abolition of the 300-percent tax on cars (part of the abolition of all taxes) have had spectacular results. Used cars are flooding into the country. The number of vehicles of all sorts registered in Basra province is up from 21,000 prewar to 50,000 now, and many vehicles are not registered.

Construction is also booming. There is a serious pollution problem in the south from the many new small brick factories that have sprung up in response to the ten-fold increase in brick prices as the demand for construction materials soars. We were told in Sulaymaniya that so many people are putting additions on their homes that there is a shortage of construction workers. Everyone ascribes the construction boom to greater confidence in the future.

But the economic progress is dependent on the security situation. If the mafias shaking down businessmen get bolder, or if the resistance gets strong enough to shut down economic development projects (in April, kidnappings practically did that), all the economic progress could be washed away. That would open a vicious cycle of growing despair, growing resistance, and diminished confidence in the future. A security vacuum could shut the economy down. It is hard to overstate the importance of the economic issue; as one Iraqi politician put it, "the belly is more important than the tongue," meaning people care more about meeting basic needs than about their new-found freedom of speech.

Ethnic Politics

In the new politics, the most important factors are ethnicity, religion, and tribe. Because Hussein banned the institutions of civil society and instilled fear of speaking openly even to one's friends, Iraqis begin their new political life with few political connections outside the family. CPA polling has found that the family is the most important source of identity for the great majority of Iraqis. When they look outside the family, Iraqis still have few places to turn except their primordial links, i.e. to ethnic, religious, and tribal ties. Primordial groups define politics in zero-sum terms where every gain for one group is a loss for all the others. It is hardly surprising that the transition to a participatory system is producing increased ethno-religious and tribal tensions.

A major problem is the lack of Sunni Arab leadership. There are no signs that the Sunni community has widely respected leaders ready to work with the CPA, and it is not clear who could negotiate on their behalf. In the worst-case scenario, Sunnis could accept the resistance as their authentic voice. Such a Sunni leadership, with a radical pan-Arab ethos, could resonate deeply throughout the (Sunni) Arab world.

As for the Kurds, the signs are mixed. We heard many encouraging words from Kurdish leaders, including KDP ministers who are regarded as "difficult" by the CPA. We heard about the KDP's determination to create a Kurdistani identity, not a Kurdish one; about the KDP's close cooperation with the police in the rest of Iraq; and about the KDP volunteering to implement border policies declared by the national interior minister. The PUK is even more promising. PUK leader Jalal Talabani is the only Governing Council member to have traveled all over the country, and he is obviously campaigning to be president of Iraq (or at least one of the two deputy presidents).

Yet there are many worrying signs. We had Kurdish cabinet ministers tell us, "Iraq is something foreign to us," and "Without Saddam, there can be no Iraq of the sort they [the Sunnis] perceive." We were told that if Decree 137 (the Governing Council's proposed revamping of family law to allow recourse to religious courts) became law, the Kurdish governments would flatly refuse to apply it, claiming a right to civil disobedience.

The Arab residents encouraged by Hussein to move north present the most worrying problem. They are known as the 10,000-dinar Arabs—that is the sum Hussein offered them as an incentive to move north, at a time when it was real money. Every Kurdish official we met told us that these people must be encouraged to leave. Some hinted that the encouragement would be vigorous; others thought it would be sufficient to compensate Arabs, thereby allowing the original Kurdish homeowners to return. Some people have expansive ideas about which Arabs must leave; one senior official said the Arabization campaigns began in 1936, so Arabs who came after that should go.

No Kurdish official was willing to see the 10,000-dinar Arabs vote where they now live, and some strongly hinted that the Kurds would take action to assure that they wouldn't. The obvious problem area is Kirkuk, to which tens of thousands of Kurds have returned (despite the claim of the PUK to the contrary). And there are other flash points, such as the rich agricultural plain surrounding the city of Mosul and the Syrian border zone.

The proposal to leave things unchanged during the transition period is based on the fiction that there is a status quo. In fact, the Kurds are creating new facts on the ground. Kurdish militiamen (*peshmerga*) are manning the road checkpoints dozens of miles south of Kirkuk, way beyond the area of nominal Kurdish control. The ethnic balance of Kirkuk has been visibly changed by the Kurdish influx.

We detected a clear difference in approach between the KDP and PUK. The KDP leaders exude confidence that they can survive nicely on their own; their attitude is that Baghdad has to make them an attractive offer if it wants their cooperation. The PUK is much more committed to working out a solution with Baghdad. The reason is simple: as their ministers told us, without funds from the center, the PUK would be broke within a few months. However, if things in the south begin to go south, even the PUK will be tempted to pull up the drawbridge.

Turning to the Shi'ite community, at the time of our visit there was an almost universal conviction in the CPA that the Shi'ites would work with the United States; we met no one in the CPA who was worried about implications of a Shi'ite-dominated government. There was also a widespread conviction in the CPA that when the Shi'ites vote, secular voices will prevail. CPA officials told us several times that Ayatollah Sistani is more powerful in the pages of the *New York Times* and *Washington Post* than he is in Iraq. And we heard from several mainstream Shi'ite clerics that this time, the Shi'ites will not miss their opportunity for power. As one Shi'ite cleric put it, "the United States is now our mother," and they must look to it for guidance and help.

Nonetheless, the emergence of radical Shi'ite politics, personified by Muqtada as-Sadr, has put some of these assumptions in doubt. His popularity may be very limited, but he has a dedicated following. As of this writing, he is locked in a showdown with the United States in Najaf. The episode has demonstrated that while the traditional leadership in Najaf reviles him, it has not been willing to confront him directly. Until Sadr loses a test of arms, he will remain a serious challenge. (An encouraging development is the rise of an Iraqi group opposed to him.)

In the short run, the pull of ethnicity, religion, and tribe will challenge the central government and could reduce it to negotiating with powerful local leaders who are largely autonomous, and who maintain and keep that autonomy by force. However disappointing that might be, it would be preferable to the reemergence of a powerful central government, tightly held by one small clique. That has been the pattern of modern Iraqi history, for a simple reason: massive oil revenues inflate the power of whoever controls the central government.

Such a scenario is still a possibility. No matter how democratic the wording of the new constitution, a newly elected leader could manipulate the system to stay in power indefinitely, relying on ethno-religious solidarity to consolidate control. Such a figure—a Saddam Hussein-lite—could come from any community, but his emergence would spell the defeat of prospects for democracy....

The U.S. and Transition

The November 15 agreement envisaged a tight timetable for writing a constitution and moving to a permanent government. It called for three elections in the eighteen months after June 30: (a) selecting delegates to the constitutional convention; (b) a referendum on the constitution; and (c) election of the new government (presumably a president as well as a legislature). Additionally, there are plans to hold local elections.

But holding elections at all will be a challenge. Few Iraqis are confident that the winners might be turned out later in another election, or see the process as a win-win proposition for all participants. The first elections therefore will be highly contested, and there is a real risk that whoever loses the elections may reject their very legitimacy, charging that the process was rigged by the Americans to favor the winners. (After all, sham elections are the norm in the region.)

Likewise, it will be a major problem to assure security on election days and even more so during campaign rallies. There is a real possibility that resistance attacks will intensify after the handover. It would only be rationale for the resistance to strike hard, precisely to show the new Iraqi government as a puppet of the United States, propped up by its military might.

These concerns explain what we heard from many Iraqis, and not only from the Kurds and persons claiming to speak for Sistani: take the extra time to get it right. They believe the United States is rushing the process, and for the least honorable of reasons: to get it done before the U.S. presidential election.

The United States is thus on the horns of a dilemma. By any objective assessment, the time is not right for the transfer of authority. But the United States faces a subjective reality: the latent fear of Iraqis that self-government could be deferred indefinitely, or perpetuated under guises familiar from the days of British indirect rule. For that reason—and that reason alone—there will be a transfer of sovereignty on June 30, whether Iraq is ready or not.

But that need not mean that the later dates, laid out for the subsequent months, should be accorded the same sanctity as June 30. Indeed, it would be appropriate for U.S. policymakers to cast the rest of the process as a kind of "road map," which lays out a preferred course but a flexible timetable. From our conversations with Iraqis, there is no doubt that they will loudly complain about delays and will privately thank the United States for prolonging the process. Even a protracted timetable is not a guarantee of success, but the compressed one laid out in the November 15 agreement is a guarantee of failure—one that will be laid at the door of the United States and that the United States can hardly afford.

Jonathan Schanzer

66
Challenges in Iraq: Learning from Yemen?

The Yemeni media recently reported that thousands of Iraqis who fled Saddam Hussein's brutal regime and have lived in Yemen for more than a decade are now thinking about returning home. Many of these individuals are encouraged by signs of new infrastructure and a recovering economy in Iraq. If and when they return, they will see a number of stark similarities between their old homeland and Yemen, including primordial federalism, a "triangle" of terrorism, and questions of Sunni-Shiite relations. Although Yemen is certainly not a model to which Iraq should aspire, San'a does have experience in dealing with challenges similar to those currently facing Iraq. Yemen's handling of these challenges provides reasons for cautious optimism about Iraq's future.

Primordial Federalism

The Iraqi government that will assume authority after June 30, 2004, is not expected to be strong. Given the influence of Iraq's primordial social structure, the first few years of self-governance will likely be characterized by weak central authority. In particular, tribal and ethnic factors will dominate Iraqi politics, making the future president's job a difficult one.

Despite having to operate within similar social and cultural conditions, Yemen's relatively weak central government has remained functional since President Ali Abdallah Salih came to power in 1978. Salih's government is not bound by strict regional, sectarian, or tribal lines. Yemen's political system, although not a democracy, is representative. It is modeled after one of the most basic forms of government in the region: "primordial federalism." As former U.S. ambassador to Yemen Barbara Bodine noted, "By maintaining a balanced and informally representative cabinet, Yemen has avoided the sectarian or ethnic divisions that have sundered other governments in the region and has given Yemenis a shared interest in the survival of the state." In other words, although Yemenis are aware of their sectarian, tribal, and regional identities, these identities are not politically determinative.

The new Iraq may need to conduct its politics in a similar fashion, particularly during its first few years of self-governance. Since Saddam's fall and the resultant power vacuum, the Iraqi people have increasingly fallen back on the most basic authority structures:

Originally published as *PolicyWatch* no. 850, March 26, 2004. Jonathan Schanzer is a Soref fellow at The Washington Institute.

family, clan, and tribe. Local patriarchs are seen as the primary powerbrokers, particularly in rural areas. The longer instability plagues Iraq, the more entrenched their power will become. Hence, when the Iraqi Governing Council yields power to the eventual Iraqi president, the new leader will likely have to negotiate with local authorities in order to earn a mandate.

The case of Yemen shows that a weak government is not necessarily a failing government. Even if it is initially reliant on a primordial system, the forthcoming Iraqi government will still be able function. Its effectiveness will depend on the ability of Iraq's leaders to learn how to play tribal politics until the central government gains strength.

'Triangles' of Terrorism

In Yemen, the contiguous governorates of Marib, Shibwa, and Jawf form a "triangle" (it is actually more of a rectangle) that is rife with kidnappings, terrorism, and attacks on oil installations. Moreover, due to the central authority's limited reach, this area is susceptible to nefarious outside influences, including Saudi Wahhabis and al-Qaeda militants. Adding to Yemen's security problems are its porous borders, particularly in Jawf, which abuts Saudi Arabia.

Iraq is currently struggling with similar issues. U.S. officials contend that the most problematic areas of the Iraqi insurgency are Falluja, Ramadi, and other spots within the so-called Sunni Triangle, where extremism and terrorism are most prevalent. Security authorities also struggle with preventing infiltration of Iraq's porous borders with Syria, Saudi Arabia, and Iran. As a result, al-Qaeda militants and other foreign fighters have penetrated Iraq in the same way they penetrated Yemen from 1998 to 2002. During that period, al-Qaeda elements in Yemen attacked both Western targets (the USS *Cole* and the French tanker *Limburg*) and local targets (hotels, liquor sellers, and courts).

Similarly, both Western and local targets in Iraq have been victimized by terrorist attacks over the past year. Iraq's security forces, once they are fully operational, would do well to learn from Yemen, which has not experienced a terrorist attack since the October 6, 2002, bombing of the *Limburg*. Yemen has deported hundreds of illegal immigrants and suspected terrorists, expended greater efforts in monitoring mosques and Islamic organizations, stepped up its border control efforts, and launched a domestic public relations campaign warning of terrorism's cost to the economy. Yemen provides a good example of how an Arab security force can be trained and influenced by the United States while still maintaining its strong national and Arab identity. For example, on November 5, 2002, CIA-Yemeni cooperation reached its zenith when six al-Qaeda operatives were killed by a CIA-launched Hellfire missile from a Predator unmanned aerial vehicle. Similarly, U.S. Special Forces have backed up Yemeni forces in operations against al-Qaeda fighters in the Hattat region. Yemen's armed forces have established strong security ties with the United States even while maintaining trust among a population that may not be enamored with U.S. policies in the region. The Iraqi military will face this same challenge in the months and years to come.

Sunni-Shiite Relations

Much has been made about the tensions between Sunnis and Shiites in Iraq. Under Saddam, the minority Sunnis ruled over the majority Shiites, whom they oppressed. Animosity has festered between the two groups in Iraq since as early as the 1920s, when Britain occupied the nascent country. The challenge for the new Iraqi government will be to allow for greater Shiite political participation while not alienating the Sunnis, who lost power overnight upon Saddam's fall.

Yemen's predominantly Islamic landscape is also split between two schools, Shafi'i (a Sunni sect claiming 53 percent of Yemeni Muslims) and Zaydi (a Shiite sect with 47 percent of Yemeni Muslims). Prior to the unification of Yemen in 1990, the Zaydis dominated politics and cultural life in the country of North Yemen. Although the demographic balance shifted dramatically following unification and the integration of South Yemen's almost entirely Shafi'i population, inter-Muslim strife was not a problem. Indeed, Yemenis are relatively oblivious to Shiite-Sunni enmity; they recognize that the interests of individual members of these sects are anything but monolithic. Currently, tensions between Yemenis exist mostly on the tribal level, irrespective of whether the individuals in question are Sunni or Shiite. Even though Shiite tribes have long dominated the country's political and tribal life, Sunnis do not resent this arrangement. In fact, Shiites and Sunnis pray together in Yemen's mosques.

Despite a host of other problems, San'a has found a way to de-emphasize religious differences among Yemenis, focusing instead on a common Yemeni identity. Unfortunately, there are no shortcuts for Iraq to reach this kind of social arrangement; the balance between Yemen's Shiite and Sunni communities has evolved over hundreds of years within a unique culture. Yemen can serve as an inspiration, however, proving that ethnicity and religion do not have to dominate the Iraqi political landscape.

Conclusion

To be sure, there are many differences between Iraq and Yemen. First and foremost, Iraq is endowed with substantial oil wealth. "Black gold" will provide the country with a fiscal edge and likely propel it forward at a faster pace than Yemen, where poverty has undoubtedly hindered progress. Iraq will also benefit from the expertise of thousands of U.S. officials, as well as billions of dollars from U.S. coffers designed to get Iraq up and running. Still, Iraq and Yemen shoulder some of the same burdens. For its part, Yemen has shown that a unique approach to some of these challenges can generate working solutions. As Iraq nears sovereignty, these Yemeni examples serve as a reminder that Iraq can and will find organic solutions to some of its toughest problems.

Dennis Ross

67
Sovereignty Now

There have been several positive developments in Iraq in the past several weeks: An interim government was formed and the largely discredited Iraqi Governing Council was disbanded. The U.N. Security Council unanimously embraced the new Iraqi government and declared that it should be sovereign even on security matters. After months of putative Iraqi leaders distancing themselves from us, the new prime minister, Iyad Allawi, and president, Ghazi al-Yawer, publicly thanked the United States for what it had done.

Are we now on the path to success in Iraq? The short answer is we don't yet know. What we do know is that the challenge before us is enormously difficult. Start with an Iraqi public that has largely turned against the U.S. presence. Wars against insurgencies cannot be won when the indigenous population is either actively hostile to the outside power or passively supportive of the insurgents. Our problem is that most Iraqis—as revealed in the polls—are more opposed to the U.S. presence than they are to those who are trying to force us out.

Does that mean all is lost? No, but we run that risk if we cannot change the Iraqi image of us, and soon. While there are many reasons for our predicament—not the least of which was not being sufficiently concerned with establishing security in the aftermath of Saddam Hussein's fall and denying that we faced a genuine insurgency—our task now is to recognize that our success depends on creating an Iraqi sense of ownership for what is at stake.

This will not be done with words or declarations. On the contrary, there must be demonstrations of sovereignty, not pronouncements about it. Iraqis will look for unmistakable signs of Iraqi control at the handover of power June 30, when the problem will be very difficult. The insurgents will do all they can to prove that the occupation isn't over and that the United States continues to pull the strings and to make all the key decisions. To discredit the interim government, the insurgents will increase the violence to prove that Mr. Allawi and his Cabinet are ineffective and control very little of significance.

The end of the Coalition Provisional Authority might be welcome to most Iraqis, but so long as there is a sizable U.S. and coalition military presence and it is regarded as being responsible for security, there will be doubt that much has changed. Unfortunately, the Iraqi government will be in no position to provide security for the country anytime soon.

Originally published in the *Baltimore Sun*, June 18, 2004. Ambassador Dennis Ross is counselor and Ziegler distinguished fellow at The Washington Institute.

Nonetheless, from the outset, we must make sure that there are sufficient Iraqi forces capable of providing for the personal security of the government. Our training and support must be geared toward this urgent task. Nothing would discredit the new leaders more quickly than the image that they are completely dependent on the U.S. military, including for their personal security.

There must be demonstrations that the government is able to veto what the U.S. commander may want to do. Having a de facto veto is not sufficient. Mr. Allawi must be able to point to decisions he has made to stop certain operations or to alter U.S. military behavior. Only in this way can the new government prove it is calling the shots. Ironically, it is as much in U.S. interests as theirs for Mr. Allawi and his colleagues to demonstrate this capability. They need it for purposes of credibility, while we need it to show we are carrying out the will of the Iraqi government, not the reverse. This will mean the government is assuming responsibility for what our forces do. While Mr. Allawi may prefer to preserve some distance from certain operations—reserving the possibility of criticizing some of our actions—such a posture would be self-defeating in the end. They need credibility—not demonstrations of impotence—and we need Iraqi sanction for what we do. Words alone won't be enough. The Iraqi government must be seen as delivering on security, and there is no substitute for that. But in the meantime, the issue of elections is something that we could use to shift the balance of psychological forces in the country.

Today, most Iraqis seem to agree on two key points: that we are occupiers and that elections are essential. Indeed, roughly 85 percent of Iraqis in polls are in favor of elections. This reflects not only the desire of the Shiites to have elections that will give them their due as a majority of the Iraqi population but also a deeper willingness of all groups in the country to fashion a new day; elections have become the symbol of that, in their eyes.

Elections are to be held for a transitional National Assembly no later than Jan. 31, 2005. Why not take the Iraqi desire for elections and show that U.S. forces are an enabler, not an impediment, to them? Why not have a rolling set of elections starting this fall? Why not declare—or, better yet, have the new Iraqi government declare—that wherever the environment is secure enough for elections, they will be held before the end of the year? Certainly, this could be true in the Kurdish region, some of the Shiite areas and even some of the Sunni areas in Mosul, Kirkuk and Baghdad. Rather than appearing as if the United States is delaying what Iraqis want, the onus could be put squarely on the insurgents, who would be demonstrating for Iraqis to see that they are the ones blocking the Iraqi people from expressing their will.

There should be no illusions. Even if the new Iraqi government is viewed as asserting control and there are rolling elections, our challenge in Iraq will not be easy. But June 30 represents both an opportunity and a danger, and our prospects for the future depend on Iraqis believing that they are acquiring sovereignty—and not in name only.

68
Iraq Reconstruction

Saddam Hussein's Iraqi regime fell to U.S.-led coalition forces on April 9, 2003, after three weeks of war. Washington, however, soon learned that "winning the peace," or stabilizing Iraq, was far more difficult than winning the war. Despite billions of dollars and the full attention of the U.S. Department of Defense, America's postwar challenges quickly mounted. Planners had anticipated and tackled several challenges, but they also made several critical miscalculations. Thus, crucial issues remained unresolved in a high-stakes reconstruction effort arguably more ambitious than any other in recent history. Indeed, efforts in Haiti (1991) or Somalia (1993) pale in comparison to the scope and breadth of U.S. reconstruction in Iraq. This is a massive undertaking, rivaling the transformations that were required in the Marshall Plan. By summer 2004, more than one year into the project, it was clear that U.S. efforts were only just getting underway.

Prewar Plans for Reconstruction

Washington never provided a prewar blueprint of Iraq's reconstruction. Various officials prior to the war, however, announced parts of the plan. Thus, U.S. reconstruction efforts, on the surface, appear to have been ad hoc. Eventually, when classified documents are made public, analysts may gain a better sense of initial U.S. plans.

U.S. Central Command (CENTCOM) began reviewing plans for an Iraq war shortly after the attacks of September 11. Numerous war games were played and various scenarios were rehearsed over some eighteen months. By contrast, Washington had designated a lead agency to prepare for post-war reconstruction only two or three months before the war. Moreover, officials appeared to rely upon the mistaken assumption that after the initial U.S. invasion, Iraqis would remove Saddam themselves. Another mistaken assumption was that, even after a full-scale war, state structures under Saddam would still exist, leading to a short and relatively easy occupation described as "three months up and out."[1]

Another issue weighing Washington down was the ongoing Pentagon vs. State Department rivalry, which increasingly played out in the areas of prewar build-up and postwar reconstruction. The civilian leadership at the Pentagon, largely labeled "neoconservatives," favored an aggressive approach to toppling Saddam and Iraqi reconstruction, whereas the State Department was more cautious. This conflict played out

From Meyrav Wurmser (ed.), *Building Free Societies in Iraq and Afghanistan—Lessons from Post–World War Two Transitions in Germany and Japan* (Washington, D.C.: Hudson Institute, forthcoming in 2004). Reprinted with permission. Jonathan Schanzer is a Soref fellow at The Washington Institute.

in the administration's decision-making process on everything from choosing the civil administrator to the UN's role in the postwar environment.[2]

The Bush administration commissioned a series of workshops in March 2002, entitled the "Future of Iraq Project." In consultation with Iraqi exiles, U.S. officials discussed transnational justice, public finance, democratic principles, public health, humanitarian issues, public outreach, environmental issues, economy, infrastructure, local governance, defense policy, oil, education, anticorruption, institution building, media outlets, refugees, foreign policy, and cultural preservation.[3] This project, however, was not the only prewar initiative. Condoleezza Rice appointed Zal Khalilzad, special assistant to the president for the Near East and South Asia, to chair interagency coordination meetings that brought together the State Department, Defense Department, Treasury, Office of Management and Budget, and various other departments. Interagency Deputies and Principals Committees brought together cabinet secretaries and CIA director George Tenet to discuss Iraq. Further, upon an order handed down from Secretary of Defense Donald Rumsfeld to the Joint Chiefs of Staff, a taskforce named JTF4 (Joint Task Force Phase Four) was created on December 19, 2002. That office was initially made up of fifty-eight individuals from the four arms of the military, and was told that it would be the future core of Iraq's reconstruction team. The group had a few Arabic speakers, and most knew little about Iraq. Still, this was the first time that the military had assembled a posthostilities planning force for reconstruction, rather than assembling one after conflict. JTF4 busied itself with virtually every aspect of postwar planning, from creating a constitution and legal system to police and the military, but did not present its work to the other National Security Council and interagency committees also charged with postwar planning. About a month into its work, the group was sent to Kuwait to await orders.[4]

Meanwhile, a number of other agencies within the U.S. government also began drawing up plans. They included the United States Agency for International Development (USAID), the Office of the Vice President, the Treasury, and the CIA.[5] Many of these plans were scrapped, however. On January 20, 2003, after several months of discussion, the president unveiled a new office—the Office of Reconstruction and Humanitarian Assistance (ORHA). This "expeditionary" office, funded with an initial $15 million, was thereafter seen as the central postwar planning office, superseding the others like it, designed to work closely with the UN, other countries, and nongovernmental organizations.[6]

Why postwar planning was duplicated several times over is not known. Why the designation of the responsible agency was made only two months before the war is also a mystery. One possibility is that the State Department had long resisted the creation of what was effectively an office of postwar planning, fearing that preparation for war might undermine diplomatic goodwill. But questions also remain as to why the multiple U.S. efforts were not fully integrated. Indeed, in the first week of operation, ORHA had but "three or four people."[7] In February 2003, ORHA had only started to estimate the cost of postwar humanitarian assistance.[8] By early March, only several hundred people, including a number of "free Iraqis" constituted the Pentagon's ORHA office.[9] Only in April, when JTF4 was effectively dissolved, were ORHA's top positions announced. A few of the JTF4 people were used in ORHA; most of their research was not.[10] Simultaneously, the Joint Chiefs of Staff refused to cable interagency policies and instructions to its leadership in Iraq. In one example, Ambassador Bill Eagleton departed for Kirkuk with an international property restitution team, only to learn that the Joint Chiefs of Staff in the Pentagon, notified two weeks previously, had failed to inform the U.S. military of their imminent arrival.[11]

From ORHA to CPA

ORHA, for its part, was split into three divisions: Humanitarian Relief, Reconstruction, and Civil Administration. All of these divisions reported to retired Lieutenant General Jay Garner, head of ORHA. Garner had been involved at the highest levels in humanitarian operations for Iraq at the end of the 1991 Gulf War. Supporting him was a team of former diplomats, intelligence operatives, and military men. This team was also supported by a small group of Iraqis from the United States and around the world.[12]

ORHA immediately fell into a Catch-22 situation. General David McKiernan, commander of the ground forces, refused to allow ORHA's deployment, arguing that security conditions were not yet ripe. Indeed, confusion over when the war (phase three) ended and when postwar reconstruction (phase four) began also created problems for ORHA. Garner argued that ORHA needed to get on the ground quickly. He soon asserted that the failure to allow the civil administration to begin work was the reason for the security situation's deterioration. This may have been the case; Garner and scores of ORHA staff remained in Kuwait as they received reports of crowds looting and burning the ministries to which they were waiting to deploy.

Once on the ground, it became apparent that ORHA was administrating a society that it little understood. Prior to the war, one official believed Iraq was a "more sophisticated country.... It has the structure and the mechanisms in there to run that country and run it fairly efficiently."[13] Some officials before the war also believed that they would rely on the Iraqi army to take part in major reconstruction efforts.[14] In reality, most Iraqi institutions were disintegrating or nonexistent after more than three decades of brutal Baathist rule and more than a decade of U.N. sanctions. The plan to utilize the army evaporated as the majority of Iraqi conscripts deserted. Many remaining officers were compromised by corruption, senior Baath party ties, and past human rights violations.

Garner began by dividing Iraq into four sectors, which loosely coincided with the borders of Iraq's sensitive sectarian groups: Kurds in the north, Sunni Arabs in the center, Shia in the south, and Baghdad as its own unit. The United States expected cooperation from these groups, but underestimated the impact of the 1991 failure to support the Shia uprising. As a result, many Iraqis preferred to sit on the sidelines, fearful well into the autumn that the United States would allow Saddam to return (U.S. failure to take down four massive busts of Saddam from the roof of their palace headquarters may have lent credence to the paranoia). Making things worse, as analyst Kenneth Pollack notes, Americans also "alienated Iraqis through arrogance and bad judgment" in the early-goings.[15] Raids on mosques angered locals, as did the confiscation of charity, physical searches of Iraqi women by U.S. military men, and the use of police dogs, which Muslims deem as unclean.[16] Meanwhile, State Department-Pentagon tensions festered, with key issues of philosophy and governance remaining undecided at the National Security Council.

Steps Forward

The Bush administration responded to the initial hardships in Iraq by making a change in command. In May 2003, L. Paul Bremer III replaced Garner, whose replacement is a story shrouded in mystery. Some say he was fired because he lacked the charisma and toughness to rule Iraq. Other officials report that Garner's "rotation" out of Iraq was planned from the start. It is widely believed, however, that Garner's political tin ear, his weakness on de-Baathification, and especially his friendship with Saad al-Janabi, the private secretary to Saddam's late son-in-law Hussein Kamal, angered the White House. Bremer's subsequent arrival was a welcomed change among both Americans and Iraqis. Bremer was close to the Bush administration, but was also a former foreign service officer. Thus, he was able to work with both quibbling sides of the occupation administration. As administrator of the CPA, Bremer also comfortably acted the part of commander and chief of Iraq with the right to exercise "executive, legislative, and judicial authority."[17]

Supporting Bremer's efforts on the military side was four-star General John Abizaid, commander of U.S. Central Command (CENTCOM), who reported directly to Secretary of Defense Donald Rumsfeld.[18] Abizaid, an Arabic speaker who took command of CENTCOM on July 7, 2003, served in northern Iraq during the 1991 Gulf War, as well as Bosnia and Kosovo. He was also deputy commander of the Combined Forces Command during Operation Iraqi Freedom.[19] Under his command, CENTCOM's primary goal was to ensure the security of the United States and international civilian administrators and aid workers, to secure the borders, to train and oversee the Iraqi Civil Defense Corps (ICDC) as well as other Iraqi security forces, to neutralize former Baath officials and terrorists, and to search for WMD.

Also working with the CPA was USAID, a government agency coordinating economic, humanitarian, and democratic assistance to other countries in need. In Iraq, USAID focused on six aspects of reconstruction: assistance to Internally Displaced Persons (IDPs) and refugees through the Disaster Assistance Response Team (DART); education, in conjunction with UNICEF to rebuild and renovate schools; emergency humanitarian relief in conjunction with the World Food Program, which distributed the largest food aid supply in history; health services, including rehabilitating hospitals and providing crucial vaccinations; rebuilding infrastructure, from schools and hospitals to airports, harbors, and energy lines; and democratization, by working with local administrators, interim representative bodies, and civic organizations.[20] USAID, however, had developed its own governance plans outside of the interagency process and ran into trouble first with ORHA and then with the CPA, by trying to execute policies without coordination.

Under the auspices of the CPA, USAID and other agencies delegated reconstruction to private companies by awarding contracts and grants for education, agriculture, health services, construction, and consulting. Some contracts were awarded under the aegis of the Iraq Infrastructure Reconstruction Program (IIRP) for the rebuilding of vital infrastructure, services, and institutions throughout Iraq. One program, run by Research Triangle Institute (RTI), made funds directly available to local governing councils throughout Iraq. Indeed, more than 1,000 grants were made available to a great number of Iraq's 250 local councils to make tangible infrastructure changes on the ground.[21] Other projects in Iraq were headed up by Development Alternatives International (DAI) and the Commanders Emergency Response Program (CERP), allocating Iraqi funds to the U.S. military that were disbursed to Iraqis to carry out various projects. Surprisingly, many of the successful reconstruction programs in Iraq were administered not through USAID, but through CERP.

Progress in Iraq

After more than a year on the ground in Iraq, tangible changes were evident, thanks to U.S. efforts and the tenacity of the Iraqi people. To be sure, progress fell far short of initial U.S. expectations. On July 4, 2004, the *Washington Post* reported that the US had only spent two percent of an $18.4 billion aid package approved by congress in October 2003.[22] Still, progress in Iraq was significant.

Education. Getting children back to school was one of the first priorities of the U.S. administration, in an attempt to return the country to a schedule and a sense of relative normalcy. All of Iraq's twenty-two major universities and forty-three technical schools were quickly opened, and more than 2,500 schools were rehabilitated, with another 1,200 expected to be refurbished by the end of 2004.[23] Meanwhile, the salaries of teachers jumped twelve to twenty-five times higher, while textbooks and curricula were reformed with the intent to promote liberal and democratic values.[24] As a result, the educational system was finally able to address new academic fields without the strictures of Saddam Hussein, who controlled every aspect of daily life and isolated Iraq's scholars from the outside world. More opportunities were also available for promising Iraqi scholars to study in the United States; the Fulbright program was made available to Iraqis after liberation following a fourteen-year interruption.[25]

One cannot mention education in Iraq without mentioning the fact that USAID awarded a $1 million, twelve-month contract to Creative Associates International, Inc. (CAII) for a project called Revitalization of Iraqi Schools and Stabilization of Education (RISE).[26] The project seeks to train teachers and implement reforms, while also focusing on the rapid dissemination of school materials, equipment, and supplies in Iraq.[27] RISE aims to train an estimated 75,000 teachers and 5,000 administrators.[28] By summer 2004, more than 32,000 of those school teachers and 3,000 supervisors had been put through

U.S. training courses. Iraqi students had also completed their final exams, marking an end to their first full year of studies since the fall of Saddam.[29]

Health Services. By October 3, 2003, Iraq reached 100 percent of prewar levels of healthcare throughout the country, but health services were not meeting U.S. projections. After the Gulf War and U.S. sanctions, Saddam drastically cut spending on healthcare for his people, which devastated public health. Spending in this sector after the war increased twenty-six times; doctors' salaries increased to eight times what they were under Saddam; some 240 hospitals and 1,200 clinics opened; pharmaceutical imports went up; and child vaccination programs dramatically increased.[30] Indeed, 85 percent of all Iraqi children were immunized by July 2004.[31]

Still, by March 2004, Iraq still suffered from a critical shortage of basic medical equipment and drugs. Babies died of infections for lack of antibiotics, surgeries were delayed because of a lack of oxygen, and patients were turned away when a hospital lacked proper facilities.[32] The Iraqi ministry of Health approved a $11.5 million emergency drug purchase in 2004, but shortages remained.[33]

Water. Iraq's prewar water system was antiquated, after some twenty to thirty years of neglect. Looters and vandals even further damaged this system during the war. After the war, the CPA and the Iraqi Ministry of Irrigation repaired some 1,700 critical breaks in Baghdad's water system,[34] while also working to rebuild Iraq's sanitation and municipal services.[35] However, much work remained to establish reserves in the water supply, and to clear out and maintain irrigation canals for the agricultural sector. There was more optimism that such projects could be accomplished with the addition of some $232 million in water projects allocated by the CPA, designed to benefit more than 14 million people.[36]

Telecommunications. Iraq's communication was in terrible condition before the war. With a system dating back to the 1970s, Iraq had only four telephones per one hundred people. Further, "Iraq had no data network, and Internet access was provided to only a handful of the power elite. This lack of a mature telecommunications system has a direct impact on the development of an advanced financial and banking sector."[37] After the war, the CPA, USAID, and contractor Bechtel struggled to reconnect Iraqi phone coverage. Bechtel reestablished a north-south fiber optic line from Dahuk to Umm Qasr.[38] However, an opaque bidding process, alleged corruption, localized monopolies, and noncompliance with contracts has hampered the success of the cellular phone networks. By July 2004, the total number of telephone subscribers in Iraq was estimated at over 1,250,000, including some 460,000 cell phone subscribers.[39]

Economy. The CPA aggressively set out to build a foundation for an open Iraqi economy. That included new financial market structures; a transparent Iraqi treasury; and infrastructure for investment, tax reform, and a new payment system for civil servants.[40] It also included creating new employment opportunities for Iraqis. Within less than a year, over 9,100 new jobs were created in the private sector, and over 100,000 in the public sector, providing some relief after the devastating dismissal of hundreds of thousands of soldiers and Baathists. Some CPA officials speculated that within two years of liberation, Iraq would need to import manual labor.

Further, the Iraqi Central Bank licensed six foreign banks to operate in the country. Since the new currency was released on October 15, 2003, dollars and Dinars kept the economy going. While the new currency was a success, increases in salaries led to inflation, while static pensions made it more difficult for the elderly and retired to get by without support from family networks. As U.S. aid money trickled into Iraq, jobs were expected to be bountiful, and economic infrastructure was expected to grow. Officials, however, expressed concern about sustaining the Iraqi economy after the initial bubble.

In January 2004, Iraq's ministry of planning reported that unemployment was hovering at 28 percent, while some 21 percent of Iraqis were underemployed. Iraqis were optimistic, however. In a spring poll, 59 percent of Iraqis believed that the economic situation was improving, and that it would continue to improve. The Iraqi stock exchange opened on June 24, 2004, providing what can only be seen as symbolic hope for Iraq's economic future.[41]

Oil. The Iraqi economy, of course, will have to be sustained by Iraq's most abundant natural resource-oil. According to CPA estimates, Iraq's oil industry, despite repeated attacks from insurgents and attempts to slow it down, was producing some 2 million barrels per day, and was exporting more than a million barrels per day in January 2004.[42] By June 27, 2004, crude oil exports were projected to be $8 billion for 2004. Revenues in June and July, however, were hindered by insurgency attacks against northern and southern pipelines.[43]

Diesel and kerosene supplies were hovering near their projected levels, as were the gasoline and liquid propane supplies. Lines for fueling stations, however, were still long throughout most of Iraq in early 2004, but began to shorten through the summer. As Iraqis buy more cars (a sign of an improving economy), the demand for fuel is expected to increase.

Electricity. Iraq's infrastructure for water, oil, and other critical areas is dependant upon electricity. Having this system operational could make Iraqi reconstruction considerably easier. After inheriting a decrepit system that had been run down by Saddam's regime, the United States worked hard to restore electricity to all of Iraq. Making that task more challenging was the growing need for electricity as Iraq expanded its infrastructure. Thus, electricity blackouts were common throughout Iraq a year after liberation, although they decreased in frequency and the duration of the outage.

Outages withstanding, electricity output surpassed the prewar level of 4,400 megawatts to 4,518.[44] Electricity remained sporadic through early 2004, however, and demand throughout Iraq surged with the influx of appliances like televisions, washing machines, and air conditioners. Goals for June 2004 were not met due to "unforeseen problems," but maintenance was scheduled to continue through the summer.[45] Looking toward the future, CPA officials estimate that some $5 billion in U.S. aid to Iraq will be used to revamp the electricity infrastructure.

Military and Police. Despite the billions of dollars earmarked for police and the New Iraqi Army (NIA), U.S. authorities have likely faced some of their toughest challenges in rebuilding the Iraqi Ministry of Interior and Ministry of Defense. Iraqi forces under Saddam, estimated at some 600,000, needed to be cut drastically, since Iraq only needs to have a defense force (with no chance of successfully tangling with the Iranian or Turkish militaries).[46] The new Iraqi army was initially slated to have twenty-seven battalions of 800 soldiers apiece by fall 2004.[47] By June 2004, Iraq's security forces numbered just over 200,000.[48] Those forces, however, still lacked adequate equipment and training, as well as a chain of command between top Iraqi officers and boots on the ground. Many of Iraqi's security forces were operating with supervision from U.S. forces, but Abizaid had no fixed timetable when they would begin operating independently.[49]

By March 2004, there were some 70,000 policemen in the Iraqi Police Service (IPS), but only a few hundred had received sufficient training. By summer 2004, several thousand had completed their training courses, but too many others were untrained. Iraqi Border Enforcement consisted of some 9,000 men, but border patrol was still weak in early 2004.

The United States in April 2004 was working to form a 400-person counterterrorism unit by the end of that year.[50] In July 2004, the Iraq Intervention Force (IIF) deployed to Baghdad for counterinsurgency operations.[51] The challenge will be to dismantle the networks of Baath Party loyalists and foreign terrorists. These networks clearly threaten the country's prosperity; civilian and military reconstruction aide is dependent upon security. A more interesting challenge for Iraqis will be the power allotted to a future "Mukhabarrat." The intelligence and security forces under Saddam existed primarily to promote Saddam's brutal regime. Iraqis will need this force to fight terror effectively, but will also want to keep its power in check.

Challenges for the Future

With or without the UN, the U.S. administration in Baghdad faces an uncertain future. Despite significant gains in infrastructure, de-Baathification, and even democratization, ethnic tensions remain raw and security is uncertain at best.... As the Iraqi government learns to stand on its own, it will likely be weak. Whoever rules Iraq as the first president will have many challenges. In addition to the Iraqi parliament, other Arab actors, and Western governments, the president will likely have to work with the tribal brokers of power. It will be these people who determine the support base for any president, giving Iraq some of the same political characteristics as a country like Yemen, where the government is based on a "primordial federation." This weak period will be critical for the new Iraq. If the new Iraq does not survive its first few years, due to lack of international support, terrorist attacks, or internecine violence, the region will suffer the effects of yet another failed state. Moreover, 25 million Iraqis would again look forward to a bleak future. If the new Iraq can survive that initial test, with the influx of oil revenues and U.S. tax dollars, Baghdad could be a center of Middle Eastern influence once again, only this time with help from the United States.

Notes

1. Quote from Jay Garner, as cited in Adam Garfinkle, "The Daunting Aftermath: L. Paul Bremer & Co. Have a Different Kind of War on their Hands," *National Review,* July 28, 2003, 29.
2. Carlos Yordan, "Failing to Meet Expectations in Iraq: A Review of the Original U.S. Post-War Strategy," *Middle East Review of International Affairs* (MERIA) 8, no. 1 (March 2004).
3. "Post Saddam Iraq," Testimony from Marc Grossman, Under Secretary for Political Affairs, before the Senate Foreign Relations Committee, February 11, 2003.
4. Author's interview with senior military official, Washington, DC, March 17, 2004.
5. "Post War Planning," Testimony from Douglas J. Feith, Under Secretary of Defense for Policy, before the Senate Foreign Relations Committee, February 11, 2003.
6. Yordan, "Failing to Meet Expectations in Iraq."
7. "Backgrounder on Reconstruction and Humanitarian Assistance in Post-War," Senior Defense Official, March 11, 2003, www.defenselink.mil/news/Mar2003/t03122003_t0311bgd.html
8. "Post War Planning," Testimony from Douglas J. Feith.
9. "Backgrounder on Reconstruction and Humanitarian Assistance in Post-War," Senior Defense Official.
10. Author's interview with senior military official, Washington, DC, March 17, 2004.
11. Author's interview with former CPA official, Washington, DC, April 2, 2004.
12. Toby Dodge, "US Intervention and Possible Iraqi Futures," *Survival* 45, no. 3 (Autumn 2003): 112.
13. "Backgrounder on Reconstruction and Humanitarian Assistance in Post-War," Senior Defense Official.
14. Ibid.
15. Kenneth M. Pollack, "After Saddam: Assessing the Reconstruction of Iraq," Saban Center for Middle East Policy, Analysis Paper no.1, January 2004, 5.
16. "Governing Iraq," International Crisis Group, *Middle East Report* no. 17, August 25, 2003, 4.
17. Coalition Provisional Authority, CPA/REG/16, May 2003/01.
18. "About CENTCOM," http://www.centcom.mil/aboutus/centcom.htm
19. "General John Abizaid," www.centcom.mil/aboutus/cdrbio_print_ver.htm
20. "Assistance for Iraq," http://www.usaid.gov/iraq/activities.html

21. Pollack, "After Saddam: Assessing the Reconstruction of Iraq," 1.
22. Rajiv Chandrasekaran, "U.S. Funds for Iraq are Largely Unspent," *Washington Post*, July 4, 2004.
23. "Working Papers: Iraq Status," Department of Defense, July 2004, p.11.
24. www.cpa-iraq.org/essential_services/education.html
25. www.cpa-iraq.org/essential_services/higher-ed.html
26. "USAID Awards Contract to Revitalize Education in Iraq," USAID Press Office, April 11, 2003, www.usaid.gov/press/releases/2003/pr030411_2.html
27. "Creative Associates to Help Rebuild Iraq Education Sector," April 14, 2003, www.caii.net/News/Iraq_news.htm
28. "Dedicated to Strengthening Education and Local Governance in Iraq," December 25, 2003, http://www.caii-dc.com/News/Iraq_news09_25_03.htm
29. "Working Papers: Iraq Status," Department of Defense, July 2004, p.11.
30. www.cpa-iraq.org/essential_services/health.html
31. "Working Papers: Iraq Status," Department of Defense, July 2004, p.10.
32. Ariana Eunjung Cha, "Iraq Hospitals on Life Support," *Washington Post*, March 5, 2004.
33. "Working Papers: Iraq Status," Department of Defense, July 2004, p. 10.
34. www.usaid.gov/iraq/accomplishments/
35. www.cpa-iraq.org/essentail services/water-management.html
36. www.usaid.gov/iraq/accomplishments/
37. http://www.cpa-iraq.org/ES/comms.html
38. "USAID Announced the Completion of Iraq Telephone Exchange Rehabilitation," USAID Press Release, March 2, 2004.
39. "Working Papers: Iraq Status," Department of Defense, July 2004, p.6.
40. www.cpa-iraq.org/economy.html
41. "Working Papers: Iraq Status," Department of Defense, July 2004, pp.17-18.
42. Andy Critchlow, "Show Me the Money," *Middle East Economic Digest* 48, no. 3 (January 16-22, 2004): 6.
43. "Working Papers: Iraq Status," Department of Defense, July 2004, p.17.
44. www.usaid.gov/iraq/accomplishments/
45. "Working Papers: Iraq Status," Department of Defense, July 2004, p.20.
46. Daniel Byman, "Building the New Iraq: The Role of Intervening Forces," *Survival* 45, no. 2 (Summer 2003): 59.

47. Michael Knights, “Militias and the Monopoly of Force in Transitional Iraq,” *PolicyWatch* no. 842, Washington Institute for Near East Policy, March 16, 2004.
48. Eric Schmitt & Susan Sachs, “NATO Agrees to Help Train Iraqi Forces,” *New York Times,* June 29, 2004.
49. Bradley Graham, “Iraqi Forces Lack Chain of Command,” *Washington Post,* March 5, 2004.
50. Knights, “Militias and the Monopoly of Force in Transitional Iraq.”
51. “Working Papers: Iraq Status,” Department of Defense, July 2004, p.29.

Part Seven

Regional Implications

Patrick Clawson

Introduction

For Iraq, the most significant regional issue has been the attitude of neighbors toward the new political order. Kuwait and, less publicly, Jordan have vigorously committed themselves to Iraq's reconstruction. The governments of both countries have taken considerable political risk to assist the new Iraqi authorities and the U.S.-led multinational coalition; after all, there are significant communities in both Jordan and Kuwait that are distinctly unhappy with the occupation. The two governments have once again proven that they are indeed America's friends. More troubling has been the attitude of Saudi Arabia and Syria. Riyadh and Damascus have at best stood aloof while radical elements from their societies have joined the Iraqi resistance and committed some of the country's worst terrorist attacks.

In analyzing the regional impact of Iraqi reconstruction, Washington Institute scholars focused on Iraq's two non-Arab neighbors, Turkey and Iran. The Turkish government has not been particularly involved. To be fair, Ankara did offer to send 15,000 troops despite domestic objections, only to see the offer rejected by the Iraqi Interim Governing Council. Perhaps most important is what Ankara did not do: the Turks have refrained from actively stirring the pot in Kurdish northern Iraq, despite the continued presence there of Kurdistan Workers Party (PKK) terrorists.

By contrast, Iran has been very active inside Iraq. Not only have Iranian government agents established a large-scale presence there, but it would appear that Iran disbursed more aid in Iraq in the first year following the war than did the United States—a sad commentary on the inefficiency of the U.S. reconstruction effort. That said, Iran's attitude toward the new Iraqi authorities seems quite ambiguous. The formal Iranian government has been quite supportive of the new authorities. At the same time, however, influential hardline clerics and powerful revolutionary institutions in Iran have positioned themselves to cause much trouble for the coalition. For example, since spring 2004, they have often called for attacks on U.S.-led forces. Each of these issues is discussed in detail by the selections in part 7.

Two other major themes predominate in the articles appearing in this section. First is the impact of developments in Iraq on Arab politics and society at large, including Arab media. The main conclusion is that the better things go in Iraq, the better the prospects for reform across the Arab world. Second is the relationship between the Iraqi resistance and broader terrorist movements. Here the main theme has been that the radical Islamist jihadists of the world have made a major commitment to terror in Iraq (though, as noted in parts 3 and 4, there is no clear evidence that these foreign jihadists have made a major contribution to the insurgency). It is unclear to what extent the jihadists' activities in Iraq have diverted them from other attacks they might have carried out (for example, in the West) or to what extent Iraq has served as a rallying cry, allowing the jihadists to mobilize additional recruits and resources.

Many have suggested that developments in Iraq will affect, or be affected by, the Israeli-Palestinian conflict. Arguments have been put forward regarding both directions of the causal link; that is, how progress in Iraq would facilitate progress on the Israeli-Palestinian front, or how progress on the Israeli-Palestinian front would facilitate progress in Iraq. In reality, although the demise of Saddam Hussein's regime is an unquestioned boon to Israel's security posture, it is difficult to see how the problems in either arena have made a major impact on the other. In any case, developments in 2003-2004 have been less encouraging than hoped for on both fronts. Some might argue that the U.S. government has been so busy with Iraq that it has not devoted as much attention as it would have otherwise to the Israeli-Palestinian issue. A strong counterargument could also be made, however. After all, senior National Security Council and State Department officials have made many trips and received many visitors in relation to Israeli-Palestinian issues, attempting to build on the positive aspects in Israeli prime minister Ariel Sharon's proposal to withdraw from the Gaza Strip and isolated settlements in the northern West Bank. Yet, in the extensive work done by Institute scholars on the Israeli-Palestinian conflict, Iraq has not loomed large.

Matthew Levitt, Roger Cressey, and Avi Jorisch

69
A Terrorist Front in Iraq?

MATTHEW LEVITT

The widespread notion that the war on terror cannot be pursued simultaneously with the war in Iraq is erroneous, a fact that was bolstered by the capture of al-Qaeda leader Khalid Sheikh Muhammad on the eve of Operation Iraqi Freedom. Counterterror operations continue, with wide international support from European governments as well as numerous Arab and Muslim countries (e.g., Yemen, Pakistan).

Al-Qaeda has been quiet since its February 2003 statement calling on Iraqis to carry out suicide attacks against Americans. In fact, al-Qaeda has an interest in allowing hatred and frustration to fester throughout the region, while continuing to instigate tension via radical Islamist organizations. Through this tactic, al-Qaeda hopes to validate its claim that the international jihad is not a terrorist-driven campaign but a mass Islamic and Arab movement against the West's imperialist and anti-Muslim intentions. Yet, al-Qaeda's recent silence should not be interpreted as an inability to carry out operations; its attacks are likely to resume during postwar reconstruction in Iraq.

Syria and various Palestinian terrorist groups pose a more pressing and unexpected threat. Unlike al-Qaeda, they are reacting out of an acute fear of being next on the antiterror hit list and have therefore attempted to derail the war on terror by encouraging anti-American attacks during the war in Iraq. Breaking with its longstanding strategy of pursuing limited cooperation with the United States (e.g., against al-Qaeda) while simultaneously supporting Hizballah and Palestinian groups, Syria has decided to stand with Saddam Hussein against the United States. Syria's foreign ministry has expressed its desire to see the United States defeated in Iraq, and it is backing up its rhetoric with action by issuing passports to irregular volunteers and night vision goggles and tractor engines to Iraqi fighters. For their part, several Palestinian groups have called for strikes against Western interests. They believe that a U.S. victory in Iraq will lead to a renewed peace process, which would end the two-year terrorist nirvana that has flourished in the West Bank and Gaza.

On April 4, 2003, Matthew Levitt, Roger Cressey, and Avi Jorisch addressed The Washington Institute's Special Policy Forum. Mr. Levitt is the Institute's senior fellow in terrorism studies and author of its 2002 monograph *Targeting Terror: U.S. Policy toward Middle Eastern State Sponsors and Terrorist Organizations, Post–September 11.* Mr. Cressey is president of Good Harbor Consulting and former director of transnational threats at the National Security Council. Mr. Jorisch is a Soref fellow at the Institute and author of *Beacon of Hatred: Inside Hizballah's al-Manar Television* (The Washington Institute, 2004). This rapporteur's summary (originally published as *PolicyWatch* no. 745, April 8, 2003) was prepared by Eran Benedek.

ROGER CRESSEY

Despite U.S.-European fissures over building a coalition against Iraq, most European governments recognize the threat of terror. As such, the antiterror alliance is strong and will continue to pursue radical Islamist organizations such as al-Qaeda. Although transatlantic intelligence and counterterror maneuvers have diminished al-Qaeda's ability to execute attacks, the organization still poses a threat to U.S. forces in Iraq and other Western targets worldwide. Operation Enduring Freedom achieved its strategic aim of ensuring that Afghanistan could no longer be used as a sanctuary for Osama bin Laden's group. Yet, al-Qaeda maintains functional capability in Iraq. The coalition is unable to seal all border crossings and prevent all terrorist infiltrators. Moreover, al-Qaeda members are experts at forging official documents and could enter Iraq through the front door. Following regime change, the U.S. occupation of Iraq is likely to fuel regional animosity toward the West, generating widespread sympathy and recruits for al-Qaeda's mission. U.S. allies such as Jordan are also at risk of attack given al-Qaeda's antipathy toward regimes that collaborate with the West.

Several wild cards may also increase the threat of terror in Iraq. First, indigenous terrorism is a serious concern, particularly if the U.S. occupation is prolonged. Second, Iran may perceive the U.S. presence along its border as an imminent threat, prompting Tehran to commission al-Qaeda or its affiliates to attack U.S. soil or interests in order to decrease American willpower and send a signal that the Islamic Republic will not collapse as easily as Saddam's regime. Third, although graduates of al-Qaeda training camps are quiet at the moment, they are still active and will continue to seek new recruits. Fourth, despite historical Sunni-Shiite animosity, regional terrorist groups are likely to form an alliance of some sort, given that they can operate relatively freely in Iran, Syria, and Lebanese and Palestinian refugee camps.

AVI JORISCH

Hizballah disseminates its message through its Beirut-based al-Manar television station, which is broadcast globally via satellite to an audience of approximately 10 million viewers. Since the Bush administration began to target Iraq, a portion of al-Manar programming has focused on what it calls American imperialism and oppression, highlighting what Hizballah believes are Washington's five main goals in Iraq:

Destroy an Arab regime. To Hizballah, the only way to stop U.S. oppression is resistance. Israel's withdrawal from southern Lebanon in May 2000 proved to Hizballah that resistance works. This mantra is therefore repeated at most Hizballah functions and throughout al-Manar programming.

Deep American involvement in the region (i.e., a new world order). To Hizballah, the United States is public enemy number 1 (with Israel cast as public enemy number 1-B). The organization is opposed to Western culture and American values; its members believes that American culture, if given free rein, will restrict them as a movement and curtail the influence of Islam.

Restrict Iranian and Syrian support of terrorism. Although Hizballah was originally an Iranian creation, its continued freedom of mobility depends on Syria. The group realizes that it is an expendable asset in the Iranian arsenal of war; Tehran could sacrifice Hizballah if that were the necessary price for gaining access to its Shiite brethren in southern Iraq. Similarly, Syria and Hizballah know that once the military campaign in Iraq is over, pressure will build on Damascus to stop supporting terrorist organizations; if and when a new Middle East is created, Syria may have no choice but to suppress Hizballah.

Arab-Israeli peace. Since the May 2000 withdrawal, the destruction of Israel has become Hizballah's ideological cornerstone. The organization justifies its existence by trumpeting this goal and by exporting its resistance ideology to the Palestinians. Hizballah has repeatedly declared that the only way for Palestinians to achieve total liberation is through armed resistance, and that they should accept nothing less than complete victory.

Wage the war against terror. Until September 11, Hizballah was responsible for more American deaths than any other terrorist organization. The organization knows that America's war on terror might eventually come its way, either through a direct attack or by giving the Israelis carte blanche. Whatever the case, the prospect of such action could have a debilitating effect on Hizballah's standing in Lebanon.

Hafez al-Mirazi, Mouafac Harb, and Jonathan Schanzer

70
Arabs View the War: Images, Attitudes, and Opinions

HAFEZ AL-MIRAZI

War remains a horrifying event and al-Jazeera will cover it realistically. Images carried by the network are graphic, but do not discriminate in showing American and Iraqi casualties. Similarly, al-Jazeera has covered both the unprecedented airpower brought to bear by the allied forces and the Iraqi government's own version of "shock and awe" in airing videotapes of American prisoners of war; failure to do so would challenge the station's credibility.

In the Middle East, al-Jazeera is unique in that it has provided American officials with an unprecedented platform to air their views, live and uncensored, directly to an Arab audience. Whereas the 1991 Gulf War witnessed a close correlation between Arab and American opinion, the current conflict with Iraq has proven much more divisive. Accordingly, images of suffering will inflame sentiments, irrespective of the explanations provided by either side. The American effort to minimize civilian casualties has not appreciably altered the mood on the street. Conversely, identifying Iraqi citizens and soldiers as hostages of Saddam's tyranny has proven detrimental to Washington's efforts to win Arab hearts and minds.

During the Clinton years, public outrage fueled by televised images of American soldiers dragged through the streets of Somalia spurred the United States to withdraw its forces, despite admonitions against doing so from official circles. If independent media can influence policy in countries with well-established democratic institutions, its effect will be magnified in those without them. In this respect, the United States should continue its relationship with al-Jazeera. Official engagement will convince the Arab public that their opinions matter to Washington and that American support for free speech applies to the Middle East as it does elsewhere. In addition, the more American opinions are available to Arab audiences, the more difficult it becomes for terrorist organizations to

On March 27, 2003, Hafez al-Mirazi, Mouafac Harb, and Jonathan Schanzer addressed The Washington Institute's Special Policy Forum. Mr. al-Mirazi is the Washington bureau chief for al-Jazeera television and host of the weekly program *From Washington.* Mr. Harb is director of network news for the U.S. government's Middle East radio network, Radio Sawa. Mr. Schanzer is a Soref fellow at the Institute, specializing in Arab and Islamic politics. This rapporteur's summary (originally published as *PolicyWatch* no. 742, April 4, 2003) was prepared by Evan Langenhahn.

depict the United States as a monolithic force inimical to Arab interests. Finally, al-Jazeera can serve as a channel for conveying Arab opinion to the United States. In this regard, the station may play a role in discouraging miscalculation, as occurred when the American and British governments misjudged the reaction of Iraqi citizens to the presence of foreign soldiers.

MOUAFAC HARB

Unfortunately, the proliferation of Arab satellite networks has done little to improve the quality of Arab media. These new media organizations have at times been provocative and unethical in their reportage, indulging the emotions of the "Arab street." Such distortions do not reflect the biases of Arab reporters, most of whom have worked in Western media, but are an extension of the dysfunctional Arab political system upon which these networks remain dependent. Such concern is particularly relevant with regard to al-Jazeera, the Arab world's most popular satellite news network. Despite unprecedented viewership levels, it has failed to establish itself as a credible and objective media institution, remaining dependent on subsidies from the Qatari government.

While it must be conceded that an American point of view is available on al-Jazeera, most of the time it is taken out of context or subject to distortion. For example, promotions for the nightly news contrast American military power with the suffering of Iraqi civilians, while interviews with counterelites staunchly opposed to American policy and even to America itself follow briefings by American officials. Meanwhile, al-Jazeera provides terrorist organizations with a platform from which to wage their own public relations campaigns. Continued American involvement with the Qatari station may encourage further radicalization of the Arab media. This also has a hand in convincing rival stations that the best way to attract Washington's attention is through negative coverage of American policy.

While al-Jazeera poses a long-term threat to Arab-American relations, the effects of its coverage should not be overstated. For one, al-Jazeera remains a station that has built a reputation on successive crises: Osama bin Laden, the Palestinian intifada, and the war with Iraq. As these events dissipate, people will turn elsewhere for news. Second, while public outrage threatens American interests, it has rarely resulted in political change. In this regard, the American military campaign in Iraq will not appreciably endanger the stability of allied regimes. Regardless, the United States must continue to address the Arab public, but in a manner that ensures the American point of view will be presented clearly and in context.

Given the complexity of government-media relations in the Middle East, it is unlikely that Arab media would depict democratic change in Iraq favorably. It is an obvious threat to regional autocracies. As such, America must look to its own resources for balance. It is in this context that the U.S. government hopes to launch its own satellite news channel in the Arab world.

JONATHAN SCHANZER

Images broadcast by Arab satellite television depict a volatile Arab public, an apparent vindication of those who warned of the debilitating effect of any American-led war on regional stability. Yet, there is reason to believe that such sentiments may not pose a long-term threat to the stability of Arab governments. Historically, most protests in the Arab world have been fueled by economic crises, and those that have been political have rarely resulted in regime change. In the months prior to war, most demonstrations remained relatively small, numbering no more than several hundred participants. It was not until regimes began sanctioning protests in February and March that the numbers climbed into the hundreds of thousands, and most of the demonstrations were clearly orchestrated by Arab leaders to co-opt public opposition to the war for political gain.

Once war broke out, the Arab street seemed to erupt. Regime tolerance of public dissent may actually benefit both American interests and Arab governments. Regime acceptance of nonconformist opinion may allow social protest to take the place of radical violence, thus frustrating the spread of terrorism. Equally important, any relaxation of regime controls on dissent may encourage further political liberalization. The Tunisian government, for example, recently allowed opposition parties to organize their first demonstration in over ten years. Such changes are significant and should not be overlooked.

Still, areas of concern persist. Areas of weak political authority—such as the refugee camps, southern Jordan, Upper Egypt, and parts of Yemen—remain political hotspots where persistent instability could degenerate into antiregime violence. A more important factor, however, is how Arab media—in particular al-Jazeera as the most watched Arab news source—depict the Iraq crisis. Al-Jazeera, while clearly possessing higher levels of journalistic integrity than many of its counterparts, continues to fuel public outrage through provocative images and inflammatory rhetoric. This may complicate American efforts for postwar rapprochement.

Patrick Clawson

71
First Steps to Remake Iraq

What to do in Iraq postwar could easily become the next crisis within the Western alliance. Canada has the credibility as a close friend of the United States, a strong supporter of international institutions, and an experienced peacekeeper to play an important role in urging all sides to make the necessary difficult compromises.

In theory, everyone agrees on the way forward. After U.S. Secretary of State Colin Powell met with his European counterparts Thursday at NATO headquarters in Brussels, NATO Secretary-General Lord George Robertson declared, "We are seeing the emergence of a consensus" about postwar Iraq.

In reality, we are more likely to see the same process that unfolded at the United Nations about disarming Iraq: first, an agreement in principle that everyone endorses; then a bitter dispute once it becomes apparent how different are the understandings of what that agreement means. Already on Friday, the French, German, and Russian foreign ministers meeting in Paris made clear they would insist on the centrality of the UN, while U.S. National Security Adviser Condoleezza Rice warned, "Iraq is not East Timor, Kosovo, or Afghanistan" (in which new administrations were established under UN auspices).

Compromise about the role of the UN will not come easily, because both the U.S. and the European critics of the war think they are in the driver's seat, and that the other side will inevitably have to let them chose which route to take. The United States is convinced that it has the responsibility and the capability to administer Iraq during a brief transition while order is re-established, and an Iraqi interim authority is set up. In this conception, the United Nations has an important humanitarian role, along the lines of the prewar oil-for-food program, but the United States and its wartime allies will make the key political decisions and reap the credit from transforming Iraq. A more active role for the UN, it is felt, would detract from the U.S. claim of victory, and retard the handover to Iraqis. As well, the United States wants no limit on its ability to pursue remnants of the Saddam Hussein regime, including tracking down its weapons-of-mass-destruction programs.

European critics of the war, such as France and Russia, as well as the UN bureaucracy and the non-governmental organization (NGO) community, think the United States badly needs the world community for postwar reconstruction. Only a UN-run transition with a substantial NGO role would, they argue, have the political legitimacy to gain acceptance

Originally published in the *Globe and Mail* (Toronto), April 8, 2003.

from the Iraqi people, as well as to forestall Arab outrage at what would otherwise be seen as American imperialist domination. As well, they argue that the reconstruction is going to require substantial donor funding and humanitarian expertise beyond what the U.S. government will provide.

And they argue that the transition will take years, pointing to how the solemn U.S. pledges to Congress that America would quickly be out of first Bosnia, and then Kosovo, turned out to be empty words. Indeed, the Balkans experience convinces European critics of the war that no matter what Washington now says, the Bush administration will have to come cap in hand to the United Nations and Europe asking for their assistance. They are prepared to concede that so long as the security situation is unstable, the United States will be running the show—and that even after that, it will continue to have the main role for ensuring security. But the political task of rebuilding the Iraqi government is a different matter.

Each side tells a story it finds convincing about why it will inevitably be having an important role but not the central role. The conflicting views are not going to make it easy to reach a compromise—and the still-raw feelings about the events leading up to the war will not help. The potential is all too real that there could be another major disagreement. The biggest losers from a deadlock over a UN role would be the Iraqi people. Absent a role for the United Nations, the United States would be tempted to turn over responsibility very quickly to Iraqis, in order to put to rest fears of a prolonged colonial occupation. That might not leave the time for the new government to gain the trust of Iraq's neighbours. If the Sunni Arab minority no longer dominates Iraq as it has for many decades, Saudi Arabia and Turkey will be wary, if not hostile: The Saudi government has no love for the Shiites and it worries about the impact of empowered Iraqi Shiites on the Saudi Shia minority—in much the same way that Turkey feels about the Iraqi Kurds.

And a quick handover would require giving a prominent role to returning exiled Iraqis, whom some would be quick to paint as U.S. puppets. Meanwhile, it would not leave enough time to develop new leaders from among the many skilled Iraqi professionals who stayed in the country but kept as far removed from politics as they could during Saddam's rule. Nor would a quick transition leave the time to develop the institutions of civil society-such as a free press and political parties—that are necessary to make democracy work. So the new Iraq would inevitably be, at best, a benevolent dictatorship, no matter how many democratic-sounding trappings are set up. Iraq deserves better. This is why a UN-assisted transition process would be the better way to go, if that can be made consistent with a pre-eminent role for the wartime states.

The British are making a valiant effort to promote compromise. They are pressing for Security Council approval of the least-controversial matters first, while setting aside, for the moment, the more difficult issues. But the British will need support to forge a broad international consensus that includes countries that were not active in the fighting. And Security Council action is more likely if countries with experience in postconflict situations, such as Canada and Japan, step forward to volunteer, whether it be to organize an international conference about humanitarian assistance, or to provide for work in Iraq respected officials whom all parties will trust to implement the Security Council resolutions in a neutral spirit, neither hostile to the U.S.-led war effort nor endorsing it.

72
Impact of Success in Iraq on Gulf States

The end of Saddam Hussein's regime offers several key benefits with regard to U.S. interests. World oil supplies will increase as Iraq—which has not been a major oil exporter since the beginning of the 1980-1988 war with Iran—raises its oil production capacity to its full potential, which may amount to 5-6 million barrels per day. Cheap oil will boost the global economy, reduce Arab control of the oil market, and allow the United States to become less dependent on Saudi Arabia and better positioned to demand reforms from Middle Eastern regimes. In addition, postwar Iraq will no longer pose a weapons-of-mass-destruction (WMD) threat to the region. The end of Saddam's regime will also reduce Russian and French influence in the region.

Impact of the War on the Gulf Monarchies

The military activity of the past few weeks would not have been possible without the aid of Bahrain, Kuwait, Qatar, and Oman, each of which made important contributions to the military effort. Although the Saudis were instrumental to the Iraq war in that they agreed to increase oil production—demonstrating that they are a reliable state willing to cooperate with Washington—the Saudis were not as helpful as they could have been. The strengthening of the U.S. relationship with the smaller Gulf Cooperation Council (GCC) states, combined with the weakening of the relationship with the Saudis, is likely to alter the balance of power in the Persian Gulf. The smaller GCC states have increased in power and may begin to resist Saudi dominance in the Gulf. This will challenge the unity and strength of the GCC itself.

Because the United States is still heavily dependent on Saudi Arabia for oil, Riyadh may be able to maintain the upper hand in the region. This makes decreasing dependence on Middle Eastern oil an important goal for Washington. Even if the United States purchases its oil from Russia, South America, and Central Asia, however, other countries will continue to buy oil from the Middle East, which will therefore retain its central role as a region in determining world oil supply and price.

On April 15, 2003, Simon Henderson addressed The Washington Institute's Special Policy Forum. Mr. Henderson is a London-based associate of the Institute, a former *Financial Times* journalist, and author of the biography *Instant Empire: Saddam Hussein's Ambition for Iraq* (Mercury House, 1991) as well as the Washington Institute perennial classic *After King Fahd: Succession in Saudi Arabia* (1994). This rapporteur's summary (originally published as *PolicyWatch* no. 752, April 24, 2003) was prepared by Shoshana Haberman.

Concerns of the GCC States

The United States has a clearer idea of its goals in the region than do the GCC states. Given this fact, the latter are waiting to evaluate the implications of the Iraq war. The United States is committed to political reform in the region and will demand that these governments devote more attention to the concerns of their people.

The GCC states will remain concerned about the U.S. military presence in their territory, and they will expect American forces to leave the region soon. The United States does not need a large, permanent presence in the Gulf in order to respond quickly and effectively to crises; the U.S. military has shown that it can be effective when operating under time pressure and in small numbers. Therefore, it would be wise to sharply reduce the presence of U.S. forces before the GCC states publicly suggest a reduction or full withdrawal.

Another concern for GCC states is the effect that the Iraq war will have on their populations. Currently, people in the region are being inundated with confusing images of Iraqi liberation and freedom. The governments have lost control over the kinds of images that reach their populations, and may therefore be faced with increased public pressure to enact reform.

Barriers to U.S. Goals

The biggest short-term challenge facing the United States is that of making sure the chaos in Iraq subsides. Soon, however, Washington will face at least two other major challenges in the Gulf.

First, GCC states may be unenthusiastic about U.S. attempts to broker a Middle East peace deal that addresses Israel's security concerns. Public opinion in GCC countries—as in much of the rest of the world—is mostly hostile to U.S. policy on this issue. They blame the Bush administration for the lack of progress rather than the Israelis, the Palestinians, or terrorist groups.

Second, Iran and other countries with WMD programs may take the wrong lesson from U.S. success in Iraq, especially in comparison with U.S. policy toward North Korea. Specifically, such states may decide that they should develop a nuclear arsenal as quickly as possible—before the United States can come after them—so as to deter U.S. intervention. To prevent the development of this scenario, the United States will need to take strong, quick, and deliberate measures against states tempted to pursue such a course of action.

Meanwhile, Washington should realize that its relationship with the United Kingdom is far more fragile than it seems. Much of the recent bilateral cooperation has been dependent on the personality of Prime Minister Tony Blair. Blair has successfully maintained the relationship thus far, but he will continue to need help from the United States. Specifically, he will need Washington's support with regard to the peace process, British commercial gains from Iraq, and recommitment to creating a global community. Although Blair does not face national elections for another three years, the local elections scheduled to occur this summer will be a test of British reaction to his policies. In order to shore up its current relationship with the United Kingdom, the United States will need to do more than pay lip service to Blair's political needs.

73
Iraq and Iran: Crosswinds?

A. WILLIAM SAMII

Although there are various players with different agendas in Iran's foreign policy bureaucracy, all those with real power agree on the unattractiveness of the situation in Iraq. Hence, Tehran has become increasingly involved in postwar Iraq. In addition to providing humanitarian assistance to Iraqis, Iran has been very active in spreading its message throughout the country, especially through direct radio and television broadcasting. Most of the radio stations that can be heard in Baghdad are sponsored by Iran, and the television signal that can be most readily received there is from an Iranian-run station. The theme on most of the Iranian radio and television programs is that Iraqis and Palestinians are facing similar conditions, that the coalition troops are occupying Iraq to help the "Zionist entity," and that the Iraqi people should confront these forces. Iran also tries to influence events in Iraq through its proxies in the Supreme Council for Islamic Revolution in Iraq (SCIRI), whose Badr Brigades military wing is linked with Iran's Islamic Revolutionary Guard Corps.

Washington could take several significant steps to counter Tehran's attempts to destabilize Iraq. First, the United States could help improve Iraqis' day-to-day lives through the restoration of law and order and essential social services. Second, U.S. personnel could engage leading Iraqi *ulama* and secure their support. Third, officials in Iraq could launch a vigorous radio and print media campaign to make Iraqis aware of the advantages that a stable post-Saddam Hussein regime could present.

The relationship between the United States and Iran has raised important political questions about who determines Iranian foreign policy: the executive branch (i.e., the president and the foreign minister) or the unelected revolutionary power centers. In particular, former president Hashemi Rafsanjani, who heads the Expediency Council, remains a powerful figure. His recent statements about restoring relations with the United States have often been misinterpreted; what he actually said was that this issue should be taken out of the hands of the executive branch and decided by a referendum or by the Expediency Council under his direction. Expediency Council Secretary Mohsen Rezai, an

On May 21, 2003, A. William Samii and Nasser Hadian addressed The Washington Institute's Special Policy Forum. Dr. Samii is an analyst at Radio Free Europe/Radio Liberty, where he prepares the Iran Report. Dr. Hadian is a professor of political science at Tehran University and a visiting scholar at the Middle East Institute of Columbia University. This rapporteur's summary (originally published as *PolicyWatch* no. 763, May 30, 2003) was prepared by Pemra Hazbay.

important Rafsanjani aide, recently met with a just-retired U.S. official responsible for Iran policy, furthering the council's bid to assume control over foreign relations. Although Foreign Minister Kamal Kharazi frequently argues that the executive branch is responsible for handling relations with the United States, he must justify any contacts with Washington against hardline attacks. Hence, he is careful to stress that his contacts are made in the context of international sessions, not bilateral meetings.

NASSER HADIAN

Iranian opinions on post-Saddam Iraq vary. The pragmatic view suggests that Iran should cooperate with the United States to ensure the rights of the Iraqi Shiite population, while the cooperative view focuses on the importance of Iran's well-established infrastructure of influence in Iraq. The radicals, however, would like to see the United States experience problems in Iraq; such problems, they argue, would impede U.S. intentions to topple the Iranian regime or to dramatically alter Tehran's policies.

Overthrowing Saddam was the easier part of the Iraqi crisis. The more difficult aspect for the United States is to avoid being perceived as an occupying force, which could in turn help prevent the growth of radicalism in the form of terrorism. In this regard, the United States has an interest in supporting moderate clerics in Iraq. The clerics have the potential to become an organized force, setting the agenda for a shattered Iraqi society. Rivalries led to intense fights among clerics prior to the occupation, but they are now trying to reconcile their differences because of the U.S. presence, which they all see as unacceptable. It is in Washington's interest to steer the clerics toward uniting around a position that discourages Iraqi imitation of Iran's system of clerical rule.

Ayatollah Muhammad Baqr al-Hakim of SCIRI is close to Tehran, but he knows from his years living in Iraq that clerical rule is a disaster for both the state and for Islam. It is uncertain to what extent SCIRI and al-Hakim will do Iran's bidding. For instance, the Badr Brigades have been trained, armed, and supported by Iran, but it is not at all clear what they would do if a disagreement emerged between al-Hakim and Iran.

In addition to discussing postwar Iraq, Tehran and Washington should address claims about the presence in Iran of senior al-Qaeda officials, Iran's growing nuclear program, and Tehran's role in supporting terrorism and disrupting Israeli-Palestinian peace talks. The current atmosphere in the region presents a very good rationale for the two states to engage in talks. One can imagine a deal of some sort unfolding. For instance, President Muhammad Khatami went to Lebanon recently and asked Hizballah to be a political rather than a military force; such actions could form the basis for an understanding.

Yet, any such understanding would require the United States to recognize Iran's legitimate security concerns. For example, Iranian missiles currently have a range sufficient to hit not only Baghdad but Israel. The United States could first acknowledge Iran's need for such missiles, then ask Tehran to deploy them only in the eastern part of the country, where they could still reach all of Iraq without threatening Israel. Similarly, in order to convince Tehran to abandon its nuclear ambitions, Washington should be prepared to address broader Iranian security concerns. For instance, the United States could guarantee that it would protect Iran from nuclear attack; alternatively, Washington could facilitate the establishment of a collective security arrangement for the region that reduces all parties' forces and military postures.

Another delicate issue in the U.S.-Iranian relationship is the Mujahedin-e Khalq (MEK) in Iraq. The United States made a great mistake in agreeing to a ceasefire with the group, both morally and politically. MEK has killed civilians as part of its opposition to the leadership in Tehran, and such actions are wrong regardless of how terrible the regime in question is. By agreeing to a ceasefire, the United States creates justifications for others to act in the same manner. Moreover, MEK supported Saddam, and the United States should not be siding with Saddam's allies.

Most important, the United States should make clear that it does not view the U.S.-Iranian relationship as a zero-sum game and that it is not pushing the Iranian government into a corner. Iran is not in a prerevolutionary state in which there could soon be a social upheaval that topples the Islamic Republic. It is in Washington's interests to promote a moderate Iran by talking to the Iranian government and elite. Cutting off the talks with Iran, as the Bush administration did recently, is in neither side's interests.

Hazem Saghie

74
An Arab Liberal Looks at the Post-Saddam Middle East

The fall of Saddam Hussein's regime is a seminal moment in the Middle East. President George W. Bush has called for democratization in the region, and the predicted results vary widely, ranging from Arab radicalization to Islamist militancy to rapid political and economic liberalization. Although liberalism is a minority voice in the Arab and Muslim worlds, a liberal agenda aimed at replacing pan-Arabism, recognizing the preeminence of the nation-state, and revitalizing civil society is critical for political and economic development in the Middle East. Such an agenda must focus on reducing poverty and improving the welfare of individual Arabs in different countries. It must not emphasize a vague ideology or narrow, sectarian interests.

Obstacles to Liberalism

In the Arab world, liberals are widely viewed as political dissidents, advocating the wrong ideas and values in a region that is illiberal, if not antiliberal. The majority of the Arab world has never fully embraced liberal Western ideologies, regarding them as vestiges of colonial domination. Indeed, the continuous struggle to reconcile these ideologies with Arab values has often exposed the region to decidedly illiberal foreign ideologies, which many regimes incorporated into their governing systems and national agendas. Saddam's regime was the most malevolent example of this phenomenon: a combination of Arab tribal loyalty and Western socialism, nationalism, and totalitarianism. Arab liberals are an oasis in a desert, confronted with the difficult task of reconstructing a region that has little experience with liberal developmental models. Hence, the Arab mainstream has yet to internalize President Bush's vision of democratization.

Given this backdrop, Arab liberals face a daunting challenge, not only because they seek political and economic reforms, but also because they must reform social and cultural values that are hostile to modernity. As a prerequisite to political modernity, Arabs—populations and regimes alike—must be disabused from their belief in pan-Arabism as a romantic dream uniting the Middle East. They must focus on reform—political, economic, and civil—in their own nation-states. Moreover, the debate on the

On May 8, 2003, Hazem Saghie addressed The Washington Institute's Special Policy Forum. Mr. Saghie has served as editor of the weekly supplement of the London-based daily *al-Hayat*, as a staff member for the Lebanon daily *al-Safir*, as a visiting fellow at the Institute, and as editor of *The Predicament of the Individual in the Middle East* (Saqi Books, 2000). This rapporteur's summary (originally published as *PolicyWatch* no. 756, May 13, 2004) was prepared by Eran Benedek.

compatibility of Islam and liberal democracy is irrelevant. It is not religion that is incompatible with modernity, but rather its practitioners who are hostile to change. Democracy and liberalism should not try to present themselves as being compatible with Islam. Instead, Arabs should create tolerant and liberal societies that are open to free religious expression.

Rebuilding Post-Saddam Iraq

Although the U.S.-led war in Iraq has had some positive results, the response of the Arab mainstream has been catastrophic. Two views dominate the Arab world. The minority view holds that the region's main problems (e.g., corrupt regimes, poverty) are an Arab responsibility, to be solved in cooperation with the West. The majority view, however, is primarily concerned with nationalism as a tool for combating foreign enemies, real or imaginary. Consequently, most Arabs in the region see regime change in Iraq more as an imperial exercise than as a liberation or a passport to modernity and development. The mainstream Arab view contends that the United States cannot help Arab states because it is allied with Israel, and that Europe cannot help because it is a colonial power. This resistance to Western liberalism may also be rooted in the continued prevalence of tribalism in mainstream Arab sociopolitical circles.

Democratization and liberalization in Iraq are possible as a long-term project, but the example of Central and Eastern European advances over the past fifteen years is inapplicable in this context. Arab liberals should join with the United States, Britain, and their allies in encouraging nation building as well as constitutional, rather than chauvinistic, nationalism.

More practically, the United States has an obligation to remain in Iraq and assist in the rebuilding process. Yet, U.S. forces should be ready to depart as soon as they accomplish their explicitly identified tasks in order to avoid becoming permanent occupiers. The challenges are formidable. First, the United States must help revitalize the Iraqi middle class, in part by inviting middle-class Iraqi expatriates to assist in reconstruction. Second, although de-Baathification is a critical step in creating distance between the new state and Saddam's Iraq, a distinction must be drawn between Baath Party officials and party members. Whereas the officials were responsible for oppression and violence and should be barred from public service, approximately five million Iraqis became party members exclusively for professional viability. These Iraqis are not responsible for, and in fact may have suffered from, Saddam's tyranny, and they should be included in public service and reconstruction efforts. Third, U.S. forces must prevent Sunni-Shiite discord, which could draw in Syria and Iran due to Sunni connections with the former and Shiite ties with the latter.

Regionwide Challenges

The first and foremost task for the United States and Europe is to help resolve the Palestinian issue. Bitterness arising from the Israeli-Palestinian conflict prevents Arabs from viewing U.S. policy favorably. Pressure on Palestinian Authority Chairman Yasser Arafat and efforts to end anti-Semitic incitement in the Arab world must be accompanied by equal pressure on Israeli Prime Minister Ariel Sharon and efforts to halt the expansion of Jewish settlements. Although the Palestinian leadership should be reprimanded for its actions and decisions, the Israeli leadership must stop speaking of negotiations in a manner that casts Israel as the sole proprietor of the land; such rhetoric comes across as colonialism and racism. A peaceful, evenhanded, negotiated resolution is essential if future U.S. policies are to succeed in the region and if Arab liberals are to pursue reforms.

Second, fissures between the United States, France, and Germany pose serious concerns for Arab liberals. Such divisions weaken the cause of liberalism worldwide, and efforts to mend these relationships are critical for Iraqi reconstruction and Middle Eastern democratization in general. The United States should not behave as, or become, a power that pursues its interests unilaterally, with callous disregard for the concerns of other nations.

Third, free-market capitalism, while good for rich people in the West, is not perfectly compatible with the Middle East. An element of social welfare is essential for the region, and social democracy is a must in order to lower poverty rates and improve individual welfare.

Fourth, U.S. domestic practices following the events of September 11 have reduced that tragedy to an ideology. Security-based fears have eroded certain civil liberties in America—a bad example for Middle Easterners who are fighting against regimes that restrict civil liberties. Ultimately, the United States is the jewel of liberty, democracy, private enterprise, and multiculturalism, and no true liberal can be anti-American. Yet, liberals cannot be expected to support everything Washington does. Dissent is not anti-Americanism; it is liberalism.

75
Can Americans, Turks, and Kurds Get Along in Northern Iraq? A Vision

Recently, the bitterness between Ankara and Washington over Turkey's failure to extend full support to the Iraq campaign culminated in a much-feared quagmire. On July 4, U.S. Army forces detained eleven Turkish special operations troops in Sulaymaniya, northern Iraq, possibly based on Iraqi Kurdish intelligence that they were planning to harm Kurdish officials in Kirkuk. Fortunately, no shots were fired and no one was hurt in the incident. Still, the fact remains that U.S. troops arrested soldiers from Turkey, a NATO ally viewed as one of America's staunchest friends until late 2002. Moreover, the Turks were allegedly conspiring against Kurds, America's best friends in Iraq. How to interpret this unpleasant episode? What can be done to prevent similar incidents in the future? Most important, can the United States and Turkey move forward in northern Iraq?

Background

When the July 4 incident was first reported, Washington refrained from high-level remarks except for State Department spokesman Richard Boucher's July 7 comment that Turkish troops had been involved in "upsetting activities" in northern Iraq. In contrast, Ankara reacted vigorously. Turkish foreign minister Abdullah Gul called Secretary of State Colin Powell, dismissing allegations that the Turkish soldiers were involved in rogue activities and requesting the release of the detainees. The Turkish Army went even further, expressing discontent with the United States. On July 7, Chief of Staff General Hilmi Ozkok stated that the incident "had triggered the most serious crisis of confidence yet between the two NATO allies" and demanded the release of the Turkish soldiers.

Where Do the United States and Turkey Stand?

Fortunately, the crisis withered quickly on July 7. Following a conversation between Vice President Dick Cheney and Turkish prime minister Tayyip Erdogan, the detainees were released. Even so, the incident's implications for future U.S.-Turkish relations must be examined. In particular, the following questions need to be answered: Was the incident initiated on a local basis, with U.S. troops taking spontaneous action against

Originally published as *PolicyWatch* no. 772, July 10, 2003. Soner Cagaptay is coordinator of The Washington Institute's Turkish Research Program.

independently minded Turkish troops and informing Washington after the fact? Or were Ankara and Washington involved in this chain of events from the very beginning?

It is difficult to ascertain Washington and Ankara's exact involvement in the episode before the bilateral investigation commission, currently in session, releases its findings. Yet, even if we assume that the incident was of local origin—that some Turkish soldiers engaged in anti-Kurdish activities without Ankara's knowledge, and that U.S. soldiers detained them without either Washington's authorization or due cause—it would still be a disturbing development, highlighting the raw frustration that midrank field officers on both sides feel toward each other. In other words, the Iraq crisis has fundamentally recast the mutual perceptions of U.S. and Turkish soldiers: they see each other more as adversaries than allies.

If, however, the events unfolded with Washington and Ankara's full knowledge, it would point at an even worse situation, namely, that the chess game over northern Iraq and the nature of Kurdish governance there have poisoned U.S.-Turkish relations to an inconceivable level.

What Next?

Clearly, the current state of U.S.-Turkish relations leaves much to be desired, largely due to the manner in which Washington and Ankara perceive each other's agenda in postwar Iraq. Many in Ankara believe that Washington will eventually create a Kurdish state in northern Iraq, while many in Washington are convinced that Ankara is attempting to confuse matters there. This presents a major challenge: as long as the United States and Turkey are at odds in northern Iraq, there is good a chance that their relations will deteriorate further with incidents similar to that of July 4. What can be done to prevent such deterioration?

Clearly, rebuilding confidence between Washington and Ankara regarding northern Iraq will not be easy. Yet, it would help if the two parties and the Iraqi Kurds agreed to enter a period of extended cool-down in order to consider the following policy recommendations.

Recommendations for Turkey:

- *Work with Washington to end Kurdish terrorism in northern Iraq.* Turkey ought to take comfort in the fact that it has successfully won an uphill fight against the terrorist Kurdistan Workers Party (PKK). The group was able to wreak havoc in southeastern Turkey during the 1990s in part because of its capacity to operate with relative freedom in the power vacuum that emerged in northern Iraq following the Gulf War. Now, the Turks can take advantage of the improved security situation in northern Iraq and work with the United States in disarming the PKK, recently renamed the Kurdistan Freedom and Democracy Congress (KADEK).
- *Begin to view the Iraqi Kurds, like the Turkmens, as part of the Turkish family.* For months before the Iraq war, Ankara took an active and justified interest in the Turkmens, who are closely related to the Turks. Yet, the fact remains that the Kurds are

family to the Turks as well. Turkey is a nation in which people of various religious and ethnic backgrounds take pride in being Turkish (more than a few generals and politicians who fought against the PKK were themselves of Kurdish origin). These factors should be the basis of Turkey's attitude toward the Iraqi Kurds.

Recommendations for the Kurds:

- *View Turkey as an avenue to the outside world and an anchor to the West.* The Kurdish area of northern Iraq is sandwiched between Iran to the east and Syria to the west. In the short run, this leaves Iraqi Kurds with two channels to the outside world: Baghdad and Turkey. Hence, Turkey is well poised to offer Iraqi Kurds access to the West, whether for trading with Europe or exporting oil (the major pipeline running from northern Iraq into the Mediterranean Sea passes through Turkey). Moreover, as long as democracy deficits and radical Islam plague the Middle East, Turkey's secular and democratic traditions will provide the Iraqi Kurds—whose own vigor in establishing an open society has received much acclaim—with an ideological anchor in the West.

Recommendations for the United States:

- *Remember that allies such as Turkey are rare to come by, even if they are not perfect.* Although many in Washington are upset by Turkey's belated support for the Iraq war, offending Turkey further (e.g., with the pending "Genocide Resolution" in the Senate, which would create nationalist, anti-American backlash in Turkey) would not further U.S. interests. Lately, Turkish public opinion, traditionally among the most pro-American, has become more anti-American. Such sentiments do not seem to be entrenched; rather, they are a product of the events of the past year. If left to brew, however, anti-Americanism could lay deep roots in Turkey. This is especially significant at a time when pro-Americanism is at a premium in the Middle East and when the situation in Iraq is not yet stable.
- *Remember that Turkey's importance for the United States extends well beyond Iraq.* The Turkish-Israeli partnership, for example, is a valuable asset for U.S. strategic thinking in the Middle East. Ankara's support is also needed in the energy-rich Caspian basin. For instance, given Turkey's many historical and cultural ties with Azerbaijan, Ankara can play a role in securing a peaceful transition there in light of long-time leader Haydar Aliyev's fragile health. The alternative to U.S.-Turkish cooperation in the Caspian region is Russian-Iranian influence.

By working soberly and incrementally to bring Turkey back into the fold, Washington may eventually be able to establish a working relationship with Ankara. The alternative is a Turkey gone in the wrong direction.

Raymond Tanter

76
Iran's Threat to Coalition Forces in Iraq

On January 13, 2004, Eli Lake of the *New York Sun* reported that two senior members of Iran's Islamic Revolutionary Guard Corps (IRGC) had defected to coalition forces in Iraq. This defection constitutes a good opportunity to reflect on several issues, including Iran's efforts to infiltrate the Iraqi Shiite community, Tehran's potential plans to target (either directly or by proxy) U.S. forces in Iraq, and the appropriate U.S. policy response to this potential Iranian threat.

Iran's Support for Anti-American Terrorism

According to the State Department's *Patterns of Global Terrorism 2002* (issued in April 2003), Tehran provides the Lebanon-based Hizballah with "funding, safe haven, training, and weapons." Such support (estimated at $80 million per year) has given Iran a terrorist proxy of global reach. For example, Hizballah suicide bombings against the U.S. Marine barracks and the U.S. embassy annex in Beirut (in October 1983 and September 1984, respectively) killed some 300 U.S. diplomats and soldiers. In addition, the twenty-two individuals on the FBI's list of Most Wanted Terrorists include three Hizballah operatives accused of the 1985 hijacking of TWA Flight 847, during which a U.S. Navy diver was murdered. The hijacking featured the infamous image of an American pilot peering out of the cockpit with a gun to his head. Moreover, according to a November 1, 1996, report by the *Washington Post*, Saudi intelligence concluded that a local group calling itself Hizballah was responsible for the June 1996 truck bombing of the Khobar Towers U.S. military housing complex on the kingdom's Persian Gulf coast. The Saudis also asserted that this local group was a wing of Lebanese Hizballah. More recently, Hizballah secretary-general Hassan Nasrallah made the following remarks in a speech given one week before coalition forces launched Operation Iraqi Freedom (as broadcast on al-Manar, the organization's Beirut-based satellite television station): "In the past, when the Marines were in Beirut, we screamed, 'Death to America!' Today, when the region is being filled with hundreds of thousands of American soldiers, 'Death to America!' was, is, and will stay our slogan."

Iran's support for anti-American terrorism is not limited to Hizballah, however. According to the State Department, some al-Qaeda operatives have obtained safe haven in Iran. U.S. intelligence believes that one such operative is Abu Musab al-Zarqawi, for whose capture the State Department's "Rewards for Justice" program offers up to $5 million.

Originally published as *PolicyWatch* no. 827, January 15, 2004. Raymond Tanter is an adjunct scholar of The Washington Institute.

Iran's links to al-Qaeda may predate the organization's post-September 11 flight from Afghanistan. At the trial for those suspected of bombing the U.S. embassies in Kenya and Tanzania in 1998, one of the defendants testified that he had provided security for meetings between al-Qaeda and Hizballah operatives. In addition, phone records revealed at the trial demonstrated that, during the period preceding the bombings, 10 percent of the calls made from Osama bin Laden's satellite phone were to Iran.

Iranian Efforts in Postwar Iraq

Over 2,000 Iranian-sponsored clerics have crossed into Iraq from Iran since the cessation of major combat in May 2003. Many of them carry books, compact discs, and audiotapes that promote militant Islam. Moreover, according to Iranian dissident sources, the IRGC's Quds (Jerusalem) Force is establishing armed underground cells across the Shiite southern region of Iraq, often using the Iranian Red Crescent as a front. Such sources also contend that the Jerusalem Force has established medical centers and local charities in Najaf, Baghdad, Hillah, Basra, and Amara in order to gain support from the local population. In addition, according to a September 2003 *Washington Times* report, IRGC agents have been deployed to Najaf in order to gather intelligence on U.S. forces. Tehran has also permitted members of Ansar al-Islam, a terrorist faction with close links to al-Qaeda, to cross back into Iraq and join the anti-American resistance.

Even as Tehran began to send Iranian operatives into postwar Iraq, members of Hizballah infiltrated the country as well. Because most of Hizballah's members are Arab, they may constitute an even more effective Iranian proxy in Iraq than Iranian agents trained in Arabic. According to Iranian dissident sources (and confirmed in part by U.S. intelligence), Tehran tasked Hizballah with sending agents and clerics across a major portion of southern Iraq. Indeed, once major combat operations came to an end, Hizballah "holy warriors" crossed into the country not only from Syria, but from Iran as well. Initially, these operatives numbered nearly 100, but this relatively small figure belies their potential impact on behalf of Tehran. Hizballah has established charitable organizations in Iraq in order to create a favorable environment for recruiting, a tactic that the organization had previously tested in southern Lebanon with Iranian assistance. Moreover, according to Muhammad al-Alawi, Hizballah's chief spokesman in Iraq, the organization's agents act as local police forces in many southern cities (e.g., Nasariya, Ummara), ignoring an official U.S. ban on militias. Overall, Tehran seems to be using Hizballah to supplement its own penetration of local Iraqi governing offices and judiciaries.

In addition, Iranian dissident sources report that Tehran has used Hizballah to smuggle Iraqis living in Iran back into their native country. A significant number of Iraqis have dual nationality and have resided in Iran for many years; some have even served as IRGC commanders. Hizballah can help conceal their long association with Iran; indeed, some of these individuals have apparently joined Iraqi police forces since the end of major combat.

Iranian dissident sources also contend that Hizballah is casing coalition assembly centers in Iraq and tracking the timing and order of movements by various coalition vehicles, including tanks, armored personnel carriers, and motorcades (this assertion has yet to be confirmed by U.S. intelligence officials). Hizballah agents are reportedly videotaping various locations in two-person teams, often using public transportation such as taxis. Footage of targets is sometimes concealed between banal imagery (e.g., wedding festivities) in order to avoid detection by coalition forces. Such reports echo Hizballah's own public statements, voiced as early as mid-April 2003, regarding its willingness to attack U.S. forces in Iraq and its increasing ability to do so.

Talks with Iran?

The devastating earthquake that struck Iran in December 2003 renewed the debate over whether Washington should resume its quiet dialogue with Tehran. That dialogue was suspended in spring 2003 after intelligence linked al-Qaeda operatives held in Iran to a series of suicide bombings in Saudi Arabia. Now that Tehran has agreed in principle to some limits on its nuclear program, Iranian-sponsored terrorism heads the list of topics that Washington needs to discuss with Tehran.

Another key issue is Tehran's efforts to build an intelligence infrastructure in Iraq. Prior to resuming U.S.-Iranian dialogue, Washington should not only insist that Iran expel al-Qaeda, but also demand that Ansar al-Islam, Hizballah, and the IRGC's Jerusalem Force withdraw from Iraq. With over 10,000 coalition forces stationed in southern Iraq, force-protection planners should be particularly wary of Hizballah's intelligence efforts, given the organization's past attacks against U.S. military forces in Lebanon and Saudi Arabia.

Matthew Levitt

77

USA Ties Terrorist Attacks in Iraq to Extensive Zarqawi Network

According to General John Abizaid, commander of US operations in Iraq, the three major elements fighting Coalition forces are former regime elements, transnational terrorists and religious extremists or jihadists.

Gen Abizaid told the US House Armed Services Committee on 4 March 2004: "Transnational terrorists such as the Zarqawi network, Ansar al-Islam and Al-Qaeda are attempting to destabilise Iraq by increasing both ethnic and sectarian strife with the intention of inciting chaos and a civil war. These terrorists are operating in the same areas as the former regime elements, which are largely former Ba'athist strongholds. They also have a presence in northern Iraq and are launching attacks into southern Iraq targeting the Shi'a population, the international community, and security forces."

Two days before Abizaid's briefing, on 2 March, an estimated 185 Shi'ite worshippers celebrating the religious festival of Ashura were killed in bombings in Karbala and Baghdad, attacks that Abizaid said bore the hallmarks of operations planned by Abu Musab al-Zarqawi (alias Fadel Nazzal al-Khalayleh).

US Central Command expects that terrorist activities by Zarqawi's network in Iraq will increase as the country moves towards sovereignty. In his testimony, Abizaid drew attention to a letter believed to have been written by Zarqawi, suggesting: "Zero hour must be at least four months before the new government gets into place. We are racing time."

The letter was found on a compact disc when Coalition forces captured senior Al-Qaeda operative Hasan Ghul in January 2004. Written as a response to an inquiry from Al-Qaeda operative Abd al-Had al Iraqi (alias Abdallah Khan), it detailed operations and planning in Iraq. It also called for more Al-Qaeda operatives to enter the country and increase attacks on Coalition forces as well as Iraq's Shi'a community.

Zarqawi's Role

Not known as a bomb maker or financier, Zarqawi appears to function as a co-ordinator involved with several Islamist networks. According to a 23 February report by Brian Bennett and Vivienne Walt in *Time* magazine, Zarqawi is believed to have been "given

Originally published in *Jane's Intelligence Review*, April 1, 2004. Reprinted with permission from Jane's Information Group/*Jane's Intelligence Review*. Matthew Levitt is a senior fellow in terrorism studies at The Washington Institute.

responsibility for rotating Al-Qaeda troops between Chechnya and Afghanistan, through the mountains of northern Iraq", as well as running a training camp in Afghanistan.

According to the US Treasury, after fighting against Soviet forces in Afghanistan in the 1980s, Zarqawi returned to Jordan in 1991 and founded Jund al-Shams, an Islamic extremist group operating primarily in Syria and Jordan. He was jailed in Jordan in 1992, apparently for a combination of his history as an "Afghan-Arab" and his activities with Jund al-Shams, he was released in 1999. He promptly angered authorities again by his support for a radical Jordanian cleric who called for the overthrow of the monarchy and the establishment of an Islamic state in Jordan, and subsequently fled to Peshawar, Pakistan and Afghanistan.

At least 116 alleged terrorists linked to Zarqawi have been arrested in Europe and the Middle East with detentions having been made in France, Italy, Spain, the UK, Germany, Turkey, Jordan and Saudi Arabia.

Turkey: On 15 February 2002, Turkish police intercepted two Palestinians and a Jordanian who entered Turkey illegally from Iran on their way to conduct bombing attacks in Israel. Zarqawi is believed to have dispatched the three men, believed to be members of Beyyiat al-Imam, who fought for the Taliban and received terrorist training in Afghanistan. More recently, Abdelatif Mourafik (alias Malek the Andalusian, or Malek the North African), a Moroccan Zarqawi associate wanted for his role in the May 2003 Casablanca suicide bombings, was arrested in Turkey in late 2003. According to early assessments by Turkish officials, Zarqawi was the planner behind the two sets of double suicide bombings in Istanbul in November 2003.

Germany: Although the al-Tawheed terrorist cell apprehended in Germany in April 2002 has been tied to Abu Qatada in the UK, Zarqawi controlled its activities. Eight men were arrested, and raids yielded hundreds of forged passports from Iran, Iraq, Jordan, Denmark and other countries. According to German prosecutors, the group facilitated the escape of terrorist fugitives from Afghanistan to Europe and planned to attack US or Israeli interests in Germany. The 2002 annual report of the Office for the Protection of the Constitution (OPC) noted that Zarqawi, who "has close links with Al-Qaeda", also "commanded a mujahidin [sic] network in the Federal Republic of Germany, amongst other countries". The US Treasury said that members of Zarqawi's German cell included Mohamed Abu Dhess, Shadi Abadallah, Aschraf Al-Dagma, Djamel Moustafa and Ismail Shalabi.

Jordan: While in Syria, Zarqawi planned and facilitated the October 2002 assassination of Lawrence Foley, a US Agency for International Development official, in Amman. Jordanian prime minister Abu Ragheb Ali announced that the Libyan and Jordanian suspects arrested in December in connection with the attack received funding and instructions from Zarqawi and had intended to conduct further attacks against "foreign embassies, Jordanian officials, some diplomatic personnel, especially Americans and Israelis". The captured assassin, Salem Said Bin Sewid, confessed that Zarqawi provided funding and weapons for the murder. According the indictment, Zarqawi entered Jordan before the attack to select 11 recruits, and provided "$60,000, as well as machine guns, silencers, tear gas, gloves and a vehicle to use for terrorist operations". During his UN address on 5 February 2003, US Secretary of State Colin Powell said "an associate of the assassin left Jordan to go to Iraq to obtain weapons and explosives for further operations" at a time when a Zarqawi-run network was operating in Baghdad. In addition, a key Zarqawi deputy called Foley's assassins on a satellite phone to congratulate them while he was driving out of Iraq toward Turkey, a mistake that led to his capture and confirmation that a terrorist cell was operating out of Iraq.

Powell also disclosed that Abuwatia, a detainee who graduated from Zarqawi's terrorist camp in Afghanistan, admitted to dispatching at least nine North African extremists to Europe to conduct poison and explosive attacks. According to the intelligence Powell revealed, terrorists detained in Europe not only provided information about the targets of Zarqawi's European network, but also the names of many of the network's members. Central Intelligence Agency Director George Tenet told the Senate Select Committee on Intelligence on 6 February 2002 that the Zarqawi network was behind poison plots in Europe. European officials have confirmed that Zarqawi is the co-ordinator for attacks there, including chemical attacks that were thwarted in the UK, France and Italy.

According to Colin Powell, Zarqawi's European network—heavily populated by Ansar al-Islam operatives—included the German cell noted above; Merouane Benahmed and Menad Benchellall in France; Abderrazak Mhadjoub, Mohammed Tahi Hamid, Radi Ayashi and Chise Mohammaed in Italy; seven unnamed North Africans arrested in the January 2003 ricin plot in the UK; and, according to US officials, unnamed operatives in Spain. US and European authorities have also tied Zarqawi to terrorists in Georgia's Pankisi Gorge (including Abu Atiya, arrested in September 2003 in Baku, Azerbaijan) and Chechnya. Zarqawi's reported experience with chemical weapons makes his role as the co-ordinator between such networks especially worrisome to law-enforcement and intelligence officials.

Transnational Support Network

In Congressional testimony on 9 March 2004, Tenet included "the Zarqawi network"—along with Ansar al-Islam, the Libyan Islamic Fighting Group and the Islamic Movement of Uzbekistan—in a list of what he termed "smaller international Sunni extremist groups who have benefited from Al-Qaeda links".

The range of actors who have given Zarqawi safe haven and support illustrate the loose and mutable nature of the terrorist networks involved. Zarqawi has been a fugitive since 1999 when Jordanian authorities first tied him to radical Islamic activity leading Jund al-Shams. In 2000, a Jordanian court sentenced him in absentia to 15 years of hard labour for his role in the millennial terror plot targeting Western interests in Jordan. Ahmad Mahmoud Saleh al-Riyati, an Ansar al-Islam member captured by Coalition forces in northern Iraq and deported to Jordan in April 2003, was also sentenced in absentia for his role in the millennial plots.

According to information declassified by the US Treasury Department, Zarqawi sent members of Jund al-Shams from Jordan to train at the al-Faruq Camp in 1999, where they received full support from Al-Qaeda. US authorities maintain that Zarqawi met Al-Qaeda leaders in Kandahar that year and then, in late 2000, left Pakistan for Afghanistan. There he oversaw his own cell and training camp near Herat where cadres, many from his own Bani Hassan tribe in Jordan, worked on chemical and biological weapons.

The US Treasury Department has also linked Zarqawi to Iran and Iraq, claiming that he met an associate named Mohamed Abu Dhess in Iran in early September 2001 "and instructed him to commit terrorist attacks against Jewish or Israeli facilities in Germany with 'his [Zarqawi's] people'". Early the following year, Zarqawi was wounded in the leg while fighting against US-led forces in Afghanistan. He escaped to Iran, then travelled to Iraq in May 2002, where his leg was amputated and replaced with a prosthetic device. According to Powell, Zarqawi then spent two months recovering in Baghdad, during which time "nearly two dozen extremists converged on Baghdad and established a base of operations there". Prior to the war in Iraq, Zarqawi had returned to the Ansar al-Islam camp in northern Iraq run by his Jund al-Shams lieutenants. There, he enjoyed safe haven and free passage into and out of Ansar-held areas. In late 2003 European intelligence officials believed that Zarqawi was in Iran, from where he co-ordinated operations in Iraq. One of his key lieutenants, Abu Mohammed Hamza, an accomplished bomb maker, was killed in a firefight with Coalition forces near Baghdad in February 2004.

Between leaving Baghdad and reappearing in Iran, Zarqawi is believed to have travelled to Syria and possibly Lebanon. US intelligence officials have linked Zarqawi to Hizbullah, magnifying their concerns about an ad hoc tactical relationship brewing between Iran's Shi'a proxy and the loosely affiliated Al-Qaeda network. In September 2003, when US authorities designated Zarqawi and several of his associates as 'Specially Designated Global Terrorist' entities, the Treasury said that Zarqawi not only had "ties" to Hizbullah, but that plans were in place for his deputies to meet with both Hizbullah and Asbat al-Ansar (a Lebanese Sunni terrorist group), "and any other group that would enable them to smuggle mujaheddin [sic] into Palestine". The Treasury claimed that Zarqawi received "more than $35,000" in mid 2001 "for work in Palestine", which included "finding a mechanism that would enable more suicide martyrs to enter Israel" as well as "to provide training on explosives, poisons, and remote controlled devices".

Zarqawi also relied on associates in Syria to facilitate travel to Iraq and other logistics for members of his European network. According to Italian prosecutors "Syria has functioned as a hub for an Al-Qaeda network" linked to Zarqawi. Transcripts of operatives' conversations "paint a detailed picture of overseers in Syria co-ordinating the movement of recruits and money" between cells in Europe and Ansar al-Islam training camps in northern Iraq. The cell's leaders in Syria facilitated the recruits' travel and provided their funding, while the European members gave false travel documents to recruits and fugitives and monitored their travel. At least some of the recruits travelling to the Ansar camps stayed at the Ragdan Hotel in Aleppo for some time and later stopped in Damascus. The

Italian investigation revealed that Zarqawi's operatives in Europe were acting on the instruction of his lieutenants in and around Damascus and Aleppo, including Muhammad Majid (also known as Mullah Fuad and described as the "gatekeeper in Syria for volunteers intent on reaching Iraq"), and two men referred to as "Abdullah" and "Abderrazak". For example, in one conversation, an operative assures a comrade that sending money via Fuad is safe, saying: "I have sent so many transfers to Mullah Fuad and they always got there, no problem."

The Nature of Terrorism

Zarqawi's activities and his matrix of relationships illustrate the current nature of international terrorism and the complex threat it poses. For example, while there are no known 'headquarters-to-headquarters' links between Al-Qaeda and Hizbullah, senior personnel linked to the two groups are known to have held meetings over the past decade and ad hoc, person-to-person ties in the areas of training and logistical support activities have been maintained.

As recent attacks in Casablanca, Istanbul and Iraq re-emphasised, it is these relationships, rather than particular group affiliations, that are facilitating Al-Qaeda's ability to conduct devastating terrorist attacks. As Tenet has testified, the counterterrorism successes of the past three years have "transformed the organisation into a loose collection of regional networks", but intelligence analysts note that while Al-Qaeda itself has been weakened, "there has been no comparable weakening in the wider Islamic jihadists movement".

While this wider movement continues to provide willing recruits, operatives like Zarqawi will be able to co-ordinate their movement and activities and use related networks and support bases to provide logistics and financial aid for operations.

78
Tehran's Hidden Hand: Iran's Mounting Threats in Iraq

The State Department's annual "Patterns of Global Terrorism" report was issued earlier this month, complete with its usual hit parade of terrorist groups, state sponsors and emerging trends. Predictably, Iran was singled out for the "planning of and support for terrorist acts," as well as assistance to "a variety of groups that use terrorism to pursue their goals." The report also fingers Iran for pursuing "a variety of policies in Iraq aimed at securing Tehran's perceived interests there, some of which ran counter to those of the Coalition." A statement castigating Iran for such activities was long overdue. However, Washington must now challenge Iran over this growing list of nefarious activities in Iraq that have been plaguing coalition reconstruction efforts.

Conventional Fighting

Ash-Sharq al-Awsat ran this headline on March 16, 2004: "American and Iranian Forces Exchange Fire on the Border." American officials claimed that one Iranian border guard was killed, and other reports indicated that three Iranians were killed, but Tehran denied that any such incident took place. This was not the first time that open hostilities were reported. Coalition officials indicated in January and February that Abu al-Khasib, the port just below Basra on the Shatt al-Arab, has been the scene of Iranian violence against Iraqis. Iranian Revolutionary Guards have opened fire upon Iraqi water patrols along the estuary separating their two countries. Iranian fighters are also inside Iraq, and they may or may not be sanctioned by Tehran. On February 14, when a number of guerrillas attacked a police station in Fallujah, it was learned that two of the slain guerrillas were Iranian. An insurgency attack the week before, according to U.S. sources, was an attempt to free a number of Iranians who had only recently been arrested in Fallujah.

Hezbollah & IRGC

In February 2004, during a Washington Institute fact-finding mission to Iraq, one Coalition official reported that Iranian Revolutionary Guards Corps (IRGC) offices were spotted in the holy cities of Najaf and Karbala. Moreover, officials noted an immense amount of Hezbollah activity in the city of Karbala. Most of the activity was "intimidation

Originally published in the *National Review Online*, May 10, 2004. Jonathan Schanzer is a Soref fellow at The Washington Institute.

and threats of intimidation...Mafia-type stuff." During our delegation's one day in Basra, we spotted a building that openly advertised the offices of Hezbollah. Members of this organization insisted that their Hezbollah was not tied to Tehran, and that the name, which means "Party of God," is a common one. According to one report in the Arabic paper *al-Hayat,* Iran sent some 90 Hezbollah fighters into Iraq shortly after Saddam's Iraq fell. The group now receives financing, training and weapons from Iran, and has a rapidly growing presence in the Shi'a south. Western intelligence officials also allege that the man who planned the recent suicide attacks in Basra is Imad Mughniyeh, the Hezbollah operative responsible for bombing the U.S. embassy in Beirut in the early 1980s.

Propaganda

Even before the U.S.-led war on Iraq, Iran had begun beaming in Arabic-language television programming in an effort to gain a strategic propaganda foothold in the country—and it has not stopped. Indeed, American labors to win hearts and minds through the television station, al-Iraqiyya, and Radio Sawa have been steadily undermined by these efforts. In April 2003, an Iranian journalist reported that Iranian Revolutionary Guards brought into Iraq radio-transmission equipment, posters, and printed matter for the militia known as the Badr Corps. The Badr Corps is a militia that has not yet challenged the U.S., but it is run by SCIRI (the Supreme Council for Islamic Revolution in Iraq), which is known to have close ties to the Iranian regime.

Ansar al-Islam

Not enough attention has been given to the established ties between Iran and Ansar al-Islam, a Kurdish al Qaeda affiliate. Before the war, Iran allowed Ansar al-Islam to operate openly along its borders in the extreme northeast mountains of Iraqi Kurdistan, just shy of the Iranian border. Kurdish intelligence, with corroboration from imprisoned Ansar fighters, has established that Iran provided logistical support to the group by allowing the flow of goods and weapons. During periods of conflict with Kurdish militia units, the Peshmerga, Iran further provided a safe haven for these Islamist fighters. One Turkish newspaper also notes that Ansar al-Islam militants actually checked cars going into Iran (rather than coming into their stronghold), indicating close security coordination with the Islamic Republic. When the U.S. struck the Ansar al-Islam enclave in March 2003, Iran permitted many Kurdish fighters to flee across the border. They were later assisted back over the border—with the help of Iran's Revolutionary Guards—so that they could fight against American soldiers in the heart of Iraq. Kurdish intelligence has since intercepted between three and ten foreign fighters crossing Iranian border each week.

Moqtada al-Sadr

Iran sent a delegation to Iraq in mid-April to mediate between the rogue cleric and the U.S. administration. However, at the same time, Hassan Kazemi Qumi, an Iranian agent, has been supporting al-Sadr's anti-American efforts. A source from *ash-Sharq al-Awsat* estimates that Iran may have provided al-Sadr some $80 million in recent months.

Further, Sadr's Mahdi army may now be getting training from Hezbollah, according to new intelligence reports. One Iranian source told *ash-Sharq al-Awsat* that Iran created three training camps along the Iran-Iraq border to train fighters from Sadr's militia.

In sum, Iran may be spending up to $70 million per month in Iraq. This pales in comparison to the billions spent by the U.S. Still, it is enough to undermine U.S. efforts. As such, Washington needs not only to better patrol the Iranian border, but also to confront clandestine Iranian activity within Iraq itself. Failure to do so will only encourage Iran to redouble its efforts to destabilize Iraq.

79
Incident in the Shatt al-Arab Waterway: Iran's Border Sensitivities

After several days of diplomatic tension between London and Tehran, eight British military personnel who had been captured by Iran's Islamic Revolutionary Guard Corps (IRGC) were released and flown out of Iran on June 24. The men, who served with the coalition forces in Iraq, had been in three boats intercepted in the Shatt al-Arab waterway, the confluence of the Tigris and Euphrates Rivers that forms the border with Iran. (Tehran, which dislikes the Arab name, calls the waterway the Arvand River.) The incident comes after several weeks of minor clashes in the Persian Gulf and at a time when Iran is facing strong international pressure due to concerns about its suspected nuclear weapons program.

The exact circumstances of the capture of the British personnel are not clear. Tehran has claimed that the men were carrying weapons and sophisticated communications equipment, while British officials have stated that they had only their personal weapons and, at the time of their capture, were merely delivering one of the boats to Iraq's new river patrol service in Basra. The men had apparently crossed into the Iranian portion of the Shatt al-Arab unintentionally. By a 1975 treaty, the border between Iran and Iraq lies along the so-called "thalweg line," the midpoint of the deepwater channel. The precise status of this treaty is currently unclear, however, as Saddam Hussein abrogated it when he launched the Iran-Iraq War in 1980.

Historical Grudges

The fact that British forces were involved made the incident especially sensitive for Iran. A 1937 treaty, brokered at a time when imperial Britain still held sway in Iraq, placed the Iraqi-Iranian border at the low-water line on the Iranian side of the waterway, putting Iran at a considerable disadvantage. (The waterway is tidal up to and north of Basra, which is located fifty miles from the Persian Gulf.) Although the 1937 treaty allowed free passage for all shipping, the effect was that ships heading for the Iranian port of Khorramshahr and the oil refinery at Abadan were placed under Iraqi control, forced to carry Iraqi pilots and pay transit fees to the harbor authorities in Basra. Iran resented this display of British dominance.

Originally published as *PolicyWatch* no. 879, June 28, 2004. Simon Henderson is a London-based associate of The Washington Institute.

The 1975 treaty was negotiated between the Shah of Iran and Saddam (at the time Iraq's de facto second-in-command). In return for Tehran halting its support for a Kurdish rebellion in northern Iraq, Saddam conceded the thalweg line as the border.

Taken by itself, last week's incident could be viewed as a case of poor British navigation and opportunistic zeal by the IRGC, whose fast boats patrol the waterway. Yet, such a view would ignore the fact that there had been previous incidents of this sort in the Shatt al-Arab. According to a senior British officer in Basra, Iraqi patrols attempting to navigate the waterway since the fall of Saddam's regime have been shot at by Iranian forces, whichever side of the thalweg line they have been on. In an attempt to defuse this and other border tensions, the British have placed a senior military "liaison officer" (i.e., not a military attaché) in Tehran to deal directly with the Iranian Ministry of Defense.

Other Incidents in the Persian Gulf

In another worrisome trend, other portions of the Persian Gulf have witnessed an outbreak of maritime incidents during the first three weeks of June. On June 2, the United Arab Emirates (UAE) detained an Iranian fishing boat for allegedly sailing into UAE territorial waters around the island of Abu Musa. Iran has long claimed the island, which lies in an area where revenues from the local oil field are shared between the two countries. Iran seized Abu Musa, along with the small islands known as the Greater and Lesser Tunbs, in 1971. The Tunbs are located near the main shipping lanes for oil tankers.

Soon after the June 2 incident, the IRGC stopped seven fishing boats from the UAE and detained twenty-two crew members for entering Iranian waters. On June 11, Iran claimed that a Qatari patrol boat had fired on Iranian fishing boats accused of entering Qatari waters. (One of the world's largest reserves of natural gas lies under the maritime boundary between the two countries.) One Iranian was killed and two were injured, and the boats were seized, according to an Iranian report. The Qatari ambassador in Tehran was summoned to the foreign ministry for an explanation and to inform him that the Iranian fisherman had permits. On June 15, the IRGC seized a UAE fishing boat and its five crew members near the island of Sirri, home to an Iranian oil terminal.

These incidents followed a June 5 meeting between foreign ministers of the Gulf Cooperation Council (i.e., Saudi Arabia, Kuwait, Bahrain, Qatar, the UAE, and Oman), at which Gulf leaders expressed regret that contacts with Iran over Abu Musa and the Tunbs had "so far failed to achieve results" (i.e., with regard to returning them to Arab sovereignty). A day later, an Iranian Foreign Ministry statement asserted that the "islands are and will remain an inseparable and eternal part of [Iran]."

In the Iranian parliament, one deputy speculated that the United States was behind the UAE's June 2 seizure of the Iranian fishing boat. Another deputy suggested the action was timed to coincide with international pressure on Iran over its nuclear facilities. Meanwhile, the managing director of one Iranian newspaper argued that Tehran's sovereignty over the islands could be traced back to official British maps of 1836 (for good measure, he added that the Shah of Iran had no right to give up Iranian claims to the island-state of Bahrain in 1970).

All of these controversial maritime actions by Iran appear to be attributable to the IRGC, the military unit that is most loyal to the regime. The IRGC has land, naval, and air components, along with increasing political power. It answers directly to Iranian Supreme Leader Ali Hossein Khamenei, and several dozen former members were recently sworn in as members of parliament. The IRGC has also been active in Iraq, where it trained the main Shiite militia (the Badr Brigades) and where it continues to send operatives.

Challenge for the United States

British foreign secretary Jack Straw described the quick resolution of the Shatt al-Arab incident as proof that Britain's "policy of engagement with the government of Iran is the best approach." Sometimes dubbed "Ayatollah Straw" by his critics because of his frequent visits to Tehran, Straw was one of the architects of the European Union agreement with Iran aimed at halting its enrichment of uranium. In fact, Tehran's agreement to surrender the British detainees (instead of, as was suggested at first, putting them on trial) can easily be seen as an effort to earn diplomatic points as the crisis of its alleged nuclear ambitions develops. For Washington, Iran's recent actions demonstrate that Tehran is determined to be seen as a major regional power and that it has an interest in the shape of postoccupation Iraq.

Soner Cagaptay

80
Allied Forces

With the U.S. having transferred sovereignty to Iraqis earlier this week, the Kurds find themselves in a more precarious position than at any time in the last year. On June 8, the U.N. Security Council accepted a new resolution dictating the guidelines for post-U.S. Iraq. The resolution did not mention the autonomy that Kurds have meticulously constructed in northern Iraq since 1991; nor did it refer to the Kurds' growing independence in Iraq since the end of the most recent war. The absence of such acknowledgments from the resolution went a long way toward confirming the Kurds' worst fears about the direction of post-Saddam Iraq: that the country's majority Arab population will take the nation's destiny into its own hands, without regard for the aspirations of the Kurdish minority. With the U.S. gone, Kurds increasingly face the prospect of political isolation in their own country.

Confronting hostility from their neighbors to the south, Kurds may now seek friendship to their north. During much of the 1990s, Kurds enjoyed a mostly chilly relationship with the Turkish government in Ankara, which has always been wary of Kurdish nationalism. So it may seem odd that an alliance, or at least a warming of relations, with Turkey is now very much in the Kurds' interest. But the Kurds cannot afford to be isolated on both their southern and northern flanks at the same time. They need allies in a region generally hostile to their aspirations. As a result, it would not be surprising to see the Kurds make overtures to Ankara in the months ahead.

The Kurds, of course, have enjoyed autonomy and relative success in building their society during the last thirteen years. But relations with their neighbors have not always been smooth. Operations during the 1990s by the terrorist Kurdistan Workers Party (PKK)—which used northern Iraq as a base to attack southeastern Turkey—led to a deterioration of relations between Ankara and the two governing entities in that region, the Kurdistan Democratic Party (KDP) and the Patriotic Union of Kurdistan (PUK). And since the ouster of Saddam, the Kurds have frequently been at odds with Iraqi Arabs to their south. At the onset of war, when Turkey refused to allow the U.S. to open up a northern front against Saddam, the Kurds moved to fill the void. The two Kurdish parties, already close with the U.S., became America's only and best allies in Iraq, hoping that in return Washington would reward them. Shortly after the war, the KDP and PUK expanded their territorial control, grabbing parts of north-central Iraq, including the city of Kirkuk,

Originally published in the *New Republic Online,* June 30, 2004. Soner Cagaptay is coordinator of The Washington Institute's Turkish Research Program.

which sits atop 40 percent of Iraq's oil. In Baghdad, the two parties made clear that the rest of Iraq would have to take them seriously. According to one member of the Iraqi Governing Council whom I spoke to while traveling in Iraq this past winter, "When the Council discusses business regarding northern Iraq, the Kurds do not allow anyone else to join in the debate." The KDP and PUK made sure their autonomy was mentioned in Iraq's interim constitution. More importantly, the Kurds won the right to veto the permanent Iraqi constitution if they found it detrimental to their interests.

Not surprisingly, these gains by the Kurds have only frustrated non-Kurdish Iraqis. Such privileges are unfair, they say, because the Kurds are a relatively small minority in Iraq, making up just 15 to 20 percent of Iraq's population. Iraqi Arabs resent that Kurds secured their rights through U.S. favor. When I spoke last winter to Shiite notables and tribal and religious leaders in southern Iraq, many referred to the Kurds as "infidel" collaborators and seemed very unhappy with their gains in post-war Iraq. This feeling is as potent among the Sunnis as among the Shiites. On June 14, five Kurdish fighters whose car broke down outside the Arab city of Samarra in the Sunni triangle were ambushed and killed. The episode was similar to the brutal slaying of U.S. contractors in Fallujah on March 31: The corpses of the five Kurdish men were abused and burnt beyond recognition. If this atrocity indicates anything, it is that a simmering hatred for Kurds endures among many Arabs.

Arab distrust of Kurds has undermined U.S. efforts to secure Iraq. Washington has started to appreciate the fact that its constituency in Iraq includes not only the Kurds, but also the country's Arab majority population, especially Shiites. Back in March, when Shiite cleric Grand Ayatollah Sistani expressed dissatisfaction with Kurdish veto powers in the interim constitution, Washington first tried to placate him. When that strategy backfired, however, the U.S. acquiesced to Shiite demands and approved the June 8 U.N. resolution that failed to mention the Kurds.

Now that Iraqis have reclaimed their sovereignty, Kurds will likely find themselves opposing the rest of Iraq on a number of issues, ranging from secularism to the future of the Kirkuk oil fields. The Kurds seem unlikely to budge on secularism. The PUK Minister of Cooperation and Foreign Affairs, Abdul Rezzak Mirza, says that "secularism is an outstanding issue between the PUK and the rest of Iraq. If secularism is not written into Iraq's constitution, we will use all our means to fight and resist that."

As for Kirkuk, although the city is multi-ethnic, at least one Coalition Provisional Authority official suggested to me that Kurds want to keep it for themselves. By laying exclusive claims to Kirkuk, the Kurds have united all their adversaries—the Turkmens, Shiite and Sunni Arabs, and even Moqtada al-Sadr from southern Iraq—around a common cause. Banners of Sadr loyalists and Turkmen parties flew together at a recent anti-Kurdish demonstration in Kirkuk. To keep Kirkuk, the Kurds will have to confront the whole of Iraq. In fact, so long as the Kurds are perceived as America's favorites, all of their moves will be checked by a broad alliance of unlikely bedfellows.

Enter Turkey. Because America's primary interest at the moment is in stabilizing Iraq, the Kurds can no longer count on our unqualified support; and as a result they need other allies. The Kurds' two other neighbors, Iran and Syria, seem unlikely to fill this role. Tehran is wary of the Kurds' secularism and pro-western orientation; and Syria, which recently experienced a Kurdish uprising, is growing anxious over Kurdish nationalism. But Turkey could fit this bill. But for that to happen, the Kurds will have to placate Turkey on two issues: the PKK and Kirkuk.

The PKK lies at the heart of Turkey's distrust of the Kurds. The group renounced its unilateral ceasefire on June 1 and substantially increased attacks on Turkey after a five-year lull. PKK offensives will increasingly become a major cause of concern for Ankara. In order to win Turkish support, the KDP and PUK will need to crack down on the approximately 5,300 PKK terrorists currently residing in areas under their control. Should the PKK launch sensational attacks into Turkey, as it did in the 1990s, the Turkish government will come under popular pressure to enter northern Iraq to destroy the group's bases. Such a scenario poses a major challenge to Iraqi Kurds who would find themselves battling on two fronts—against Turkey in the north, and against Arab Iraq in the south. But if the KDP and PUK were to help the U.S. and Turkey shut down the PKK, they would achieve two goals. First, the parties would signal to the U.S. that they are willing to fight terrorism even when it is Kurdish terrorism. Second, by acting against the PKK, the KDP and PUK could restore themselves to the good graces of Ankara.

Then there is the problem of Kirkuk. Exclusive Kurdish control of the city would be unpopular in Turkey because of the city's substantial population of Turkmens. For the Kurds, reaching out to Turkey would likely mean working out some kind of power-sharing arrangement in Kirkuk with Arabs and Turkmens. Of course, such a settlement would make obsolete one of the reasons for Kurdish estrangement from Baghdad—and that estrangement is, in turn, the reason the Kurds need an alliance with Ankara. But with so many other sources of tension between the Kurds and the rest of Iraq—namely, secularism, the degree of Kurdish autonomy, and the perception among Arabs that the U.S. favors the Kurds—the Kurdish relationship with Baghdad would still be rocky even with a resolution on Kirkuk. So a settlement on Kirkuk would bolster the chances of a Turk-Kurd alliance without obviating the need for that alliance in the first place.

Contrary to common wisdom, the gap between the Iraqi Kurds and Turkey is neither wide nor unbridgeable. Rather, it is a recent phenomenon related to the PKK's emergence in northern Iraq. In the early 1990s, the Iraqi Kurds had a cordial relationship with Ankara. Turkey supported U.S. efforts to protect them against Saddam Hussein and extended a helping hand to KDP leader Massoud Barzani and PUK leader Jalal Talabani. The two visited Ankara often and traveled all over the world with Turkish diplomatic passports. Throughout much of the 1990s, the KPD and the PUK were allied with Turkey. Relations between the two parties and Ankara soured only when the PKK became a significant force in northern Iraq, creating worries that the KDP and the PUK were more interested in helping the PKK than in their partnership with Turkey. If the Iraqi Kurdish parties were to take decisive action against the PKK now, they would once again earn Turkey's confidence.

Turkey, it turns out, also has an important reason of its own to want improved relations with the Iraqi Kurds: Both Ankara and the Iraqi Kurds are very interested in a secular government in Baghdad. In this endeavor, then, Turkey, the KPD, and the PUK are natural allies. Which is why there is reason to believe that should the Kurds make overtures to Ankara, the Turkish government would be more than willing to listen. In any event, the Kurds' alternative—to remain sandwiched between an unfriendly Turkey to the north and a hostile, powerful alliance of non-Kurdish Iraqis to the south—is not an attractive one.

Chronology

2003

March 17: President George W. Bush delivers a final ultimatum to Saddam Hussein and his sons, Uday and Qusay, demanding that they leave Iraq within forty-eight hours.

March 19: The United States launches a predawn strike on al-Dora farm south of Baghdad in a failed bid to eliminate Saddam and other key regime figures.

March 20: U.S. and British forces enter Iraq, taking control of areas bordering Kuwait and parts of the al-Faw Peninsula.

March 21: The coalition begins its "shock and awe" bombing campaign against Saddam's palaces and ministries. U.S. Marines capture the port of Umm Qasr; British forces surround Basra.

March 22: A Saudi suicide bomber from the Ansar al-Islam enclave in Kurdish territory kills an Australian cameraman at a checkpoint near Halabja.

March 23: Iraq's military scores a rare victory when it repulses U.S. attack helicopters at Karbala. Kurdish fighters, with backing from U.S. Special Forces, unmanned aerial vehicles, and airstrikes, attack Ansar al-Islam's stronghold, destroying most of the enclave.

March 31: Ansar al-Islam's enclave is occupied.

April 2: Fighting reaches the suburbs of Baghdad.

April 5: U.S. "thunder runs" into Baghdad begin.

April 8-9: U.S. forces secure Baghdad and pull down the statue of Saddam in al-Fardus Square. Intense looting begins.

April 11: Moderate Shiite cleric Ayatollah Abdul Majid al-Khoei is murdered by henchmen of rival cleric Muqtada al-Sadr in Najaf.

April 14: U.S. forces gain control of Tikrit, the last major Iraqi city to fall.

April 21-27: The first signs of insurgent resistance to coalition forces emerge. Ten incidents of armed resistance are reported.

April 23: Retired general Jay Garner arrives in Iraq to manage the Office of Reconstruction and Humanitarian Assistance (ORHA).

May 1: President Bush declares an end to major combat operations in Iraq on the deck of the USS *Abraham Lincoln.*

May 12: L. Paul Bremer replaces Jay Garner as the U.S. administrator of Iraq. ORHA becomes the Coalition Provisional Authority (CPA).

May 22: The UN Security Council ends economic sanctions against Iraq and formalizes the role of the CPA with the passage of Resolution 1483.

May 23: The CPA simultaneously dissolves all Iraqi security institutions.

June 2: Chief UN weapons inspector Hans Blix submits his final report to the Security Council.

June 12: The twenty-five-member Iraqi Interim Governing Council (IGC) is established.

June 14: Five Kurdish fighters whose car broke down outside the Arab city of Samara in the Sunni Triangle are ambushed and killed, their corpses abused and burned beyond recognition.

June 24: Shiites riot in the southern town of Majar al-Kabir, leaving six British military police and an unknown number of Iraqis dead.

June 25: The United States decides to establish a new range of Iraqi security forces, forming the Iraqi Civil Defense Corps and the Iraqi Police Service.

July 22: Uday and Qusay Hussein are killed in a gunfight with U.S. troops in Mosul.

August 7: The Jordanian embassy in Baghdad is hit with a suicide truck bomb, killing sixteen and wounding more than fifty.

August 19: The UN's Baghdad headquarters is attacked by suicide bombers. Twenty-four are killed (including UN envoy Sergio Vieira de Mello) and more than 100 are wounded.

August 29: A car bomb outside the Imam Ali Mosque in Najaf kills Ayatollah Muhammad Baqr al-Hakim, a prominent Shiite leader, and eighty others.

September 7: President Bush requests $87 billion for additional military and reconstruction costs in Iraq.

September 25: IGC member Akila al-Hashimi, one of three women on the council, dies of wounds suffered in an ambush on September 20.

October 2: In testimony before Congress, David Kay, head of the Iraq Survey Group, reveals that no weapons of mass destruction have been discovered.

October 16: The UN Security Council unanimously approves Resolution 1511, which supports the maintenance of a multinational force under U.S. command.

October 19: The UN and World Bank create the International Reconstruction Fund Facility for Iraq to administer reconstruction aid.

October 23-24: Eighty nations attend the Madrid Conference, pledging an additional $13 billion to fund reconstruction in Iraq.

October 26: Missiles launched by resistance elements kill one U.S. soldier and wound eighteen other people at the Rashid Hotel in Baghdad during a visit by U.S. deputy secretary of defense Paul Wolfowitz.

October 27: Suicide bombings at the Red Crescent headquarters and various police stations in Baghdad kill 43 and wound more than 200 on the first day of Ramadan.

October 30: The UN evacuates its non-Iraqi staff from Baghdad pending a security assessment.

November 2: Iraqi insurgents down a Chinook helicopter, killing sixteen U.S. soldiers and wounding twenty-one in the single deadliest military attack since the beginning of the war.

November 12: A truck bomb kills eighteen Italian soldiers and nine Iraqis at a base in Nasariya.

November 15: The CPA and IGC sign an agreement to transfer sovereignty to an interim Iraqi government by July 2004.

December 13: U.S. troops capture Saddam, who had been hiding in a hole at a farm near his hometown of Tikrit.

December 16-21: France, Germany, Italy, Russia, Britain, the United Arab Emirates, Qatar, Kuwait, and Saudi Arabia agree to write off and restructure part of Iraq's $120 billion debt.

2004

January 15: Grand Ayatollah Ali Hussein al-Sistani reportedly threatens to issue a *fatwa* against the U.S. transition plan if his demands for direct election of an interim government are not met. Tens of thousands protest in Basra in support.

January 17: Japan sends 1,000 troops on a humanitarian mission to Iraq in its largest military deployment since World War II.

February 1: Two suicide bombers strike the Irbil offices of the Kurdish Democratic Party and the Patriotic Union of Kurdistan, killing 105 and wounding more than 200.

February 23: Carina Perelli, the UN delegate tasked with evaluating the feasibility of elections before June 30, issues a report concluding that they will have to be postponed until late 2004 or early 2005, and that an alternate method for transferring sovereignty by June 30 will have to be devised.

March 1: The IGC finalizes the Transitional Administrative Law (TAL), which protects the "inalienable rights of all Iraqis."

March 2: Multiple bombings in Baghdad and Karbala during the Shiite holy festival of Ashura kill more than 180.

March 4: In testimony delivered to the House Armed Services Committee, Gen. John Abizaid characterizes "transnational terrorists" as the most dangerous element of the resistance effort.

March 8: The IGC signs the TAL, which includes a bill of rights, grants the Kurds a degree of autonomy, and calls for nationwide elections by January 31, 2005. Grand Ayatollah al-Sistani expresses dissatisfaction with Kurdish veto powers in the interim constitution.

March 12: Muqtada al-Sadr's militia—called the Mahdi Army—conducts a well-prepared and coordinated strike on the village of Qawliya, attacking it with mortars and infantry, occupying and razing it, and dispersing its population.

March 14: The Socialist Party wins the Spanish elections. Prime Minister-elect Jose Luis Rodriguez Zapatero vows to withdraw Spanish troops if the UN does not assume control in Iraq by July.

March 16: U.S. and Iranian forces exchange border fire. American officials claim that one Iranian border guard was killed, but Tehran denies that any such incident took place.

March 28: U.S. forces shut down al-Sadr's newspaper, *al-Hawza*, due to its anti-American incitement. Thousands of his supporters protest in Baghdad.

March 29: Faced with the challenge of al-Sadr's militia, the IGC inserts into the interim constitution the provision, "Armed forces and militias not under the command structure of the Iraqi Transitional Government are prohibited except as provided by federal law."

March 31: Four American security contractors are ambushed and killed in Falluja. Their corpses are mutilated, dragged through the streets, and hung from a bridge.

April 2: In a sermon in Kufa, al-Sadr instructs his followers to fight "the occupiers" and "strike them where you meet them."

April 3: Coalition authorities arrest Mustafa al-Yaqubi, an aide to al-Sadr, for his alleged connection to the April 2003 killing of rival cleric al-Khoei.

April 4: Al-Sadr calls on his followers to "terrorize your enemy," sparking uprisings in Nasariya, Karbala, Najaf, and Baghdad's Sadr City neighborhood.

April 5: U.S. Marines launch Operation Vigilant Resolve to pacify Falluja. The city is surrounded by 1,200 Marines and two battalions of Iraqi security forces, who immediately engage the militants.

April 7: Al-Sadr followers continue their uprising, attacking Iraqi security forces in Kufa, Najaf, Nasariya, Basra, and Baghdad and occupying several government offices. The city of Kut falls to the Mahdi Army as Ukrainian forces flee, leaving their armaments and facilities to be used by al-Sadr.

April 9: Facing light resistance, U.S. forces retake Kut and begin to concentrate their presence outside Najaf.

April 11: U.S. forces agree to a ceasefire with militants in Falluja.

April 14: Al-Sadr begins to speak of a negotiated settlement, seemingly abandoning his previous declarations of fighting to the death.

April 15: South Korea reaffirms its commitment to send 3,600 troops to Iraq. These forces are slated to assist with reconstruction rather than offensive security operations.

April 16: Secretary of Defense Donald Rumsfeld extends the tours of duty of 20,000 U.S. troops who had been preparing to rotate out of Iraq.

April 18: Sunnis and Shiites participate in demonstrations in Baghdad against the occupation.

April 19: President Bush nominates John Negroponte, the U.S. ambassador to the UN, to be the new ambassador in Iraq.

April 21: Suicide bombings kill 50 and wound more than 100 in Basra.

April 23: CPA administrator L. Paul Bremer announces that thousands of former members of the Baath Party who had been barred from government service following Operation Iraqi Freedom will be allowed to return to positions in the military and the bureaucracy.

April 26: U.S. forces launch offensive operations intended to suppress and destroy the Mahdi Army and remove its leadership.

April 29: Graphic pictures are released showing U.S. military personnel abusing and humiliating detainees at Abu Ghraib prison.

April 29: U.S. Marines announce an agreement to end the siege of Falluja, transferring security control of the city to a former general in Saddam's army.

April 29: A U.S. airstrike against al-Sadr's forces in Kufa kills forty militiamen.

May 1: A militia called the Falluja Protection Army assumes security control over the city.

May 5: U.S. forces launch a major assault against al-Sadr loyalists in Karbala. CBS airs the Abu Ghraib abuse photos.

May 8: Ayatollah Sadreddin Kubanji delivers a sermon calling for al-Sadr to leave Najaf.

May 10: U.S. forces demolish al-Sadr's Baghdad headquarters.

May 11: Ayatollah Kubanji delivers a second sermon calling for al-Sadr to leave Najaf.

May 15: Al-Sadr attempts to reenergize his revolt against coalition forces with small uprisings in Baghdad, Nasariya, and Amara.

May 17: A U.S. AC-130 gunship launches a strike in Karbala, killing sixteen Mahdi Army militiamen mere meters away from the city's Shrine of Abbas.

May 17: Izzedine Salim, then-holder of the rotating IGC presidency, is killed by a suicide bomber.

May 18: Ayatollah al-Sistani calls for al-Sadr's militia and coalition forces to leave Najaf.

May 27: A ceasefire agreement is reached between coalition forces and al-Sadr in Najaf and Kufa.

May 28: Iyad Allawi, a former Baathist who became the leader of the Iraqi National Accord after being exiled by Saddam, is named prime minister of the interim government slated to assume authority on June 30.

June 1: Sheikh Ghazi al-Yawar, a Sunni tribal leader, is named president of the forthcoming interim government. Allawi names the members of his cabinet. The IGC is dissolved.

June 8: The UN Security Council unanimously approves Resolution 1546, ending the formal occupation of Iraq on June 30 and formalizing the transfer of "full sovereignty to the interim Iraqi government." The resolution also mandates the presence of a U.S.-led multinational force, scheduled to end when a constitutionally elected government takes power. It omits any mention of Kurdish autonomy, however.

June 8: Nine of Iraq's largest militias announce their intention to disband. Neither the Mahdi Army nor the paramilitary Falluja Protection Army takes part in the announcement.

June 17: Al-Sadr orders his Mahdi Army to temporarily disband.

June 23: John Negroponte is sworn in as the new U.S. ambassador to Iraq.

June 24: The Iraqi Stock Exchange opens.

June 24: Eight British military personnel who had been captured by Iran's Islamic Revolutionary Guard Corps are released.

June 28: The coalition transfers sovereignty to the Iraqi Interim Government two days early. Bremer leaves Iraq.

June 28: At a meeting in Istanbul, NATO leaders announce that they will provide assistance for the training of Iraqi security forces.

June 30: The Iraqi Interim Government takes legal custody of Saddam and eleven of his top associates, although they remain in the physical custody of U.S. forces.

Index

A

Abizaid, Gen. John, 93, 116, 122, 313, 317, 348, 366
Abu Ghraib prison, 232, 237, 367
Afghanistan, 24, 33, 84, 127, 238, 250, 253, 266, 331, 356
- and al-Qaeda, 81, 82, 85, 146, 148, 326, 346, 349, 351

air bases, U.S.
- basing restrictions, 53-55

air power, 62
- air superiority during Operation Iraqi Freedom, 29, 59
- response to Iraqi threats in no-fly zones, 41, 42

Allawi, Iyad, 308, 309, 368, 376
al-Qaeda, 22, 81-83, 131, 132, 137, 152, 223, 306, 325, 326, 345-347
- and Ansar al-Islam, 81-83, 85, 126-128, 146
- in Iraq, 81-83, 85, 126, 136, 146, 150, 283, 326, 348-352, 354

Ansar al-Islam, 81-83, 85, 107, 126-128, 145-153, 223, 283, 293, 294, 299, 348-351, 363
- links to Iran, 83, 137, 148, 346, 347, 354
- *see also* Iraqi Kurdistan

Arab countries
- media, 323
  - Al-Jazeera, 328-330
- politics, 68, 323, 329

Arab-Israeli conflict, 16, 17, 22, 68, 84, 327, 340, 341
Arabs, 22, 282, 284, 288, 302, 339-341, 359-361
- *see also* Sunnis

B

Baath Party, 340
- leadership, 59, 92, 340
- loyalists, 29-31, 225, 317

Baath regime
- Arabization policy, 262-264, 302
- collapse of, 59, 60
- de-Baathification, 78, 201, 260, 340
- defense strategy, 44, 45, 51
- effectiveness during battle for Baghdad, 45
- response to Operation Iraqi Freedom, 29-31

Badr Brigades, 58, 190, 218, 336, 337, 358
Baghdad
- battle for, 45, 47-49, 59
- population in, 60

Bahrain, 334, 357
Basra, 44, 45, 51, 53, 59, 60, 97, 162-164, 169, 209, 272, 356
"battle for Baghdad"
- strategies in, 48, 49

battlefield preparation
- Operation Iraqi Freedom, 41-43

bin Laden, Osama, 85, 146, 151, 329
Bremer, L. Paul, 145, 151, 214, 222, 274, 280, 313, 364, 367, 368
Britain
- alliance with United States, 146, 226, 335
- British Empire experience in Iraq, 13-23, 136, 137, 240
- coalition troops in Iraq, 227
  - in Basra, 59, 226
  - in Majar al-Kabir, 95, 163, 221, 226, 364
- impact on Iraq, 16

mandate period, 15, 16, 136, 137, 251, 287, 307, 356
Bush, George W., 94, 210, 240, 250, 253, 339, 363, 364, 367
speech, 16, 23

C

Cairo Conference (1921), 19
Central Intelligence Agency (CIA), 145, 306, 311
chemical weapons, 65, 66, 82, 147, 148, 150, 350
coalition forces
casualties, 47, 99, 110, 165
mission after Operation Iraqi Freedom, 70-74, 95, 203
mission during Operation Iraqi Freedom, 29, 56
tactics, post-war, 30, 31
weapons, 36, 37, 42, 120
Coalition Provisional Authority (CPA), 78, 93, 214, 229, 272, 364, 365
alliances with Iraqis, 111, 138, 236
de-Baathification, 78, 201, 313
and Iraqi politics, 201
objectives, 68
Office of Reconstruction and Humanitarian assistance, 311-314, 363, 364
postwar security policy, 191, 201, 211, 214-216, 220, 232
transfer of sovereignty to IIG, 217, 239, 240, 282, 299-304, 308, 309, 365, 368
collateral damage, 36, 43, 57, 115, 198
false claims debunking, 43
communications network, 22
targeting of, 36, 37
constitutions, 290-292
coup
considerations for, 38-40, 48, 207
CPA. *see* Coalition Provisional Authority

D

Dawa. *see* Islamic Dawa Party
democracy, 16, 17, 20-22, 70-74, 126, 184, 207, 231, 247, 249, 251, 256, 257
dual-use facilities
targeting of, 35, 36

E

economics
policy, 315, 316
reconstruction, 275-278
electricity infrastructure
targeting of, 35, 36
extremism, 127, 307

F

Falluja
battle for, 133-135, 139, 140, 366, 367
Faysal I, King of Iraq, 13, 19-21
Fedayeen Saddam, 29, 45, 48, 49, 51, 59, 69, 87, 91, 117

G

Garner, Jay, 312, 313, 363, 364
geography
Iraqi exploitation, 33
Gulf Cooperation Council (GCC), 53, 54, 206, 277, 334, 335, 357
Gulf States
U. S. relations, 53-55, 334, 335
Gulf War (1991), 32, 44, 53, 68, 260, 313, 328

H

hostage taking, 134, 143
humanitarian assistance, 17, 57, 311, 331, 333, 336
Hussein, Saddam. see Saddam

I

information networks
control prior to Operation Iraqi Freedom, 42

infrastructure
  destruction as defense tactic, 34, 37, 51
  targeting during Operation Desert Fox, 35-37
  targeting during Operation Desert Storm, 35, 37
insurgency
  background, 117
  growth of, 118, 230
  see also Muqtada al-Sadr, resistance
intelligence
  prewar, 7
International Atomic Energy Agency
  weapons of mass destruction, 66, 67
International Reconstruction Fund Facility, 364
invasion. *see* Operation Iraqi Freedom
Iran, 16, 323, 345-347, 353-355
  Shiites in, 259, 260
  support for resistance, 58, 83
  and United States, 66, 240, 241, 258, 336-338, 347
Iran-Iraq War (1980-1988), 137, 260
Iraq
  civil society, 21, 245, 247, 257, 285
  constitution, 238, 257, 260, 292
  democratic institutions, 20, 21
  economy, 94, 143, 315, 316
  elections, 303, 304, 309, 365
  employment, 252, 268, 272-274
  invasion of Kuwait (1990), 7
  mandate period, 15, 16, 251, 287
  nationalism, 16, 17, 49, 251, 260
  neighboring countries, 42, 58, 71, 275, 284, 323
  political parties, 126, 256
  sanctions against, 17, 57, 271, 280, 312, 364
  tribes, 15, 20, 49, 249
Iraqi Civil Defense Corps, 125, 129, 140, 201, 215, 217, 220, 224, 235, 313, 364
Iraqi Governing Council, 94, 109, 131, 138, 166, 169, 229, 237, 239, 268, 270, 281, 290, 294, 306, 360, 364
  dissolution of, 308
Iraqi Interim Government (IIG), 70, 202, 203, 232, 237, 239-241, 368
Iraqi Kurdistan, 81, 82, 85, 146, 252, 262-264, 282-284, 288, 293-298
Iraqi military, 22, 34, 36, 45, 47, 63, 84, 235
  antiaircraft fire, 45, 52
  consequences of Operation Iraqi Freedom, 205-214, 217-219, 253, 258, 260, 306
  defense strategy in mandate period, 21, 22
  "outside-in" strategy, 29
  willingness to fight, 46
Iraqi Police Service, 125, 128, 140, 160, 176, 198, 200, 216, 220, 221, 227, 235, 285, 300, 317, 364
Iraqi security forces, 13, 77, 116, 119, 126, 128, 134, 135, 140, 170, 174, 194, 198, 201-203, 227, 228, 231, 235, 240, 364, 366
  in Baath regime
    dissolution of, 201, 364
  postwar, 214-222
    reform of, 77, 201, 213
    training of, 202, 203, 224, 225, 235, 313, 368
  see also Fedayeen Saddam, Republican Guard, Special Republican Guard
Iraqis
  views of U.S. role, 34, 57, 70, 71, 269-271
Islamic Dawa Party, 23, 109, 162, 169, 175, 190, 259
Islamic fundamentalism, 78
Islamic Revolutional Guard Corps, 163, 336, 346, 353, 356-358

Israel, 47, 51, 70, 137, 326, 327, 337, 340, 341, 349, 351
Israeli-Palestinian conflict. see Arab-Israeli conflict
Italy, 152, 226, 227, 349, 350, 365

J
Japan, 227, 241, 251, 254, 277, 333, 365
Jordan, 53, 54, 85, 127, 148, 212, 219, 247, 253, 274, 323, 326, 330, 349-351

K
Karbala, 16, 72, 88, 131, 139, 159, 165-167, 174, 177, 181, 182, 188-190, 193-195, 233, 234, 259, 294, 295, 348, 353, 363, 367-368
    U. S. losses in, 166
Khoei, Ayatollah Abdul Majid al-
    murder of, 159, 163, 209, 230, 363, 366
Kurds, 147, 257, 293-298, 302, 342-344, 359-362
    see also Iraqi Kurdistan
Kuwait, 50, 51, 53-55, 257, 323

L
League of Nations, 15, 16, 22
local security, 232-233
loyalty, 51, 61, 87
    and coup potential, 39, 40
    maintenance efforts, 33

M
Madrid Conference, 276, 365
Mahdi Army
    U. S. offensives against, 178, 179, 190-192, 233, 234, 367
media
    Al-Jazeera, 328-330
militias, 69, 70, 203, 217-219, 236, 240, 366-368
missiles
    coalition attacks on, 42
multinational forces, 141, 228, 237, 238, 364, 368
    performance, 140, 202, 226-228
Muslim countries
    constitutions, 290-292

N
Najaf, 52, 261
Nasariya, 44, 45, 50, 51
nationalism
    Iraqi appeals to, 46
NATO, 32, 84, 140, 141, 202, 226, 228, 238, 331, 368
no-augmentation zones
    described, 41
no-fly zones, 41-43
    authority for, 41

O
Occupation. see Coalition Provisional Authority, Operation Iraqi Freedom
Occupied Territories, 82, 127, 137
Office of Reconstruction and Humanitarian Assistance. see Coalition Provisional Authority
oil fields, 15, 48, 208
oil industry, 265, 273, 274, 316
    targeting of, 36, 37, 110
oil-for-food program. see UN
101st Airborne Division, 44, 223, 224, 227
Operation Desert Fox
    infrastructure targeting, 37
Operation Desert Storm
    infrastructure targeting, 37
Operation Iraqi Freedom
    airstrikes, 29
    battlefield preparation, 41, 42
    ground forces, 29, 50, 59, 63
    initial successes, 47, 50, 68
    international reaction, 60
    overview, 29
    postwar transition, 30, 31, 68-74

prewar planning, 62, 63, 310-313
regional implications, 54, 55, 321-362
"shock and awe," 43, 45, 51, 363
U.S. objectives, 16, 56
war-fighting phase, 29-64
Ottoman Empire, 13, 18, 248
"outside-in" strategy, 44-46
described, 29, 44

P

Pakistan, 67, 151, 325, 349, 351
Palestinian
intifada, 275, 329
militants, 81, 82, 147, 149, 151, 152, 325
territories, 82, 127, 137
Persian Gulf, 53, 357
Poland, 140, 166, 226
population, Iraqi
as shield, 44-46, 51, 52, 78, 79, 195
use as cover, 33
post-war combat
counterinsurgency, 62, 124
objectives, 117
setbacks, 178
tactics, 120
weapons, 120
Powell, Colin, 126, 145, 147, 148, 331, 342, 350, 351
power grid
targeting of, 36
propaganda, 58, 69, 125, 210, 354
debunking strategies, 43
psychological operations, 33, 37, 51, 209, 248, 265
prior to Operation Iraqi Freedom, 42
public opinion, 22, 23, 48, 60, 237, 254, 256, 269-271, 335, 344

Q

Qaeda. see al-Qaeda
Qatar, 53-55, 253, 329, 334, 357, 365

R

reconstruction
Commanders Emergency Reconstruction Program (CERP), 224
economy, 275-278, 286, 287
funding, 224, 275-278, 323
progress, 143, 314-317
regional security, 206, 213, 258, 337, 338
religion
as driver of resistance, 106, 162
Republican Guard, 47-49, 59, 248
resistance movements, 77-123, 365, 366
capabilities, 115, 118-119
challenge to CPA, 93-103, 114-120, 162, 165, 172, 173, 176, 363
coalition response, 78, 79, 144, 189
emergence, 87-89
evolution of, 77, 78, 92, 114-119, 126
foreign elements among, 85, 89, 107, 233
funding, 79
groups, 107, 108
and Iraqi politics, 249, 253
leadership, 122
in mandate period, 16, 17
organization, 88, 90, 105
popular support, 33, 106, 114, 119, 233
Shiite, 108, 109, 164, 201
suicide bombers, bombings, 78, 100, 108, 115, 118, 131, 145, 149-151, 166, 181, 194, 363, 365, 367
Sunni, 77-80, 90-92, 195, 196, 234, 267, 268
tactics, 91, 100-103, 108, 109, 115, 118-120, 125, 128, 129, 139, 143
targets, 91, 104, 108, 109, 115, 116, 118, 143
U.S. operations against, 78
see also Mahdi Army, Muqtada al-Sadr
restraint
Iraqi exploitation of, 45, 51, 195
Rumsfeld, Donald, 93, 290, 311, 313, 367

S

Saddam
  capture of, 121-123, 365, 368
  coup against, potential for, 38-40
  loyalty to, potential for, 33
  trial of, 279-284
Sadr, Grand Ayatollah Muhammad Baqr al-, 159, 184
Sadr, Muqtada al-, 160, 161, 165-167, 172-183, 233, 234, 354, 367
  followers, 160, 184
  Mahdi Army, 139, 160, 166-169, 187-191, 194, 195, 366, 368
  threat to CPA, 109, 159, 160, 166-192
Sadr City, 159-166, 177, 178, 182, 187, 189, 191, 194, 233, 234, 269, 366
Samson option
  described, 30
sanitation resources
  maintenance efforts, 36
Saudi Arabia, 16, 53-55, 68, 69, 73, 79-81, 84, 85, 89, 137, 147, 152, 253, 258, 277, 291, 306, 323, 332, 334, 347, 349, 357, 365
Shatt al-Arab waterway, 356-358
Shiites
  Iraqi
    Baath policy toward, 259
    leadership, 159, 261
    as minority, 259
    resistance, 87, 88, 164, 182, 183
  in neighboring countries, 259, 260
  opposition to occupation, 162-164
  and Sunnis, 136-138, 340
  support of coalition, war, 159
Sistani, Grand Ayatollah Ali Hussein al-, 109, 138, 160, 166, 181, 189, 193, 233, 234, 303, 304
  relations with CPA, 162, 168, 169, 175, 176, 187, 239, 286, 360, 365, 366, 368
South Korea, 227, 241, 367
space-for-time trading strategy, 34, 44
Spain, 226, 227, 236, 237, 277, 349, 350, 366
special operations
  Iraqi countermeasures, 33
Special Republican Guard, 48, 59, 69
Sulaymaniya, 82, 137, 147, 150, 284, 287, 293, 294, 298, 299, 301, 342
Sunni, Sunnis
  leadership, 94, 246, 302
  minority, 248, 259, 267, 268
  relations with Shiites, 136-138, 340
  resistance, 77-80, 90-92, 195, 196, 234, 267, 268
Sunni Triangle, 49, 69, 79, 142-144, 227, 267, 268
Supreme Council for Islamic Revolution in Iraq, 109, 162, 175, 218, 234, 236, 336, 337, 354
Syria, 16, 58
  and al-Qaeda, 351
  support for resistance, 79, 86
  and United States, 266, 325
  and weapons of mass destruction, 66, 71

T

terrorism
  foreign irregulars in Iraq, 69-71, 77, 84-86, 107
Tikrit, 87, 88, 91, 92, 98, 105, 114, 116, 126, 135, 151, 209, 210, 252, 363, 365
Transitional Administrative Law (TAL), 169, 237-239, 240, 290-292, 365, 366
transportation network
  maintenance efforts, 36, 142-144
Turkey, 288, 289, 323, 349, 361-362
  basing restructions, 53-55, 58
  and Turkmens, 262, 264
  and United States, 342-344
Turkmens, 262-264, 282, 284, 343, 360, 361

U

Ukraine, 47
UN, 60, 73, 140, 206, 207, 227, 228, 237, 239-241, 256, 266, 279, 282, 283, 331, 332, 364-367
  Baghdad headquarters, 280, 364
UN Security Council
  oil-for-food, 37, 216, 257, 273, 276, 277, 295, 296
  weapons of mass destruction inspections, 65, 83, 364
UN Security Council Resolution 949 provisions, 41
UN World Bank Needs Assessment, 272-278
United Arab Emirates (UAE), 54, 241, 270, 357, 365
United States
  coalition troops, 202, 226, 234
  Middle East policy, 16, 71, 73, 335
urban warfare. *see* "battle for Baghdad"
U.S. Agency for International Development (USAID), 36, 37, 148, 272, 273, 296, 311, 313-316
U.S. Air Force, 35, 36, 253
U.S. Army, 36, 37, 253, 342
U.S. Central Command (CENTCOM), 93, 96, 122, 129, 208, 310, 313
U.S. Department of Defense, 310

W

Wahhabis, 261, 283, 306
water supplies, 163, 274, 315
  maintenance efforts, 35, 36, 315
weapons of mass destruction (WMD), 208, 249-251, 255, 258, 364
  biological weapons, 51, 65, 66, 351
  chemical weapons, 51, 65, 66, 82, 351
  nuclear weapons, 66, 67, 71, 356
  postwar analyses and intelligence, 65, 66, 71
  proliferation, 65-67, 71
  see also UN
World War I, 13, 15, 17, 23

Y

Yaqubi, Mustafa al-, 169, 185, 366
Yemen, 127, 137, 292, 305-307, 317, 325, 330

Z

Zarqawi, Abu Musab al-, 82, 131, 132, 136, 137, 148, 150, 345, 348-352